THUCYDIDES

HISTORY II

edited with translation and commentary by

P. J. RHODES

© P.J. Rhodes 1988. All rights reserved. No part of this publication may be reproduced, stored in a retrieval system, or transmitted in any form by any means without the prior written permission of the publishers. *Greek text* adapted from the Oxford Classical Texts edition with the permission of Oxford University Press.

British Library Cataloguing in Publication Data
Thucydides.
 [History of the Peloponnesian War: Book 2]
 Thucydides histories of book II.
 1. Peloponnesian War
 I. [History of the Peloponnesian War: Book 2]
 II. Title
 938'.05

ISBN 0 85668 396 5 *cloth*
ISBN 0 85668 397 3 *limp*

Classical Texts ISSN 0953–7961

Printed and published in England by ARIS & PHILLIPS Ltd., Teddington House, Warminster, Wiltshire, BA12 8PQ, England.

CONTENTS

Preface   v

References   vii

Maps
   1. Greece and the Aegean   x
   2. Central and Southern Greece   xi

Introduction
   1. Thucydides and his History   1
   2. The Peloponnesian War   20
   3. Summary of Book II   29
   4. Abbreviations used in *Apparatus Criticus*   30

Bibliography   32

Text and Translation   37

Commentary   179

Appendix
   Athenian Population Figures   271

Index   278

PREFACE

The *Historical Commentary on Thucydides* of Gomme, Andrewes and Dover is addressed to advanced readers, and its first volume was published more than forty years ago. Other English-speaking readers of Thucydides have to make do, except for books VI and VII, with editions which are nearly a century old and which, even when equipped with new introductions, do not cater for the needs and interests of the present day. Hence this new edition of book II, the book in which, having completed his introduction, Thucydides begins his main narrative of the Peloponnesian War.

In common with other Aris & Phillips editions of classical texts, this edition supplies introduction and bibliography; Greek text and *apparatus criticus* with facing translation; and a commentary which does not neglect the Greek text but is based on the translation. The Greek text and *apparatus criticus* are my own, but in the interest of economy the publishers have produced the text by adaptation of the Oxford Text (with the kind permission of the Oxford University Press): on p. 100 (52. 2) it was impossible to make an insertion which I believe is needed, and what I regard as the correct text is indicated in the *apparatus*; throughout the Greek text it has been necessary to retain the paragraph divisions of the Oxford Text, and for my own paragraph divisions readers should refer to the translation.

I am grateful to Mr. J. A. Aris for inviting me to write this book and for general advice, and to Mr. P. Mudd for technical help over the preparation of camera-ready copy; to Mr. A. Corner of Durham University's Department of Geography, who drew the maps; to Dr. J. P. Coleman, Sir Kenneth Dover, Dr. M. H. Hansen and Prof. M. M. Willcock; and above all to my colleague Prof. A. J. Woodman, who read a preliminary draft and the final typescript and helped me to improve both.

University of Durham   P.J.R.
Epiphany Term 1988

REFERENCES

Greek authors and their works are in general abbreviated as in the second edition of the *Oxford Classical Dictionary*, but notice:

Ath. Pol. (with no indication of author)
 [Aristotle], *Athenaion Politeia*
Din. Dinarchus

The following collections of inscriptions have been used:

Agora xvii *The Athenian Agora*, xvii. *Inscriptions: The Funerary Monuments*, by BRADEEN, D.W. Princeton: Am. Sch. Class. Stud. Ath., 1974.

ATL *The Athenian Tribute Lists*, revised collection of texts in vol. ii (1949). See final section of Bibliography under MERITT, B.D.

IG *Inscriptiones Graecae*. Berlin: Reimer / de Gruyter, 1873– . Vol. i^3, by a team of editors headed by LEWIS, D.M., bringing up to date the collection of Athenian inscriptions down to 404/3, is in course of publication (Part 1, 1981).

M&L MEIGGS, R., & LEWIS, D.M. *A Selection of Greek Historical Inscriptions to the End of the Fifth Century B.C.* Oxford U.P., 1969.

TAM i *Tituli Asiae Minoris*, i. Vienna: Akademie der Wissenschaften, 1901.

Tod TOD, M.N. *A Selection of Greek Historical Inscriptions*. Volumes i^2, ii. Oxford U.P., 1946-8.

(Many of the inscriptions cited are translated in:

Fornara FORNARA, C.W. *Translated Documents of Greece and Rome*, i. *Archaic Times to the End of the Peloponnesian War*. Johns Hopkins U.P., 1977; ^{2}Cambridge U.P., 1983.)

The papyri from Oxyrhynchus cited for the text of book II are published in:

P. Oxy. *The Oxyrhynchus Papyri*. London: Egypt Exploration Fund / Society, 1898– .

Other collections of texts which have been used are:

FGrH JACOBY, F. *Die Fragmente der griechischen Histori-*

	ker. Berlin: Weidmann / Leiden: Brill, 1926-58.
Kock	KOCK, T. *Comicorum Atticorum Fragmenta*. Leipzig: Teubner, 1880-8.
(Edmonds	EDMONDS, J.M. *The Fragments of Attic Comedy*. Leiden: Brill, 1957-61. For the most part uses the same numeration as Kock; unreliable, but includes English translations.)
Vorsokr.	DIELS, H., rev. KRANZ, W. *Die Fragmente der Vorsokratiker*. Berlin: Weidmann, ^{6}1951-2.
(Freeman	FREEMAN, K. *Ancilla to the Pre-Socratic Philosophers*. Oxford: Blackwell, 1952. Provides English translations of the fragments in *Vorsokr.*, using the same numeration.)

Otherwise, details of modern books cited, apart from editions of Thucydides cited only for their emendations of the Greek text, will be found in the Bibliography, on pp. 32-6. "Gomme" without further specification denotes vol. ii of his *Historical Commentary on Thucydides*; a few other books, cited frequently in the commentary on a group of chapters, are (after due warning at their first appearance) cited in that part of the commentary by author's name without further specification.

The following periodicals are cited. Superior figures (e.g. CQ^2) denote the second and subsequent series of a periodical.

AAA	*Athens Annals of Archaeology*
AJA	*American Journal of Archaeology*
Ath.	*Athenaeum*
BCH	*Bulletin de Correspondance Hellénique*
BICS	*Bulletin of the Institute of Classical Studies*
BSA	*Annual of the British School at Athens*
C&M	*Classica et Mediaevalia*
Chiron	*Chiron*
CQ	*Classical Quarterly*
CRAI	*Comptes-rendus de l'Académie des Inscriptions et Belles-lettres*
CSCA	*California Studies in Classical Antiquity*
G&R	*Greece and Rome*
GR&BMon.	*Greek, Roman and Byzantine Monographs*
GR&BS	*Greek, Roman and Byzantine Studies*
Hermes	*Hermes*
Hesp.	*Hesperia*
Hist.	*Historia*
HSCP	*Harvard Studies in Classical Philology*
HTR	*Harvard Theological Review*

JHS	*Journal of Hellenic Studies*
JRS	*Journal of Roman Studies*
Klio	*Klio*
LCM	*Liverpool Classical Monthly*
Mnem.	*Mnemosyne*
NJhB	*Neue Jahrbücher für Philologie und Pädagogik*
PCPS	*Proceedings of the Cambridge Philological Society*
Phoen.	*Phoenix*
YCS	*Yale Classical Studies*
ZPE	*Zeitschrift für Papyrologie und Epigraphik*

Map 1 Greece and the Aegean

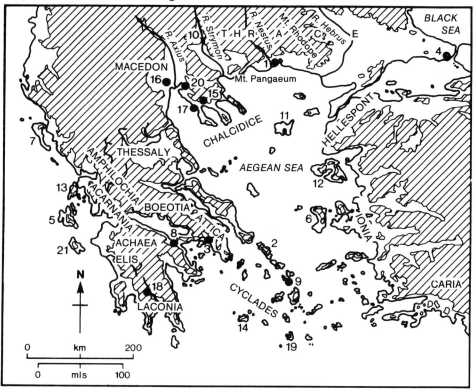

1	Abdera	8	Corinth	15	Olynthus
2	Andros	9	Delos	16	Pella
3	Athens	10	Doberus	17	Potidaea
4	Byzantium	11	Lemnos	18	Sparta
5	Cephallenia	12	Lesbos	19	Thera
6	Chios	13	Leucas	20	Therme
7	Corcyra	14	Melos	21	Zacynthus

Map 2 Central and Southern Greece

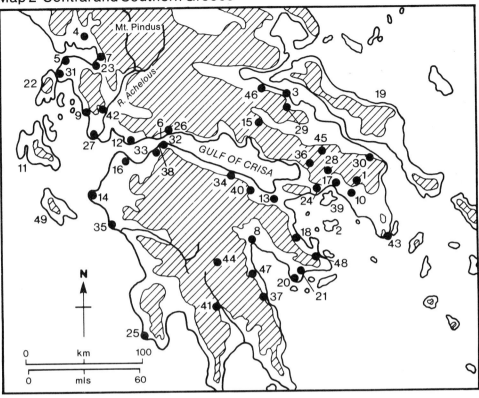

1 Acharnae	18 Epidaurus	35 Pheia
2 Aegina	19 Euboea	36 Plataea
3 Alope	20 Halieis	37 Prasiae
4 Ambracia	21 Hermione	38 Rhium
5 Anactorium	22 Leucas	39 Salamis
6 Antirrhium	23 Limnaea	40 Sicyon
7 Argos	24 Megara	41 Sparta
8 Argos	25 Methone	42 Stratus
9 Astacus	26 Naupactus	43 Sunium
10 Athens	27 Oeniadae	44 Tegea
11 Cephallenia	28 Oenoe	45 Thebes
12 Chalcis	29 Opus	46 Thronium
13 Corinth	30 Oropus	47 Thyrea
14 Cyllene	31 Palaerus	48 Troezen
15 Daulis	32 Panormus	49 Zacynthus
16 Dyme	33 Patrae	
17 Eleusis	34 Pellene	

INTRODUCTION

1. Thucydides and his History

Thucydides

Thucydides the Athenian historian tells us that he was the son of Olorus, and had mining interests in Thrace (IV. 104. 4 - 105. 1). Since the Miltiades who commanded the Athenians at Marathon in 490 married the daughter of a Thracian king called Olorus (Hdt. VI. 39. 2), and the Thucydides who opposed Pericles in the 440s belonged to that family (e.g. *Ath. Pol.* 28. 2), it is likely that Thucydides the historian belonged to that family too. The relationships shown in the following table are possible but not certain.

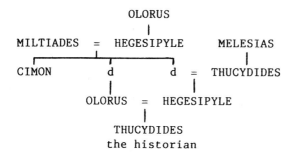

Thucydides served as an Athenian general in 424/3, so if generals had to be at least thirty years old (which is likely but not certain) he was born not later than 454. He failed to prevent Amphipolis from falling into the hands of the Spartans, but was in time to save Ëion for Athens (IV. 104. 6 - 106). He was exiled for his failure, and did not return to Athens until an amnesty was proclaimed at the end of the Peloponnesian War, in 404 (V. 26. 5, cf. e.g. Xen. *Hell.* II. 2. 20). It is assumed that he died within a few years of his return: a recent attempt to prolong his life by arguing that the Lichas who was archon in Thasos in 398/7 is the Lichas of Sparta whose death he records in VIII. 84. 5[1] is unlikely to be correct.

Although he was an aristocrat, from the family which had provided the leading opponents of Pericles in the middle of the century, it is clear that Thucydides became an ardent admirer of Pericles, the aristocrat who presided over the Athenian democracy (see 65. 5-13 with notes). His admiration seems to have been personal rather than ideological: comments on Sparta and Chios (I. 18. 1, VIII. 24. 4), and on the fickleness of the Athenian assembly and on the régime under which Athens lived in 411/0 (II. 65. 4, VIII. 97. 2), suggest that he was no enthusiast for democracy. He strongly disliked Cleon, the ostentatiously populist politician who dominated Athens in the 420s (III. 36. 6, IV. 21. 3, 27-8, V. 16. 1), and Hyperbolus, who tried to succeed to Cleon's position (VIII. 73. 3): Cleon favoured energetic action against Sparta in the north-east, and the statement of an ancient biographer that he was the prosecutor of Thucydides (Marcellin. *Vit. Thuc.* 46) may well be true.

His History

The writing of historical narrative in prose was a product of the intellectual awakening which seems to have begun among the Greeks living on the west coast of Asia Minor and the offshore islands in the sixth and fifth centuries. The one predecessor of Thucydides whose work survives is Herodotus of Halicarnassus (*c*. 480s - 420s), who wrote a history focused on the conflicts between Greeks and Persians at the beginning of the fifth century, in a discursive manner which gave him ample opportunity for digressions on places, peoples and earlier history. He was an intelligent and energetic enquirer (though doubts have been raised as to whether he visited all the places he claims to have visited and saw all the things he claims to have seen); he had an interest but not a totally credulous interest in legends of the gods and the remote past, and in his account of events he combined human motivation with a notion of divine justice. His manner was that of a story-teller, and he had the reputation of being "most Homer-like" ('Ομηρικώτατος). Thucydides does not mention him by name, but in I. 20. 3 criticises statements of his.

Other early historians are known only from quotations and allusions by later writers, and many are little more than names to us. Three deserve to be mentioned here. Hecataeus of Miletus, at the beginning of the fifth century, wrote an account of the Mediterranean world, which was used by Herodotus, and a book on families claiming a divine origin. Hellanicus of Lesbos compiled systematised accounts of myths, and works of local history and chronology: Thucydides in I. 97. 2 says that he was the one previous writer to deal with the period between the Persian Wars and the Peloponnesian War, but his account was brief and not chronologically precise (the reader of I. 89 - 118. 2 is apt to make the same criticism of that account). The eastern enlightenment quickly spread to the west: Antiochus of Syracuse wrote histories of Sicily and Italy, and his work on Sicily may be the source of what Thucydides says in VI. 2 - 5 on Greek colonisation there.

Thucydides states at the outset of his history that he started work on the history of the Peloponnesian War at the beginning of the war, expecting it to be a great war and more noteworthy than any of its predecessors: "this was the greatest upheaval among the Greeks and some of the barbarians, indeed one might say among most of the human race" (I. 1. 1-2: the whole of I. 1 - 23. 3 is intended to justify this statement). This suggests an objective not unlike that of Herodotus, who had written "so that the deeds of men should not be obliterated in the course of time, and that great and wonderful achievements both of the Greeks and of the barbarians should not be lost from memory" (Hdt. I. *praef.*), and had claimed that the force with which the Persians invaded Greece in 480 was greater than any previous force either in the historical period or in the legendary (Hdt. VII. 20).

Though Thucydides' narrative manner is commonly thought of as matter-of-fact, he is actually very willing to use superlatives. At the outbreak of the Peloponnesian War the Greek states were more powerful than ever before (I. 1. 3, 18. 3 - 19, Archidamus in II. 11. 1); never before had there been such destructions of cities, banishment and slaughter of people, earthquakes, eclipses, famine and diseases (I. 23. 3); the losses of Ambracia in the battle at Idomene were "the greatest disaster to befall a single city in the same number of days in this war" (III. 113. 6); the massacre at Mycalessus was "a lamentable disaster, second to none in the war for the size of the place" (VII. 30. 3); and the disaster suffered by the great Athenian invasion of Sicily was the greatest ever (VII. 75. 7, 87. 5-6). In book II, there had never been such a fatal disease as the plague at Athens (47. 3), but the summer of 430 was exceptionally free from disease until the plague struck (49. 1); the Athenians had never had such a leader as Pericles (65); the Spartans' attempt to set fire to Plataea produced the greatest man-made blaze ever known (77. 4), and their landing on Salamis resulted in a panic in Athens second to none in the war (94. 1); in terms of prosperity the Odrysian kingdom is the greatest in Europe, while for military strength the Scythians when united are greater than any other people in Europe and even than any single nation in Asia (97. 5-6);

Archelaus did more for Macedon than all the eight kings who preceded him (100. 2).

But it is not as a recorder of superlatives that Thucydides is commonly remembered. Most of his narrative is sober and serious in manner, and he has impressed readers as a man determined to establish the truth. In I. 22 he gives a statement on his method and purpose, which deserves to be quoted in full:

καὶ ὅσα μὲν λόγῳ εἶπον ἕκαστοι ἢ μέλλοντες πολεμήσειν ἢ ἐν αὐτῷ ἤδη ὄντες, χαλεπὸν τὴν ἀκρίβειαν αὐτὴν τῶν λεχθέντων διαμνημονεῦσαι ἦν ἐμοί τε ὧν αὐτὸς ἤκουσα καὶ τοῖς ἄλλοθέν ποθεν ἐμοὶ ἀπαγγέλλουσιν· ὡς δ' ἂν ἐδόκουν ἐμοὶ ἕκαστοι περὶ τῶν αἰεὶ παρόντων τὰ δέοντα μάλιστ' εἰπεῖν, ἐχομένῳ ὅτι ἐγγύτατα τῆς ξυμπάσης γνώμης τῶν ἀληθῶς λεχθέντων, οὕ-
2 τως εἴρηται. τὰ δ' ἔργα τῶν πραχθέντων ἐν τῷ πολέμῳ οὐκ ἐκ τοῦ παρατυχόντος πυνθανόμενος ἠξίωσα γράφειν, οὐδ' ὡς ἐμοὶ ἐδόκει, ἀλλ' οἷς τε αὐτὸς παρῆν καὶ παρὰ τῶν ἄλλων ὅσον
3 δυνατὸν ἀκριβείᾳ περὶ ἑκάστου ἐπεξελθών. ἐπιπόνως δὲ ηὑρίσκετο, διότι οἱ παρόντες τοῖς ἔργοις ἑκάστοις οὐ ταὐτὰ περὶ τῶν αὐτῶν ἔλεγον, ἀλλ' ὡς ἑκατέρων τις εὐνοίας ἢ μνή-
4 μης ἔχοι. καὶ ἐς μὲν ἀκρόασιν ἴσως τὸ μὴ μυθῶδες αὐτῶν ἀτερπέστερον φανεῖται· ὅσοι δὲ βουλήσονται τῶν τε γενομένων τὸ σαφὲς σκοπεῖν καὶ τῶν μελλόντων ποτε αὖθις κατὰ τὸ ἀνθρώπινον τοιούτων καὶ παραπλησίων ἔσεσθαι, ὠφέλιμα κρίνειν αὐτὰ ἀρκούντως ἕξει. κτῆμά τε ἐς αἰεὶ μᾶλλον ἢ ἀγώνισμα ἐς τὸ παραχρῆμα ἀκούειν ξυγκεῖται.

The words uttered by individual speakers, both before the outbreak of the war and once the war was under way, I could not easily report with accuracy either in cases where I heard the speeches myself or in cases where I depended on reports made to me from the various places. The speeches here represent what I judged it most appropriate for the individual speakers to say with regard to the current circumstances, while keeping as closely as possible
2 to the general sense of what was actually said. The actions performed in the war I did not think it right to narrate on the basis of chance informants or in accordance with my own judgment, but I have based the narrative on my own observation and on the most precise investigation possible of what I could learn from others about each event.
3 The task proved burdensome, because those who were present at the various events gave conflicting reports of the same occurrences, in accordance with each man's prejudice and

memory. The absence of a fabulous element in the history may make it less attractive to listen to, but if it is judged useful by those who want to study a clear account of what has happened, the like of which in accordance with human nature will some time happen again, that will be sufficient. What I have written is a possession for all time rather than a prize composition for a single hearing.

Thucydides' claim is that his history is intended to be useful (cf. II. 48. 3, on his account of the plague at Athens), and that although it is hard to get behind the differing accounts of witnesses (cf. VII. 44. 1-2, 71, but he does not often insert such cautionary remarks in his narrative) he has made a great effort to achieve accuracy. He is proud of his achievement, and very willing to criticise those who do not get the facts right (cf. I. 20, 97. 2, VI. 54. 1, 55): in I. 23. 6 he claims that Sparta's truest reason for going to war against Athens was most concealed, but he will give a definitive account of the causes of the war; in II. 48. 3 he says he will eschew speculation on the plague and keep to the facts; in V. 68. 2 he complains that it was hard to discover the size of the armies which fought at Mantinea in 418 — but then he proceeds to calculate the size of the Spartan army.

For the most part he has relied on oral sources, as he had to do (documents might tell him who commanded the Athenians in a battle and how many soldiers were sent, but they would not give him an account of the course of the battle); and that, and the facts that his history immediately became a classic and no one else wrote an independent history of the Peloponnesian War, make it very hard for us to check his account. Normally he does not, as Herodotus sometimes does, reveal the sources of his information, or give alternative versions before stating which he prefers (there is a striking exception in VIII. 87, and in II. 5. 6 he reports two versions without stating a preference). We know he was aware that witnesses could be biased, and he tells us that his exile gave him the opportunity to speak to people on the anti-Athenian side (V. 26. 5). We know that he made some use of documents: with the treaty quoted in V. 47 we can compare a version inscribed on stone (Tod 72 = *IG* i^3 83), which differs from his version only in small verbal details. Documents are directly quoted only in books IV - V and VIII, but this may be a fact about the composition of his history rather than about the research done for his history. He explains events entirely in human terms, without any suggestion of intervention by the gods or fulfilment of divine plans (cf. pp. 12-13), and his account of what happened and of how and why it happened is almost always credible. (Many, however, have thought that the unexpectedness of the Spartans' encounter with the enemy at Mantinea, mentioned in V. 66. 1-2, does not make sense unless their view was blocked by a wood whose existence is not mentioned by Thucydides, or by any writer earlier than the traveller Pausanias, in the second century A.D.)

He reveals more of how he thought one should set about establishing the truth in the passages where he deals with events earlier than the fifth century. In the opening chapters of book I he reviews the growth of power in Greece, to support his claim that the Peloponnesian War was greater than any previous war. The fact that there was no single name for the Greeks, or distinction between Greeks and barbarians, shows that the earliest Greeks were not a united people who engaged in joint actions (3). The customs which still prevail in the more primitive parts of Greece show what life used to be like in the parts which are no longer primitive (5-6). When corpses were removed from Delos, it was seen that many had been buried in the Carian manner, and this shows that the Aegean islands were once occupied by Carians (8). Powerful states do not necessarily leave impressive physical remains: Athens would seem even more powerful than it actually is, but one would not take Sparta to be powerful; so the unimpressiveness of Mycenae does not disprove the tradition that it was once powerful (10. 1-2). Poets are given to exaggeration, but their stories of the past, and even the details in their stories, can be used if they are approached in a rational spirit (10. 3-5).

In a digression in book VI on the ending of the Athenian tyranny Thucydides confirms that Hippias was the eldest son of Pisistratus by citing an inscription in which Hippias is the first son to be listed, and the only one to be listed with sons of his own (55. 1-2). He also quotes the couplet recording the younger Pisistratus' dedication of the altar of Apollo (54. 7), and puzzles those who have seen the surviving inscription (M&L 11 = IG i^3 948) by describing its lettering as faint. Less happily, in telling the dubious story of the Spartan regent Pausanias he quotes not only the boastful couplet which the Spartans deleted from the Serpent Column (I. 132. 2-3: cf. M&L 27), but also letters allegedly, but hardly in fact, exchanged between Pausanias and the Persian King Xerxes in 478 (I. 128. 6 - 129).

Various statements which Thucydides makes are supported by *tekmeria*, confirmatory pieces of evidence. The fact that originally the city of Athens was on and to the south of the Acropolis is supported by the *tekmerion* that that is where the oldest temples are to be found (II. 15. 3-4). To confirm that birds and animals were vulnerable to the plague at Athens he adduces the *tekmerion* that birds of prey stayed away from the victims and dogs caught the disease from their owners (II. 50). He is also prepared to argue from *eikos*, reasonable likelihood. There is no connection (one had perhaps been alleged by a dramatist) between Teres the Thracian, father of Sitalces, and Tereus of Greek legend, the husband of Procne: apart from other arguments, it is likely that an Athenian king would be more interested in a son-in-law from Daulis than in one from distant Thrace (II. 29). If Hipparchus had been the reigning tyrant in 514, it is unlikely that Hippias would have been able to establish himself when Hipparchus was murdered (VI. 55. 3: in this instance the word *eikos* is not used).

Thucydides is not infallible. Archaeologists do not now believe that the Aegean islands were once occupied by Carians. He ought not to have been taken in by the letters between Pausanias and Xerxes (there was no time for the exchange of letters while Pausanias was in Byzantium in 478, and the letters seem to improve on a rumour reported by Hdt. V. 32). In VI. 54-9 he argues that until 514 the tyranny at Athens was not unpopular, and Harmodius and Aristogiton murdered Hipparchus for purely personal reasons, yet he gives them some fellow-plotters and the hope that when they had struck the first blow the rest of the Athenians would want to reclaim their freedom. His belief that a rational enquirer can extract historical truth from epic poetry is too simple-minded.

Even in the contemporary history which was his main concern we occasionally have reason to think him mistaken on points of detail. An inscription (M&L 61 = *IG* i³ 364) suggests that he is wrong about the commanders of an Athenian expedition in I. 51. 4. Later writers (Androt. *FGrH* 324 F 43, *Ath. Pol.* 29. 2, Philoch. *FGrH* 328 F 136) disagreed with VIII. 67. 1 on the composition of the committee which paved the way for the oligarchy of the Four Hundred in 411, and were probably right to do so. Under the influence of the sophists, the teachers of rhetoric and philosophy who were important in Greek intellectual life in the second half of the fifth century, he was very fond of contrasts such as that between surface appearance and underlying reality (λόγῳ μὲν . . . ἔργῳ δὲ . . .), and we may suspect that sometimes the appearance which he rejects was not wholly false (as in VIII. 89. 2-3, where Theramenes and Aristocrates were no doubt personally ambitious but may not have been totally insincere in the arguments which they used against the Four Hundred). Nevertheless, Thucydides' determination to establish the truth, and the range of evidence and arguments which he employed in his investigations of past history, are most impressive.

The statement on method in I. 22, before proceeding to "the actions performed in the war", begins with "the words uttered by individual speakers". Thucydides' history incorporates a considerable number of speeches, and whereas elsewhere he "did not think it right to narrate . . . in accordance with his own judgment", the speeches "represent what he judged it most appropriate for the individual speakers to say with regard to the current circumstances, while keeping as closely as possible to the general sense of what was actually said". Serious modern historians do not use direct speech except for *verbatim* quotations, and readers who recognise Thucydides' attitude to historical truth as similar to their own are disturbed to find that in the speeches he confessedly allows himself an element of free composition.

Herodotus earlier had used direct speech, but he made no overt claim to authenticity, and in his case the speeches suit the story-telling manner and have not worried modern readers. Direct speech is used also in the other narrative forms of early Greek literature, epic and drama, but of course they make no pretence to factual accuracy. With these precedents it is not surprising that Thucydides should have decided to include speeches in his narrative, but he has caused perplexity by professing two apparently conflicting aims, to follow his own judgment of what was appropriate and to adhere to the general sense of what was actually said. Clearly he was better informed in some cases than in others: he is likely to have heard speeches delivered in Athens before his exile, but he will have had difficulty in finding survivors who had heard and remembered Nicias' speeches in Sicily. Even in cases where he is likely to know what was said in the original speech, he tends to make a speech delivered in one place echo or respond to a speech delivered in another place, as the original cannot have done (compare II. 64. 3, from a speech of Pericles in Athens in 430, with I. 70, from a Corinthian speech in Sparta in 432). The similarity of style between speeches makes it clear that the language is on the whole Thucydides' own, though some striking expressions may have been remembered and incorporated from the original speeches (a Spartan speech in I. 86 begins, "I don't understand the long speech of the Athenians"; Pericles in II. 62. 3 tells the Athenians to regard their land and houses as "a pleasure-garden or adornment of their wealth"). The kind of argument found in the speeches is appropriate to a generation taught by the sophists, and has parallels in speeches in contemporary drama, but we may suspect that the amount of attention devoted to the nature of Athenian power in Thucydides' speeches reflects his own obsession with the subject rather than the amount of attention devoted to it in speeches actually delivered (cf. pp. 13-14).

What room is left for authentic reporting? Most scholars would accept that men did make a speech on occasions when they are said to have done so; and some resolve the problem of conflicting aims by supposing that the "general sense" for which Thucydides claims authenticity is no more than the main point of the speech, e.g. that at Sparta in 432 king Archidamus was opposed to an immediate declaration of war but the ephor Sthenelaidas was in favour.[2] However, so small a degree of authenticity is hardly worth claiming, and it is better to think that Thucydides aimed at more than that, and that the general line of argument is the line which the speaker was known to have taken or could genuinely be expected to have taken — though where Thucydides did not know he may have misjudged, and even where he did know his sense of what was appropriate may have led to his giving more or less prominence to particular arguments than the original speaker gave them. Thucydidean speakers contradict one another on points of fact and interpretation (contrast III. 39. 6 with 47. 2-4 in the Athenian debate on Mytilene): it should never be assumed automatically that what a speaker says is true, or is believed by Thucydides to be true.

Every historian, however strongly committed to factual accuracy, has to decide which facts to include, which facts to treat prominently and which to treat in passing, how one fact should be seen in relation to others. There can be no history without interpretation. Thucydides not only had to interpret, but his family background and involvement in the war make it impossible that his interpretations should be unprejudiced. The tendency of recent scholarship has been not to set him on a pedestal as a totally accurate and objective historian (as earlier generations did) but to present him as an "artful reporter",[3] who though his manner is often matter-of-fact has used great artistry in selecting and presenting his material so as to have the desired effect on his readers.[4]

The use of Athens' might to crush Melos, the last island in the Aegean to hold out against her, is written up at length, with a dialogue between representatives of the two sides, at the end of book V (84 - 116), and immediately afterwards books VI and VII give us a lengthy account of Athens' great expedition to Sicily, which set out with extravagant ambitions but ended in total disaster, while just before the section on Melos Sparta's equally cruel treatment of Hysiae in the Argolid is disposed of in a single sentence (V. 83. 2). Thus Athens' treatment of Melos, though neither important for the course of the war nor unparalleled in its cruelty, is used as an opportunity to give the most cynical presentation of Athens' imperialism before that imperialism overreaches itself in the attempt to conquer Sicily. In book II, the display of Athenian ideals in Pericles' funeral speech (35 - 46) is followed almost immediately by the collapse of moral standards which accompanied the plague (47. 3 - 54, esp. 53: see notes); the campaigns of 429/8 are presented in such a way that each makes a particular point about the contenders (79 - 103: see note on 79).

Thucydides' history is unfinished (cf. pp. 14 - 16), and in a world lacking not only the word-processor and the card index, but even the modern form of book, comparison of one passage with another will have been much harder both for author and for readers than it is today. There have been many highly ingenious studies of Thucydides' artistry which have erred no less than those attributing total objectivity to him, by seeing an implausible degree of intention behind every word in the text as it has come down to us. Not everything in Thucydides' writing in which we can find significance was put there so that we should find that significance; but it is certainly true that he often wrote one passage in full awareness of what he had written in another, and that he has not mechanically compiled a chronicle but has written a well considered history.

The modern reader may complain of Thucydides' omissions. The problem is not so much that he omits explanations which we need but the first generation of his readers did not. Sometimes he does that, as when he fails to make clear what rights the Athenian generals had with regard to convening the assembly (II. 22. 1, 59. 3); but he is presumably remembering that not all his readers will be contemporary Athenians when he gives his account of Athens' public funeral of those who died in war (34), or writes of "what is called the coastal territory, . . . as far as Laurium, where the Athenians have their silver mines" (55. 1); and he gives geographical notes on places in the north-east (96 - 97. 2, 99. 2-6), in the north-west, not always very satisfactorily (30. 2, 66. 1, 102. 2-6), and even in the Peloponnese (27. 2, 56. 5). Nor should we complain too strongly that, by our standards, he takes too narrow a view of what should be included in a history of the Peloponnesian War, that although he devotes a great deal of attention to the morality of the Athenian empire (cf. pp. 13 - 14) he devotes very little to its working, that he does not tell us how far the contenders depended on imports for basic materials or how much damage was done to Athenian agriculture by the Peloponnesian invasions: at that level, what he has not done is what no ancient writer would have thought of doing.

Other kinds of omission are more irritating. In 433 the Athenians received an appeal from Corcyra for support, and a counter-appeal from Corinth, and the assembly devoted two days to considering these appeals; on the first day they tended to favour Corinth, but on the second they changed their minds and made a limited alliance with Corcyra (I. 44. 1) — but how many changed their minds, who spoke on which side, and what was Pericles' position? In book II, not every Athenian approves of Pericles' policy of refusing to meet the Peloponnesian invaders in battle, but no opponent is named: in 431 the men of the deme Acharnae collectively are dissatisfied (21. 3, cf. 20. 4); in 430 "the Athenians" change their mind, attempt to negotiate with Sparta, depose Pericles from his generalship (which Thucydides does not actually state) and fine him, but later reelect him (59. 1-2, 65. 3-4). In cases like these it looks as if the artist has got the better of the reporter, and facts which Thucydides must have known are omitted to show Athens moving towards war in 433, Pericles towering over the other Athenians in 431 and 430. Great perplexity has been caused by the fact that Thucydides does not make much of, and does not make sense of, Athens' large-scale naval expeditions in 431 and 430 (cf. p. 25).

There are lesser omissions too. Ships urgently needed in 429 to reinforce Phormio at Naupactus were sent, but with instructions to go via Crete and take part in a war there: Thucydides does not explain why the Athenians chose to involve themselves in that war, or to use the ships destined for Phormio rather than other ships, but writes of the episode as if it were unremarkable (85. 5-6, 92. 7). Although those reinforcements did not reach him in time, and he was heavily outnumbered, Phormio defeated the Peloponnesians, and the last chapter of book II records his return to Athens in the spring of 428 (103. 1); a little later, in III. 7. 1, his son is sent to Naupactus "because the Acarnanians urged that a son or kinsman should be sent to them as commander", but Thucydides does not explain why Phormio himself was no longer available (possibly he thought he had explained earlier: cf. p. 15).

His Beliefs

Already by the beginning of the fifth century many Greeks were unhappy with the gods as depicted by Homer, beings who resembled but surpassed mortals in every respect including their misbehaviour, and some intellectuals, such as Xenophanes (*Vorsokr.* 21 B 11-12, 14-16, 23-6) and Heraclitus (*Vorsokr.* 22 B 42, 128), were prepared to believe in a divine power but complained that human beings create gods in their own image. Protagoras in the middle of the century proclaimed that man is the measure of all things, and that it is impossible to know whether or not gods exist or what they are like (*Vorsokr.* 80 B 1, 4). Critias at the end of the century wrote a play in which one speaker says that originally there were no restraints on human nature; then laws were invented; but men took to breaking the laws when there was no risk of detection, so gods were invented to put a stop to that (*Vorsokr.* 88 B 25). Herodotus was prepared to say that a channel was certainly the result of an earthquake, and can be called the work of Poseidon if one likes to attribute earthquakes to him (Hdt. VII. 129. 4); but he did not deny the existence of the anthropomorphic gods, and he certainly believed in a divine power which punished impiety, was jealous of great human prosperity and had long-term plans which were fulfilled in human affairs, and he believed in the messages conveyed to human beings through oracles.[5]

There is no indication that Thucydides had any religious beliefs. Events are explained in human terms, beyond which there is only the factor which he calls *tyche* or expresses by means of the impersonal verb *xymbainei*. In some instances these terms refer to the totality of what happens to a community or individual (e.g. II. 74. 1, IV. 14. 3). In others they refer to "chance" in the sense of what cannot be foreseen (e.g. II. 87. 2-3, or, on the weather, III. 49. 4): in I. 140. 1 Pericles remarks on the habit of blaming *tyche* for what *xymbainei* contrary to reasonable expectation (*logos*); in II. 61. 3 he classes the plague at Athens among "happenings which are sudden, unforeseen and contrary to all reasonable expectation".

Religion is a phenomenon which plays a part in the life of some people — but in Pericles' funeral speech festivals have only social value, not religious (II. 38. 1), and when the plague strikes Athens the pious are not spared and religious belief does not prevent people from pursuing their immediate advantage by unjust means (47. 4, 53. 4). Oracles, likewise, are facts to be taken into account when relevant (e.g. 54. 2-5): occasionally the rationalist can find in them a sense other than their surface sense (17. 1-2); only with an oracle that the Peloponnesian War was to last thrice nine years does Thucydides seem inclined to go further (V. 26. 3-4). Sometimes he suppresses a religious dimension: when in 428/7 the men who escape from Plataea do so with their right foot bare, he suggests only a practical reason (III. 22. 2) but probably there was a religious or superstitious reason.[6] Natural phenomena are just natural phenomena, with no significance for human conduct (e.g. II. 28, VII. 50. 4, on eclipses; III. 89. 2-5, on an earthquake and tidal waves; VII. 79. 3, on autumn thunderstorms): exceptionally, at the end of his introduction on the greatness of the Peloponnesian War, he is tempted to see significance in the earthquakes, eclipses, famines and diseases which accompanied it (I. 23. 3).[7]

We have already noticed Thucydides' attitude to Pericles and Periclean democracy (pp. 1-2). The nature of Athenian power is a prominent theme in his speeches, and I have suggested that this is because he was obsessed with the subject. Contemporary sophists were fond of the distinction between *physis*, unrestrained nature, and *nomos*, human convention (notice III. 45. 3, 7, from Diodotus' speech in the debate on Mytilene: "It is the *physis* of all men to err, both individually and collectively, and there is no *nomos* which will prevent them from doing so ... quite simply it is impossible, and extremely naïve, to suppose that when men's *physis* is strongly impelled to do anything it can be deterred by the might of *nomoi* or any other threat"). Some men argued that, although laws (*nomoi*) and moral rules were matters of human convention, they were nevertheless desirable (e.g. Protagoras in Pl. *Prt.* 320 C - 322 D, 326 C-E); others claimed that they were undesirable, as a device to prevent those who were strong by nature from acting as they wished (e.g. Antiphon the Sophist, *Vorsokr.* 87 B 44. 12-34). It is clear that Thucydides, though he did not believe in divine sanctions for human behaviour, did believe that as far as the conduct of individuals is concerned compliance with moral standards and obedience to law is better than rejection of moral standards and defiance of law (see especially II. 53, in the account of the plague at Athens, III. 82-3, generalising from a civil war in Corcyra;[8] and compare II. 37. 3, in Pericles' funeral speech).

However, the Athenian empire presented him with a dilemma: as a patriotic Athenian, he was proud of his city's achievement (his admiration of Pericles clearly extends to Pericles' empire: II. 65. 5-7); yet the means by which the empire was acquired and retained might well be seen as acts of unrestrained *physis*, as rejection of moral standards and defiance of law on the largest scale: the Athenians in Sparta in 432 say, "We have done nothing surprising or alien to human ways . . . men deserve praise if they take advantage of human *physis* to rule over others but behave with more justice than the strength which they have would allow" (I. 76. 2-3). In his speeches Thucydides represents the Athenians as having no illusions about the nature of their empire: it is described as a tyranny not only by the Corinthians (I. 122. 3), and by Cleon, of whom he disapproves, but also by Pericles, of whom he approves (II. 63. 2: cf. also the unknown Euphemus in VI. 85. 1). As he suggests that the Athenians naturally exercised their power in their own interests, he suggests that their subjects naturally hated this (e.g. the Athenians in I. 75. 4 - 76. 1, Pericles in II. 63. 1, 64. 5). I believe that the element of reporting in his speeches is to be taken seriously (cf. pp. 8 - 9): in concentrating on this view of the empire Thucydides may be exaggerating, but he is not fundamentally wrong.[9] And I suspect that he returns to the subject so often because he could not resolve the dilemma to his own satisfaction.

The Composition of his History

Thucydides' history is unfinished. Though he lived beyond the end of the war (cf. p. 1), the text which we have breaks off abruptly in the autumn of 411; and, since Xenophon's *Hellenica* and other histories which have not survived began at that far from obvious point (cf. pp. 18 - 19), we may safely assume that what we have is, if not all that Thucydides wrote, at any rate all of his writing that was ever made public. Since he started work at the beginning of the war (I. 1. 1) and lived beyond the end, we may reasonably wonder about the timetable of his work. Did he write up the events of each year or half-year (cf. note on II. 1. 1) shortly afterwards and then close that section, did he merely make notes during the course of the war, and wait until the war was over to begin composing his history, or did he do something between those two extremes?

The question is complicated by the fact that for some time the Peloponnesian War seemed to have been ended by the Peace of Nicias, in 421: although Athenians and Spartans fought against one another in the intervening years, it was possible to pretend that the peace was still in force until Athens joined Argos in a raid on Spartan territory, in 414 (VI. 105, cf. VII. 18. 3). V. 20 discusses the length of this first phase of the war in a manner appropriate to the ending of the war; but the chapter ends by referring to "this first war", and therefore cannot have been written in its present form until Thucydides realised that the Peace of Nicias had not ended the war. V. 24. 2, with another reference to "the first war", begins Thucydides' eleventh year; ch. 25 remarks that even immediately there was not a complete settlement, and the situation worsened until open war resumed; and then in ch. 26 we have Thucydides' second preface, which echoes I. 1. 1 and II. 1. 1, says that he continued his history to the dismantling of the Athenian empire and the destruction of the long walls and Piraeus fortifications (which as far as his published text is concerned is not true), and justifies his decision to treat the whole twenty-seven-year period as a single war.

In book II, the obituary notice on Pericles in ch. 65 refers to events after Pericles' death, including the great Sicilian expedition of 415 - 413, and the support for Sparta of the Persian prince Cyrus in and after 407 (§§10-12); 100. 2 mentions the reign of Archelaus in Macedon, which lasted from 413 to 399. On the other hand, 23. 3 says that Oropus "is occupied by the Oropians as subjects of Athens", which ceased to be true in 412/1 (and it is arguable that the last sentence of 54. 3 was written before the end of the war and not revised afterwards). Therefore neither of the extreme solutions mentioned above is acceptable: throughout the history there are both passages which were written well before the end of the war, and were not revised in the light of subsequent events, and passages which were not written until after the war had ended.

Moreover, there are internal discrepancies which show that the whole work is not the product of a single spell of thinking. Most strikingly, II. 65. 11 suggests that the Sicilian expedition was not at fault in its conception but failed owing to a lack of proper support from Athens; but books VI - VII give the impression that the expedition was at fault in its conception yet even so short-term success might have been achieved but for the blunders of Nicias. At the level of detail, a note on Thyrea and the settlement of the Aeginetans there, in II. 27. 2, is repeated in IV. 56. 2; and it seems possible that when Thucydides wrote III. 7. 1 he imagined that in II. 103. 1 he had explained what became of Phormio (cf. p. 11).

V. 25 - 83 and book VIII are disjointed as the rest of the history is not, and it can plausibly be argued that these represent a relatively primitive stage in the process of composition, a first draft which Thucydides hoped to revise later. IV.

102 - V. 13, V. 84 - 116 and books VI - VII contain polished accounts of events in the north-east, in Melos and in Sicily respectively: they are not obviously unfinished, but comparison with the rest of the narrative suggests that they need to have combined with them more information on what was happening elsewhere at the same time, and that Thucydides may have intended to supply that information in due course. II. 1 - IV. 101 appear to be the most finished part of books II - VIII, neither unpolished nor limited to particular episodes, but within book II we have noticed at least one passage which came to need revision but did not receive it, and other passages which were not written until the end of the war. Book I, on the greatness of the war and the causes of the war, is thought by some to betray an attempt to superimpose a later view of the causes on an earlier, but I believe that it does not do so, but embodies a carefully worked out design.[10] It is, however, possible that the section on Pausanias and Themistocles in chs. 128-38 is an early essay, incorporated because Thucydides had written it rather than written in order to be incorporated.

The number of passages which are demonstrably early or late is not large. It is likely that the account of the years 431 - 421 was worked up to almost its present form in the years after the Peace of Nicias, when the war seemed to be at an end, and that the accounts of Melos and of the Sicilian expedition were similarly worked up soon after the events in question. No section of the history was definitively finished: later events might cause Thucydides to go back and revise a passage which already existed in a polished form, but he never reached the final stage of going through all that he had written to bring everything up to date and remove all inconsistencies.

His Language

Detailed treatment of Thucydides' language, and of the history of the text, is outside the scope of this series, but a little must be said here about these subjects.[11] In narrative passages his manner is for the most part very straightforward; as in the chapters on Plataea (II. 2 - 6, 71-8, III. 20-4, 52 - 68) it can be extremely vivid. In speeches his style is elaborate and idiosyncratic, making great and sometimes forced use of antithesis, but (unlike his contemporary, the Sicilian orator Gorgias) preferring variation in detail to an exact balance between the contrasted elements, and it is a compressed style, in which "he often tries to say too much in too few words",[12] so that the meaning may be hard to fathom. He is fond of abstract concepts, which he expresses sometimes by means of abstract nouns, sometimes by means of a neuter adjective or participle with the definite article, and he is fond of verbs compounded by one or more prefixes, often producing forms which have few or no parallels in surviving classical literature. Though not always perfectly lucid, he was a writer of great skill, at a time when writing in prose was still a young art in Greece. There is little contemporary prose for us to compare with his, but if more existed we should expect to find many features which were distinctively his own: when we look for parallels in surviving texts, we can often find them more easily in contemporary drama than in later prose.

The Text

No scribe at any date is likely to have copied a substantial portion of the text in front of him without making errors of his own, and perhaps also emending (whether correctly or incorrectly) what he took to be errors in the text in front of him, so no copy of Thucydides' text is likely to be identical either with any other copy or with the text which Thucydides himself wrote. It is not always easy for us to identify and correct our predecessors' errors, and neither this nor any other modern edition is likely to have succeeded at every point in recovering what Thucydides himself wrote.

Thucydides' text is known to have existed in the ancient world in a number of different versions: our mediaeval manuscripts transmit a version which divides the text into eight books, but there is no indication of a division made by Thucydides himself, and we know that other versions existed which divided the text into a larger number of books.

Several papyrus fragments, written between the third century B.C. and the sixth century A.D., contain parts of the text. In this edition I cite Π^8, a commentary on II. 1 – 45, and Π^{21}, Π^{25} and Π^{34}, each of which contains a few chapters of book II.

For book II there are seven mediaeval manuscripts of primary importance, C, G, M, E, F, A and B: they appear to be derived in the main from a single ancestor, Θ, but to account for the differences between the surviving manuscripts scholars have been led to postulate several lost manuscripts which are independent of Θ but have affected one or more descendants of Θ. P is a manuscript containing a text of II. 75-8 which appears to be independent of Θ; H is a manuscript which in book II derives its original text from Θ through B but has had corrections made from a source independent of Θ. Because the relationship between the manuscripts is complex, it is impossible to identify a group of "the best manuscripts", whose authority could be followed when we had alternative readings both of which were intrinsically acceptable.

We also have indirect evidence for the text of Thucydides. There are places where ancient authors and commentators (themselves transmitted to us by generations of copyists) quote or expound Thucydides, and sometimes their text is different from that of our surviving copies. For example, on 42. 4 and 102. 4 I cite scholiasts (commentators) on Thucydides; on 13. 3 I cite a scholiast on Aristophanes' *Plutus* who quotes Thucydides; on 42. 4 and elsewhere I cite Dionysius of Halicarnassus, a critic who wrote in the time of Augustus. Lorenzo Valla, who completed a Latin translation of Thucydides in 1452, had access to manuscripts independent of those which now survive, and on 21. 1 and 39. 5 I cite his translation.

In this edition I provide an *apparatus criticus* at all points where my text differs from the Oxford Classical Text of H. Stuart Jones, and at some points where I accept the Oxford Text but significant doubts have been raised. For a catalogue of the papyri and manuscripts cited, see p. 30.

After Thucydides

Thucydides' history immediately became a classic: other historians deliberately began their work where his ended (cf. p. 14), and as far as we know no one wrote a history of the Peloponnesian War which was essentially independent of his.

Some subsequent writers produced general Greek histories, covering a shorter or longer period. Xenophon, an Athenian who spent much of his life as a dependant of Sparta, in his *Hellenica* continued the story from 411 to 362: he was not an energetic enquirer; on many points other sources disagree with him and are sometimes to be preferred to him; he tended to deal with matters which could not be presented in a manner creditable to Sparta by omitting them altogether. He also wrote the *Anabasis*, on an exciting episode in which he was involved, and an account of his hero, the Spartan king *Agesilaus*. Ephorus, of Cyme in Asia Minor, wrote a general Greek history from the legendary period to the middle of the fourth century, and although that has not survived the section on the fifth and fourth centuries was extensively used in the universal history of Diodorus Siculus (cf. p. 20): after 411 he is a valuable alternative to Xenophon, but for the earlier part of the Peloponnesian War his account was based on that of Thucydides, with some deviations to the greater glory of Athens from another source or his own invention. Theopompus of Chios wrote *Hellenica*, covering the period 411 - 394, and *Philippica*, presenting a universal history in a series of digressions from Philip II of Macedon. All of these were more given than Thucydides to moralising; Ephorus and Theopompus were both believed to have been pupils of the Athenian orator Isocrates, and Theopompus wrote speeches before he turned to history. Many of the later Greek historians succumbed to rhetorical influence, and were more interested in pleasing their readers and in moralising than in investigating what had happened and explaining why it had happened.

Those who were still interested in investigation tended to work on a smaller scale, compiling local histories, records of eponymous priests or Olympic victors, and the like: the first to write in this way was Thucydides' older contemporary, Hellanicus of Lesbos (cf. pp. 2-3). In and after the time of Alexander the Great some of the leading generals wrote accounts of the affairs in which they had been involved: writers like Nearchus and Ptolemy on Alexander and Hieronymus on the late fourth and early third centuries were at any rate in a position to know much of the truth, and were less given to rhetorical embellishment than the later writers who used them as sources.

The last great Greek historian was another man of affairs, the Arcadian Polybius, who in the second century was taken to Rome as a hostage, became an admirer of Rome, and wrote an account of the growth of Rome's empire from 264 to 146. Polybius like Thucydides professed a serious purpose and criticised those who did not come up to his standards. He believed that history should be useful, and frequently protested that it should keep to the truth, of speeches as well as actions: Phylarchus is criticised for writing history like tragedy, which aims to be plausible and does not mind being false (Polyb. II. 56); Timaeus is criticised for composing rhetorical exercises and passing over the speeches that were actually made (XII. 25b, cf. i). The historian needs research in libraries and archives, exploration of the terrain and personal experience of affairs (XII. 25e): Polybius' details of the Carthaginian forces at the beginning of the Second Punic War are not plausible invention but are derived from an inscription (III. 33. 17-18); other accounts of Hannibal's crossing of the Alps are both false and contradictory, but Polybius credits him with a reasonable plan, and has himself interrogated witnesses and explored the terrain (III. 47. 6 – 48). Two concessions are made: to report miracles is childish credulity, but what will support the piety of the masses can be pardoned as long as it does not go too far (XVI. 12. 3-11); and the historian may yield to patriotic bias as long as it does not lead him into actual falsehood (XVI. 14. 6-10). Polybius, like Thucydides, was human and should not be placed on a pedestal, but he had a sense of the historian's responsibility which was like that of Thucydides and not far from that of a modern historian.

From the time of Polybius the Greek world was part of the Roman, and historians writing in Greek were concerned as much with Rome as with Greece. Diodorus (cf. p. 19) wrote a universal history down to 54 B.C.: for the most part he followed one main source at a time for each region, rearranging the material in annalistic form (without taking much care to assign events to the correct years) and adding moralising passages of his own. Appian of Alexandria, in the second century A.D., wrote regional histories of the wars through which Rome's empire grew; and Cassius Dio of Bithynia, in the third, rose to be twice consul and wrote a history of Rome. Meanwhile, c. A.D. 100, Plutarch, of Chaeronea in Boeotia, wrote parallel *Lives* to display the characters of famous Greeks and famous Romans; and in the second century Arrian, like Dio a man from Bithynia who had a political career under the Romans, wrote histories of Alexander the Great and his successors in which he went back to early and well-informed sources. Greek had become the language of educated men throughout the eastern Mediterranean, and histories written in Greek include the *Jewish War* and *Jewish Antiquities* of Josephus (first century A.D.), who used non-Jewish as well as Jewish sources, and ended his life as a Roman citizen living in Rome.

2. The Peloponnesian War

The Origins of the War

By the beginning of the fifth century B.C. Sparta and Athens were the largest and strongest of the many city states into which Greece was divided, and most of the other states in the Peloponnese, the southern part of the Greek mainland, were organised under Sparta's leadership in a league of allies, known to modern scholars as the Peloponnesian League. In the 480s the

Athenians took advantage of surplus revenue from their silver mines to equip themselves with two hundred warships, a much larger navy than any other state possessed. When the Persians embarked on a major invasion of Greece, in 480, Sparta was accepted with little dispute as the leader of the loyalist cities, and Athens provided by far the largest contingent in the loyalists' navy. Though successful at first, the Persians were defeated at sea in 480, at Salamis, and on land in 479, at Plataea.

The Persians were never in fact to invade Europe again, but in 479 that could not have been predicted, and it seemed important to strike back at the Persians, in order to obtain revenge and to liberate the Greeks of western Asia Minor, who were still under Persian rule, and also to guard against subsequent Persian attacks. Already in 479 Greek forces landed on Cape Mycale, on the mainland of Asia Minor, and defeated the Persians there; later that year, when the Spartans and some of the allies had returned home, the Athenians led others in capturing Sestos, on the European side of the Hellespont. In 478 the war continued, still under Spartan leadership; but the Spartan commander Pausanias, who first campaigned in Cyprus and then captured Byzantium, made himself unpopular. The original anti-Persian alliance was not dissolved, but in the winter of 478/7 a new alliance (with its headquarters on the island of Delos, where there was an important sanctuary of Apollo, so the alliance is known to us as the Delian League) was founded under the leadership of Athens to continue the war against Persia. Sparta and the other Peloponnesian states did not join this league, but did not at first feel threatened by it. (Cf. Thuc. I. 89, 94-7.)

The Delian League began as an alliance of free states with a common purpose, in which the executive power was vested in Athens, and those among the members who remembered the Ionian Revolt against Persia in the 490s (to which Athens had sent assistance, but only for one year) may have been more afraid that Athens would lose interest in the war against Persia than that she would abuse her position and infringe their independence. However, though the Athenians probably did not set out with selfish intentions, even in the earliest campaigns of the league they found themselves presented with, and accepted, opportunities to advance the particular interests of Athens. The alliance had been made for all time, but the allies' enthusiasm for an unending war was not so durable, and as the Athenians insisted on the obligations of reluctant allies they became increasingly domineering: in particular, more and more members chose or were required to contribute cash (*phoros*, "tribute") rather than ships of their own to the league's forces, and in this way they were weakened while Athens was strengthened. (Cf. I. 98 - 101.)

After the defeat of the Persian invasion of Greece, the Athenian Themistocles had seen Sparta as a rival of Athens (cf. I. 90-3, and other stories in which Themistocles is credited with an anti-Spartan stance); but he was on the losing side in Athenian politics, and the league's early campaigns were directed by Cimon, who favoured good relations with Sparta. After an earthquake in 464, when they were confronted with a revolt of their subject peoples in Laconia and Messenia, the Spartans appealed for help to all who had been their allies against Persia in 480 - 478, including Athens, and Cimon took a substantial Athenian army to the Peloponnese. But men associated with Themistocles (who had himself been driven into exile with the Persians) gained the upper hand in Cimon's absence, in 462/1, and achieved a major democratic reform. They had been opposed to the sending of help to Sparta, and the Spartans, distrusting the new régime, dismissed Cimon and his army. The Athenians then broke off their alliance with Sparta, and joined instead with Sparta's enemies on the Greek mainland. (Cf. I. 101-2.)

Between 460 and 454 the Athenians continued the war against Persia, in Cyprus (which was half Greek) and Egypt (where there had been Greek settlers for two hundred years), and at the same time fought to build up a powerful position on the Greek mainland: members of the Delian League were called on to help them, in Greece as well as against the Persians. However, the Egyptian campaign ended in disaster, and Cimon was killed in a further campaign in Cyprus, while Athens' expansion in Greece lost momentum. (Cf. 1. 103-12.) From inscriptions we learn that in the late 450s and early 440s Athens had to face a good deal of disaffection from league members, some of whom had Persian support, and that in dealing with this she took several further steps along the road which led her from being leader of an alliance to being ruler of an empire. With the Persians driven out of the Aegean, and Cimon dead, there was no longer enthusiasm in Athens for continuing war against Persia, and *c*. 450 the war which the league had been founded to fight came to an end (whether *de facto* or by a formal treaty). Nevertheless, the league was not disbanded.

In 447/6 subjects in Greece whom Athens had acquired in the early 450s rebelled, and a Peloponnesian army commanded by a Spartan king invaded Attica. He turned back without attacking

Athens, but the Athenians came to terms. By the Thirty Years' Peace of 446/5 (mentioned in II. 2. 1) Athens gave up her possessions on the mainland but her domination of the Aegean through the Delian League was recognised: Greece was divided into a Spartan-led, land-based bloc and an Athenian-led, sea-based bloc. (Cf. I. 113 - 115. 1.) But, if expansion on the mainland was forbidden, Athens was still interested in expanding wherever she could: in the years after 446/5 we hear of colonies founded at Thurii, in southern Italy, at Amphipolis, in Thrace (IV. 102. 2-3), and on the shores of the Black Sea. The equilibrium which the Thirty Years' Peace sought to establish was unstable.

Thucydides' narrative of the events leading directly to the outbreak of the war (I. 24 - 88, 118. 3 - 126. 1, 139-46) begins with a war between Corinth, the most powerful member of the Peloponnesian League after Sparta, and Corcyra, an island state off the north-west coast of Greece which had remained outside both blocs: in 433 each appealed to Athens for support, and in the hope of weakening Corinth but avoiding a direct breach of the Thirty Years' Peace Athens granted limited aid to Corcyra. In 433/2 Athens put pressure on Potidaea, which was a member of the Delian League but had strong links with Corinth, and Potidaea revolted: there was a battle in which once more Athenians fought against Corinthians, and Athens began a long and expensive siege of Potidaea, which finally capitulated in 430/29 (cf. II. 2. 1, 13. 3, 31. 2, 58, 67, 70). Also trouble arose between Athens and Megara; and Aegina, forced into the Delian League in the 450s, complained of unfair treatment (cf. II. 27). Among the members of the Peloponnesian League, Corinth took the lead in protesting against Athens' conduct and putting pressure on Sparta, and in 432 first Sparta and then the Peloponnesian League formally decided to go to war against Athens, and to try to break the Athenian empire (for this objective cf. II. 8. 4-5).

Thucydides insists three times that what persuaded the Spartans was their fear of Athens' power, rather than the validity of the particular complaints against Athens (I. 23. 4-6, 88, 118. 2). Technically the Peloponnesians were the aggressors (cf. II. 2. 3, 10 - 12, 18 - 20, and VII. 18. 2), and except perhaps in the case of Aegina, whose complaint Thucydides reports without comment (I. 67. 2, cf. 139. 1, 140. 3), Athens seems to have been careful not to break the letter of the Thirty Years' Peace. Some modern scholars accept that Athens was indeed in the right.[13] However, it can be argued that the Athenians knew that there was bound to be war with Sparta unless they gave up their ambitions (which of course they could not do), that in the late 430s they took a line which was provocative while remaining technically correct, in order to bring about the inevitable war in circumstances favourable to themselves, and that Thucydides has written not an impartial but a patriotically Athenian account of the causes of the war.[14] For "the Athenians" we may read "Pericles". He was one, but not yet the leading one, of the democrats who triumphed over Cimon in 462/1; and, although he never became the universally accepted leader that Thucydides in II. 65. 4-10 would have us believe, he became increasingly influential, and for the most part the policies pursued by Athens from *c.* 460 to 429 were his policies.

Strategy; The Archidamian War

Sparta was fighting to break the Athenian empire and liberate the Greeks from actual or threatened rule by Athens (cf. II. 8. 4-5), so she needed a positive victory: Athens needed only to survive unscathed. Sparta was a land power and Athens was a sea power: we are given figures for Athens' own forces in II. 13. 6-8, and although we have no comparable figures for Athens' allies or for the Spartan side it is a reasonable assumption that the Athenians had a 3 : 1 superiority in ships (and the more skilled sailors) but the Spartans had a 3 : 1 superiority in heavy infantry (and no other city's soldiers were a match for Sparta's).

Sparta began the war with the traditional Greek strategy, of invading the enemy's territory with a large army in the hope that they would come outside their fortifications to fight and be beaten (in book II, chs. 10 - 12, 18 - 23; 47. 1-2, 55, 57). These invasions were led by the Spartan king Archidamus, and the first phase of the war is known as the Archidamian War. However, the long walls built in the middle of the century had made a single fortified area of Athens and the harbour town of the Piraeus, and as long as they controlled the sea and had the money to pay for their purchases (and financially the Athenians were far stronger than their opponents: cf. 13. 2-5) the Athenians could afford to neglect their farms in Attica. Pericles' strategy for Athens, which tried the patience of some men, was therefore to stay inside the fortifications and not give the Spartans the infantry battle which they wanted (13. 2, 14 - 17, 22; 55. 2). Beyond that, according to Thucydides, he merely thought that she should maintain her naval strength, keeping a firm grip on the empire she already had but not seeking to extend it (13. 2, 62. 2-3, 65. 7).

In fact, in the first two years of the war Athens sent out large-scale, expensive naval expeditions, and if she had continued to operate on that scale she would have exhausted her funds long before the Peace of Nicias brought the war to an apparent end in 421 — but Thucydides' narrative of these expeditions is disjointed and perfunctory, implying that they were casual raiding expeditions of no great importance (17. 4, 23. 2, 25-6, 30; 56, 58). Almost all commentators have agreed that these expeditions are hard to reconcile with the picture of Periclean strategy painted by Thucydides: my own view is that Thucydides reflects Pericles' public statements and that those were more cautious than Pericles' private hopes (see on 25. 1).

The area under Peloponnesian influence which was most vulnerable to attack by a naval power was north-western Greece, where there were many Corinthian colonies but also some friends of Athens, and this area saw a good deal of activity in the early years of the war. The expedition which Athens sent round the Peloponnese in 431 continued beyond the Gulf of Corinth to Acarnania (30); in the winter of 431/0 a Corinthian expedition was sent in reply (33); and in 430 another Peloponnesian force attacked Zacynthus (66), and Ambracia and its barbarian neighbours made an attack on Athens' ally, Amphilochian Argos (68). In 429 Ambracia invited the Peloponnesians to join in a major attack on Acarnania, but the impetuosity of their barbarian allies led to disaster, and the attempt to send help to this force by sea resulted in further disasters for the Peloponnesians in the Gulf of Corinth (80 - 92); an Athenian force campaigned in Acarnania in the winter of 429/8 (102-3). Fighting in the north-west continued for a while, and on the whole Athens had the better of it, but her allies on the mainland grew afraid of her and in 426/5 made a hundred-year treaty of neutrality with their opponents (III. 113. 6 - 114), and on the island of Corcyra a bitter civil war left Athens' supporters victorious but badly weakened (III. 69 - 85, IV. 2 - 5, 46-8).

The one part of the Athenian empire which could be reached from Greece by a land power was the coast of Macedon and Thrace: when the war began, Potidaea was under siege and its neighbours were in revolt from Athens, and king Perdiccas of Macedon in the interests of his own security wavered between friendship and hostility towards Athens. The siege of Potidaea ended with the city's capitulation in the winter of 430/29 (II. 31. 2, 58, 67. 1, 70). In 431 Athens made an alliance with the

Thracian king Sitalces (29): in 430 his son handed over to the Athenians a party of Peloponnesian envoys making for Persia (67: on Persia cf. p. 27); but he did not help them against Potidaea, or in a campaign in 429 (79), and they sent no help to him when he invaded Macedon with a large army in the winter of 429/8 (95 - 101). The Spartan Brasidas, who makes his first appearances in book II, where he is already shown to be more enterprising than most Spartans (25. 2, 85-6, 93. 1), took a small force through Greece to Thrace in 424. Support from Sparta was luke-warm, on account of the Athenians' success at Pylos in 425 (cf. p. 27), but he was so successful in detaching north-eastern cities from their allegiance to Athens that special terms had to be provided for several of them in the Peace of Nicias, and Athens' colony Amphipolis, which should have been returned to Athens, defied the treaty (IV. 78 - 88, 102-32, 135, V. 2 - 3, 6 - 13, 18. 5-6, 21).

Thucydides treats as the first episode of the war an attack by Thebes on Plataea, in the spring of 431 (II. 2 - 6). Plataea was on the Boeotian side of the mountain range separating Boeotia from Attica, but since the late sixth century had refused to join the Boeotian federation dominated by Thebes, and had been an ally of Athens. In 429 Sparta began a siege of Plataea (71-8), and in 427 the city was captured and destroyed (III. 20-4, 52 - 58). This was clearly to the advantage of Thebes, and made for easier communications between Thebes and the Peloponnese, but the importance of the destruction of Plataea for the course of the Peloponnesian War does not justify the amount of attention which Thucydides devotes to it (see on 6. 4 and 71. 1). Although Athens could not hope to defeat the combined forces of her enemies on land, she might have been able to defeat the Thebans in circumstances where they could not quickly obtain help from the Peloponnese. Twice, it seems, Athens tried to strike at Thebes from several directions simultaneously, in 426 and in 424/3 (III. 91. 3-6 with 94-8, but Thucydides does not make the connection; IV. 76-7, 89 - 101. 2), but she was not successful on either occasion.

Sparta would have hurt Athens more than she did by her annual invasions if she had been able to establish a permanent fortress within Attica as a base from which to attack the Athenians all the year round (*epiteichismos*). This possibility is mentioned both by the Corinthians and by Pericles in speeches in book I (122. 1, 142. 2-4), but it was only in 413, after the Athenians had committed the most flagrant breach of the Peace of Nicias, and had sent so large a proportion of their manpower to Sicily that the risk seemed worth taking, that the Spartans established a post at Decelea, in northern Attica (VII. 18, 27-8). Similarly, Athens could most effectively have acted against Sparta by establishing a stronghold in Spartan territory, to interfere with Spartan agriculture and incite disaffection among the Spartans' large subject population. There is no sign that the Athenians contemplated this when they sent their large naval expeditions round the Peloponnese in the first two years of the war (cf. on 56. 6); but in 425 Demosthenes was able to establish an Athenian base at Pylos, on the coast of Messenia, and in the fighting which followed the Athenians captured a number of Spartan citizen soldiers, who became an important bargaining counter (IV. 3 - 23, 26 - 41). In 424 a second Athenian base was added, on the island of Cythera, off the coast of Laconia (IV. 53-7).

Athens was better prepared than Sparta to endure a long war (II. 13, cf. I. 80. 3-4, 121-2, 141. 2 - 143). If the war was prolonged, Sparta's best hope of outlasting Athens was to gain access to the comparatively unlimited resources of Persia; and Athens needed, if not to obtain Persian support for herself, at any rate to prevent Sparta from obtaining it (II. 7. 1, cf. I. 82. 1). In 430 Peloponnesian envoys to Persia were betrayed to the Athenians in Thrace (II. 67), and in 425/4 a Persian envoy to Sparta was captured by the Athenians (IV. 50. 1-2). Presumably some Athenian approach to Persia lies behind the mockery of one in Aristophanes, *Acharnians*, 61 - 125, of 425. The Athenians sent back the Persian whom they captured with representatives of their own: these turned back on learning of the King's death (IV. 50. 3), but, although Thucydides does not mention it, other evidence makes it certain that once the new King was securely established Athens did succeed in obtaining a treaty.

In 430 Athens was struck by a plague, which persisted until 426/5, killed about a third of the population and weakened many others (II. 47 - 54, cf. 58. 2-3, III. 87). The effect of this was so demoralising that in 430 the Athenians attempted to make peace with Sparta and deposed Pericles from the office of general; but Pericles revived their determination to fight, and was reelected general, though eventually he was one of those killed by the plague (II. 59. 1-2, 65. 2-6). However, after the capture of their soldiers at Pylos in 425, the Spartans in turn were willing to admit defeat and offered to make peace (cf. IV. 15 - 22). A one-year truce was made in 423 (IV. 117-9), but failed to hold in the Thracian region; the death of the Spartan Brasidas and the Athenian Cleon in a battle outside Amphipolis in 422 removed the men most strongly opposed to a settlement, and in 421 the Peace of Nicias, attempting with a few exceptions to return to the position of 431, seemed to mark the end of the war (V. 14 - 24).

The End of the War

What followed may be narrated briefly here. Sparta's allies did not share her reason for wanting peace, and some of them refused to accept the Peace of Nicias. Argos, Sparta's chief opponent within the Peloponnese, had been kept out of the Archidamian War by a thirty-year peace treaty, but that expired in 421. In 420 Athens, unhappy with Sparta's half-hearted implementation of the Peace of Nicias, made an alliance with Argos and other Peloponnesian states currently opposed to Sparta: this combination offered the chance of an encounter on land in which Athens might be victorious; but in fact the battle of Mantinea, in 418, was a victory for Sparta and enabled her to reassert her supremacy in the Peloponnese.

Most of the Greek cities in the west had been colonised from the Peloponnese, and at the beginning of the war were reckoned among Sparta's allies (II. 7. 2). During the Archidamian War they sent no help to Sparta, and Athens' intervention in support of the Sicilian city of Leontini had to be abandoned when Syracuse persuaded the other Sicilian cities to reject all outside interference (scattered passages between III. 86 and IV. 58 - 65, and V. 4 - 5). In 415 Athens accepted another invitation to intervene in Sicily: large and ambitious forces were sent, and came close to capturing Syracuse; support for Syracuse from the Peloponnese, though not on a large scale, arrived just in time to prevent the Syracusans from surrendering, and in 413 the Athenians were disastrously defeated. This was a great blow to their morale, and the drain on their resources seriously weakened them (VI - VII). Meanwhile, in 413 the Spartans established their raiding base at Decelea (cf. pp. 26-7).

Although in the late 420s the Athenians had made a treaty with the Persians, about 414 they supported a rebel called Amorges against the Persian King. After this provocation, the Persians were prepared to support the Spartans against Athens; and although not all Spartans were happy to pay Persia's price (the return of the Asiatic Greeks to Persian rule), and at some times some Athenians thought that Persia's support could be diverted to them, Persia's support did eventually enable Sparta to defeat Athens. After Athens' failure at

Syracuse, her subjects in the Aegean were less afraid to challenge her. Fighting there began in 412; and, although there were times when it looked as if the war might yet be won by Athens, Sparta's victory at Aegospotami in 405 left her in control of the Hellespont and able to cut off Athens' vital imports, and left Athens unable to build, equip and man another fleet. Athens was blockaded during the winter of 405/4, and capitulated in the spring. She lost her empire (the Asiatic Greeks were claimed by Persia, the other members passed at any rate for a few years into the hands of Sparta), her long walls and nearly all her navy, and became a subordinate ally of Sparta. But this was not a final settlement of the balance of power in Greece: in 395 Athens was to join former allies of Sparta in a new war against Sparta, and in 378 she was to found a new league, of states wishing to defend their independence against Sparta, while in 371 - 369 Sparta was to suffer at the hands of Thebes defeats of a kind which Athens had not been able to inflict on her.

3. Summary of Book II

1	Formal beginning of war
2 - 32	FIRST SUMMER (431)
2 - 6	Thebes' attempt to seize Plataea
7 - 17	Final preparations and resources
18 - 23	The Peloponnesian invasion of Attica
24 - 32	Athenian counter-measures
33 - 46	FIRST WINTER (431/0)
33	A Corinthian campaign in the north-west
34 - 46	The public funeral in Athens
47 - 68	SECOND SUMMER (430)
47 - 54	The plague in Athens
55 - 58	The summer's campaigns (i)
59 - 65	Pericles under attack
66 - 69	The summer's campaigns (ii)
69 - 70	SECOND WINTER (430/29)
71 - 92	THIRD SUMMER (429)
71 - 78	The siege of Plataea
79	An Athenian campaign in the north-east
80 - 82	A Spartan campaign in the north-west
83 - 92	Naval battles in the Gulf of Corinth

93 - 103	THIRD WINTER (429/8)	
93 - 93	The Peloponnesian fleet	
95 - 101	A campaign by Sitalces the Odrysian	
102 - 103	Phormio in Acarnania	

4. Abbreviations used in Apparatus Criticus

(cf. pp. 17 - 18)

Π^8	Pap. *Oxyrhynchius* 853 (London) (commentary on II. 1 - 45)	C2
Π^{21}	Pap. *Oxyrhynchius* 1622 (London) (II. 65, 67)	C2
Π^{25}	Pap. Berolinensis 13236 (Berlin) (II. 65, 67-8, 79 - 82) (A. H. Salonius, *Ein Thucydidespapyrus*. Soc. Scient. Fenn. Comm. Hum. Litt. 2. ii (1927))	C4
Π^{34}	Pap. Mediolanus Voglianus 205 (Milan) (II. 73-4) (V. Bartoletti, *Studi in onore di L. Castiglioni* (Florence: Sansoni, 1960), i. 59 - 66)	C2
C	Cod. Laurentianus LXIX. 2 (Florence)	C10
G	Cod. Monacensis gr. 228 (Munich)	C13
\<G\>	readings inferred for G but not now legible in it	
M	Cod. Britannicus add. 11727 (London)	C11
E	Cod. Palatinus gr. 252 (Heidelberg)	C11
F	Cod. Monacensis gr. 480 (Munich)	C11
A	Cod. Parisinus suppl. gr. 255 (Paris)	C11/12
B	Cod. Vaticanus gr. 126 (Vatican)	C11
P	Cod. Parisinus suppl. gr. 607 (Paris) (foll. 102-3 contain II. 75-8)	C10
H	Cod. Parisinus gr. 1734 (Paris)	C14
codd.	consensus of CGMEFAB	
cett.	consensus of CGMEFAB except as otherwise stated	
rec.	one or more of the manuscripts not listed above	
ac	before correction	
pc	after correction	
Valla	L. Valla, Latin translation of Thucydides, in Cod. Vaticanus lat. 1801	1452

Notes

1. J. Pouilloux & F. Salviat, *CRAI* (1983), 376 - 403.
2. E.g. de Ste Croix, *The Origins of the Peloponnesian War*,

    7 - 16.

3. The phrase is borrowed from the title of a book by V. J. Hunter.

4. This aspect of early Greek literature is stressed by Kitto in *Poiesis*: he notes that the author "relies on his reader to read with that degree of imaginative cooperation that makes direct statement unnecessary and the result more effective " (p. 249, referring at that point to Plato).

5. See de Ste Croix, *G&R*^{2} 24 (1977), 130-48.

6. See Vidal-Naquet, *Le Chasseur noir*, 101-2, 116-7, L. Edmunds, *Studies . . . S. Dow* (GR&BMon. 10 (1984)), 71-5.

7. On the Greeks' interest in recording natural disasters see E. Gabba, *JRS* 71 (1981), 50 - 62, at 56.

8. But III. 84 is an interpolation.

9. For the contrary view see especially de Ste Croix, *Hist.* 3 (1954-5), 1 - 41.

10. I argue this in *Hermes* 115 (1987), 154-65.

11. A list of distinctive features of Thucydides' style may be found in K. J. Dover's small editions of books VI and VII, pp. xiii - xviii / xiii - xvii.

12. Dover, *opp. citt.* xviii / xvi - xvii. Similar criticism was made by ancient writers, such as Cicero and Dionysius of Halicarnassus.

13. E.g. de Ste Croix, *The Origins of the Peloponnesian War*.

14. Cf. my article in *Hermes* 115 (1987), 154-65.

BIBLIOGRAPHY

Details of articles in periodicals are given where they are cited. Here I give details of all books which I cite, apart from editions of Thucydides cited only for their emendations of the Greek text, and of a limited selection of other books: when a book has different publishers in the U.K. and the U.S.A., the American publisher is named second, in parentheses.

Greek Text

The most recent major editions are:
Books I - II ed. ALBERTI, G.B. (Academia Lynceorum.) Rome: Istituto Poligrafico dello Stato, 1972.
Books I - II ed. LUSCHNAT, O., after HUDE, K. (Bibl. Teubneriana.) Leipzig: Teubner, 1954; ^{2}1960.
ed. ROMILLY, J. DE, with WEIL, R., & BODIN, L. (Coll. Budé.) 6 volumes (book II by de Romilly, in vol. ii, 1962). Paris: Les Belles Lettres, 1953-72; i^2 1958.
ed. STUART JONES, H., with *apparatus criticus* revised by POWELL, J.E. (Oxford Classical Texts.) 2 volumes (book II in vol. i). Oxford U.P., 1942.

Commentary

DOVER, K.J. *Thucydides Book VI* and *Thucydides Book VII, with an Introduction and Commentary*. Oxford U.P., 1965.
GOMME, A.W., ANDREWES, A., & DOVER, K.J. *A Historical Commentary on Thucydides*. 5 volumes (book II by Gomme, in vol. ii, 1956). Oxford U.P., 1945-81; i corrected 1950.

English Translation

by CRAWLEY, R. Longmans, 1874; reissued (Everyman's Library) Dent (New York: Dutton), 1910.
by SMITH, C.F. (Loeb Classical Library: with Greek text) 4 volumes (book II in vol. i). Heinemann (Harvard U.P.), 1919-23; revised 1928-35.
by WARNER, R. (Penguin Classics) Penguin, 1954; revised, with introduction and appendixes by FINLEY, M.I., 1972.

On Thucydides

CONNOR, W.R. *Thucydides.* Princeton U.P., 1984.
DOVER, K.J. *Thucydides. Greece and Rome: New Surveys in the Classics* 7 (1973).
FINLEY, J.H. *Three Essays on Thucydides.* (Reprinted from HSCP 49 (1938), 50 (1939) and Supp. 1 (1940).) Harvard U.P., 1967.
—— *Thucydides.* Harvard U.P., 1942; paperback reprint U. of Michigan P., 1963.
FLASHAR, H. *Der Epitaphios des Perikles. Sitzungsberichte Heidelberg* 1969, i.
GOMME, A.W. *Essays in Greek History and Literature* (chs. vi - ix). Blackwell, 1937.
—— *More Essays in Greek History and Literature* (pp. 92 - 138). Blackwell, 1962.
HORNBLOWER, S. *Thucydides.* Duckworth, 1987.
HUNTER, V.J. *Thucydides, the Artful Reporter.* Toronto: Hakkert, 1973.
KITTO, H.D.F. *Poiesis: Structure and Thought* (ch. vi). (Sather Class. Lectures, 36.) U. of California P., 1966.
MACLEOD, C.W. *Collected Essays* (chs. viii - xiii). Oxford U.P., 1983.
MOXON, I.S., SMART, J.D., & WOODMAN, A.J. (edd.) *Past Perspectives: Studies in Greek and Roman Historical Writing* (pp. 1 - 35). Cambridge U.P., 1986.
ROMILLY, J. DE, trans. Thody, P. *Thucydides and Athenian Imperialism.* Blackwell, 1963.
STADTER, P.A. (ed.) *The Speeches in Thucydides.* U. of N. Caro- P., 1973.
WESTLAKE, H.D. *Essays on the Greek Historians and Greek History* (chs. i - xii). Manchester U.P. (New York: Barnes & Noble, 1969.
—— *Individuals in Thucydides.* Cambridge U.P., 1968.
ZIOLKOWSKI, J.E. *Thucydides and the Tradition of Funeral Speeches at Athens.* New York: Arno, 1981.

General Histories

BURY, J.B., rev. MEIGGS, R. *A History of Greece to the Death of Alexander the Great.* Macmillan (New York: St. Martin's P.), ⁴1975.
BUSOLT, G. *Griechische Geschichte bis zur Schlacht bei Chaeroneia.* Volumes I^2, II^2, III.i, III.ii (to 404). Gotha:

Perthes, 1893 - 1904.
Cambridge Ancient History, vol. v. Cambridge U.P., 1927; new edition forthcoming.
HAMMOND, N.G.L. *A History of Greece to 322 B.C.* Oxford U.P., ^{3}1986.
HENDERSON, B.W. *The Great War between Athens and Sparta.* Macmillan, 1927.
HORNBLOWER, S. *The Greek World, 479 - 323 B.C.* Methuen, 1983.
KAGAN, D. *The Outbreak of the Peloponnesian War.* Cornell U.P., 1969.
—— *The Archidamian War.* Cornell U.P., 1974.
—— *The Peace of Nicias and the Sicilian Expedition.* Cornell U.P., 1981.
—— *The Fall of the Athenian Empire.* Cornell U.P., 1987.
SEALEY, R. *A History of the Greek City States, ca. 700 - 338 B.C.* U. of California P., 1976.

Other Books Cited

BELOCH, K.J. *Die attische Politik seit Perikles.* Leipzig: Teubner, 1884.
BEST, J.G.P. *Thracian Peltasts and their Influence on Greek Warfare.* Groningen: Wolters-Noordhoff, 1969.
BOMMELAER, J.-F. *Lysandre de Sparte.* (B.E.F.A.R., 240.) Paris: Boccard, 1981.
BURKERT, W., trans. Raffan, J. *Greek Religion, Archaic and Classical.* Blackwell (Harvard U.P.), 1985.
COALE, A.J., & DEMENY, P. *Regional Model Life Tables.* Princeton U.P., 1966.
DAVIES, J.K. *Athenian Propertied Families, 600 - 300 B.C.* Oxford U.P., 1971.
DE STE CROIX, G.E.M. *The Origins of the Peloponnesian War.* Duckworth (Cornell U.P.), 1972.
—— *Crux: Essays presented to G. E. M. de Ste Croix.* Imprint Academic (as *History of Political thought* 5. i-ii) / Duckworth (Longwood), 1985.
DINSMOOR, W.B., after ANDERSON, W.J., & SPIERS, R.P. *The Architecture of Ancient Greece.* Batsford, 1950; reissued with new preface and photographs, Batsford (Norton), 1975.
DODDS, E.R. *The Greeks and the Irrational.* (Sather Class. Lectures, 25.) U. of California P., 1951.
DOW, S. *Studies presented to S. Dow.* (GR&BMon. 10.) Duke U., 1984.
FORNARA, C.W. *The Athenian Board of Generals from 501 to 404.*

Hist. Einzelschrift 16 (1977).
GOMME, A.W. *The Population of Athens in the Fifth and Fourth Centuries B.C.* (Glasgow U. Pub. 28.) Blackwell, 1933.
HAMMOND, N.G.L. *Epirus.* Oxford U.P., 1967.
—— *Studies in Greek History.* Oxford U.P., 1973.
HAMMOND, N.G.L., GRIFFITH, G.T., & WALBANK, F.W. *A History of Macedonia.* 3 volumes. Oxford U.P., 1972– . (I cite vol. i, by Hammond, 1972, and vol. ii, by Hammond & Griffith [but all passages cited are by Hammond], 1979.)
HANSEN, M.H. *The Athenian Assembly in the Age of Demosthenes.* Blackwell, 1987.
—— *Demography and Democracy.* Herning: Systime, 1986.
HANSON, V.D. *Warfare and Agriculture in Ancient Greece.* (Bibl. di Stud. Ant. 45.) Pisa: Giardini, 1983.
HOPPER, R.J. *The Acropolis.* Weidenfeld & Nicolson (Macmillan), 1971.
ISAAC, B. *The Greek Settlements in Thrace until the Macedonian Conquest.* Leiden: Brill, 1986.
JACOBY, F. *Abhandlungen zur griechischen Geschichtschreibung.* Leiden: Brill, 1956.
JONES, A.H.M. *Athenian Democracy.* Blackwell (Praeger), 1957.
MARSDEN, E.W. *Greek and Roman Artillery,* [i]. *Historical Development.* Oxford U.P., 1969.
MEIGGS, R. *The Athenian Empire.* Oxford U.P., 1972.
MERITT, B.D. *The Athenian Calendar in the Fifth Century.* Harvard U.P. for Am. Sch. Class. Stud. Ath., 1928.
—— Φόρος: *Tribute to B. D. Meritt.* Locust Valley, N.Y.: Augustin, 1974.
MERITT, B.D., WADE-GERY, H.T., & McGREGOR, M.F. *The Athenian Tribute Lists.* 4 volumes. Harvard U.P. for Am. Sch. Class. Stud. Ath. / Princeton: Am. Sch. Class. Stud. Ath., 1939–53.
MIKALSON, J.D. *The Sacred and Civil Calendar of the Athenian Year.* Princeton U.P., 1975.
MITCHELL, B.R. *European Historical Statistics, 1750 - 1950.* Macmillan (Columbia U.P.), 1975.
MORRISON, J.S., & COATES, J.F. *The Athenian Trireme.* Cambridge U.P., 1986.
MORRISON, J.S., & WILLIAMS, R.T. *Greek Oared Ships, 900 - 322 B.C.* Cambridge U.P., 1968.
OBER, J.S. *Fortress Attica.* Mnem. Supp. 84 (1985).
Oxford Classical Dictionary. Oxford U.P., ^{2}1970.
PARKE, H.W. *Festivals of the Athenians.* Thames & Hudson (Cornell U.P.), 1977.
PATTERSON, C. *Pericles' Citizenship Law of 451-50 B.C.* New

York: Arno, 1981.
PICKARD-CAMBRIDGE, A.W., rev. GOULD, J.P.A., & LEWIS, D.M. *The Dramatic Festivals of Athens*. Oxford U.P., 1968.
PRITCHETT, W.K. *The Greek State at War*. 4 volumes (vol. i originally published as *Ancient Greek Military Practices*, i. U. Calif. Pub. Class. Stud. 7 [1971]). U. of California P., 1974-85.
RHODES, P.J. *The Athenian Boule*. Oxford U.P., 1972.
—— *The Athenian Empire*. *Greece & Rome: New Surveys in the Classics* 17 (1985).
ROBINSON, E.S.G. *Essays in Greek Coinage presented to S. Robinson*. Oxford U.P., 1968.
STUPPERICH, R. *Staatsbegräbnis und Privatgrabmal im klassischen Athen*. (Dissertation.) U. of Münster, 1977.
TRAILL, J.S. *The Political Organization of Attica*. Hesp. Supp. 14 (1975).
TRAVLOS, J. *Pictorial Dictionary of Ancient Athens*. Thames & Hudson for Deutscher Archäologischer Institut, 1971.
UNITED NATIONS, Dept. of Social Affairs. *Age and Sex Patterns of Mortality: Model Life-Tables for Under-Developed Countries*. (Population Studies, 22.) New York: United Nations, 1955.
VIDAL-NAQUET, P. *Le Chasseur noir*. Paris: La Découverte / Maspero, 1983.
WHITEHEAD, D. *The Demes of Attica, 508/7 - ca. 250 B.C.* Princeton U.P., 1986.
WOODMAN, A.J. *Velleius Paterculus, Edited with a Commentary*. Cambridge, U.P., 1977- .
WYCHERLEY, R.E. *The Stones of Athens*. Princeton U.P., 1978.

ΘΟΥΚΥΔΙΔΟΥ

ΞΥΓΓΡΑΦΗΣ   Β

THUCYDIDES

HISTORY   II

ΘΟΥΚΥΔΙΔΟΥ

ΞΥΓΓΡΑΦΗΣ Β

1 Ἄρχεται δὲ ὁ πόλεμος ἐνθένδε ἤδη Ἀθηναίων καὶ Πελοποννησίων καὶ τῶν ἑκατέροις ξυμμάχων, ἐν ᾧ οὔτε ἐπεμείγνυντο ἔτι ἀκηρυκτεὶ παρ' ἀλλήλους καταστάντες τε ξυνεχῶς ἐπολέμουν· γέγραπται δὲ ἑξῆς ὡς ἕκαστα ἐγίγνετο κατὰ θέρος καὶ χειμῶνα.

2 Τέσσαρα μὲν γὰρ καὶ δέκα ἔτη ἐνέμειναν αἱ τριακοντούτεις σπονδαὶ αἳ ἐγένοντο μετ' Εὐβοίας ἅλωσιν· τῷ δὲ πέμπτῳ καὶ δεκάτῳ ἔτει, ἐπὶ Χρυσίδος ἐν Ἄργει τότε πεντήκοντα δυοῖν δέοντα ἔτη ἱερωμένης καὶ Αἰνησίου ἐφόρου ἐν Σπάρτῃ καὶ Πυθοδώρου ἔτι τέσσαρας μῆνας ἄρχοντος Ἀθηναίοις, μετὰ τὴν ἐν Ποτειδαίᾳ μάχην μηνὶ δεκάτῳ καὶ ἅμα ἦρι ἀρχομένῳ Θηβαίων ἄνδρες ὀλίγῳ πλείους τριακοσίων (ἡγοῦντο δὲ αὐτῶν βοιωταρχοῦντες Πυθάγγελός τε ὁ Φυλείδου καὶ Διέμπορος ὁ Ὀνητορίδου) ἐσῆλθον περὶ πρῶτον ὕπνον ξὺν ὅπλοις ἐς Πλάταιαν τῆς Βοιωτίας οὖσαν Ἀθηναίων

2 ξυμμαχίδα. ἐπηγάγοντο δὲ καὶ ἀνέῳξαν τὰς πύλας Πλαταιῶν ἄνδρες, Ναυκλείδης τε καὶ οἱ μετ' αὐτοῦ, βουλόμενοι ἰδίας ἕνεκα δυνάμεως ἄνδρας τε τῶν πολιτῶν τοὺς σφίσιν ὑπεναντίους διαφθεῖραι καὶ τὴν πόλιν Θηβαίοις προσποιῆσαι.

3 ἔπραξαν δὲ ταῦτα δι' Εὐρυμάχου τοῦ Λεοντιάδου, ἀνδρὸς Θηβαίων δυνατωτάτου. προϊδόντες γὰρ οἱ Θηβαῖοι ὅτι ἔσοιτο ὁ πόλεμος ἐβούλοντο τὴν Πλάταιαν αἰεὶ σφίσι διάφορον οὖσαν ἔτι ἐν εἰρήνῃ τε καὶ τοῦ πολέμου μήπω φανεροῦ καθεστῶτος προκαταλαβεῖν. ᾗ καὶ ῥᾷον ἔλαθον

4 ἐσελθόντες, φυλακῆς οὐ προκαθεστηκυίας. θέμενοι δὲ ἐς τὴν ἀγορὰν τὰ ὅπλα τοῖς μὲν ἐπαγαγομένοις οὐκ ἐπείθοντο ὥστε εὐθὺς ἔργου ἔχεσθαι καὶ ἰέναι ἐπὶ τὰς οἰκίας τῶν ἐχθρῶν, γνώμην δ' ἐποιοῦντο κηρύγμασί τε χρήσασθαι

---
10. τέσσαρας Krüger: δύο codd.
11. δεκάτῳ Hude: ἕκτῳ codd., ἕκτῳ καὶ δεκάτῳ Lipsius.

THUCYDIDES

History II

Here we reach the starting-point of the war between the Athenians and the Peloponnesians, each with their allies. Now they no longer communicated with each other without a herald, and they entered on a state of continuous war. I have recorded the events in the order in which they occurred, by summers and winters.

The thirty-year truce which followed the capture of Euboea lasted for fourteen years. In the fifteenth year (when Chrysis was in her forty-eighth year as priestess at Argos, Aenesias was ephor at Sparta and Pythodorus still had four months to run as archon at Athens), in the tenth month after the battle at Potidaea, and at the beginning of spring, an armed entry into Plataea was made at the time of the first watch by slightly more than three hundred men from Thebes, led by the boeotarchs Pythangelus son of Phyleides and Diemporus son of Onetorides. Plataea was situated in Boeotia but allied to Athens. They were invited and the gate was opened to them by men of Plataea, Nauclides and his party, who in order to gain power for themselves wanted to eliminate those of the citizens who were opposed to them and align the city with Thebes. The arrangements were made through Eurymachus son of Leontiades, who was very influential in Thebes.

The Thebans saw that war was coming. Plataea had always been hostile to them, and they wanted to strike first and seize it while the peace still held and war had not yet openly broken out. Because of that no guard had yet been set, and it was easier for them to enter undetected. They grounded their arms in the main square, and rather than immediately turning to action and making for the houses of their enemies, as those who invited them had advised, they decided to make an amicable pro-

ἐπιτηδείοις καὶ ἐς ξύμβασιν μᾶλλον καὶ φιλίαν τὴν πόλιν ἀγαγεῖν (καὶ ἀνεῖπεν ὁ κῆρυξ, εἴ τις βούλεται κατὰ τὰ πάτρια τῶν πάντων Βοιωτῶν ξυμμαχεῖν, τίθεσθαι παρ' αὑτοὺς τὰ ὅπλα), νομίζοντες σφίσι ῥᾳδίως τούτῳ τῷ τρόπῳ προσ-
3 χωρήσειν τὴν πόλιν. οἱ δὲ Πλαταιῆς ὡς ᾔσθοντο ἔνδον τε ὄντας τοὺς Θηβαίους καὶ ἐξαπιναίως κατειλημμένην τὴν πόλιν, καταδείσαντες καὶ νομίσαντες πολλῷ πλείους ἐσεληλυθέναι (οὐ γὰρ ἑώρων ἐν τῇ νυκτί) πρὸς ξύμβασιν ἐχώρησαν καὶ τοὺς λόγους δεξάμενοι ἡσύχαζον, ἄλλως τε καὶ ἐπειδὴ
2 ἐς οὐδένα οὐδὲν ἐνεωτέριζον. πράσσοντες δέ πως ταῦτα κατενόησαν οὐ πολλοὺς τοὺς Θηβαίους ὄντας καὶ ἐνόμισαν ἐπιθέμενοι ῥᾳδίως κρατήσειν· τῷ γὰρ πλήθει τῶν Πλαταιῶν
3 οὐ βουλομένῳ ἦν τῶν Ἀθηναίων ἀφίστασθαι. ἐδόκει οὖν ἐπιχειρητέα εἶναι, καὶ ξυνελέγοντο διορύσσοντες τοὺς κοινοὺς τοίχους παρ' ἀλλήλους, ὅπως μὴ διὰ τῶν ὁδῶν φανεροὶ ὦσιν ἰόντες, ἁμάξας τε ἄνευ τῶν ὑποζυγίων ἐς τὰς ὁδοὺς καθίστασαν, ἵνα ἀντὶ τείχους ᾖ, καὶ τἆλλα ἐξήρτυον ᾗ ἕκαστον
4 ἐφαίνετο πρὸς τὰ παρόντα ξύμφορον ἔσεσθαι. ἐπεὶ δὲ ὡς ἐκ τῶν δυνατῶν ἕτοιμα ἦν, φυλάξαντες ἔτι νύκτα καὶ αὐτὸ τὸ περίορθρον ἐχώρουν ἐκ τῶν οἰκιῶν ἐπ' αὐτούς, ὅπως μὴ κατὰ φῶς θαρσαλεωτέροις οὖσι προσφέροιντο καὶ σφίσιν ἐκ τοῦ ἴσου γίγνωνται, ἀλλ' ἐν νυκτὶ φοβερώτεροι ὄντες ἥσσους ὦσι τῆς σφετέρας ἐμπειρίας τῆς κατὰ τὴν πόλιν. προσ-
4 έβαλόν τε εὐθὺς καὶ ἐς χεῖρας ᾖσαν κατὰ τάχος. οἱ δ' ὡς ἔγνωσαν ἐξηπατημένοι, ξυνεστρέφοντό τε ἐν σφίσιν αὐτοῖς
2 καὶ τὰς προσβολὰς ᾗ προσπίπτοιεν ἀπεωθοῦντο. καὶ δὶς μὲν ἢ τρὶς ἀπεκρούσαντο, ἔπειτα πολλῷ θορύβῳ αὐτῶν τε προσβαλλόντων καὶ τῶν γυναικῶν καὶ τῶν οἰκετῶν ἅμα ἀπὸ τῶν οἰκιῶν κραυγῇ τε καὶ ὀλολυγῇ χρωμένων λίθοις τε καὶ κεράμῳ βαλλόντων, καὶ ὑετοῦ ἅμα διὰ νυκτὸς πολλοῦ ἐπι-

---

3. τῶν πάντων Βοιωτῶν codd.: fortasse τοῖς πᾶσι Βοιωτοῖς.
28. προσβαλλόντων H pc rec.: προσβαλόντων codd.

clamation and if possible bring the city to a friendly agreement. The herald's announcement was that any one who wished to be an ally in accordance with the tradition of the whole of Boeotia should set down his weapons with them. They thought that in this way they would easily win over the city.

When the Plataeans realised that the Thebans were inside and the city had been suddenly occupied, they took fright, thinking that far more men had entered than was actually the case, and being unable to see them because it was night. So they came to an agreement and accepted the terms peacefully, especially because no act of violence was committed against anybody. However, in the course of this they discovered that the Thebans were few in number, and reckoned that if they made an attack they would easily win: the majority of the Plataeans were not in favour of defecting from Athens. So they decided they should make the attempt. They joined up with one another by digging through the party walls, to avoid moving through the streets and being detected; and they placed carts without the draught animals in the streets, to serve as a barricade, and arranged everything else in the way that seemed most convenient in the circumstances. When they had made all the preparations they could, they waited until the time when it was still night but dawn was imminent, and then moved from their houses against the Thebans. They did not want to attack by daylight, when their opponents would be more confident and on a level with them, but to catch them at night, when they would be more frightened and unable to match the Plataeans' familiarity with the city. So they made a sudden attack, and quickly came to fighting at close quarters.

The Thebans, realising that they had been tricked, tried to close in upon themselves and repel the attacks wherever they were made. Two or three times they drove the Plataeans back; but a loud noise was made both by the actual attackers and by the women and household slaves, who shouted and cheered and threw stones and tiles at them, and in addition it rained heavily throughout the

γενομένου, ἐφοβήθησαν καὶ τραπόμενοι ἔφευγον διὰ τῆς πόλεως, ἄπειροι μὲν ὄντες οἱ πλείους ἐν σκότῳ καὶ πηλῷ τῶν διόδων ᾗ χρὴ σωθῆναι (καὶ γὰρ τελευτῶντος τοῦ μηνὸς τὰ γιγνόμενα ἦν), ἐμπείρους δὲ ἔχοντες τοὺς διώκοντας τοῦ
3 μὴ ἐκφεύγειν, ὥστε διεφθείροντο οἱ πολλοί. τῶν δὲ Πλαταιῶν τις τὰς πύλας ᾗ ἐσῆλθον καὶ αἵπερ ἦσαν μόναι ἀνεῳγμέναι ἔκλῃσε στυρακίῳ ἀκοντίου ἀντὶ βαλάνου χρησάμενος ἐς τὸν μοχλόν, ὥστε μηδὲ ταύτῃ ἔξοδον ἔτι εἶναι.
4 διωκόμενοι δὲ κατὰ τὴν πόλιν οἱ μέν τινες αὐτῶν ἐπὶ τὸ τεῖχος ἀναβάντες ἔρριψαν ἐς τὸ ἔξω σφᾶς αὐτοὺς καὶ διεφθάρησαν οἱ πλείους, οἱ δὲ κατὰ πύλας ἐρήμους γυναικὸς δούσης πέλεκυν καὶ διακόψαντες τὸν μοχλὸν λαθόντες ἐξῆλθον οὐ πολλοί (αἴσθησις γὰρ ταχεῖα ἐπεγένετο), ἄλλοι
5 δὲ ἄλλῃ τῆς πόλεως σποράδες ἀπώλλυντο. τὸ δὲ πλεῖστον καὶ ὅσον μάλιστα ἦν ξυνεστραμμένον ἐσπίπτουσιν ἐς οἴκημα μέγα, ὃ ἦν τοῦ τείχους καὶ αἱ θύραι ἀνεῳγμέναι ἔτυχον αὐτοῦ, οἰόμενοι πύλας τὰς θύρας τοῦ οἰκήματος εἶναι καὶ
6 ἄντικρυς δίοδον ἐς τὸ ἔξω. ὁρῶντες δὲ αὐτοὺς οἱ Πλαταιῆς ἀπειλημμένους ἐβουλεύοντο εἴτε κατακαύσωσιν ὥσπερ ἔχου-
7 σιν, ἐμπρήσαντες τὸ οἴκημα, εἴτε τι ἄλλο χρήσωνται. τέλος δὲ οὗτοί τε καὶ ὅσοι ἄλλοι τῶν Θηβαίων περιῆσαν κατὰ τὴν πόλιν πλανώμενοι, ξυνέβησαν τοῖς Πλαταιεῦσι παραδοῦναι σφᾶς τε αὐτοὺς καὶ τὰ ὅπλα χρήσασθαι ὅτι ἂν
8 βούλωνται. οἱ μὲν δὴ ἐν τῇ Πλαταίᾳ οὕτως ἐπεπράγεσαν.
5 οἱ δ' ἄλλοι Θηβαῖοι, οὓς ἔδει ἔτι τῆς νυκτὸς παραγενέσθαι πανστρατιᾷ, εἴ τι ἄρα μὴ προχωροίη τοῖς ἐσεληλυθόσι, τῆς ἀγγελίας ἅμα καθ' ὁδὸν αὐτοῖς ῥηθείσης περὶ τῶν γεγενη-
2 μένων ἐπεβοήθουν. ἀπέχει δὲ ἡ Πλάταια τῶν Θηβῶν σταδίους ἑβδομήκοντα, καὶ τὸ ὕδωρ τὸ γενόμενον τῆς νυκτὸς ἐποίησε βραδύτερον αὐτοὺς ἐλθεῖν· ὁ γὰρ Ἀσωπὸς ποταμὸς
3 ἐρρύη μέγας καὶ οὐ ῥᾳδίως διαβατὸς ἦν. πορευόμενοί τε ἐν ὑετῷ καὶ τὸν ποταμὸν μόλις διαβάντες ὕστερον παρεγένοντο, ἤδη τῶν ἀνδρῶν τῶν μὲν διεφθαρμένων, τῶν δὲ
4 ζώντων ἐχομένων. ὡς δ' ᾔσθοντο οἱ Θηβαῖοι τὸ γεγενη-

---

5. ὥστε διεφθείροντο οἱ πολλοί secl. Steup.
12. λαθόντες post πέλεκυν exhibent codd., huc transposuit Classen: ἐρήμους λαθόντες <καὶ> γυναικὸς Richards.
16. καὶ αἱ θύραι C G: καὶ αἱ πλησίον θύραι cett., Π⁸, πλησίον καὶ αἱ θύραι Haase.

42

night, so they took fright. They abandoned their resistance and tried to escape through they city, but most of them did not know in the dark and the mud which were the routes leading through to safety (these events took place at the end of the month), while their pursuers did know how to prevent them from escaping, and so most of them were killed. One of the Plataeans closed the gate by 3 which they had come in, the only one which remained open, inserting the butt-end of a spear instead of a pin into the bolt, and so made it impossible to get out even there. As the Thebans were being pursued through the 4 city, some climbed the wall and hurled themselves outside, but most of these perished. Others at an unguarded gate were given an axe by a woman and cut the bolt: a few got out undetected, but discovery came quickly. Others perished scattered in different parts of the city. The 5 largest number, who formed the most cohesive body, burst into a large building which formed part of the wall and whose door was open, thinking that the door of the building was a city gate and that there was a way through to the outside. The Plataeans saw that they were trapped, 6 and debated whether to set fire to the house and burn them just as they were or to do something else with them. Eventually these men, and such other Thebans as survived 7 wandering about the city, came to terms with the Plataeans, that they should surrender themselves and their weapons and be treated in whatever way the Plataeans chose. That is what happened to the men in Plataea. 8

The rest of the Thebans were supposed to arrive in 5 full force while it was still night, in case anything went wrong for the men inside. The news of what had happened reached them while they were on the road, and they hurried ahead to help. Plataea is seventy stades away 2 from Thebes, and the rain which fell during the night made their journey slower: the River Asopus was in full flood, and was not easy to cross. So, after proceeding 3 through the rain and crossing the river with difficulty, they arrived too late, when some of the men were dead and the others were alive but under arrest. When the Thebans 4

μένον, ἐπεβούλευον τοῖς ἔξω τῆς πόλεως τῶν Πλαταιῶν·
ἦσαν γὰρ καὶ ἄνθρωποι κατὰ τοὺς ἀγροὺς καὶ κατασκευή,
οἷα ἀπροσδοκήτου κακοῦ ἐν εἰρήνῃ γενομένου· ἐβούλοντο
γὰρ σφίσιν, εἴ τινα λάβοιεν, ὑπάρχειν ἀντὶ τῶν ἔνδον, ἢν
ἄρα τύχωσί τινες ἐζωγρημένοι. καὶ οἱ μὲν ταῦτα διενοοῦντο, 5
5 οἱ δὲ Πλαταιῆς ἔτι διαβουλευομένων αὐτῶν ὑποτοπήσαντες
τοιοῦτόν τι ἔσεσθαι καὶ δείσαντες περὶ τοῖς ἔξω κήρυκα
ἐξέπεμψαν παρὰ τοὺς Θηβαίους, λέγοντες ὅτι οὔτε τὰ πεποιη-
μένα ὅσια δράσειαν ἐν σπονδαῖς σφῶν πειράσαντες καταλαβεῖν τὴν πόλιν, τά τε ἔξω ἔλεγον αὐτοῖς μὴ ἀδικεῖν· εἰ 10
δὲ μή, καὶ αὐτοὶ ἔφασαν αὐτῶν τοὺς ἄνδρας ἀποκτενεῖν οὓς
ἔχουσι ζῶντας· ἀναχωρησάντων δὲ πάλιν ἐκ τῆς γῆς
6 ἀποδώσειν αὐτοῖς τοὺς ἄνδρας. Θηβαῖοι μὲν ταῦτα λέγουσι
καὶ ἐπομόσαι φασὶν αὐτούς· Πλαταιῆς δ᾽ οὐχ ὁμολογοῦσι
τοὺς ἄνδρας εὐθὺς ὑποσχέσθαι ἀποδώσειν, ἀλλὰ λόγων 15
πρῶτον γενομένων ἤν τι ξυμβαίνωσι, καὶ ἐπομόσαι οὔ φασιν.
7 ἐκ δ᾽ οὖν τῆς γῆς ἀνεχώρησαν οἱ Θηβαῖοι οὐδὲν ἀδικήσαντες·
οἱ δὲ Πλαταιῆς ἐπειδὴ τὰ ἐκ τῆς χώρας κατὰ τάχος ἐσεκο-
μίσαντο, ἀπέκτειναν τοὺς ἄνδρας εὐθύς. ἦσαν δὲ ὀγδοήκοντα
καὶ ἑκατὸν οἱ ληφθέντες, καὶ Εὐρύμαχος εἷς αὐτῶν ἦν, πρὸς 20
6 ὃν ἔπραξαν οἱ προδιδόντες. τοῦτο δὲ ποιήσαντες ἔς τε τὰς
Ἀθήνας ἄγγελον ἔπεμπον καὶ τοὺς νεκροὺς ὑποσπόνδους
ἀπέδοσαν τοῖς Θηβαίοις, τά τε ἐν τῇ πόλει καθίσταντο πρὸς
2 τὰ παρόντα ᾗ ἐδόκει αὐτοῖς. τοῖς δ᾽ Ἀθηναίοις ἠγγέλθη
εὐθὺς τὰ περὶ τῶν Πλαταιῶν γεγενημένα, καὶ Βοιωτῶν τε 25
παραχρῆμα ξυνέλαβον ὅσοι ἦσαν ἐν τῇ Ἀττικῇ καὶ ἐς τὴν
Πλάταιαν ἔπεμψαν κήρυκα, κελεύοντες εἰπεῖν μηδὲν νεώτερον
ποιεῖν περὶ τῶν ἀνδρῶν οὓς ἔχουσι Θηβαίων, πρὶν ἄν τι καὶ
3 αὐτοὶ βουλεύσωσι περὶ αὐτῶν· οὐ γὰρ ἠγγέλθη αὐτοῖς ὅτι
τεθνηκότες εἶεν. ἅμα γὰρ τῇ ἐσόδῳ γιγνομένῃ τῶν Θηβαίων 30
ὁ πρῶτος ἄγγελος ἐξῄει, ὁ δὲ δεύτερος ἄρτι νενικημένων τε

discovered what had happened, they planned to act against the Plataeans who were outside the city: for there were men in the fields and also equipment, as was natural since trouble had struck unexpectedly in time of peace. They wanted to capture any of these that they could, in order to have them to exchange for any of the men inside who had been taken alive. That is the plan they decided on; but while they were still considering what to 5 do the Plataeans suspected that something of this kind would happen and grew afraid for their property outside. So they sent a herald to the Thebans, to say that their action in trying to take the city in time of truce was not right, and to order them not to do any harm to their property outside; otherwise, the Plataeans said, they would kill the men whom they held alive. When the Thebans had withdrawn from their territory, they would return the men to them. This is what the Thebans say, and they claim 6 that the Plataeans confirmed it by an oath; but the Plataeans deny that they promised to return the men immediately, claiming that there were first to be talks to try to reach an agreement, and they say that they did not swear an oath. At any rate, the Thebans did withdraw from 7 the territory without doing any harm. The Plataeans quickly conveyed inside their property in the country, and then immediately killed the men. The number of captives was a hundred and eighty, among them Eurymachus, the man with whom the Plataean traitors had dealt. After 6 doing this they sent a messenger to Athens, returned the bodies to the Thebans under truce, and organised things in the city as seemed best in the circumstances.

What happened at Plataea was reported immediately 2 to the Athenians. They promptly arrested all the Boeotians who were in Attica, and sent a herald to Plataea with instructions to say that no drastic action was to be taken with regard to the Theban prisoners until the Athenians also had been able to deliberate about them. (The 3 Athenians had not yet heard that the men were dead. The first messenger set out at the time of the Thebans' entry, and the second as soon as they had been defeated and

καὶ ξυνειλημμένων· καὶ τῶν ὕστερον οὐδὲν ᾔδεσαν. οὕτω
δὴ οὐκ εἰδότες οἱ Ἀθηναῖοι ἐπέστελλον· ὁ δὲ κῆρυξ ἀφικό-
4 μενος ηὗρε τοὺς ἄνδρας διεφθαρμένους. καὶ μετὰ ταῦτα οἱ
Ἀθηναῖοι στρατεύσαντες ἐς Πλάταιαν σῖτόν τε ἐσήγαγον
καὶ φρουροὺς ἐγκατέλιπον, τῶν τε ἀνθρώπων τοὺς ἀχρειοτά-
τους ξὺν γυναιξὶ καὶ παισὶν ἐξεκόμισαν.

7 Γεγενημένου δὲ τοῦ ἐν Πλαταιαῖς ἔργου καὶ λελυμένων
λαμπρῶς τῶν σπονδῶν οἱ Ἀθηναῖοι παρεσκευάζοντο ὡς
πολεμήσοντες, παρεσκευάζοντο δὲ καὶ Λακεδαιμόνιοι καὶ
οἱ ξύμμαχοι, πρεσβείας τε μέλλοντες πέμπειν παρὰ βασιλέα
καὶ ἄλλοσε πρὸς τοὺς βαρβάρους, εἴ ποθέν τινα ὠφελίαν
ἤλπιζον ἑκάτεροι προσλήψεσθαι, πόλεις τε ξυμμαχίδας
2 ποιούμενοι ὅσαι ἦσαν ἐκτὸς τῆς ἑαυτῶν δυνάμεως. καὶ
Λακεδαιμονίοις μὲν πρὸς ταῖς αὐτοῦ ὑπαρχούσαις ἐξ Ἰταλίας
καὶ Σικελίας τοῖς τἀκείνων ἑλομένοις ναῦς ἐπετάχθη ποιεῖσθαι
κατὰ μέγεθος τῶν πόλεων, ὡς ἐς τὸν πάντα ἀριθμὸν πεντακοσίων νεῶν ἐσομένων, καὶ ἀργύριον ῥητὸν ἑτοιμάζειν, τά
τε ἄλλα ἡσυχάζοντας καὶ Ἀθηναίους δεχομένους μιᾷ νηὶ
3 ἕως ἂν ταῦτα παρασκευασθῇ. Ἀθηναῖοι δὲ τήν τε ὑπάρ-
χουσαν ξυμμαχίαν ἐξήταζον καὶ ἐς τὰ περὶ Πελοπόννησον
μᾶλλον χωρία ἐπρεσβεύοντο, Κέρκυραν καὶ Κεφαλληνίαν
καὶ Ἀκαρνᾶνας καὶ Ζάκυνθον, ὁρῶντες, εἰ σφίσι φίλια ταῦτ'
εἴη βεβαίως, πέριξ τὴν Πελοπόννησον καταπολεμήσοντες.
8 ὀλίγον τε ἐπενόουν οὐδὲν ἀμφότεροι, ἀλλ' ἔρρωντο ἐς τὸν
πόλεμον οὐκ ἀπεικότως· ἀρχόμενοι γὰρ πάντες ὀξύτερον
ἀντιλαμβάνονται, τότε δὲ καὶ νεότης πολλὴ μὲν οὖσα ἐν τῇ
Πελοποννήσῳ, πολλὴ δ' ἐν ταῖς Ἀθήναις οὐκ ἀκουσίως ὑπὸ
ἀπειρίας ἥπτετο τοῦ πολέμου, ἥ τε ἄλλη Ἑλλὰς ἅπασα
2 μετέωρος ἦν ξυνιουσῶν τῶν πρώτων πόλεων. καὶ πολλὰ
μὲν λόγια ἐλέγετο, πολλὰ δὲ χρησμολόγοι ᾖδον ἔν τε τοῖς
3 μέλλουσι πολεμήσειν καὶ ἐν ταῖς ἄλλαις πόλεσιν. ἔτι δὲ
Δῆλος ἐκινήθη ὀλίγον πρὸ τούτων, πρότερον οὔπω σεισθεῖσα

rounded up. The Athenians knew nothing of what had happened after that, and so sent their message in ignorance.) On his arrival the messenger found that the men had been put to death. After this the Athenians marched out to Plataea, stocked it with corn, left a garrison, and evacuated the least fit men along with the women and children.

After the episode at Plataea, which was an open breach of the treaty, the Athenians started preparing to embark on the war; and so too did the Spartans and their allies. Both sides intended to send deputations to the Persian King, and anywhere else among the barbarians where they thought they might obtain help; and they tried to make allies of cities which were outside the sphere of their own power. The Spartans ordered the cities which took their side in Italy and Sicily to build ships, in proportion to their size, to supplement those available in Greece and bring their total number of ships up to five hundred. These cities were also to make ready a stated sum of money; and in other respects, until these preparations were complete, were to remain at peace and receive the Athenians only if they came in a single ship. The Athenians reviewed their existing alliance, and made a point of sending deputations to Corcyra, Cephallenia, Acarnania and Zacynthus, beyond the Peloponnese, since they reckoned that if these were firm friends of theirs they could carry on the war all round the Peloponnese.

Neither side made plans on a small scale in any respect: they approached the war with enthusiasm. This was not surprising. People always take a matter up more eagerly at the beginning; and on this occasion there were large numbers of young men, both in the Peloponnese and in Athens, who had no experience of war and embarked on it without reluctance, and all the rest of Greece was excited at this clash between the leading cities. Many oracles were on people's lips, and many were pronounced by oracle-mongers, both in the cities that were going to fight and in the others. Moreover, a short time before this there was an earthquake on Delos, where there had

ἀφ' οὗ Ἕλληνες μέμνηνται· ἐλέγετο δὲ καὶ ἐδόκει ἐπὶ τοῖς μέλλουσι γενήσεσθαι σημῆναι. εἴ τέ τι ἄλλο τοιουτότροπον 4 ξυνέβη γενέσθαι, πάντα ἀνεζητεῖτο. ἡ δὲ εὔνοια παρὰ πολὺ ἐποίει τῶν ἀνθρώπων μᾶλλον ἐς τοὺς Λακεδαιμονίους, ἄλλως τε καὶ προειπόντων ὅτι τὴν Ἑλλάδα ἐλευθεροῦσιν. ἔρρωτό τε πᾶς καὶ ἰδιώτης καὶ πόλις εἴ τι δύναιτο καὶ λόγῳ καὶ ἔργῳ ξυνεπιλαμβάνειν αὐτοῖς· ἐν τούτῳ τε κεκωλῦσθαι ἐδόκει ἑκάστῳ τὰ πράγματα ᾧ μή τις αὐτὸς παρέσται. 5 οὕτως ⟨ἐν⟩ ὀργῇ εἶχον οἱ πλείους τοὺς Ἀθηναίους, οἱ μὲν τῆς ἀρχῆς ἀπολυθῆναι βουλόμενοι, οἱ δὲ μὴ ἀρχθῶσι φοβούμενοι.

9 Παρασκευῇ μὲν οὖν καὶ γνώμῃ τοιαύτῃ ὥρμηντο. πόλεις δὲ ἑκάτεροι τάσδε ἔχοντες ξυμμάχους ἐς τὸν πόλεμον καθί-2 σταντο. Λακεδαιμονίων μὲν οἵδε ξύμμαχοι· Πελοποννήσιοι μὲν οἱ ἐντὸς Ἰσθμοῦ πάντες πλὴν Ἀργείων καὶ Ἀχαιῶν (τούτοις δὲ ἐς ἀμφοτέρους φιλία ἦν· Πελληνῆς δὲ Ἀχαιῶν μόνοι ξυνεπολέμουν τὸ πρῶτον, ἔπειτα δὲ ὕστερον καὶ ἅπαντες), ἔξω δὲ Πελοποννήσου Μεγαρῆς, Βοιωτοί, Λοκροί, 3 Φωκῆς, Ἀμπρακιῶται, Λευκάδιοι, Ἀνακτόριοι. τούτων ναυτικὸν παρείχοντο Κορίνθιοι, Μεγαρῆς, Σικυώνιοι, Πελληνῆς, Ἠλεῖοι, Ἀμπρακιῶται, Λευκάδιοι, ἱππέας δὲ Βοιωτοί, Φωκῆς, Λοκροί· αἱ δ' ἄλλαι πόλεις πεζὸν παρεῖχον. αὕτη μὲν 4 Λακεδαιμονίων ξυμμαχία· Ἀθηναίων δὲ Χῖοι, Λέσβιοι, Πλαταιῆς, Μεσσήνιοι οἱ ἐν Ναυπάκτῳ, Ἀκαρνάνων οἱ πλείους, Κερκυραῖοι, Ζακύνθιοι, καὶ ἄλλαι πόλεις αἱ ὑποτελεῖς οὖσαι ἐν ἔθνεσι τοσοῖσδε, Καρία ἡ ἐπὶ θαλάσσῃ, Δωριῆς Καρσὶ πρόσοικοι, Ἰωνία, Ἑλλήσποντος, τὰ ἐπὶ Θρᾴκης, νῆσοι ὅσαι ἐντὸς Πελοποννήσου καὶ Κρήτης πρὸς ἥλιον ἀνίσχοντα, πᾶσαι αἱ Κυκλάδες πλὴν Μήλου καὶ Θήρας. 5 τούτων ναυτικὸν παρείχοντο Χῖοι, Λέσβιοι, Κερκυραῖοι, οἱ 6 δ' ἄλλοι πεζὸν καὶ χρήματα. ξυμμαχία μὲν αὕτη ἑκατέρων καὶ παρασκευὴ ἐς τὸν πόλεμον ἦν.

10 Οἱ δὲ Λακεδαιμόνιοι μετὰ τὰ ἐν Πλαταιαῖς εὐθὺς περιήγγελλον κατὰ τὴν Πελοπόννησον καὶ τὴν ἔξω ξυμμαχίδα

never before been an earthquake as far as the Greeks could remember: it was said, and was believed, that this was significant for what was going to happen. In addition, anything else of this kind that occurred was investigated. A large majority of people showed the greater *4* good will towards the Spartans, especially because they proclaimed that they were going to liberate Greece. Every individual and every city was eager to join in on the Spartan side if possible, both in word and deed, and every one thought that the work would be hampered in so far as he was not present in person. So great was the *5* anger which most men felt towards Athens: they were either desirous of being freed from the Athenian empire or fearful of being incorporated in it. That was the *9* scale of preparation and planning with which they started moving.

The following were the allies with which each side entered the war. The allies of Sparta were: all the Peloponnesians south of the Isthmus except Argos and Achaea *2* (which had friendly relations with both sides: Pellene was the only Achaean state to join in at the beginning, but later they all did); and, outside the Peloponnese, Megara, Boeotia, Locris, Phocis, Ambracia, Leucas and Anactorium. Ships were provided by Corinth, Megara, Sicyon, *3* Pellene, Elis, Ambracia and Leucas, and cavalry by Boeotia, Phocis and Locris; the other cities provided infantry. That was the Spartan alliance. The allies of Ath- *4* ens were: Chios, Lesbos, Plataea, the Messenians at Naupactus, most of the Acarnanians, Corcyra and Zacynthus; and also the cities subject to them among the peoples of coastal Caria, the Dorians bordering on Caria, Ionia, the Hellespont, the Thraceward region, the islands between the Peloponnese and Crete to the east, and all the Cyclades except Melos and Thera. Of these, Chios, Lesbos *5* and Corcyra provided ships, and the rest provided infantry and money. Those were the two sides' alliances and *6* resources for the war.

Immediately after the events at Plataea the Spartans *10* sent round instructions throughout the Peloponnese and

στρατιὰν παρασκευάζεσθαι ταῖς πόλεσι τά τε ἐπιτήδεια οἷα εἰκὸς ἐπὶ ἔξοδον ἔκδημον ἔχειν, ὡς ἐσβαλοῦντες ἐς τὴν 2 Ἀττικήν. ἐπειδὴ δὲ ἑκάστοις ἑτοῖμα γίγνοιτο, κατὰ τὸν χρόνον τὸν εἰρημένον ξυνῇσαν τὰ δύο μέρη ἀπὸ πόλεως 3 ἑκάστης ἐς τὸν Ἰσθμόν. καὶ ἐπειδὴ πᾶν τὸ στράτευμα ξυνειλεγμένον ἦν, Ἀρχίδαμος ὁ βασιλεὺς τῶν Λακεδαιμονίων, ὅσπερ ἡγεῖτο τῆς ἐξόδου ταύτης, ξυγκαλέσας τοὺς στρατηγοὺς τῶν πόλεων πασῶν καὶ τοὺς μάλιστα ἐν τέλει καὶ ἀξιολογωτάτους παρῄνει τοιάδε.

11 "Ἄνδρες Πελοποννήσιοι καὶ ξύμμαχοι, καὶ οἱ πατέρες ἡμῶν πολλὰς στρατείας καὶ ἐν αὐτῇ Πελοποννήσῳ καὶ ἔξω ἐποιήσαντο, καὶ ἡμῶν αὐτῶν οἱ πρεσβύτεροι οὐκ ἄπειροι πολέμων εἰσίν· ὅμως δὲ τῆσδε οὔπω μείζονα παρασκευὴν ἔχοντες ἐξήλθομεν, ἀλλὰ καὶ ἐπὶ πόλιν δυνατωτάτην νῦν ἐρχόμεθα καὶ αὐτοὶ πλεῖστοι καὶ ἄριστοι στρατεύοντες. 2 δίκαιον οὖν ἡμᾶς μήτε τῶν πατέρων χείρους φαίνεσθαι μήτε ἡμῶν αὐτῶν τῆς δόξης ἐνδεεστέρους. ἡ γὰρ Ἑλλὰς πᾶσα τῇδε τῇ ὁρμῇ ἐπῆρται καὶ προσέχει τὴν γνώμην, εὔνοιαν ἔχουσα διὰ τὸ Ἀθηναίων ἔχθος πρᾶξαι ἡμᾶς ἃ ἐπινοοῦμεν. 3 οὔκουν χρή, εἴ τῳ καὶ δοκοῦμεν πλήθει ἐπιέναι καὶ ἀσφάλεια πολλὴ εἶναι μὴ ἂν ἐλθεῖν τοὺς ἐναντίους ἡμῖν διὰ μάχης, τούτων ἕνεκα ἀμελέστερόν τι παρεσκευασμένους χωρεῖν, ἀλλὰ καὶ πόλεως ἑκάστης ἡγεμόνα καὶ στρατιώτην τὸ καθ' 4 αὑτὸν αἰεὶ προσδέχεσθαι ἐς κίνδυνόν τινα ἥξειν. ἄδηλα γὰρ τὰ τῶν πολέμων, καὶ ἐξ ὀλίγου τὰ πολλὰ καὶ δι' ὀργῆς αἱ ἐπιχειρήσεις γίγνονται· πολλάκις τε τὸ ἔλασσον πλῆθος δεδιὸς ἄμεινον ἠμύνατο τοὺς πλέονας διὰ τὸ καταφρονοῦντας 5 ἀπαρασκεύους γενέσθαι. χρὴ δὲ αἰεὶ ἐν τῇ πολεμίᾳ τῇ μὲν γνώμῃ θαρσαλέους στρατεύειν, τῷ δ' ἔργῳ δεδιότας παρεσκευάσθαι· οὕτω γὰρ πρός τε τὸ ἐπιέναι τοῖς ἐναντίοις εὐψυχότατοι ἂν εἶεν πρός τε τὸ ἐπιχειρεῖσθαι ἀσφαλέ- 6 στατοι. ἡμεῖς δὲ οὐδ' ἐπὶ ἀδύνατον ἀμύνεσθαι οὕτω πόλιν ἐρχόμεθα, ἀλλὰ τοῖς πᾶσιν ἄριστα παρεσκευασμένην, ὥστε χρὴ καὶ πάνυ ἐλπίζειν διὰ μάχης ἰέναι αὐτούς, εἰ μὴ καὶ

their alliance outside it that the cities were to get ready an army and the provisions needed for an expedition away from home, in order to invade Attica. When they had all made their preparations, a two-thirds levy from each city assembled at the Isthmus at the appointed time. When the whole army was gathered together, Archidamus the Spartan king, who was the commander of this expedition, called together the generals of all the cities, and the principal office-holders and most important men, and made this speech of encouragement.

"Peloponnesians and allies, our fathers have undertaken many campaigns both within the Peloponnese and outside it, and the older men among ourselves are not without experience of war. Nevertheless, we have never set out with a greater force than this one: the object of our present campaign is the most powerful city, and this is the largest and best force of ours. We ought, then, not to appear inferior to our fathers or to our own reputation. The whole of Greece has been aroused by this movement of ours, and is watching it closely and, because of the Athenians' unpopularity, with good wishes for us to achieve what we intend. So, even if some people think that our invading force is enormous, and that there is no danger that our opponents will risk a battle with us, we ought not for that reason to neglect any precautions on our march, but the commanders and soldiers of every city should always be prepared for their own section to come into danger. War is full of uncertainty, and most frequently attacks are made at short notice, in a moment of passion. Often inferior numbers, afraid for themselves, have gained the upper hand in fighting superior numbers who despised them and so were unprepared. In enemy territory one should always display a confident spirit but take the precautions which are inspired by fear: in that way one will combine bravery in making attacks on the enemy with safety in resisting attacks.

"The city we are marching against is not at all unable to defend itself, but is most fully prepared in every respect, so we should have a strong expectation

νῦν ὥρμηνται ἐν ᾧ οὔπω πάρεσμεν, ἀλλ' ὅταν ἐν τῇ γῇ
7 ὁρῶσιν ἡμᾶς δῃοῦντάς τε καὶ τἀκείνων φθείροντας. πᾶσι
γὰρ ἐν τοῖς ὄμμασι καὶ ἐν τῷ παραυτίκα ὁρᾶν πάσχοντάς τι
ἄηθες ὀργὴ προσπίπτει· καὶ οἱ λογισμῷ ἐλάχιστα χρώμενοι
8 θυμῷ πλεῖστα ἐς ἔργον καθίστανται. Ἀθηναίους δὲ καὶ
πλέον τι τῶν ἄλλων εἰκὸς τοῦτο δρᾶσαι, οἳ ἄρχειν τε τῶν
ἄλλων ἀξιοῦσι καὶ ἐπιόντες τὴν τῶν πέλας δῃοῦν μᾶλλον ἢ
9 τὴν αὑτῶν ὁρᾶν. ὡς οὖν ἐπὶ τοσαύτην πόλιν στρατεύοντες
καὶ μεγίστην δόξαν οἰσόμενοι τοῖς τε προγόνοις καὶ ἡμῖν
αὐτοῖς ἐπ' ἀμφότερα ἐκ τῶν ἀποβαινόντων, ἕπεσθ' ὅπῃ ἄν
τις ἡγῆται, κόσμον καὶ φυλακὴν περὶ παντὸς ποιούμενοι καὶ
τὰ παραγγελλόμενα ὀξέως δεχόμενοι· κάλλιστον γὰρ τόδε
καὶ ἀσφαλέστατον, πολλοὺς ὄντας ἑνὶ κόσμῳ χρωμένους
φαίνεσθαι."

12 Τοσαῦτα εἰπὼν καὶ διαλύσας τὸν ξύλλογον ὁ Ἀρχίδαμος
Μελήσιππον πρῶτον ἀποστέλλει ἐς τὰς Ἀθήνας τὸν Διακρίτου ἄνδρα Σπαρτιάτην, εἴ τι ἄρα μᾶλλον ἐνδοῖεν οἱ
2 Ἀθηναῖοι ὁρῶντες σφᾶς ἤδη ἐν ὁδῷ ὄντας. οἱ δὲ οὐ
προσεδέξαντο αὐτὸν ἐς τὴν πόλιν οὐδ' ἐπὶ τὸ κοινόν· ἦν
γὰρ Περικλέους γνώμη πρότερον νενικηκυῖα κήρυκα καὶ
πρεσβείαν μὴ προσδέχεσθαι Λακεδαιμονίων ἐξεστρατευμένων· ἀποπέμπουσιν οὖν αὐτὸν πρὶν ἀκοῦσαι καὶ ἐκέλευον
ἐκτὸς ὅρων εἶναι αὐθημερόν, τό τε λοιπὸν ἀναχωρήσαντας
ἐπὶ τὰ σφέτερα αὐτῶν, ἤν τι βούλωνται, πρεσβεύεσθαι.
ξυμπέμπουσί τε τῷ Μελησίππῳ ἀγωγούς, ὅπως μηδενὶ
3 ξυγγένηται. ὁ δ' ἐπειδὴ ἐπὶ τοῖς ὁρίοις ἐγένετο καὶ ἔμελλε
διαλύσεσθαι, τοσόνδε εἰπὼν ἐπορεύετο ὅτι "ἥδε ἡ ἡμέρα τοῖς
4 Ἕλλησι μεγάλων κακῶν ἄρξει." ὡς δὲ ἀφίκετο ἐς τὸ
στρατόπεδον καὶ ἔγνω ὁ Ἀρχίδαμος ὅτι οἱ Ἀθηναῖοι οὐδέν
πω ἐνδώσουσιν, οὕτω δὴ ἄρας τῷ στρατῷ προυχώρει ἐς τὴν
5 γῆν αὐτῶν. Βοιωτοὶ δὲ μέρος μὲν τὸ σφέτερον καὶ τοὺς

that they will risk a battle with us, and that even if they are not already moving while we are not yet present they will do so when they see us in their territory, ravaging and destroying their property. Men are always inflamed with anger when they see unfamiliar damage being done to them on the spot, before their very eyes; and when they are least able to reason they are most liable to act in passion. This is likely to happen with the Athenians even more than with others, since they claim to rule over other people, and are accustomed to invade their neighbours' land and ravage that rather than see this done to their own land. It is a great city against which we are fighting; and, whichever way things turn out, we shall win the greatest glory for our ancestors and for ourselves. So follow where you are led; consider discipline and watchfulness to be all-important; and respond promptly to commands. This is the best and safest procedure, that our large numbers should appear as a single orderly body."

After saying this Archidamus closed the meeting. First he sent Melesippus son of Diacritus, a Spartiate, to Athens, to see if the Athenians would be more willing to submit when they realised that the Peloponnesians were now on their way. But the Athenians did not allow him to enter the city or meet the public authorities: a proposal of Pericles had been carried earlier, that they should not receive any herald or deputation once the Spartans had set out on campaign. They sent him away unheard, and ordered him to be outside their boundaries that same day: for the future, the Peloponnesians should return to their own territory, and then send a deputation if they wanted anything. Escorts were sent with Melesippus to prevent him from making contact with anybody. When he arrived at the frontier, and was about to cross it, before proceeding he made the pronouncement, "This day will be the beginning of great misfortune for the Greeks." When he reached the camp Archidamus, learning that the Athenians were still unwilling to submit, set out with the army and advanced towards their territory. The Boeo-

ἱππέας παρείχοντο Πελοποννησίοις ξυστρατεύειν, τοῖς δὲ
λειπομένοις ἐς Πλάταιαν ἐλθόντες τὴν γῆν ἐδῄουν.

13 Ἔτι δὲ τῶν Πελοποννησίων ξυλλεγομένων τε ἐς τὸν
Ἰσθμὸν καὶ ἐν ὁδῷ ὄντων, πρὶν ἐσβαλεῖν ἐς τὴν Ἀττικήν,
Περικλῆς ὁ Ξανθίππου στρατηγὸς ὢν Ἀθηναίων δέκατος
αὐτός, ὡς ἔγνω τὴν ἐσβολὴν ἐσομένην, ὑποτοπήσας, ὅτι
Ἀρχίδαμος αὐτῷ ξένος ὢν ἐτύγχανε, μὴ πολλάκις ἢ αὐτὸς
ἰδίᾳ βουλόμενος χαρίζεσθαι τοὺς ἀγροὺς αὐτοῦ παραλίπῃ καὶ
μὴ δῃώσῃ, ἢ καὶ Λακεδαιμονίων κελευσάντων ἐπὶ διαβολῇ
τῇ ἑαυτοῦ γένηται τοῦτο, ὥσπερ καὶ τὰ ἄγη ἐλαύνειν προεῖ-
πον ἕνεκα ἐκείνου, προηγόρευε τοῖς Ἀθηναίοις ἐν τῇ ἐκκλησίᾳ
ὅτι Ἀρχίδαμος μέν οἱ ξένος εἴη, οὐ μέντοι ἐπὶ κακῷ γε τῆς
πόλεως γένοιτο, τοὺς δὲ ἀγροὺς τοὺς ἑαυτοῦ καὶ οἰκίας ἢν
ἄρα μὴ δῃώσωσιν οἱ πολέμιοι ὥσπερ καὶ τὰ τῶν ἄλλων,
ἀφίησιν αὐτὰ δημόσια εἶναι καὶ μηδεμίαν οἱ ὑποψίαν κατὰ
2 ταῦτα γίγνεσθαι. παρῄνει δὲ καὶ περὶ τῶν παρόντων ἅπερ
καὶ πρότερον, παρασκευάζεσθαί τε ἐς τὸν πόλεμον καὶ τὰ ἐκ
τῶν ἀγρῶν ἐσκομίζεσθαι, ἔς τε μάχην μὴ ἐπεξιέναι, ἀλλὰ
τὴν πόλιν ἐσελθόντας φυλάσσειν, καὶ τὸ ναυτικόν, ᾗπερ
ἰσχύουσιν, ἐξαρτύεσθαι, τά τε τῶν ξυμμάχων διὰ χειρὸς
ἔχειν, λέγων τὴν ἰσχὺν αὐτοῖς ἀπὸ τούτων εἶναι τῶν χρημάτων τῆς προσόδου, τὰ δὲ πολλὰ τοῦ πολέμου γνώμῃ καὶ
3 χρημάτων περιουσίᾳ κρατεῖσθαι. θαρσεῖν τε ἐκέλευε προσ-
ιόντων μὲν ἑξακοσίων ταλάντων ὡς ἐπὶ τὸ πολὺ φόρου
κατ' ἐνιαυτὸν ἀπὸ τῶν ξυμμάχων τῇ πόλει ἄνευ τῆς ἄλλης
προσόδου, ὑπαρχόντων δὲ ἐν τῇ ἀκροπόλει αἰεί ποτε ἀργυρίου ἐπισήμου ἑξακισχιλίων ταλάντων (ἑξακισχίλια μέν γε
τάλαντα τριακοσίων ἀποδέοντα περιεγένετο, ἀφ' ὧν ἔς τε
τὰ προπύλαια τῆς ἀκροπόλεως καὶ τἆλλα οἰκοδομήματα
4 καὶ ἐς Ποτείδαιαν ἀπανηλώθη), χωρὶς δὲ χρυσίου ἀσήμου

---

26. αἰεί ποτε schol. Ar. *Plut.* 1193: ἔτι τότε codd.
27. ἑξακισχίλια μέν γε τάλαντα scripsi: τὰ γὰρ πλεῖστα codd., schol. Ar.
28. περιεγένετο schol. Ar.: μύρια ἐγένετο codd.

tians sent their contingent and their cavalry to join the Peloponnesians on the campaign, and with the rest of their forces they went to Plataea and ravaged its territory.

While the Peloponnesians were still assembling at 13 the Isthmus and were on the way, before they invaded Attica, Pericles son of Xanthippus, one of the ten Athenian generals, knew that the invasion was coming, and suspected that Archidamus, with whom he had relations of hospitality, might often leave his land alone and not ravage it — either on his own initiative, wanting to do Pericles a favour, or on the orders of the Spartans, to create a ground of objection to Pericles, just as previously they had commanded the Athenians to expel the accursed on account of him. He therefore announced to the Athenians in the assembly that he had relations of hospitality with Archidamus but this was not to be a source of harm to the city: if the enemy did not ravage his land and houses as they did those of others, he would give them up to be public property, and no suspicion should attach to him in connection with this.

As far as the current situation was concerned, he 2 encouraged them on the same lines as before: they were to prepare for the war and carry into the city their property from the fields; they were not to go out to battle but were to come into the city and defend that; they were to make ready the fleet, in which their strength lay; and they were to keep a firm hold on their allies. Their strength, he said, depended on the money which they received from the allies, and most successes in war were won by good judgment and ready supplies of money. They 3 should be confident, he said. The city had more or less six hundred talents tribute from the allies each year, apart from its other revenue; they had always kept on the Acropolis six thousand talents of coined silver, and there still remained three hundred talents short of the six thousand, though they had spent from this fund on the Propylaea of the Acropolis and the other buildings, and on Potidaea; and in addition they had uncoined gold and 4

καὶ ἀργυρίου ἔν τε ἀναθήμασιν ἰδίοις καὶ δημοσίοις καὶ ὅσα ἱερὰ σκεύη περί τε τὰς πομπὰς καὶ τοὺς ἀγῶνας καὶ σκῦλα Μηδικὰ καὶ εἴ τι τοιουτότροπον, οὐκ ἐλάσσονος [ἦν] ἢ πεντακοσίων ταλάντων. ἔτι 5 δὲ καὶ τὰ ἐκ τῶν ἄλλων ἱερῶν προσετίθει χρήματα οὐκ ὀλίγα, οἷς χρήσεσθαι αὐτούς, καὶ ἢν πάνυ ἐξείργωνται πάντων, καὶ αὐτῆς τῆς θεοῦ τοῖς περικειμένοις χρυσίοις· ἀπέφαινε δ᾽ ἔχον τὸ ἄγαλμα τεσσαράκοντα τάλαντα σταθμὸν χρυσίου ἀπέφθου, καὶ περιαιρετὸν εἶναι ἅπαν. χρησαμένους τε ἐπὶ σωτηρίᾳ ἔφη χρῆναι μὴ ἐλάσσω ἀντικαταστῆσαι 6 πάλιν. χρήμασι μὲν οὖν οὕτως ἐθάρσυνεν αὐτούς. ὁπλίτας δὲ τρισχιλίους καὶ μυρίους εἶναι ἄνευ τῶν ἐν τοῖς φρουρίοις καὶ τῶν παρ᾽ ἔπαλξιν ἑξακισχιλίων καὶ μυρίων. 7 τοσοῦτοι γὰρ ἐφύλασσον τὸ πρῶτον ὁπότε οἱ πολέμιοι ἐσβάλοιεν, ἀπό τε τῶν πρεσβυτάτων καὶ τῶν νεωτάτων, καὶ μετοίκων ὅσοι ὁπλῖται ἦσαν. τοῦ τε γὰρ Φαληρικοῦ τείχους στάδιοι ἦσαν πέντε καὶ τριάκοντα πρὸς τὸν κύκλον τοῦ ἄστεως, καὶ αὐτοῦ τοῦ κύκλου τὸ φυλασσόμενον τρεῖς καὶ τεσσαράκοντα (ἔστι δὲ αὐτοῦ ὃ καὶ ἀφύλακτον ἦν, τὸ μεταξὺ τοῦ τε μακροῦ καὶ τοῦ Φαληρικοῦ), τὰ δὲ μακρὰ τείχη πρὸς τὸν Πειραιᾶ τεσσαράκοντα σταδίων, ὧν τὸ ἔξωθεν ἐτηρεῖτο· καὶ τοῦ Πειραιῶς ξὺν Μουνιχίᾳ ἑξήκοντα μὲν σταδίων ὁ ἅπας περίβολος, τὸ δ᾽ ἐν φυλακῇ ὂν ἥμισυ 8 τούτου. ἱππέας δὲ ἀπέφαινε διακοσίους καὶ χιλίους ξὺν ἱπποτοξόταις, ἑξακοσίους δὲ καὶ χιλίους τοξότας, καὶ τριή- 9 ρεις τὰς πλωίμους τριακοσίας. ταῦτα γὰρ ὑπῆρχεν Ἀθηναίοις καὶ οὐκ ἐλάσσω ἕκαστα τούτων, ὅτε ἡ ἐσβολὴ τὸ πρῶτον ἔμελλε Πελοποννησίων ἔσεσθαι καὶ ἐς τὸν πόλεμον καθίσταντο. ἔλεγε δὲ καὶ ἄλλα οἷάπερ εἰώθει Περικλῆς ἐς ἀπόδειξιν τοῦ περιέσεσθαι τῷ πολέμῳ.
14 Οἱ δὲ Ἀθηναῖοι ἀκούσαντες ἀνεπείθοντό τε καὶ ἐσεκομίζοντο ἐκ τῶν ἀγρῶν παῖδας καὶ γυναῖκας καὶ τὴν ἄλλην κατασκευὴν ᾗ κατ᾽ οἶκον ἐχρῶντο, καὶ αὐτῶν τῶν οἰκιῶν καθαιροῦντες τὴν ξύλωσιν· πρόβατα δὲ καὶ ὑποζύγια ἐς τὴν

silver in private and public dedications, items of sacred equipment for processions and competitions, booty from the Medes, and other things of that kind, worth not less than five hundred talents. To these he added the 5 monies from the other sanctuaries, which they would be able to use, no small sum. Finally, if they were deprived of absolutely all their funds, they could use the gold plate cladding the goddess herself: he pointed out that on the statue there were forty talents' weight of refined gold, all removable. These resources were to be used for their safety, on condition that no less was replaced afterwards. That is what he said to encourage them on the 6 financial side.

He added that they had 13,000 hoplites, apart from the 16,000 in the garrison posts and on the battlements. (That is the number who were on guard at the beginning, 7 at the times of the enemy invasions: they were taken from the youngest and the oldest age-classes, and from those metics who were hoplites. The Phaleric Wall was thirty-five stades long to the circuit of the city; the part of the circuit which was guarded was forty-three stades, while there was also an unguarded part, the section between the Long Wall and the Phaleric; the Long Walls to the Piraeus, of which the outer wall was under guard, were forty stades; the total circumference of Piraeus with Munichia was sixty stades, and half of that was guarded.) He pointed out that they had 1,200 cavalry, in- 8 cluding the mounted archers; 1,600 archers; and 300 seaworthy triremes. These were the resources at Athens' dis- 9 posal, not less in any department, when the Peloponnesians were about to invade for the first time and they were on the point of going to war. Pericles added other arguments of the kind he normally used to demonstrate that they would prevail in the war.

The Athenians listened to this and were persuaded. 14 They brought in from the country their children, their wives, and the various items of equipment which they used in their houses, even demolishing the woodwork of the houses. They sent their cattle and beasts of burden to

Εὔβοιαν διεπέμψαντο καὶ ἐς τὰς νήσους τὰς ἐπικειμένας. 2 χαλεπῶς δὲ αὐτοῖς διὰ τὸ αἰεὶ εἰωθέναι τοὺς πολλοὺς ἐν τοῖς ἀγροῖς διαιτᾶσθαι ἡ ἀνάστασις ἐγίγνετο. ξυνεβεβήκει δὲ ἀπὸ τοῦ πάνυ ἀρχαίου ἑτέρων μᾶλλον Ἀθηναίοις τοῦτο. ἐπὶ γὰρ Κέκροπος καὶ τῶν πρώτων βασιλέων ἡ Ἀττικὴ ἐς Θησέα αἰεὶ κατὰ πόλεις ᾠκεῖτο πρυτανεῖά τε ἐχούσας καὶ ἄρχοντας, καὶ ὁπότε μή τι δείσειαν, οὐ ξυνῇσαν βουλευσόμενοι ὡς τὸν βασιλέα, ἀλλ' αὐτοὶ ἕκαστοι ἐπολίτευον καὶ ἐβουλεύοντο· καί τινες καὶ ἐπολέμησάν ποτε αὐτῶν, ὥσπερ 2 καὶ Ἐλευσίνιοι μετ' Εὐμόλπου πρὸς Ἐρεχθέα. ἐπειδὴ δὲ Θησεὺς ἐβασίλευσε, γενόμενος μετὰ τοῦ ξυνετοῦ καὶ δυνατὸς τά τε ἄλλα διεκόσμησε τὴν χώραν καὶ καταλύσας τῶν ἄλλων πόλεων τά τε βουλευτήρια καὶ τὰς ἀρχὰς ἐς τὴν νῦν πόλιν οὖσαν, ἓν βουλευτήριον ἀποδείξας καὶ πρυτανεῖον, ξυνῴκισε πάντας, καὶ νεμομένους τὰ αὐτῶν ἑκάστους ἅπερ καὶ πρὸ τοῦ ἠνάγκασε μιᾷ πόλει ταύτῃ χρῆσθαι, ἣ ἁπάντων ἤδη ξυντελούντων ἐς αὐτὴν μεγάλη γενομένη παρεδόθη ὑπὸ Θησέως τοῖς ἔπειτα· καὶ ξυνοίκια ἐξ ἐκείνου Ἀθηναῖοι ἔτι 3 καὶ νῦν τῇ θεῷ ἑορτὴν δημοτελῆ ποιοῦσιν. τὸ δὲ πρὸ τοῦ ἡ ἀκρόπολις ἡ νῦν οὖσα πόλις ἦν, καὶ τὸ ὑπ' αὐτὴν πρὸς 4 νότον μάλιστα τετραμμένον. τεκμήριον δέ· τὰ γὰρ ἱερὰ ⟨τὰ ἀρχαιότατα⟩ ἐν αὐτῇ τῇ ἀκροπόλει ⟨τῆς τε Ἀθηνᾶς⟩ καὶ ἄλλων θεῶν ἐστὶ καὶ τὰ ἔξω πρὸς τοῦτο τὸ μέρος τῆς πόλεως μᾶλλον ἵδρυται, τό τε τοῦ Διὸς τοῦ Ὀλυμπίου καὶ τὸ Πύθιον καὶ τὸ τῆς Γῆς καὶ τὸ ⟨τοῦ⟩ ἐν Λίμναις Διονύσου, ᾧ τὰ ἀρχαιότατα Διονύσια τῇ δωδεκάτῃ ποιεῖται ἐν μηνὶ Ἀνθεστηριῶνι, ὥσπερ καὶ οἱ ἀπ' Ἀθηναίων Ἴωνες ἔτι καὶ νῦν νομίζουσιν. ἵδρυται δὲ καὶ 5 ἄλλα ἱερὰ ταύτῃ ἀρχαῖα. καὶ τῇ κρήνῃ τῇ νῦν μὲν τῶν τυράννων οὕτω σκευασάντων Ἐννεακρούνῳ καλουμένῃ, τὸ δὲ πάλαι φανερῶν τῶν πηγῶν οὐσῶν Καλλιρρόῃ ὠνομασμένῃ,

---

21. νότον codd.: βορρᾶν Parsons.
    ἱερὰ <τὰ ἀρχαιότατα> Gomme post Stahl.
22. ἀκροπόλει <τῆς τε Ἀθηνᾶς> rec. pc.
25. <τοῦ> ἐν Λίμναις Cobet.
    ἀρχαιότατα Π⁸: ἀρχαιότερα codd.
    τῇ δωδεκάτῃ secl. Torstrik.

Euboea and the offshore islands. The removal was a hard 2
thing for them, because the majority had always been used
to living in the country.

This had been true of the Athenians more than of the 15
others from very ancient times. In the time of Cecrops
and the first kings, down to Theseus, the population of
Attica had been dispersed among cities which had their
own town halls and officials, and which except in times
of fear did not come to the king to deliberate together
but ran their own affairs separately and deliberated on
their own. On occasions some of them even went to war
against the king, as the Eleusinians did with Eumolpus
against Erechtheus. When Theseus became king, since he 2
was both powerful and intelligent, he organised the land
in general, and, abolishing the council-houses and offices of the other cities, he brought all the people together in the present city, designating a single council-
house and town hall. The people were to attend to their
own affairs as before, but were obliged to use this as
their one city, and now that everybody was making a contribution this became the powerful city which Theseus
handed on to posterity. As a result of what he did, the
Athenians continue to this day to celebrate the *Synoikia*
as a publicly funded festival.

In earlier times the city was the present Acropolis, 3
together with the area below it, especially towards the
south. Here is confirmation of this. The oldest temples 4
both of Athena and of the other gods are actually
on the Acropolis, and those outside have tended to be
located towards this southern part of the city — I
mean the temple of Olympian Zeus, the Pythium, the temple
of Ge, and that of Dionysus in the Marshes, where the
oldest festival of Dionysus is celebrated on the twelfth
of the month Anthesterion (as it is still observed today
by the Ionians descended from the Athenians). There are
other ancient sanctuaries here too. The fountain which 5
was built in its present form by the tyrants and is now
called *Enneakrounos*, but in antiquity when the springs
were in the open was called *Kallirhoe*, was considered by

ἐκεῖνοί τε ἐγγὺς οὔσῃ τὰ πλείστου ἄξια ἐχρῶντο, καὶ νῦν ἔτι ἀπὸ τοῦ ἀρχαίου πρό τε γαμικῶν καὶ ἐς ἄλλα τῶν ἱερῶν νομίζεται τῷ ὕδατι χρῆσθαι· καλεῖται δὲ διὰ τὴν παλαιὰν ταύτῃ κατοίκησιν καὶ ἡ ἀκρόπολις μέχρι τοῦδε ἔτι ὑπ' Ἀθηναίων πόλις. τῇ τε οὖν ἐπὶ πολὺ κατὰ τὴν χώραν αὐτονόμῳ οἰκήσει [μετεῖχον] οἱ Ἀθηναῖοι, καὶ ἐπειδὴ ξυνῳκίσθησαν, διὰ τὸ ἔθος ἐν τοῖς ἀγροῖς ὅμως οἱ πλείους τῶν τε ἀρχαίων καὶ τῶν ὕστερον μέχρι τοῦδε τοῦ πολέμου γενόμενοί τε καὶ οἰκήσαντες οὐ ῥᾳδίως πανοικεσίᾳ τὰς μεταναστάσεις ἐποιοῦντο, ἄλλως τε καὶ ἄρτι ἀνειληφότες τὰς κατασκευὰς μετὰ τὰ Μηδικά· ἐβαρύνοντο δὲ καὶ χαλεπῶς ἔφερον οἰκίας τε καταλείποντες καὶ ἱερὰ ἃ διὰ παντὸς ἦν αὐτοῖς ἐκ τῆς κατὰ τὸ ἀρχαῖον πολιτείας πάτρια δίαιτάν τε μέλλοντες μεταβάλλειν καὶ οὐδὲν ἄλλο ἢ πόλιν τὴν αὐτοῦ ἀπολείπων ἕκαστος. ἐπειδή τε ἀφίκοντο ἐς τὸ ἄστυ, ὀλίγοις μέν τισιν ὑπῆρχον οἰκήσεις καὶ παρὰ φίλων τινὰς ἢ οἰκείων καταφυγή, οἱ δὲ πολλοὶ τά τε ἐρῆμα τῆς πόλεως ᾤκησαν καὶ τὰ ἱερὰ καὶ τὰ ἡρῷα πάντα πλὴν τῆς ἀκροπόλεως καὶ τοῦ Ἐλευσινίου καὶ εἴ τι ἄλλο βεβαίως κλῃστὸν ἦν· τό τε Πελαργικὸν καλούμενον τὸ ὑπὸ τὴν ἀκρόπολιν, ὃ καὶ ἐπάρατόν τε ἦν μὴ οἰκεῖν καί τι καὶ Πυθικοῦ μαντείου ἀκροτελεύτιον τοιόνδε διεκώλυε, λέγον ὡς "τὸ Πελαργικὸν ἀργὸν ἄμεινον," ὅμως ὑπὸ τῆς παραχρῆμα ἀνάγκης ἐξῳκήθη. καί μοι δοκεῖ τὸ μαντεῖον τοὐναντίον ξυμβῆναι ἢ προσεδέχοντο· οὐ γὰρ διὰ τὴν παράνομον ἐνοίκησιν αἱ ξυμφοραὶ γενέσθαι τῇ πόλει, ἀλλὰ διὰ τὸν πόλεμον ἡ ἀνάγκη τῆς οἰκήσεως, ὃν οὐκ ὀνομάζον τὸ μαντεῖον προῄδει μὴ ἐπ' ἀγαθῷ ποτε αὐτὸ κατοικισθησόμενον. κατεσκευάσαντο δὲ καὶ ἐν τοῖς πύργοις τῶν τειχῶν πολλοὶ καὶ ὡς ἕκαστός που ἐδύνατο· οὐ γὰρ ἐχώρησε ξυνελθόντας αὐτοὺς ἡ πόλις, ἀλλ' ὕστερον δὴ τά

---

6. μετεῖχον secl. Driessen.
9. πανοικεσίᾳ post πολέμου exhibent codd., Π⁸, huc transposuit Lipsius.
22. Πελαργικὸν C: Πελασγικὸν cett.

the Athenians of that time to be of the greatest importance because it was nearby, and even today as a survival from past times it is customary to use this water before weddings and for other religious purposes. Because the ancient settlement was there, the Athenians have continued to the present day to call the Acropolis *polis*.

So for the most part the Athenians lived in independent settlements in the country. Even after the unification, custom prevailed, and most of them continued to live in the countryside in antiquity, and more recently up to the time of this war. So they did not find it easy to migrate with their whole households, especially as they had only recently restored their furnishings after the Persian Wars. It was a distressing hardship for them to abandon their houses and the family shrines which they had everywhere on account of the ancient form of government, in order to change their way of life: each man was virtually abandoning his own city.

When they arrived in the city, a few had places to live in and were able to take refuge with some of their friends or relatives; but the majority occupied the uninhabited places in the city, and all the sanctuaries of gods and heroes apart from the Acropolis, the Eleusinium and other places that were firmly closed. There was an area called the *Pelargikon*, below the Acropolis, which was protected against habitation by a curse, and by a prohibition in the fag-end of a Delphic oracle which ran, "The *Pelargikon* is better left alone": but even that was occupied under the pressure of the immediate emergency. I think the oracle was fulfilled in the opposite way to people's expectation: it is not that the disasters fell on the city because of the unlawful occupation, but that because of the war the need to occupy it arose, and the oracle was not referring specifically to this occasion but was predicting that the *Pelargikon* would never be occupied for a good purpose. Many men found a refuge even in the towers of the city walls, and wherever each of them was able. There was not enough room in the city for the people when they came together; but later they di-

τε μακρὰ τείχη ᾤκησαν κατανειμάμενοι καὶ τοῦ Πειραιῶς
4 τὰ πολλά. ἅμα δὲ καὶ τῶν πρὸς τὸν πόλεμον ἥπτοντο,
ξυμμάχους τε ἀγείροντες καὶ τῇ Πελοποννήσῳ ἑκατὸν
5 νεῶν ἐπίπλουν ἐξαρτύοντες. καὶ οἱ μὲν ἐν τούτῳ παρασκευῆς ἦσαν.

18 Ὁ δὲ στρατὸς τῶν Πελοποννησίων προϊὼν ἀφίκετο τῆς
Ἀττικῆς ἐς Οἰνόην πρῶτον, ᾗπερ ἔμελλον ἐσβαλεῖν. καὶ
ὡς ἐκαθέζοντο, προσβολὰς παρεσκευάζοντο τῷ τείχει ποιη-
2 σόμενοι μηχαναῖς τε καὶ ἄλλῳ τρόπῳ· ἡ γὰρ Οἰνόη οὖσα ἐν
μεθορίοις τῆς Ἀττικῆς καὶ Βοιωτίας ἐτετείχιστο, καὶ αὐτῷ
φρουρίῳ οἱ Ἀθηναῖοι ἐχρῶντο ὁπότε πόλεμος καταλάβοι.
τάς τε οὖν προσβολὰς ηὐτρεπίζοντο καὶ ἄλλως ἐνδιέτριψαν
3 χρόνον περὶ αὐτήν. αἰτίαν δὲ οὐκ ἐλαχίστην Ἀρχίδαμος
ἔλαβεν ἀπ' αὐτοῦ, δοκῶν καὶ ἐν τῇ ξυναγωγῇ τοῦ πολέμου
μαλακὸς εἶναι καὶ τοῖς Ἀθηναίοις ἐπιτήδειος, οὐ παραινῶν
προθύμως πολεμεῖν· ἐπειδή τε ξυνελέγετο ὁ στρατός, ἥ τε
ἐν τῷ Ἰσθμῷ ἐπιμονὴ γενομένη καὶ κατὰ τὴν ἄλλην πορείαν
ἡ σχολαιότης διέβαλεν αὐτόν, μάλιστα δὲ ἡ ἐν τῇ Οἰνόῃ
4 ἐπίσχεσις. οἱ γὰρ Ἀθηναῖοι ἐσεκομίζοντο ἐν τῷ χρόνῳ
τούτῳ, καὶ ἐδόκουν οἱ Πελοποννήσιοι ἐπελθόντες ἂν διὰ
τάχους πάντα ἔτι ἔξω καταλαβεῖν, εἰ μὴ διὰ τὴν ἐκείνου
5 μέλλησιν. ἐν τοιαύτῃ μὲν ὀργῇ ὁ στρατὸς τὸν Ἀρχίδαμον
ἐν τῇ καθέδρᾳ εἶχεν. ὁ δὲ προσδεχόμενος, ὡς λέγεται,
τοὺς Ἀθηναίους τῆς γῆς ἔτι ἀκεραίου οὔσης ἐνδώσειν τι καὶ
19 κατοκνήσειν περιιδεῖν αὐτὴν τμηθεῖσαν, ἀνεῖχεν. ἐπειδὴ
μέντοι προσβαλόντες τῇ Οἰνόῃ καὶ πᾶσαν ἰδέαν πειράσαντες
οὐκ ἐδύναντο ἑλεῖν, οἵ τε Ἀθηναῖοι οὐδὲν ἐπεκηρυκεύοντο,
οὕτω δὴ ὁρμήσαντες ἀπ' αὐτῆς μετὰ τὰ ἐν Πλαταίᾳ [τῶν
ἐσελθόντων Θηβαίων] γενόμενα ἡμέρᾳ ὀγδοηκοστῇ μάλιστα,
θέρους καὶ τοῦ σίτου ἀκμάζοντος, ἐσέβαλον ἐς τὴν Ἀττικήν·
ἡγεῖτο δὲ Ἀρχίδαμος ὁ Ζευξιδάμου, Λακεδαιμονίων βασιλεύς.
2 καὶ καθεζόμενοι ἔτεμνον πρῶτον μὲν Ἐλευσῖνα καὶ τὸ Θριάσιον πεδίον καὶ τροπήν τινα τῶν Ἀθηναίων ἱππέων περὶ

---

13. δὲ C <G> : τε cett.
28–9. τῶν ἐσελθόντων Θηβαίων secl. Classen.

vided up the long walls and most of the Piraeus, and settled there.

At the same time the Athenians began to look to military matters, collecting allies and fitting out an expedition of a hundred ships against the Peloponnese. Those are the preparations which they were making.

The Peloponnesians' army advanced, and the first point in Attica that they reached was Oenoe, by way of which they intended to invade. They established themselves there, and prepared to assault the wall with machines and in other ways. Oenoe had been fortified, since it was on the frontier between Attica and Boeotia, and the Athenians used it as a garrison post whenever war broke out. So the Peloponnesians prepared their means of assault, and in general allowed time to pass there. Archidamus particularly incurred blame for this. It was thought that he had been feeble in setting the war in motion and was favourably disposed to Athens, and men held against him the delay at the Isthmus, his slowness on the rest of the march, and especially this pause at Oenoe. During this time the Athenians were conveying their possessions inside, and the Peloponnesians thought that if they had attacked them quickly, and had not been prevented by his hesitation, they would have caught everything still outside. That is why Archidamus' inaction provoked the army to anger. It is said that he held back because he expected that the Athenians would show some willingness to submit while their land was still intact, and would not be prepared to watch it being laid waste.

When the Peloponnesians made their assault on Oenoe, but in spite of trying every contrivance they were unable to take it, and the Athenians did not begin to make overtures to them, they set out from there, and about the eightieth day after the events at Plataea, in the summer, when the corn was growing ripe, they invaded Attica. Their commander was Archidamus son of Zeuxidamus, king of Sparta. They began by establishing themselves and laying waste Eleusis and the Thriasian Plain, and they won a victory against the Athenian cavalry by what is

τοὺς Ῥείτους καλουμένους ἐποιήσαντο· ἔπειτα προυχώρουν ἐν δεξιᾷ ἔχοντες τὸ Αἰγάλεων ὄρος διὰ Κρωπιᾶς, ἕως ἀφίκοντο ἐς Ἀχαρνάς, χωρίον μέγιστον τῆς Ἀττικῆς τῶν δήμων καλουμένων, καὶ καθεζόμενοι ἐς αὐτὸ στρατόπεδόν τε ἐποιήσαντο χρόνον τε πολὺν ἐμμείναντες ἔτεμνον. γνώμῃ δὲ τοιᾷδε λέγεται τὸν Ἀρχίδαμον περί τε τὰς Ἀχαρνὰς ὡς ἐς μάχην ταξάμενον μεῖναι καὶ ἐς τὸ πεδίον ἐκείνῃ τῇ 2 ἐσβολῇ οὐ καταβῆναι· τοὺς γὰρ Ἀθηναίους ἤλπιζεν, ἀκμάζοντάς τε νεότητι πολλῇ καὶ παρεσκευασμένους ἐς πόλεμον ὡς οὔπω πρότερον, ἴσως ἂν ἐπεξελθεῖν καὶ τὴν γῆν οὐκ ἂν 3 περιιδεῖν τμηθῆναι. ἐπειδὴ οὖν αὐτῷ ἐς Ἐλευσῖνα καὶ τὸ Θριάσιον πεδίον οὐκ ἀπήντησαν, πεῖραν ἐποιεῖτο περὶ τὰς 4 Ἀχαρνὰς καθήμενος εἰ ἐπεξίασιν· ἅμα μὲν γὰρ αὐτῷ ὁ χῶρος ἐπιτήδειος ἐφαίνετο ἐνστρατοπεδεῦσαι, ἅμα δὲ καὶ οἱ Ἀχαρνῆς μέγα μέρος ὄντες τῆς πόλεως (†τρισχίλιοι γὰρ ὁπλῖται† ἐγένοντο) οὐ περιόψεσθαι ἐδόκουν τὰ σφέτερα διαφθαρέντα, ἀλλ' ὁρμήσειν καὶ τοὺς πάντας ἐς μάχην. εἴ τε καὶ μὴ ἐπεξέλθοιεν ἐκείνῃ τῇ ἐσβολῇ οἱ Ἀθηναῖοι, ἀδεέστερον ἤδη ἐς τὸ ὕστερον τό τε πεδίον τεμεῖν καὶ πρὸς αὐτὴν τὴν πόλιν χωρήσεσθαι· τοὺς γὰρ Ἀχαρνέας ἐστερημένους τῶν σφετέρων οὐχ ὁμοίως προθύμους ἔσεσθαι ὑπὲρ τῆς τῶν 5 ἄλλων κινδυνεύειν, στάσιν δ' ἐνέσεσθαι τῇ γνώμῃ. τοιαύτῃ μὲν διανοίᾳ ὁ Ἀρχίδαμος περὶ τὰς Ἀχαρνὰς ἦν.

21 Ἀθηναῖοι δὲ μέχρι μὲν οὗ περὶ Ἐλευσῖνα καὶ τὸ Θριάσιον πεδίον ὁ στρατὸς ἦν, καί τινα ἐλπίδα εἶχον ἐς τὸ ἐγγυτέρω αὐτοὺς μὴ προϊέναι, μεμνημένοι καὶ Πλειστοάνακτα τὸν Παυσανίου Λακεδαιμονίων βασιλέα, ὅτε ἐσβαλὼν τῆς Ἀττικῆς ἐς Ἐλευσῖνα καὶ Θριῶζε στρατῷ Πελοποννησίων πρὸ τοῦδε τοῦ πολέμου τέσσαρσι καὶ δέκα ἔτεσιν ἀνεχώρησε πάλιν ἐς τὸ πλέον οὐκέτι προελθών (δι' ὃ δὴ καὶ ἡ φυγὴ αὐτῷ ἐγένετο ἐκ Σπάρτης δόξαντι χρήμασι πεισθῆναι [τὴν ἀναχώρησιν])· 2 ἐπειδὴ δὲ περὶ Ἀχαρνὰς εἶδον τὸν στρατὸν ἑξήκοντα σταδίους τῆς πόλεως ἀπέχοντα, οὐκέτι ἀνασχετὸν ἐποιοῦντο, ἀλλ'

15–16. τρισχίλιοι γὰρ ὁπλῖται haud sanum: πολῖται Polle, χίλιοι καὶ διακόσιοι (XHH pro XXX) Whitehead post Gomme.
31. τὴν ἀναχώρησιν om. Valla, secl. Krüger.

known as The Streams. Then they proceeded through Cropia, keeping Mount Aegaleos on their right, until they reached Acharnae, the largest of the places in Attica called demes. Establishing themselves near Acharnae, they pitched camp there, and for a considerable time they stayed there and ravaged the land.

 It is said that Archidamus' purpose in staying near Acharnae, drawn up as if for battle, and not in this invasion going down into the plain, was as follows: he hoped that the Athenians, since they were in a flourishing state with ample numbers of young men, and were prepared for war as never before, might perhaps not watch their land being laid waste but come out against him. Since they had not come to Eleusis and the Thriasian Plain to meet him, he tried establishing himself near Acharnae to see if the Athenians would come out. He thought the terrain was suitable for a camp; and, since the Acharnians were a large part of the citizen body, with †three thousand hoplites†, he thought they would not look on when their property was destroyed, but would urge on all the rest to battle too. If the Athenians did not come out even in response to this invasion, then there would be less cause for fear in the future if he laid waste the plain and moved against the city itself: the Acharnians, already deprived of their own property, would not be so eager to take risks for the others' land, and the Athenians would be divided in their policy. That was Archidamus' intention when he was at Acharnae.

 Up to the time when the army was in the region of Eleusis and the Thriasian Plain, the Athenians still had some hope that they would not advance any nearer. They remembered that when Plistoanax son of Pausanias, king of Sparta, had invaded Attica with an army from the Peloponnese as far as Eleusis and Thria, fourteen years before this war, he had gone back again without advancing any further: on account of that he was judged to have taken bribes and was exiled from Sparta. When they saw the army near Acharnae, sixty stades from the city, they thought this was no longer tolerable. Their land was being laid

αὐτοῖς, ὡς εἰκός, γῆς τεμνομένης ἐν τῷ ἐμφανεῖ, ὃ οὔπω ἑοράκεσαν οἵ γε νεώτεροι, οὐδ' οἱ πρεσβύτεροι πλὴν τὰ Μηδικά, δεινὸν ἐφαίνετο καὶ ἐδόκει τοῖς τε ἄλλοις καὶ
3 μάλιστα τῇ νεότητι ἐπεξιέναι καὶ μὴ περιορᾶν. κατὰ ξυστάσεις τε γιγνόμενοι ἐν πολλῇ ἔριδι ἦσαν, οἱ μὲν κελεύοντες ἐπεξιέναι, οἱ δέ τινες οὐκ ἐῶντες. χρησμολόγοι τε ᾖδον χρησμοὺς παντοίους, ὧν ἀκροᾶσθαι ὡς ἕκαστος ὥρμητο. οἵ τε Ἀχαρνῆς οἰόμενοι παρὰ σφίσιν αὐτοῖς οὐκ ἐλαχίστην μοῖραν εἶναι Ἀθηναίων, ὡς αὐτῶν ἡ γῆ ἐτέμνετο, ἐνῆγον τὴν ἔξοδον μάλιστα. παντί τε τρόπῳ ἀνηρέθιστο ἡ πόλις, καὶ τὸν Περικλέα ἐν ὀργῇ εἶχον, καὶ ὧν παρῄνεσε πρότερον ἐμέμνηντο οὐδέν, ἀλλ' ἐκάκιζον ὅτι στρατηγὸς ὢν οὐκ ἐπεξά-
22 γοι, αἴτιόν τε σφίσιν ἐνόμιζον πάντων ὧν ἔπασχον. Περικλῆς δὲ ὁρῶν μὲν αὐτοὺς πρὸς τὸ παρὸν χαλεπαίνοντας καὶ οὐ τὰ ἄριστα φρονοῦντας, πιστεύων δὲ ὀρθῶς γιγνώσκειν περὶ τοῦ μὴ ἐπεξιέναι, ἐκκλησίαν τε οὐκ ἐποίει αὐτῶν οὐδὲ ξύλλογον οὐδένα, τοῦ μὴ ὀργῇ τι μᾶλλον ἢ γνώμῃ ξυνελθόντας ἐξαμαρτεῖν, τήν τε πόλιν ἐφύλασσε καὶ δι' ἡσυχίας μάλιστα
2 ὅσον ἐδύνατο εἶχεν. ἱππέας μέντοι ἐξέπεμπεν αἰεὶ τοῦ μὴ προδρόμους ἀπὸ τῆς στρατιᾶς ἐσπίπτοντας ἐς τοὺς ἀγροὺς τοὺς ἐγγὺς τῆς πόλεως κακουργεῖν· καὶ ἱππομαχία τις ἐγένετο βραχεῖα ἐν Φρυγίοις τῶν τε Ἀθηναίων τέλει ἑνὶ τῶν ἱππέων καὶ Θεσσαλοῖς μετ' αὐτῶν πρὸς τοὺς Βοιωτῶν ἱππέας, ἐν ᾗ οὐκ ἔλασσον ἔσχον οἱ Ἀθηναῖοι καὶ Θεσσαλοί, μέχρι οὗ προσβοηθησάντων τοῖς Βοιωτοῖς τῶν ὁπλιτῶν τροπὴ ἐγένετο αὐτῶν καὶ ἀπέθανον τῶν Θεσσαλῶν καὶ Ἀθηναίων οὐ πολλοί· ἀνείλοντο μέντοι αὐτοὺς αὐθημερὸν ἀσπόνδους.
3 καὶ οἱ Πελοποννήσιοι τροπαῖον τῇ ὑστεραίᾳ ἔστησαν. ἡ δὲ βοήθεια αὕτη τῶν Θεσσαλῶν κατὰ τὸ παλαιὸν ξυμμαχικὸν ἐγένετο τοῖς Ἀθηναίοις, καὶ ἀφίκοντο παρ' αὐτοὺς Λαρισαῖοι, Φαρσάλιοι, Πειράσιοι, Κραννώνιοι, Πυράσιοι, Γυρτώνιοι,

---

31. Πειράσιοι Π⁸: Περάσιοι Β, Παράσιοι cett., secl. Heringa.
Πυράσιοι rec. cf. Strabo 435.IX.5.14, Steph. Byz.: Πειράσιοι codd., secl. Alberti.

waste in full view of them, which had never happened before to the younger men, or even to the older except in the Persian Wars, and, naturally enough, they thought this was terrible. So they thought, especially the young men, that they should not look on but go out to attack. The Athenians took sides and argued violently, some insisting that they ought to go out and others insisting that they ought not. Oracle-mongers recited oracles of every kind, and every one was eager to listen to them. The men of Acharnae in particular urged that they should go out, since they reckoned that they comprised a very large part of the Athenian people, and it was their land that was being laid waste.

  The city was inflamed with every kind of excitement, and there was anger against Pericles: none of the advice that he had given earlier was remembered, but they accused him of cowardice in that, general as he was, he did not lead them out, and they held him to blame for all that they were suffering. He realised that they were discontented because of the immediate situation, and were not thinking on the right lines. Since he was confident that his decision that they ought not to go out was right, he refused to call an assembly or any kind of meeting, fearing that the people might make a mistake if they met in a spirit of passion rather than judgment. So he kept the city under guard and calm as far as he could. He did, however, keep sending out cavalry, to prevent advance parties from the invaders attacking the fields near the city and doing damage there. There was even a slight battle at Phrygii, where a squadron of the Athenian cavalry and the Thessalians with them fought against the Boeotian cavalry, and had the upper hand until the hoplites came up to support the Boeotians. Then the Thessalians and Athenians were beaten back, and a few of them were killed; they recovered the bodies the same day without a truce, and the Peloponnesians set up a trophy the next day. This help from Thessaly came to Athens in accordance with their ancient alliance. There were contingents from Larisa, Pharsalus, Pirasia, Crannon, Pyrasus,

Φεραῖοι. ἡγοῦντο δὲ αὐτῶν ἐκ μὲν Λαρίσης Πολυμήδης καὶ Ἀριστόνους, ἀπὸ τῆς στάσεως ἑκάτερος, ἐκ δὲ Φαρσάλου Μένων· ἦσαν δὲ καὶ τῶν ἄλλων κατὰ πόλεις ἄρχοντες.

23 Οἱ δὲ Πελοποννήσιοι, ἐπειδὴ οὐκ ἐπεξῇσαν αὐτοῖς οἱ Ἀθηναῖοι ἐς μάχην, ἄραντες ἐκ τῶν Ἀχαρνῶν ἐδῄουν τῶν δήμων τινὰς ἄλλους τῶν μεταξὺ Πάρνηθος καὶ Βριλησσοῦ **2** ὄρους. ὄντων δὲ αὐτῶν ἐν τῇ γῇ οἱ Ἀθηναῖοι ἀπέστειλαν τὰς ἑκατὸν ναῦς περὶ Πελοπόννησον ἅσπερ παρεσκευάζοντο καὶ χιλίους ὁπλίτας ἐπ' αὐτῶν καὶ τοξότας τετρακοσίους· ἐστρατήγει δὲ Καρκίνος τε ὁ Ξενοτίμου καὶ Πρωτέας ὁ **3** Ἐπικλέους καὶ Σωκράτης ὁ Ἀντιγένους. καὶ οἱ μὲν ἄραντες τῇ παρασκευῇ ταύτῃ περιέπλεον, οἱ δὲ Πελοποννήσιοι χρόνον ἐμμείναντες ἐν τῇ Ἀττικῇ ὅσον εἶχον τὰ ἐπιτήδεια ἀνεχώρησαν διὰ Βοιωτῶν, οὐχ ᾗπερ ἐσέβαλον· παριόντες δὲ Ὠρωπὸν τὴν γῆν τὴν Γραϊκὴν καλουμένην, ἣν νέμονται Ὠρώπιοι Ἀθηναίων ὑπήκοοι, ἐδῄωσαν. ἀφικόμενοι δὲ ἐς Πελοπόννησον διελύθησαν κατὰ πόλεις ἕκαστοι.

24 Ἀναχωρησάντων δὲ αὐτῶν οἱ Ἀθηναῖοι φυλακὰς κατεστήσαντο κατὰ γῆν καὶ κατὰ θάλασσαν, ὥσπερ δὴ ἔμελλον διὰ παντὸς τοῦ πολέμου φυλάξειν· καὶ χίλια τάλαντα ἀπὸ τῶν ἐν τῇ ἀκροπόλει χρημάτων ἔδοξεν αὐτοῖς ἐξαίρετα ποιησαμένοις χωρὶς θέσθαι καὶ μὴ ἀναλοῦν, ἀλλ' ἀπὸ τῶν ἄλλων πολεμεῖν· ἢν δέ τις εἴπῃ ἢ ἐπιψηφίσῃ κινεῖν τὰ χρήματα ταῦτα ἐς ἄλλο τι, ἢν μὴ οἱ πολέμιοι νηίτῃ στρατῷ ἐπιπλέωσι τῇ πόλει καὶ δέῃ ἀμύνασθαι, θάνατον ζημίαν **2** ἐπέθεντο. τριήρεις τε μετ' αὐτῶν ἐξαιρέτους ἑκατὸν ἐποιήσαντο κατὰ τὸν ἐνιαυτὸν ἕκαστον τὰς βελτίστας, καὶ τριηράρχους αὐταῖς, ὧν μὴ χρῆσθαι μηδεμιᾷ ἐς ἄλλο τι ἢ μετὰ τῶν χρημάτων περὶ τοῦ αὐτοῦ κινδύνου, ἢν δέῃ.

25 Οἱ δ' ἐν ταῖς ἑκατὸν ναυσὶ περὶ Πελοπόννησον Ἀθηναῖοι καὶ Κερκυραῖοι μετ' αὐτῶν πεντήκοντα ναυσὶ προσβεβοηθηκότες καὶ ἄλλοι τινὲς τῶν ἐκεῖ ξυμμάχων ἄλλα τε ἐκάκουν περιπλέοντες καὶ ἐς Μεθώνην τῆς Λακωνικῆς ἀποβάντες τῷ

Gyrton and Pherae; the commanders were Polymedes and Aristonous from Larisa, one from each party, Meno from Pharsalus, and officers from the other individual cities.

23 Since the Athenians refused to come out for a battle with them, the Peloponnesians set out from Acharnae and proceeded to lay waste some of the other demes between Parnes and Mount Brilessus. While they were in their territory, the Athenians sent out round the Peloponnese the hundred ships which they had been making ready, with a thousand hoplites and four hundred archers on board, and Carcinus son of Xenotimus, Proteas son of Epicles and Socrates son of Antigenes as generals. Those commanders, with that force, set out on their voyage. Meanwhile the Peloponnesians, after staying in Attica for the time for which they had provisions, retired, not by the way they had come but through Boeotia. As they passed Oropus, they ravaged the land called Graea, which is occupied by the Oropians as subjects of Athens. On returning to the Peloponnese they were discharged, and went back to their individual cities.

24 When the Peloponnesians had withdrawn, the Athenians set up garrisons by land and sea at the points where they intended to keep guard throughout the war. They decided to establish a separate fund of a thousand talents out of the monies on the Acropolis: this was to be set aside and not spent, while they funded the war with the rest; the death penalty was prescribed for any one who proposed or put to the vote a proposal to touch this money in any circumstances other than the need to resist if the enemy sailed against the city with their navy. They likewise kept separate their hundred best triremes each year, and trierarchs for them, and these were not to be used except with the money in the same emergency, if the need should arise.

25 The Athenians sailing round the Peloponnese in their hundred ships were joined by fifty from Corcyra and by some of their other allies in that region. They did damage in various places on their voyage round, and when they reached Methone in Laconia they disembarked and at-

τείχει προσέβαλον ὄντι ἀσθενεῖ καὶ ἀνθρώπων οὐκ ἐνόντων. 2 ἔτυχε δὲ περὶ τοὺς χώρους τούτους Βρασίδας ὁ Τέλλιδος ἀνὴρ Σπαρτιάτης φρουρὰν ἔχων, καὶ αἰσθόμενος ἐβοήθει τοῖς ἐν τῷ χωρίῳ μετὰ ὁπλιτῶν ἑκατόν. διαδραμὼν δὲ τὸ τῶν Ἀθηναίων στρατόπεδον ἐσκεδασμένον κατὰ τὴν χώραν καὶ πρὸς τὸ τεῖχος τετραμμένον ἐσπίπτει ἐς τὴν Μεθώνην καὶ ὀλίγους τινὰς ἐν τῇ ἐσδρομῇ ἀπολέσας τῶν μεθ᾽ αὑτοῦ τήν τε πόλιν περιεποίησε καὶ ἀπὸ τούτου τοῦ τολμήματος 3 πρῶτος τῶν κατὰ τὸν πόλεμον ἐπῃνέθη ἐν Σπάρτῃ. οἱ δὲ Ἀθηναῖοι ἄραντες παρέπλεον, καὶ σχόντες τῆς Ἠλείας ἐς Φειὰν ἐδῄουν τὴν γῆν ἐπὶ δύο ἡμέρας καὶ προσβοηθήσαντας τῶν ἐκ τῆς κοίλης Ἤλιδος τριακοσίους λογάδας καὶ τῶν 4 αὐτόθεν ἐκ τῆς περιοικίδος Ἠλείων μάχῃ ἐκράτησαν. ἀνέμου δὲ κατιόντος μεγάλου χειμαζόμενοι ἐν ἀλιμένῳ χωρίῳ, οἱ μὲν πολλοὶ ἐπέβησαν ἐπὶ τὰς ναῦς καὶ περιέπλεον τὸν Ἰχθῦν καλούμενον τὴν ἄκραν ἐς τὸν ἐν τῇ Φειᾷ λιμένα, οἱ δὲ Μεσσήνιοι ἐν τούτῳ καὶ ἄλλοι τινὲς οἱ οὐ δυνάμενοι 5 ἐπιβῆναι κατὰ γῆν χωρήσαντες τὴν Φειὰν αἱροῦσιν. καὶ ὕστερον αἵ τε νῆες περιπλεύσασαι ἀναλαμβάνουσιν αὐτοὺς καὶ ἐξανάγονται ἐκλιπόντες Φειάν, καὶ τῶν Ἠλείων ἡ πολλὴ ἤδη στρατιὰ προσεβεβοηθήκει. παραπλεύσαντες δὲ οἱ Ἀθηναῖοι ἐπὶ ἄλλα χωρία ἐδῄουν.

26 Ὑπὸ δὲ τὸν αὐτὸν χρόνον τοῦτον Ἀθηναῖοι τριάκοντα ναῦς ἐξέπεμψαν περὶ τὴν Λοκρίδα καὶ Εὐβοίας ἅμα φυλα-2 κήν· ἐστρατήγει δὲ αὐτῶν Κλεόπομπος ὁ Κλεινίου. καὶ ἀποβάσεις ποιησάμενος τῆς τε παραθαλασσίου ἔστιν ἃ ἐδῄωσε καὶ Θρόνιον εἷλεν, ὁμήρους τε ἔλαβεν αὐτῶν, καὶ ἐν Ἀλόπῃ τοὺς βοηθήσαντας Λοκρῶν μάχῃ ἐκράτησεν.

27 Ἀνέστησαν δὲ καὶ Αἰγινήτας τῷ αὐτῷ θέρει τούτῳ ἐξ Αἰγίνης Ἀθηναῖοι, αὐτούς τε καὶ παῖδας καὶ γυναῖκας, ἐπικαλέσαντες οὐχ ἥκιστα τοῦ πολέμου σφίσιν αἰτίους εἶναι· καὶ τὴν Αἴγιναν ἀσφαλέστερον ἐφαίνετο τῇ Πελοποννήσῳ ἐπικειμένην αὐτῶν πέμψαντας ἐποίκους ἔχειν. καὶ ἐξ-2 έπεμψαν ὕστερον οὐ πολλῷ ἐς αὐτὴν τοὺς οἰκήτορας. ἐκ-

---

32. <τῇ τε Ἀττικῇ καὶ> τῇ Πελοποννήσῳ Classen.

tacked the city wall, since it was weak and there were no soldiers inside. It happened that a Spartiate called Brasidas son of Tellis was in that area with an expeditionary force. On learning what was happening, he went to support the people there with a hundred hoplites. The Athenian force was scattered over the countryside and no longer concentrating on the city wall, so he was able to pass through them and break into Methone, though in making his entry he lost a few of his men. Thus he secured the city, and as a result of this deed of daring he was the first man to win praise in Sparta during the war.

The Athenians set out and continued their voyage. Putting in to Pheia in Elis, they ravaged the land there for two days, and when there came to the defence three hundred picked men from Hollow Elis and from the Eleans living there in the dependent territory, the Athenians defeated them in a battle. A strong wind arose, and, since the storm had caught the Athenians in a place with no harbour, most of them embarked on the ships and sailed round what is called Cape Fish to the harbour at Pheia, while the Messenians and some others who were unable to board the ships proceeded by land and captured Pheia. The ships then sailed round and picked these men up, and they left Pheia and put out to sea: by now the main army of Elis had come to the defence. The Athenians continued their voyage to other places, and ravaged them.

About this same time the Athenians sent thirty ships round Locris and to guard Euboea, under the general Cleopompus son of Clinias. He disembarked and ravaged some coastal sites, captured Thronium and took hostages from it, and at Alope won a battle against the Locrians who came to the defence.

In this same summer the Athenians expelled the Aeginetans, together with their children and wives, from Aegina. They alleged that the Aeginetans were particularly responsible for bringing the war on them, and since Aegina is situated close to the Peloponnese they thought it would be safer to occupy it with colonists sent from Athens. The settlers were sent there soon afterwards. The

πεσοῦσι δὲ τοῖς Αἰγινήταις οἱ Λακεδαιμόνιοι ἔδοσαν Θυρέαν οἰκεῖν καὶ τὴν γῆν νέμεσθαι, κατά τε τὸ Ἀθηναίων διάφορον καὶ ὅτι σφῶν εὐεργέται ἦσαν ὑπὸ τὸν σεισμὸν καὶ τῶν Εἱλώτων τὴν ἐπανάστασιν. ἡ δὲ Θυρεᾶτις γῆ μεθορία τῆς Ἀργείας καὶ Λακωνικῆς ἐστίν, ἐπὶ θάλασσαν καθήκουσα. καὶ οἱ μὲν αὐτῶν ἐνταῦθα ᾤκησαν, οἱ δ' ἐσπάρησαν κατὰ τὴν ἄλλην Ἑλλάδα.

28 Τοῦ δ' αὐτοῦ θέρους νουμηνίᾳ κατὰ σελήνην, ὥσπερ καὶ μόνον δοκεῖ εἶναι γίγνεσθαι δυνατόν, ὁ ἥλιος ἐξέλιπε μετὰ μεσημβρίαν καὶ πάλιν ἀνεπληρώθη, γενόμενος μηνοειδὴς καὶ ἀστέρων τινῶν ἐκφανέντων.

29 Καὶ ἐν τῷ αὐτῷ θέρει Νυμφόδωρον τὸν Πύθεω ἄνδρα Ἀβδηρίτην, οὗ εἶχε τὴν ἀδελφὴν Σιτάλκης, δυνάμενον παρ' αὐτῷ μέγα οἱ Ἀθηναῖοι πρότερον πολέμιον νομίζοντες πρόξενον ἐποιήσαντο καὶ μετεπέμψαντο, βουλόμενοι Σιτάλκην σφίσι τὸν Τήρεω, Θρᾳκῶν βασιλέα, ξύμμαχον γενέσθαι.
2 ὁ δὲ Τήρης οὗτος ὁ τοῦ Σιτάλκου πατὴρ πρῶτος Ὀδρύσαις τὴν μεγάλην βασιλείαν ἐπὶ πλέον τῆς ἄλλης Θρᾴκης ἐποίη-
3 σεν· πολὺ γὰρ μέρος καὶ αὐτόνομόν ἐστι Θρᾳκῶν. Τηρεῖ δὲ τῷ Πρόκνην τὴν Πανδίονος ἀπ' Ἀθηνῶν σχόντι γυναῖκα προσήκει ὁ Τήρης οὗτος οὐδέν, οὐδὲ τῆς αὐτῆς Θρᾴκης ἐγένοντο, ἀλλ' ὁ μὲν ἐν Δαυλίᾳ τῆς Φωκίδος νῦν καλουμένης γῆς ὁ Τηρεὺς ᾤκει, τότε ὑπὸ Θρᾳκῶν οἰκουμένης, καὶ τὸ ἔργον τὸ περὶ τὸν Ἴτυν αἱ γυναῖκες ἐν τῇ γῇ ταύτῃ ἔπραξαν (πολλοῖς δὲ καὶ τῶν ποιητῶν ἐν ἀηδόνος μνήμῃ Δαυλιὰς ἡ ὄρνις ἐπωνόμασται), εἰκός τε καὶ τὸ κῆδος Πανδίονα ξυνάψασθαι τῆς θυγατρὸς διὰ τοσούτου ἐπ' ὠφελίᾳ τῇ πρὸς ἀλλήλους μᾶλλον ἢ διὰ πολλῶν ἡμερῶν ἐς Ὀδρύσας ὁδοῦ. Τήρης δὲ οὐδὲ τὸ αὐτὸ ὄνομα ἔχων βασιλεὺς [τε] πρῶτος
4 ἐν κράτει Ὀδρυσῶν ἐγένετο. οὗ δὴ ὄντα τὸν Σιτάλκην οἱ Ἀθηναῖοι ξύμμαχον ἐποιοῦντο, βουλόμενοι σφίσι τὰ ἐπὶ
5 Θρᾴκης χωρία καὶ Περδίκκαν ξυνεξελεῖν αὐτόν. ἐλθών τε ἐς τὰς Ἀθήνας ὁ Νυμφόδωρος τήν τε τοῦ Σιτάλκου ξυμμα-

---

21. προσήκει cett.: προσῆκεν C G, fortasse recte.
23. ὁ Τηρεὺς secl. Herwerden.
29. βασιλεὺς [τε] Classen: <οὔτε τῆς αὐτῆς γῆς ὤν>, βασιλεὺς [τε] Krüger, βασιλεύς τε <ἐν Θρᾴκῃ καὶ οὐκ ἐν Φωκίδι ὤν> Gomme.

Aeginetans after their expulsion were allowed by the Spartans to live in Thyrea and cultivate the land, because of their hostility to Athens and because they had been benefactors of Sparta at the time of the earthquake and the helot revolt. (The land of Thyrea is on the borders of Argos and Laconia, reaching down to the sea.) Some of the Aeginetans settled there, while others were dispersed through the rest of Greece.

28 In the same summer, at the beginning of the lunar month (which appears to be the only time when it can happen), the sun was eclipsed and became crescent-shaped, and some stars appeared, and then the full moon returned.

29 In the same summer the Athenians appointed as *proxenos* Nymphodorus son of Pythes, of Abdera, and invited him to Athens. They had previously considered him an enemy, but Sitalces son of Teres, king of Thrace, was married to his sister and he had great influence with Sitalces, and they wanted to make an ally of Sitalces. This 2 Teres, Sitalces' father, was the first man to make the Odrysian kingdom powerful and extend it further into the rest of Thrace: for a large part of Thrace is independent. This Teres has no connection with Tereus, who took 3 as his wife Pandion's daughter Procne from Athens. They did not even live in that same country of Thrace: Tereus lived in Daulis, in the territory which is now called Phocis but was then inhabited by Thracians, and it was in that country that the women perpetrated the outrage on Itys, and indeed many of the poets when referring to the nightingale call it the Daulian bird. Moreover, one would expect Pandion to arrange his daughter's marriage within a limited distance, with a view to mutual assistance, rather than with the Odrysians, many days' journey away. Teres does not even have the same name as Tereus. He was the first powerful king of the Odrysians, and it was his 4 son Sitalces whom the Athenians set out to make their ally, in the hope that he would join them in capturing the Thraceward region and Perdiccas.

5 Nymphodorus came to Athens, arranged the alliance with Sitalces and Athenian citizenship for Sitalces' son

χίαν ἐποίησε καὶ Σάδοκον τὸν υἱὸν αὐτοῦ Ἀθηναῖον τόν
τε ἐπὶ Θρᾴκης πόλεμον ὑπεδέχετο καταλύσειν· πείσειν γὰρ
Σιτάλκην πέμπειν στρατιὰν Θρᾳκίαν Ἀθηναίοις ἱππέων τε
6 καὶ πελταστῶν. ξυνεβίβασε δὲ καὶ τὸν Περδίκκαν τοῖς
Ἀθηναίοις καὶ Θέρμην αὐτῷ ἔπεισεν ἀποδοῦναι· ξυνεστρά-
τευσέ τε εὐθὺς Περδίκκας ἐπὶ Χαλκιδέας μετὰ Ἀθηναίων
7 καὶ Φορμίωνος. οὕτω μὲν Σιτάλκης τε ὁ Τήρεω Θρᾳκῶν
βασιλεὺς ξύμμαχος ἐγένετο Ἀθηναίοις καὶ Περδίκκας ὁ
Ἀλεξάνδρου Μακεδόνων βασιλεύς.

30 Οἱ δ' ἐν ταῖς ἑκατὸν ναυσὶν Ἀθηναῖοι ἔτι ὄντες περὶ
Πελοπόννησον Σόλλιόν τε Κορινθίων πόλισμα αἱροῦσι καὶ
παραδιδόασι Παλαιρεῦσιν Ἀκαρνάνων μόνοις τὴν γῆν καὶ
πόλιν νέμεσθαι· καὶ Ἀστακόν, ἧς Εὔαρχος ἐτυράννει, λαβόντες κατὰ κράτος καὶ ἐξελάσαντες αὐτὸν τὸ χωρίον ἐς τὴν
2 ξυμμαχίαν προσεποιήσαντο. ἐπί τε Κεφαλληνίαν τὴν νῆσον
προσπλεύσαντες προσηγάγοντο ἄνευ μάχης· κεῖται δὲ ἡ
Κεφαλληνία κατὰ Ἀκαρνανίαν καὶ Λευκάδα τετράπολις οὖσα,
Παλῆς, Κράνιοι, Σαμαῖοι, Προνναῖοι. ὕστερον δ' οὐ πολλῷ
ἀνεχώρησαν αἱ νῆες ἐς τὰς Ἀθήνας.

31 Περὶ δὲ τὸ φθινόπωρον τοῦ θέρους τούτου Ἀθηναῖοι
πανδημεί, αὐτοὶ καὶ οἱ μέτοικοι, ἐσέβαλον ἐς τὴν Μεγαρίδα
Περικλέους τοῦ Ξανθίππου στρατηγοῦντος. καὶ οἱ περὶ
Πελοπόννησον Ἀθηναῖοι ἐν ταῖς ἑκατὸν ναυσίν (ἔτυχον γὰρ
ἤδη ἐν Αἰγίνῃ ὄντες ἐπ' οἴκου ἀνακομιζόμενοι) ὡς ᾔσθοντο
τοὺς ἐκ τῆς πόλεως πανστρατιᾷ ἐν Μεγάροις ὄντας, ἔπλευσαν
2 παρ' αὐτοὺς καὶ ξυνεμείχθησαν. στρατόπεδόν τε μέγιστον
δὴ τοῦτο ἁθρόον Ἀθηναίων ἐγένετο, ἀκμαζούσης ἔτι τῆς
πόλεως καὶ οὔπω νενοσηκυίας· μυρίων γὰρ ὁπλιτῶν οὐκ
ἐλάσσους ἦσαν αὐτοὶ Ἀθηναῖοι (χωρὶς δὲ αὐτοῖς οἱ ἐν
Ποτειδαίᾳ τρισχίλιοι ἦσαν), μέτοικοι δὲ ξυνεσέβαλον οὐκ
ἐλάσσους τρισχιλίων ὁπλιτῶν, χωρὶς δὲ ὁ ἄλλος ὅμιλος
ψιλῶν οὐκ ὀλίγος. δῃώσαντες δὲ τὰ πολλὰ τῆς γῆς ἀνε-
3 χώρησαν. ἐγένοντο δὲ καὶ ἄλλαι ὕστερον ἐν τῷ πολέμῳ
κατὰ ἔτος ἕκαστον ἐσβολαὶ Ἀθηναίων ἐς τὴν Μεγαρίδα
καὶ ἱππέων καὶ πανστρατιᾷ, μέχρι οὗ Νίσαια ἑάλω ὑπ'
Ἀθηναίων.

Sadocus, and undertook to end the war in Thrace by persuading Sitalces to send the Athenians a force of Thracian cavalry and peltasts. He also reconciled Perdiccas 6 with the Athenians and persuaded them to restore Therme to him, after which Perdiccas immediately joined the Athenians and Phormio in campaigning against the Chalcidians. That is how Sitalces son of Teres, king of Thrace, 7 and Perdiccas son of Alexander, king of Macedon, became allies of Athens.

The Athenians in the hundred ships, while they were 30 still round the Peloponnese, captured Sollium, a township belonging to Corinth, and allowed the people of Palaerus, independently of the rest of Acarnania, to occupy the territory and the city. They took by force Astacus, which was subject to the tyrant Evarchus, expelled him, and brought the place into their alliance. They sailed 2 against the island of Cephallenia, and won it over without a battle. Cephallenia lies opposite Acarnania and Leucas, and comprises four cities, Pale, Cranae, Same and Pronni. Soon after that, the ships returned to Athens.

About the autumn of this summer the Athenians invaded 31 the territory of Megara, in full force together with the metics, under the generalship of Pericles son of Xanthippus. The Athenians who had gone round the Peloponnese in the hundred ships were now at Aegina in the course of their journey home, and when they learned that the men from the city were at Megara in full force they sailed there and joined them. This was the largest Athenian 2 force ever assembled together, since the city was still flourishing and the plague had not yet struck: the Athenians themselves supplied no less than ten thousand hoplites (and in addition there were three thousand at Potidaea), the metics who joined in the invasion numbered not less than three thousand hoplites, and there was also a large body of light-armed soldiers. They laid waste most of the territory, and then withdrew. The Athenians 3 made further invasions of the Megarid, with their cavalry and with their full forces, every year during the war until they captured Nisaea.

32 Ἐτειχίσθη δὲ καὶ Ἀταλάντη ὑπὸ Ἀθηναίων φρούριον τοῦ θέρους τούτου τελευτῶντος, ἡ ἐπὶ Λοκροῖς τοῖς Ὀπουντίοις νῆσος ἐρήμη πρότερον οὖσα, τοῦ μὴ λῃστὰς ἐκπλέοντας ἐξ Ὀποῦντος καὶ τῆς ἄλλης Λοκρίδος κακουργεῖν τὴν Εὔβοιαν.

Ταῦτα μὲν ἐν τῷ θέρει τούτῳ μετὰ τὴν Πελοποννησίων 33 ἐκ τῆς Ἀττικῆς ἀναχώρησιν ἐγένετο. τοῦ δ' ἐπιγιγνομένου χειμῶνος Εὔαρχος ὁ Ἀκαρνὰν βουλόμενος ἐς τὴν Ἀστακὸν κατελθεῖν πείθει Κορινθίους τεσσαράκοντα ναυσὶ καὶ πεντακοσίοις καὶ χιλίοις ὁπλίταις ἑαυτὸν κατάγειν πλεύσαντας, καὶ αὐτὸς ἐπικούρους τινὰς προσεμισθώσατο· ἦρχον δὲ τῆς στρατιᾶς Εὐφαμίδας τε ὁ Ἀριστωνύμου καὶ Τιμόξενος ὁ 2 Τιμοκράτους καὶ Εὔμαχος ὁ Χρύσιδος. καὶ πλεύσαντες κατήγαγον· καὶ τῆς ἄλλης Ἀκαρνανίας τῆς περὶ θάλασσαν ἔστιν ἃ χωρία βουλόμενοι προσποιήσασθαι καὶ πειραθέντες, 3 ὡς οὐκ ἐδύναντο, ἀπέπλεον ἐπ' οἴκου. σχόντες δ' ἐν τῷ παράπλῳ ἐς Κεφαλληνίαν καὶ ἀπόβασιν ποιησάμενοι ἐς τὴν Κρανίων γῆν, ἀπατηθέντες ὑπ' αὐτῶν ἐξ ὁμολογίας τινὸς ἄνδρας τε ἀποβάλλουσι σφῶν αὐτῶν, ἐπιθεμένων ἀπροσδοκήτοις τῶν Κρανίων, καὶ βιαιότερον ἀναγαγόμενοι ἐκομίσθησαν ἐπ' οἴκου.

34 Ἐν δὲ τῷ αὐτῷ χειμῶνι Ἀθηναῖοι τῷ πατρίῳ νόμῳ χρώμενοι δημοσίᾳ ταφὰς ἐποιήσαντο τῶν ἐν τῷδε τῷ πολέμῳ 2 πρώτων ἀποθανόντων τρόπῳ τοιῷδε. τὰ μὲν ὀστᾶ προτίθενται τῶν ἀπογενομένων πρότριτα σκηνὴν ποιήσαντες, καὶ 3 ἐπιφέρει τῷ αὑτοῦ ἕκαστος ἤν τι βούληται· ἐπειδὰν δὲ ἡ ἐκφορὰ ᾖ, λάρνακας κυπαρισσίνας ἄγουσιν ἅμαξαι, φυλῆς ἑκάστης μίαν· ἔνεστι δὲ τὰ ὀστᾶ ἧς ἕκαστος ἦν φυλῆς. μία δὲ κλίνη κενὴ φέρεται ἐστρωμένη τῶν ἀφανῶν, οἳ ἂν 4 μὴ εὑρεθῶσιν ἐς ἀναίρεσιν. ξυνεκφέρει δὲ ὁ βουλόμενος καὶ ἀστῶν καὶ ξένων, καὶ γυναῖκες πάρεισιν αἱ προσήκουσαι 5 ἐπὶ τὸν τάφον ὀλοφυρόμεναι. τιθέασιν οὖν ἐς τὸ δημόσιον σῆμα, ὅ ἐστιν ἐπὶ τοῦ καλλίστου προαστείου τῆς πόλεως, καὶ αἰεὶ ἐν αὐτῷ θάπτουσι τοὺς ἐκ τῶν πολέμων, πλήν γε τοὺς ἐν Μαραθῶνι· ἐκείνων δὲ διαπρεπῆ τὴν ἀρετὴν κρίναντες

At the end of this summer the Athenians fortified as a garrison post Atalante, a previously uninhabited island off Opuntian Locris, to prevent raiders from sailing from Opus and the rest of Locris to damage Euboea. That is what happened in this summer after the Peloponnesians had withdrawn from Attica.

In the following winter Evarchus of Acarnania, wanting to return to Astacus, persuaded the Corinthians to sail with forty ships and fifteen hundred hoplites to reinstate him, and in addition hired some mercenaries himself. The commanders of the force were Euphamidas son of Aristonymus, Timoxenus son of Timocrates and Eumachus son of Chrysis. They made the voyage and reinstated him. They also wanted to win over some places in the rest of coastal Acarnania, but they failed in their attempt. Then they sailed back home. In the course of their voyage they put in to Cephallenia and made a descent on the territory of Cranae. They made an agreement, but were deceived by the Cranians, and lost some of their men when they attacked unexpectedly. So they put out to sea somewhat abruptly, and made their way home.

In the same winter the Athenians, in accordance with their traditional institution, held a public funeral of those who had been the first to die in the war. The practice is this. Two days before the funeral they set up a tent and lay out in it the bones of the deceased, for each man to bring what offerings he wishes to his own kin. On the day of the procession, cypress-wood coffins are carried on waggons, one for each tribe, with each man's bones in his own tribe's coffin. In addition there is one empty bier carried, laid out for the missing, that is, for those whose bodies could not be found and recovered. Every man who wishes joins the procession, whether citizen or foreigner, and the women of the families are present to lament at the grave. In this way the dead are placed in the public tomb, which is situated in the most beautiful suburb of the city. Those who die in war are always buried there, apart from those who fell at Marathon, whose virtue was judged outstanding and who

6 αὐτοῦ καὶ τὸν τάφον ἐποίησαν. ἐπειδὰν δὲ κρύψωσι γῇ, ἀνὴρ ᾑρημένος ὑπὸ τῆς πόλεως, ὃς ἂν γνώμῃ τε δοκῇ μὴ ἀξύνετος εἶναι καὶ ἀξιώσει προήκῃ, λέγει ἐπ' αὐτοῖς ἔπαινον
7 τὸν πρέποντα· μετὰ δὲ τοῦτο ἀπέρχονται. ὧδε μὲν θάπτουσιν· καὶ διὰ παντὸς τοῦ πολέμου, ὁπότε ξυμβαίη αὐτοῖς, ἐχρῶντο
8 τῷ νόμῳ. ἐπὶ δ' οὖν τοῖς πρώτοις τοῖσδε Περικλῆς ὁ Ξανθίππου ᾑρέθη λέγειν. καὶ ἐπειδὴ καιρὸς ἐλάμβανε, προελθὼν ἀπὸ τοῦ σήματος ἐπὶ βῆμα ὑψηλὸν πεποιημένον, ὅπως ἀκούοιτο ὡς ἐπὶ πλεῖστον τοῦ ὁμίλου, ἔλεγε τοιάδε.

35 " Οἱ μὲν πολλοὶ τῶν ἐνθάδε ἤδη εἰρηκότων ἐπαινοῦσι τὸν προσθέντα τῷ νόμῳ τὸν λόγον τόνδε, ὡς καλὸν ἐπὶ τοῖς ἐκ τῶν πολέμων θαπτομένοις ἀγορεύεσθαι αὐτόν. ἐμοὶ δὲ ἀρκοῦν ἂν ἐδόκει εἶναι ἀνδρῶν ἀγαθῶν ἔργῳ γενομένων ἔργῳ καὶ δηλοῦσθαι τὰς τιμάς, οἷα καὶ νῦν περὶ τὸν τάφον τόνδε δημοσίᾳ παρασκευασθέντα ὁρᾶτε, καὶ μὴ ἐν ἑνὶ ἀνδρὶ πολλῶν ἀρετὰς κινδυνεύεσθαι εὖ τε καὶ χεῖρον εἰπόντι πι-
2 στευθῆναι. χαλεπὸν γὰρ τὸ μετρίως εἰπεῖν ἐν ᾧ μόλις καὶ ἡ δόκησις τῆς ἀληθείας βεβαιοῦται. ὅ τε γὰρ ξυνειδὼς καὶ εὔνους ἀκροατὴς τάχ' ἄν τι ἐνδεεστέρως πρὸς ἃ βούλεταί τε καὶ ἐπίσταται νομίσειε δηλοῦσθαι, ὅ τε ἄπειρος ἔστιν ἃ καὶ πλεονάζεσθαι, διὰ φθόνον, εἴ τι ὑπὲρ τὴν αὐτοῦ φύσιν ἀκούοι. μέχρι γὰρ τοῦδε ἀνεκτοὶ οἱ ἔπαινοί εἰσι περὶ ἑτέρων λεγόμενοι, ἐς ὅσον ἂν καὶ αὐτὸς ἕκαστος οἴηται ἱκανὸς εἶναι δρᾶσαί τι ὧν ἤκουσεν· τῷ δὲ ὑπερβάλλοντι αὐτῶν φθονοῦντες
3 ἤδη καὶ ἀπιστοῦσιν. ἐπειδὴ δὲ τοῖς πάλαι οὕτως ἐδοκιμάσθη ταῦτα καλῶς ἔχειν, χρὴ καὶ ἐμὲ ἑπόμενον τῷ νόμῳ πειρᾶσθαι ὑμῶν τῆς ἑκάστου βουλήσεώς τε καὶ δόξης τυχεῖν ὡς ἐπὶ πλεῖστον.

36 " Ἄρξομαι δὲ ἀπὸ τῶν προγόνων πρῶτον· δίκαιον γὰρ αὐτοῖς καὶ πρέπον δὲ ἅμα ἐν τῷ τοιῷδε τὴν τιμὴν ταύτην

were given a tomb on the spot.

When they have been covered with earth, appropriate words of praise are spoken over them by a man chosen by the state for the intelligence of his mind and his outstanding reputation, and after that the people depart. That is how the funeral is conducted: this institution was followed throughout the war when occasion arose. Over these first casualties, then, Pericles son of Xanthippus was chosen to make the speech. When the time arrived, he came forward from the grave on to a high platform which had been erected so that he should be as clearly audible as possible to the crowd; and he spoke on these lines.

"The majority of those who have spoken here before have praised the man who included this speech in our institution, and have claimed that it is good that they should make a speech over those who are buried in consequence of war. However, I should have thought that when men have been good in action it is sufficient for our honours of them to be made evident in action, as you see we have done in providing for this public funeral, and that the virtues of many ought not to be put at risk by being entrusted to one man, who might speak well or ill. It is hard to speak appropriately in circumstances where even the appearance of truth can only with difficulty be confirmed. The listener who knows what has happened and is favourably disposed can easily think that the account given falls short of his wishes and knowledge, while the man lacking in experience may through jealousy think some claims exaggerated if he hears of things beyond his own capacity. Praise spoken of others is bearable up to the point where each man believes himself capable of doing the things he hears of: anything which goes beyond that arouses envy and so disbelief. Nevertheless, since in the past this has been approved as a good practice, I too must comply with our institution, and try as far as I can to coincide with the wishes and opinions of each of you.

"I shall begin first of all with our ancestors. It is right, and on an occasion like this it is appropriate,

τῆς μνήμης δίδοσθαι. τὴν γὰρ χώραν οἱ αὐτοὶ αἰεὶ οἰκοῦντες
διαδοχῇ τῶν ἐπιγιγνομένων μέχρι τοῦδε ἐλευθέραν δι' ἀρετὴν
2 παρέδοσαν. καὶ ἐκεῖνοί τε ἄξιοι ἐπαίνου καὶ ἔτι μᾶλλον οἱ
πατέρες ἡμῶν· κτησάμενοι γὰρ πρὸς οἷς ἐδέξαντο ὅσην
ἔχομεν ἀρχὴν οὐκ ἀπόνως ἡμῖν τοῖς νῦν προσκατέλιπον.
3 τὰ δὲ πλείω αὐτῆς αὐτοὶ ἡμεῖς οἵδε οἱ νῦν ἔτι ὄντες μάλιστα
ἐν τῇ καθεστηκυίᾳ ἡλικίᾳ ἐπηυξήσαμεν καὶ τὴν πόλιν τοῖς
πᾶσι παρεσκευάσαμεν καὶ ἐς πόλεμον καὶ ἐς εἰρήνην αὐταρ-
4 κεστάτην. ὧν ἐγὼ τὰ μὲν κατὰ πολέμους ἔργα, οἷς ἕκαστα
ἐκτήθη, ἢ εἴ τι αὐτοὶ ἢ οἱ πατέρες ἡμῶν βάρβαρον ἢ Ἕλληνα
πολέμιον ἐπιόντα προθύμως ἠμυνάμεθα, μακρηγορεῖν ἐν εἰδόσιν οὐ βουλόμενος ἐάσω· ἀπὸ δὲ οἵας τε ἐπιτηδεύσεως
ἤλθομεν ἐπ' αὐτὰ καὶ μεθ' οἵας πολιτείας καὶ τρόπων ἐξ
οἵων μεγάλα ἐγένετο, ταῦτα δηλώσας πρῶτον εἶμι καὶ ἐπὶ
τὸν τῶνδε ἔπαινον, νομίζων ἐπί τε τῷ παρόντι οὐκ ἂν ἀπρεπῆ
λεχθῆναι αὐτὰ καὶ τὸν πάντα ὅμιλον καὶ ἀστῶν καὶ ξένων
ξύμφορον εἶναι ἐπακοῦσαι αὐτῶν.

37 "Χρώμεθα γὰρ πολιτείᾳ οὐ ζηλούσῃ τοὺς τῶν πέλας
νόμους, παράδειγμα δὲ μᾶλλον αὐτοὶ ὄντες τισὶν ἢ μιμού-
μενοι ἑτέρους. καὶ ὄνομα μὲν διὰ τὸ μὴ ἐς ὀλίγους ἀλλ'
ἐς πλείονας οἰκεῖν δημοκρατία κέκληται· μέτεστι δὲ κατὰ
μὲν τοὺς νόμους πρὸς τὰ ἴδια διάφορα πᾶσι τὸ ἴσον, κατὰ
δὲ τὴν ἀξίωσιν, ὡς ἕκαστος ἔν τῳ εὐδοκιμεῖ, οὐκ ἀπὸ μέρους
τὸ πλέον ἐς τὰ κοινὰ ἢ ἀπ' ἀρετῆς προτιμᾶται, οὐδ' αὖ
κατὰ πενίαν, ἔχων γέ τι ἀγαθὸν δρᾶσαι τὴν πόλιν, ἀξιώ-
2 ματος ἀφανείᾳ κεκώλυται. ἐλευθέρως δὲ τά τε πρὸς τὸ
κοινὸν πολιτεύομεν καὶ ἐς τὴν πρὸς ἀλλήλους τῶν καθ'
ἡμέραν ἐπιτηδευμάτων ὑποψίαν, οὐ δι' ὀργῆς τὸν πέλας, εἰ

---

11. πολέμιον Haase: πόλεμον codd., secl. Dobree.

that this honour should be paid to their memory, for the same race of men has always occupied this land, as one generation has succeeded another, and by their valour they have handed it on as a free land until the present day. They are worthy of praise; and particularly worthy 2 are our own fathers, who by their efforts gained the great empire which we now possess, in addition to what they had received, and left this too to us of the present generation. We ourselves, who are still alive and have 3 reached the settled stage of life, have enlarged most parts of this empire, and we have made our city's resources most ample in all respects both for war and for peace. The deeds in war by which each acquisition was 4 won, the enthusiastic responses of ourselves or our fathers to the attacks of the barbarians or our Greek enemies, I do not wish to recount at length to those who already know of them, so I shall pass them over. What I shall expound first, before I proceed to praise these men, is the way of life which has enabled us to pursue these objectives, and the form of government and the habits which made our great achievements possible. I think in the present circumstances it is not unfitting for these things to be mentioned, and it is advantageous for this whole assemblage of citizens and foreigners to hear of them.

"We have a constitution which does not seek to copy 37 the laws of our neighbours: we are an example to others rather than imitators of them. The name given to this constitution is democracy, because it is based not on a few but on a larger number. For the settlement of private disputes all are on an equal footing in accordance with the laws, while in public life men gain preferment because of their deserts, when anybody has a good reputation for anything: what matters is not rotation but merit. As for poverty, if a man is able to confer some benefit on the city, he is not prevented by the obscurity of his position. With regard to public life, we live as 2 free men; and, as for the suspicion of one another which can arise from daily habits, if our neighbour behaves

καθ' ἡδονήν τι δρᾷ, ἔχοντες, οὐδὲ ἀζημίους μέν, λυπηρὰς δὲ
3 τῇ ὄψει ἀχθηδόνας προστιθέμενοι. ἀνεπαχθῶς δὲ τὰ ἴδια
προσομιλοῦντες τὰ δημόσια διὰ δέος μάλιστα οὐ παρανο-
μοῦμεν, τῶν τε αἰεὶ ἐν ἀρχῇ ὄντων ἀκροάσει καὶ τῶν νόμων,
καὶ μάλιστα αὐτῶν ὅσοι τε ἐπ' ὠφελίᾳ τῶν ἀδικουμένων 5
κεῖνται καὶ ὅσοι ἄγραφοι ὄντες αἰσχύνην ὁμολογουμένην
φέρουσιν.

38 "Καὶ μὴν καὶ τῶν πόνων πλείστας ἀναπαύλας τῇ γνώμῃ
ἐπορισάμεθα, ἀγῶσι μέν γε καὶ θυσίαις διετησίοις νομίζοντες,
ἰδίαις δὲ κατασκευαῖς εὐπρεπέσιν, ὧν καθ' ἡμέραν ἡ τέρψις 10
2 τὸ λυπηρὸν ἐκπλήσσει. ἐπεσέρχεται δὲ διὰ μέγεθος τῆς
πόλεως ἐκ πάσης γῆς τὰ πάντα, καὶ ξυμβαίνει ἡμῖν μηδὲν
οἰκειοτέρᾳ τῇ ἀπολαύσει τὰ αὐτοῦ ἀγαθὰ γιγνόμενα καρποῦ-
σθαι ἢ καὶ τὰ τῶν ἄλλων ἀνθρώπων.

39 "Διαφέρομεν δὲ καὶ ταῖς τῶν πολεμικῶν μελέταις τῶν 15
ἐναντίων τοῖσδε. τήν τε γὰρ πόλιν κοινὴν παρέχομεν, καὶ
οὐκ ἔστιν ὅτε ξενηλασίαις ἀπείργομέν τινα ἢ μαθήματος ἢ
θεάματος, ὃ μὴ κρυφθὲν ἄν τις τῶν πολεμίων ἰδὼν ὠφελη-
θείη, πιστεύοντες οὐ ταῖς παρασκευαῖς τὸ πλέον καὶ ἀπάταις
ἢ τῷ ἀφ' ἡμῶν αὐτῶν ἐς τὰ ἔργα εὐψύχῳ· καὶ ἐν ταῖς 20
παιδείαις οἱ μὲν ἐπιπόνῳ ἀσκήσει εὐθὺς νέοι ὄντες τὸ ἀν-
δρεῖον μετέρχονται, ἡμεῖς δὲ ἀνειμένως διαιτώμενοι οὐδὲν
2 ἧσσον ἐπὶ τοὺς ἰσοπαλεῖς κινδύνους χωροῦμεν. τεκμήριον
δέ· οὔτε γὰρ Λακεδαιμόνιοι καθ' ἑαυτούς, μεθ' ἁπάντων δὲ
ἐς τὴν γῆν ἡμῶν στρατεύουσι, τήν τε τῶν πέλας αὐτοὶ 25
ἐπελθόντες οὐ χαλεπῶς ἐν τῇ ἀλλοτρίᾳ τοὺς περὶ τῶν
3 οἰκείων ἀμυνομένους μαχόμενοι τὰ πλείω κρατοῦμεν. ἁθρόᾳ
τε τῇ δυνάμει ἡμῶν οὐδείς πω πολέμιος ἐνέτυχε διὰ τὴν τοῦ
ναυτικοῦ τε ἅμα ἐπιμέλειαν καὶ τὴν ἐν τῇ γῇ ἐπὶ πολλὰ
ἡμῶν αὐτῶν ἐπίπεμψιν· ἢν δέ που μορίῳ τινὶ προσμείξωσι, 30
κρατήσαντές τέ τινας ἡμῶν πάντας αὐχοῦσιν ἀπεῶσθαι καὶ

---
24. ἑαυτούς Valla (*per se tantum*), schol. Dem. II.
Ol.ii.14: ἑκαστούς codd.

with a view to his own pleasure, we do not react with anger or put on those expressions of disgust which, though not actually harmful, are nevertheless distressing. In our private dealings with one another we avoid offence, and in the public realm what particularly restrains us from wrongdoing is fear: we are obedient to the officials currently in office, and to the laws, especially those which have been enacted for the protection of people who are wronged, and those which have not been written down but which bring acknowledged disgrace on those who break them.

"Moreover, we have provided the greatest number of relaxations from toil for the spirit, by holding contests and sacrifices throughout the year, and by tasteful private provisions, whose daily delight drives away sorrow. Because of the size of our city, everything can be imported from all over the earth, with the result that we have no more special enjoyment of our native goods than of the goods of the rest of mankind.

"In military practices we differ from our enemy in this way. We maintain an open city, and do not from time to time stage expulsions of foreigners to prevent them from learning or seeing things, when the sight of what we have not troubled to conceal might benefit an enemy, since we trust not so much in our preparations and deceit as in our own inborn spirit for action. In education, they start right from their youth to pursue manliness by arduous training, while we live a relaxed life but none the less go to confront the dangers to which we are equal. Here is a sign of it. Even the Spartans do not invade our territory on their own, but with all their allies; and we attack our neighbours' territory, and for the most part have no difficulty in winning battles on their land against men defending their own property. No enemy has yet encountered our whole force together, because we simultaneously maintain our fleet and send out detachments of our men in many directions by land. If they come into conflict with a part of our forces, either they boast that they have repelled all of us when they

4 νικηθέντες ὑφ' ἁπάντων ἡσσῆσθαι. καίτοι εἰ ῥᾳθυμίᾳ μᾶλλον ἢ πόνων μελέτῃ καὶ μὴ μετὰ νόμων τὸ πλέον ἢ τρόπων ἀνδρείας ἐθέλομεν κινδυνεύειν, περιγίγνεται ἡμῖν τοῖς τε μέλλουσιν ἀλγεινοῖς μὴ προκάμνειν, καὶ ἐς αὐτὰ ἐλθοῦσι μὴ ἀτολμοτέρους τῶν αἰεὶ μοχθούντων φαίνεσθαι, καὶ ἔν τε τούτοις τὴν πόλιν ἀξίαν εἶναι θαυμάζεσθαι καὶ ἔτι ἐν ἄλλοις.

40 "Φιλοκαλοῦμέν τε γὰρ μετ' εὐτελείας καὶ φιλοσοφοῦμεν ἄνευ μαλακίας· πλούτῳ τε ἔργου μᾶλλον καιρῷ ἢ λόγου κόμπῳ χρώμεθα, καὶ τὸ πένεσθαι οὐχ ὁμολογεῖν τινὶ αἰσχρόν,
2 ἀλλὰ μὴ διαφεύγειν ἔργῳ αἴσχιον. ἔν τε τοῖς αὐτοῖς οἰκείων ἅμα καὶ πολιτικῶν ἐπιμέλεια, καὶ ἑτέροις ⟨ἕτερα⟩ πρὸς ἔργα τετραμμένοις τὰ πολιτικὰ μὴ ἐνδεῶς γνῶναι· μόνοι γὰρ τόν τε μηδὲν τῶνδε μετέχοντα οὐκ ἀπράγμονα, ἀλλ' ἀχρεῖον νομίζομεν. καὶ αὐτοὶ ἤτοι κρίνομέν γε ἢ ἐνθυμούμεθα ὀρθῶς τὰ πράγματα, οὐ τοὺς λόγους τοῖς ἔργοις βλάβην ἡγούμενοι, ἀλλὰ μὴ προδιδαχθῆναι μᾶλλον λόγῳ πρότερον ἢ ἐπὶ ἃ δεῖ
3 ἔργῳ ἐλθεῖν. διαφερόντως γὰρ δὴ καὶ τόδε ἔχομεν ὥστε τολμᾶν τε οἱ αὐτοὶ μάλιστα καὶ περὶ ὧν ἐπιχειρήσομεν ἐκλογίζεσθαι· ὃ τοῖς ἄλλοις ἀμαθία μὲν θράσος, λογισμὸς δὲ ὄκνον φέρει. κράτιστοι δ' ἂν τὴν ψυχὴν δικαίως κριθεῖεν οἱ τά τε δεινὰ καὶ ἡδέα σαφέστατα γιγνώσκοντες καὶ διὰ
4 ταῦτα μὴ ἀποτρεπόμενοι ἐκ τῶν κινδύνων. καὶ τὰ ἐς ἀρετὴν ἐνηντιώμεθα τοῖς πολλοῖς· οὐ γὰρ πάσχοντες εὖ, ἀλλὰ δρῶντες κτώμεθα τοὺς φίλους. βεβαιότερος δὲ ὁ δράσας τὴν χάριν ὥστε ὀφειλομένην δι' εὐνοίας ᾧ δέδωκε σῴζειν· ὁ δὲ ἀντοφείλων ἀμβλύτερος, εἰδὼς οὐκ ἐς χάριν, ἀλλ' ἐς

---

11. ἔν cett., Πᵇ: ἔνι C G.
12. ἑτέροις ⟨ἕτερα⟩ Richards: ἑτέροις codd., ἕτερα Classen.
15. αὐτοὶ cett., Πᵇ: οἱ αὐτοὶ C G.

have defeated only some, or if beaten they claim that it was all of us who defeated them. Yet if we are prepared 4 to face danger, though we live relaxed lives rather than making a practice of toil, and rely on courageous habits rather than legal compulsion, we have the advantage of not suffering in advance for future pain, and when we come to meet it we are shown to be no less daring than those committed to perpetual endurance. In this respect as well as in others our city can be seen to be worthy of admiration.

"We are lovers of beauty without extravagance, and 40 of wisdom without softness. We treat wealth as an opportunity for action rather than a matter for boastful words, and poverty as a thing which it is not shameful for any one to admit to, but rather is shameful not to act to escape from. The same men accept responsibility 2 both for their own affairs and for the state's, and although different men are active in different fields they are not lacking in understanding of the state's concerns: we alone regard the man who refuses to take part in these not as non-interfering but as useless.

"We have the ability to judge or plan rightly in our affairs, since we think it is not speech which is an obstacle to action but failure to expound policy in speech before action has to be taken. We are different also in 3 that we particularly combine boldness with reasoning about the business we are to take in hand, whereas for other people it is ignorance that produces courage and reasoning produces hesitation. When people have the clearest understanding of what is fearful and what is pleasant, and on that basis do not flinch from danger, they would rightly be judged to have the best spirit.

"With regard to displays of goodness, we are the op- 4 posite of most people, since we acquire our friends not by receiving good from them but by doing good to them. If you do good, you are in a better position to keep the other party's favour, as something owed in gratitude by the recipient: if you owe a return, you are less alert, knowing that when you do good it will not be as a favour

5 ὀφείλημα τὴν ἀρετὴν ἀποδώσων. καὶ μόνοι οὐ τοῦ ξυμφέροντος μᾶλλον λογισμῷ ἢ τῆς ἐλευθερίας τῷ πιστῷ ἀδεῶς τινὰ ὠφελοῦμεν.

41 "Ξυνελών τε λέγω τήν τε πᾶσαν πόλιν τῆς Ἑλλάδος παίδευσιν εἶναι καὶ καθ' ἕκαστον δοκεῖν ἄν μοι τὸν αὐτὸν ἄνδρα παρ' ἡμῶν ἐπὶ πλεῖστ' ἂν εἴδη καὶ μετὰ χαρίτων
2 μάλιστ' ἂν εὐτραπέλως τὸ σῶμα αὔταρκες παρέχεσθαι. καὶ ὡς οὐ λόγων ἐν τῷ παρόντι κόμπος τάδε μᾶλλον ἢ ἔργων ἐστὶν ἀλήθεια, αὐτὴ ἡ δύναμις τῆς πόλεως, ἣν ἀπὸ τῶνδε
3 τῶν τρόπων ἐκτησάμεθα, σημαίνει. μόνη γὰρ τῶν νῦν ἀκοῆς κρείσσων ἐς πεῖραν ἔρχεται, καὶ μόνη οὔτε τῷ πολεμίῳ ἐπελθόντι ἀγανάκτησιν ἔχει ὑφ' οἵων κακοπαθεῖ οὔτε
4 τῷ ὑπηκόῳ κατάμεμψιν ὡς οὐχ ὑπ' ἀξίων ἄρχεται. μετὰ μεγάλων δὲ σημείων καὶ οὐ δή τοι ἀμάρτυρόν γε τὴν δύναμιν παρασχόμενοι τοῖς τε νῦν καὶ τοῖς ἔπειτα θαυμασθησόμεθα, καὶ οὐδὲν προσδεόμενοι οὔτε Ὁμήρου ἐπαινέτου οὔτε ὅστις ἔπεσι μὲν τὸ αὐτίκα τέρψει, τῶν δ' ἔργων τὴν ὑπόνοιαν ἡ ἀλήθεια βλάψει, ἀλλὰ πᾶσαν μὲν θάλασσαν καὶ γῆν ἐσβατὸν τῇ ἡμετέρᾳ τόλμῃ καταναγκάσαντες γενέσθαι, πανταχοῦ δὲ
5 μνημεῖα κακῶν τε κἀγαθῶν ἀίδια ξυγκατοικίσαντες. περὶ τοιαύτης οὖν πόλεως οἵδε τε γενναίως δικαιοῦντες μὴ ἀφαιρεθῆναι αὐτὴν μαχόμενοι ἐτελεύτησαν, καὶ τῶν λειπομένων πάντα τινὰ εἰκὸς ἐθέλειν ὑπὲρ αὐτῆς κάμνειν.

42 "Δι' ὃ δὴ καὶ ἐμήκυνα τὰ περὶ τῆς πόλεως, διδασκαλίαν τε ποιούμενος μὴ περὶ ἴσου ἡμῖν εἶναι τὸν ἀγῶνα καὶ οἷς τῶνδε μηδὲν ὑπάρχει ὁμοίως, καὶ τὴν εὐλογίαν ἅμα ἐφ' οἷς
2 νῦν λέγω φανερὰν σημείοις καθιστάς. καὶ εἴρηται αὐτῆς τὰ μέγιστα· ἃ γὰρ τὴν πόλιν ὕμνησα, αἱ τῶνδε καὶ τῶν τοιῶνδε ἀρεταὶ ἐκόσμησαν, καὶ οὐκ ἂν πολλοῖς τῶν Ἑλλήνων ἰσόρροπος ὥσπερ τῶνδε ὁ λόγος τῶν ἔργων φανείη.

---

12. ἐπελθόντι secl. Classen, fortasse recte.
17–18. ἡ ὑπόνοια τὴν ἀλήθειαν βλάψει vel τῇ ὑπονοίᾳ ἡ ἀλήθεια βλάψεται Gomme.

but as the payment of a debt. We alone are fearless in helping others, not calculating the advantage so much as confident in our freedom.

"To sum up, I maintain that our city as a whole is an education to Greece; and I reckon that each individual man among us can keep his person ready to profit from the greatest variety in life and the maximum of graceful adaptability. That this is not just a momentary verbal boast but actual truth is demonstrated by the very strength of our city, which we have built up as a result of these habits. Athens alone when brought to the test proves greater than its current reputation; Athens alone does not give an enemy attacker the right to be indignant at the kind of people at whose hands he suffers, or a subject the right to complain that his rulers are unworthy of their position. Our power does not lack witnesses, but we provide mighty proof of it, to earn the admiration both of our contemporaries and of posterity. We do not need the praise of a Homer, or of any one whose poetry gives immediate pleasure but whose impression of the facts is undermined by the truth. We have compelled the whole of sea and land to make itself accessible to our daring, and have joined in setting up everywhere undying memorials both of our failures and of our successes. Such is our city. These men fought and died, nobly judging that it would be wrong to be deprived of it; and it is right that every single one of those who are left should be willing to struggle for it.

"That is why I have spoken at length about our city, to instruct you that the contest is not on the same terms for us and for those who do not similarly enjoy these advantages, and to give a firm basis of proof to my praise of the men for whom I am now speaking. The greater part of this praise has been uttered already. When I have lauded the city, it has been for qualities bestowed on it by the virtues of these men and of men like them, and there could not be many Greeks of whom it is true, as it is of these, that what is said of them is equalled by the facts.

δοκεῖ δέ μοι δηλοῦν ἀνδρὸς ἀρετὴν πρώτη τε μηνύουσα καὶ
3 τελευταία βεβαιοῦσα ἡ νῦν τῶνδε καταστροφή. καὶ γὰρ
τοῖς τἆλλα χείροσι δίκαιον τὴν ἐς τοὺς πολέμους ὑπὲρ τῆς
πατρίδος ἀνδραγαθίαν προτίθεσθαι· ἀγαθῷ γὰρ κακὸν ἀφανί-
σαντες κοινῶς μᾶλλον ὠφέλησαν ἢ ἐκ τῶν ἰδίων ἔβλαψαν. 5
4 τῶνδε δὲ οὔτε πλούτου τις τὴν ἔτι ἀπόλαυσιν προτιμήσας
ἐμαλακίσθη οὔτε πενίας ἐλπίδι, ὡς κἂν ἔτι διαφυγὼν αὐτὴν
πλουτήσειεν, ἀναβολὴν τοῦ δεινοῦ ἐποιήσατο· τὴν δὲ τῶν
ἐναντίων τιμωρίαν ποθεινοτέραν αὐτῶν λαβόντες καὶ κινδύνων ἅμα τόνδε κάλλιστον νομίσαντες ἐβουλήθησαν μετ᾽ 10
αὐτοῦ τοὺς μὲν τιμωρεῖσθαι, τῶν δὲ ἀφίεσθαι, ἐλπίδι μὲν
τὸ ἀφανὲς τοῦ κατορθώσειν ἐπιτρέψαντες, ἔργῳ δὲ περὶ τοῦ
ἤδη ὁρωμένου σφίσιν αὐτοῖς ἀξιοῦντες πεποιθέναι, καὶ ἐν
αὐτῷ τῷ ἀμύνεσθαι καὶ παθεῖν μᾶλλον ἡγησάμενοι ἢ [τὸ]
ἐνδόντες σῴζεσθαι, τὸ μὲν αἰσχρὸν τοῦ λόγου ἔφυγον, τὸ δ᾽ 15
ἔργον τῷ σώματι ὑπέμειναν καὶ δι᾽ ἐλαχίστου καιροῦ τύχης
ἅμα ἀκμῇ τῆς δόξης μᾶλλον ἢ τοῦ δέους ἀπηλλάγησαν.

43 "Καὶ οἵδε μὲν προσηκόντως τῇ πόλει τοιοίδε ἐγένοντο·
τοὺς δὲ λοιποὺς χρὴ ἀσφαλεστέραν μὲν εὔχεσθαι, ἀτολμο-
τέραν δὲ μηδὲν ἀξιοῦν τὴν ἐς τοὺς πολεμίους διάνοιαν ἔχειν, 20
σκοποῦντας μὴ λόγῳ μόνῳ τὴν ὠφελίαν, ἥν ἄν τις πρὸς
οὐδὲν χεῖρον αὐτοὺς ὑμᾶς εἰδότας μηκύνοι, λέγων ὅσα ἐν
τῷ τοὺς πολεμίους ἀμύνεσθαι ἀγαθὰ ἔνεστιν, ἀλλὰ μᾶλλον
τὴν τῆς πόλεως δύναμιν καθ᾽ ἡμέραν ἔργῳ θεωμένους καὶ
ἐραστὰς γιγνομένους αὐτῆς, καὶ ὅταν ὑμῖν μεγάλη δόξῃ εἶναι, 25
ἐνθυμουμένους ὅτι τολμῶντες καὶ γιγνώσκοντες τὰ δέοντα
καὶ ἐν τοῖς ἔργοις αἰσχυνόμενοι ἄνδρες αὐτὰ ἐκτήσαντο, καὶ
ὁπότε καὶ πείρᾳ του σφαλεῖεν, οὐκ οὖν καὶ τὴν πόλιν γε τῆς
σφετέρας ἀρετῆς ἀξιοῦντες στερίσκειν, κάλλιστον δὲ ἔρανον
2 αὐτῇ προϊέμενοι. κοινῇ γὰρ τὰ σώματα διδόντες ἰδίᾳ τὸν 30

---

11. ἀφίεσθαι Poppo: ἐφίεσθαι codd., Dion. Hal.
806–7. Thuc. Propr. 16.
14. τῷ ἀμύνεσθαι C G, Dion. Hal.: τὸ ἀμύνεσθαι cett.,
schol.
παθεῖν <δεῖν> Classen.
μᾶλλον codd.: κάλλιον Dobree.
ἡγησάμενοι codd.: ᾑρημένοι Weil.
ἢ ἐνδόντες Dion. Hal.: ἢ τὸ ἐνδόντες codd.
17. τοῦ δέους μᾶλλον ἢ τῆς δόξης perpendit Gomme.

"I believe that the way in which these men have died is a proof of their virtues, whether it was the first indication of them or the final confirmation. For even if 3 men have been less good in other respects, it is right to give priority to the courage which they have displayed for war on their country's behalf: they have wiped out the evil by good, and the harm which they did as individuals is outweighed by the benefit which they conferred together. None of these was led into cowardice by 4 the hope that he might continue to enjoy his wealth; nor did a poor man's hope that he might yet escape and grow rich prompt any one to delay the dreadful encounter. They accepted that the punishment of our enemy was more desirable than these things; and, reckoning this to be the noblest of dangers, they were willing at the price of this danger to forsake wealth and punish the enemy, to entrust to hope the uncertainty of success while thinking it right to rely on themselves in the action already before their eyes. They thought that safety lay more in the act of resistance and in suffering than in submission, and so, avoiding a disgraceful reputation and enduring bodily action, in a very brief moment, at the turning-point of fortune, they were delivered not from fear but from glory.

"These men met their fate in a manner worthy of our 43 city. The rest must judge it right to adopt an equally daring attitude towards the enemy, though you may pray for a safer outcome. You must not consider the advantages of this simply as a theoretical matter. I could spell out at length what benefits there are in resisting the enemy, but you know them as well as I. In your actions you must every day fix your eyes on the strength of our city; you must become lovers of it. When it appears great to you, you must realise that men have made it great, by daring, by recognising what was needed, and by acting with a sense of honour; and when they failed in any attempt they still did not think it right to deprive the city of their good qualities, but they offered them to it as the finest kind of free contribution. Together they offered their 2

ἀγήρων ἔπαινον ἐλάμβανον καὶ τὸν τάφον ἐπισημότατον, οὐκ ἐν ᾧ κεῖνται μᾶλλον, ἀλλ' ἐν ᾧ ἡ δόξα αὐτῶν παρὰ τῷ ἐντυχόντι αἰεὶ καὶ λόγου καὶ ἔργου καιρῷ αἰείμνηστος κατα-
3 λείπεται. ἀνδρῶν γὰρ ἐπιφανῶν πᾶσα γῆ τάφος, καὶ οὐ στηλῶν μόνον ἐν τῇ οἰκείᾳ σημαίνει ἐπιγραφή, ἀλλὰ καὶ ἐν τῇ μὴ προσηκούσῃ ἄγραφος μνήμη παρ' ἑκάστῳ τῆς γνώμης
4 μᾶλλον ἢ τοῦ ἔργου ἐνδιαιτᾶται. οὓς νῦν ὑμεῖς ζηλώσαντες καὶ τὸ εὔδαιμον τὸ ἐλεύθερον, τὸ δ' ἐλεύθερον τὸ εὔψυχον
5 κρίναντες μὴ περιορᾶσθε τοὺς πολεμικοὺς κινδύνους. οὐ γὰρ οἱ κακοπραγοῦντες δικαιότερον ἀφειδοῖεν ἂν τοῦ βίου, οἷς ἐλπὶς οὐκ ἔστιν ἀγαθοῦ, ἀλλ' οἷς ἡ ἐναντία μεταβολὴ ἐν τῷ ζῆν ἔτι κινδυνεύεται καὶ ἐν οἷς μάλιστα μεγάλα τὰ
6 διαφέροντα, ἤν τι πταίσωσιν. ἀλγεινοτέρα γὰρ ἀνδρί γε φρόνημα ἔχοντι ἡ μετὰ τοῦ [ἐν τῷ] μαλακισθῆναι κάκωσις ἢ ὁ μετὰ ῥώμης καὶ κοινῆς ἐλπίδος ἅμα γιγνόμενος ἀναίσθητος θάνατος.

44 "Δι' ὅπερ καὶ τοὺς τῶνδε νῦν τοκέας, ὅσοι πάρεστε, οὐκ ὀλοφύρομαι μᾶλλον ἢ παραμυθήσομαι. ἐν πολυτρόποις γὰρ ξυμφοραῖς ἐπίστασθε τραφέντες· τὸ δ' εὐτυχές, οἳ ἂν τῆς εὐπρεπεστάτης λάχωσιν, ὥσπερ οἵδε μὲν νῦν, τελευτῆς, ὑμεῖς δὲ λύπης, καὶ οἷς ἐνευδαιμονῆσαί τε ὁ βίος ὁμοίως καὶ ἐν-
2 τελευτῆσαι ξυνεμετρήθη. χαλεπὸν μὲν οὖν οἶδα πείθειν ὄν, ὧν καὶ πολλάκις ἕξετε ὑπομνήματα ἐν ἄλλων εὐτυχίαις, αἷς ποτὲ καὶ αὐτοὶ ἠγάλλεσθε· καὶ λύπη οὐχ ὧν ἄν τις μὴ πειρασάμενος ἀγαθῶν στερίσκηται, ἀλλ' οὗ ἂν ἐθὰς γενό-
3 μενος ἀφαιρεθῇ. καρτερεῖν δὲ χρὴ καὶ ἄλλων παίδων ἐλπίδι, οἷς ἔτι ἡλικία τέκνωσιν ποιεῖσθαι· ἰδίᾳ τε γὰρ τῶν οὐκ ὄντων λήθη οἱ ἐπιγιγνόμενοί τισιν ἔσονται, καὶ τῇ πόλει διχόθεν, ἔκ τε τοῦ μὴ ἐρημοῦσθαι καὶ ἀσφαλείᾳ, ξυνοίσει·

---

14. μετὰ τοῦ ἐν τῷ C G, ἐν τῷ μετὰ τοῦ cett.: ἐν τῷ secl. Bredow, μετὰ τοῦ secl. Schneider.
19. ἐπίστασθε Herwerden: ἐπίστανται codd.
21–2. ἐντελευτῆσαι codd.: εὖ τελευτῆσαι Poppo, <εὖ> ἐντελευτῆσαι Gomme.

bodies; individually they received eternal praise, and the most distinguished of tombs — not the one in which their bodies lie but rather the one in which their glory remains recorded for ever on every occasion for word or deed. For the whole earth is the grave of distinguished *3* men: they are commemorated not only by the inscription on the tombstone in their own land, but even in foreign territory there lives in every man's heart an unwritten memorial, of their purpose rather than their accomplishment.

"You now must emulate them, judging that happiness *4* depends on freedom, and freedom on a good spirit, and not looking anxiously at the dangers of war. It is not *5* the victims of misfortune, men with no hope of a good outcome, who are most justified in being generous with their lives, but those who risk a great downfall if their life continues, and the greatest reversal of fortune if they fail. For a man of spirit the arrival of misfortune *6* attended by cowardice is more distressing than a barely perceived death attended by firmness and hope for one's country.

"For that reason, to those of you who are here now *44* as the parents of these men I wish to offer encouragement rather than sympathy. You know that you were brought up in a world of changing fortune. It is success to achieve the most honourable end, as these men have now done (though it is a source of grief to you), and to have one's happiness in life measured out to the moment of death. I know it is hard to convince you, when you will *2* often have reminders of your grief as you see others enjoy the good fortune which you once enjoyed, and sadness comes not from missing the good things that one never had but from losing those to which one was once accustomed. Those of you who are still of an age to have children *3* must be stout-hearted in the hope of having other sons: for you as individuals, the new children will help you forget those who are no more; and for the city there will be a double benefit, deliverance from shortage of men, and a source of safety, since men who do not contribute

οὐ γὰρ οἷόν τε ἴσον τι ἢ δίκαιον βουλεύεσθαι οἳ ἂν μὴ καὶ
4 παῖδας ἐκ τοῦ ὁμοίου παραβαλλόμενοι κινδυνεύωσιν. ὅσοι
δ' αὖ παρηβήκατε, τόν τε πλέονα κέρδος ὃν ηὐτυχεῖτε βίον
ἡγεῖσθε καὶ τόνδε βραχὺν ἔσεσθαι, καὶ τῇ τῶνδε εὐκλείᾳ
κουφίζεσθε. τὸ γὰρ φιλότιμον ἀγήρων μόνον, καὶ οὐκ ἐν
τῷ ἀχρείῳ τῆς ἡλικίας τὸ κερδαίνειν, ὥσπερ τινές φασι,
45 μᾶλλον τέρπει, ἀλλὰ τὸ τιμᾶσθαι. παισὶ δ' αὖ ὅσοι τῶνδε
πάρεστε ἢ ἀδελφοῖς ὁρῶ μέγαν τὸν ἀγῶνα (τὸν γὰρ οὐκ
ὄντα ἅπας εἴωθεν ἐπαινεῖν), καὶ μόλις ἂν καθ' ὑπερβολὴν
ἀρετῆς οὐχ ὁμοῖοι, ἀλλ' ὀλίγῳ χείρους κριθεῖτε. φθόνος
γὰρ τοῖς ζῶσι πρὸς τὸ ἀντίπαλον, τὸ δὲ μὴ ἐμποδὼν ἀνανταγωνίστῳ
2 εὐνοίᾳ τετίμηται. εἰ δέ με δεῖ καὶ γυναικείας τι
ἀρετῆς, ὅσαι νῦν ἐν χηρείᾳ ἔσονται, μνησθῆναι, βραχείᾳ
παραινέσει ἅπαν σημανῶ. τῆς τε γὰρ ὑπαρχούσης φύσεως
μὴ χείροσι γενέσθαι ὑμῖν μεγάλη ἡ δόξα καὶ ἧς ἂν ἐπ'
ἐλάχιστον ἀρετῆς πέρι ἢ ψόγου ἐν τοῖς ἄρσεσι κλέος ᾖ.

46 "Εἴρηται καὶ ἐμοὶ λόγῳ κατὰ τὸν νόμον ὅσα εἶχον πρόσφορα,
καὶ ἔργῳ οἱ θαπτόμενοι τὰ μὲν ἤδη κεκόσμηνται, τὰ
δὲ αὐτῶν τοὺς παῖδας τὸ ἀπὸ τοῦδε δημοσίᾳ ἡ πόλις μέχρι
ἥβης θρέψει, ὠφέλιμον στέφανον τοῖσδέ τε καὶ τοῖς λειπομένοις
τῶν τοιῶνδε ἀγώνων προτιθεῖσα· ἆθλα γὰρ οἷς κεῖται
ἀρετῆς μέγιστα, τοῖς δὲ καὶ ἄνδρες ἄριστοι πολιτεύουσιν.
2 νῦν δὲ ἀπολοφυράμενοι ὃν προσήκει ἑκάστῳ ἄπιτε."

47 Τοιόσδε μὲν ὁ τάφος ἐγένετο ἐν τῷ χειμῶνι τούτῳ· καὶ
διελθόντος αὐτοῦ πρῶτον ἔτος τοῦ πολέμου τοῦδε ἐτελεύτα.
2 τοῦ δὲ θέρους εὐθὺς ἀρχομένου Πελοποννήσιοι καὶ οἱ ξύμμαχοι
τὰ δύο μέρη ὥσπερ καὶ τὸ πρῶτον ἐσέβαλον ἐς τὴν
Ἀττικήν (ἡγεῖτο δὲ Ἀρχίδαμος ὁ Ζευξιδάμου Λακεδαι-

children and so run the same risks as the others cannot be fair or just in their deliberation. Those who are past that age must reckon that the longer period of life in which you have had good fortune is a gain, and that the life still to come will be short and will be lightened by these men's fame. Love of honour is the only thing that does not grow old; and it is not profit, as some say, but honour which gives pleasure in the useless time of life.

"For those of you who are here as sons or brothers of the dead I see there will be a great contest: every one tends to praise those who are no more, and you will find it hard to be judged only a little inferior to these men, let alone equal to them, as their virtues come to be exaggerated. Among the living, rivalry arouses jealousy, but what is no longer present is honoured with a good will free from competition.

"If I am to say anything to those who have now been widowed, about the virtues of a wife, I can convey my whole message in a brief exhortation: your glory is great if you do not fail to live up to your own nature, and if there is the least possible talk of you among men either for praise or for blame.

"So in this speech I have said in my own way what appropriate things I could, in accordance with our institution. In our actions these men have been honoured by their burial now; and henceforward the city will undertake the upbringing of their sons until they grow up, thus conferring a valuable crown on them and on the survivors of conflicts like these. Where the prizes for valour are the greatest, there the men will be the best citizens.

"Now make your lament for your own dead, and go your way."

Such was the funeral in this winter. When that was over, the first year of this war came to an end.

At the very beginning of summer, the Peloponnesians and their allies invaded Attica, with a two-thirds force as on the first occasion, under the command of Archidamus

3 μονίων βασιλεύς), καὶ καθεζόμενοι ἐδῄουν τὴν γῆν. καὶ ὄντων αὐτῶν οὐ πολλάς πω ἡμέρας ἐν τῇ Ἀττικῇ ἡ νόσος πρῶτον ἤρξατο γενέσθαι τοῖς Ἀθηναίοις, λεγόμενον μὲν καὶ πρότερον πολλαχόσε ἐγκατασκῆψαι καὶ περὶ Λῆμνον καὶ ἐν ἄλλοις χωρίοις, οὐ μέντοι τοσοῦτός γε λοιμὸς οὐδὲ φθορὰ 5
4 οὕτως ἀνθρώπων οὐδαμοῦ ἐμνημονεύετο γενέσθαι. οὔτε γὰρ ἰατροὶ ἤρκουν τὸ πρῶτον θεραπεύοντες ἀγνοίᾳ, ἀλλ' αὐτοὶ μάλιστα ἔθνῃσκον ὅσῳ καὶ μάλιστα προσῇσαν, οὔτε ἄλλη ἀνθρωπεία τέχνη οὐδεμία· ὅσα τε πρὸς ἱεροῖς ἱκέτευσαν ἢ μαντείοις καὶ τοῖς τοιούτοις ἐχρήσαντο, πάντα ἀνωφελῆ ἦν, 10 τελευτῶντές τε αὐτῶν ἀπέστησαν ὑπὸ τοῦ κακοῦ νικώμενοι.

48 ἤρξατο δὲ τὸ μὲν πρῶτον, ὡς λέγεται, ἐξ Αἰθιοπίας τῆς ὑπὲρ Αἰγύπτου, ἔπειτα δὲ καὶ ἐς Αἴγυπτον καὶ Λιβύην
2 κατέβη καὶ ἐς τὴν βασιλέως γῆν τὴν πολλήν. ἐς δὲ τὴν Ἀθηναίων πόλιν ἐξαπιναίως ἐσέπεσε, καὶ τὸ πρῶτον ἐν τῷ 15 Πειραιεῖ ἥψατο τῶν ἀνθρώπων, ὥστε καὶ ἐλέχθη ὑπ' αὐτῶν ὡς οἱ Πελοποννήσιοι φάρμακα ἐσβεβλήκοιεν ἐς τὰ φρέατα· κρῆναι γὰρ οὔπω ἦσαν αὐτόθι. ὕστερον δὲ καὶ ἐς τὴν ἄνω
3 πόλιν ἀφίκετο, καὶ ἔθνῃσκον πολλῷ μᾶλλον ἤδη. λεγέτω μὲν οὖν περὶ αὐτοῦ ὡς ἕκαστος γιγνώσκει καὶ ἰατρὸς καὶ 20 ἰδιώτης, ἀφ' ὅτου εἰκὸς ἦν γενέσθαι αὐτό, καὶ τὰς αἰτίας ἅστινας νομίζει τοσαύτης μεταβολῆς [ἱκανὰς εἶναι] δύναμιν ἐς τὸ μεταστῆσαι σχεῖν· ἐγὼ δὲ οἷόν τε ἐγίγνετο λέξω, καὶ ἀφ' ὧν ἄν τις σκοπῶν, εἴ ποτε καὶ αὖθις ἐπιπέσοι, μάλιστ' ἂν ἔχοι τι προειδὼς μὴ ἀγνοεῖν, ταῦτα δηλώσω 25 αὐτός τε νοσήσας καὶ αὐτὸς ἰδὼν ἄλλους πάσχοντας.

49 Τὸ μὲν γὰρ ἔτος, ὡς ὡμολογεῖτο, ἐκ πάντων μάλιστα δὴ ἐκεῖνο ἄνοσον ἐς τὰς ἄλλας ἀσθενείας ἐτύγχανεν ὄν· εἰ δέ
2 τις καὶ προύκαμνέ τι, ἐς τοῦτο πάντα ἀπεκρίθη. τοὺς δὲ ἄλλους ἀπ' οὐδεμιᾶς προφάσεως, ἀλλ' ἐξαίφνης ὑγιεῖς ὄντας 30 πρῶτον μὲν τῆς κεφαλῆς θέρμαι ἰσχυραὶ καὶ τῶν ὀφθαλμῶν ἐρυθήματα καὶ φλόγωσις ἐλάμβανε, καὶ τὰ ἐντός, ἥ τε

22–3. ἱκανὰς εἶναι secl. Gomme: δύναμιν ... σχεῖν secl. Gesner.

son of Zeuxidamus, king of Sparta. They established themselves and began to ravage the land.

They had not yet spent many days in Attica when the plague first struck the Athenians. It is said to have broken out previously in many other places, in the region of Lemnos and elsewhere, but there was no previous record of so great a pestilence and destruction of human life. The doctors were unable to cope, since they were treating the disease for the first time and in ignorance: indeed, the more they came into contact with sufferers the more liable they were to lose their own lives. No other device of men was any help. Moreover, supplication at sanctuaries, resort to divination and the like were all unavailing. In the end people were overwhelmed by the disaster and abandoned their efforts against it. *3*

4

The plague is said to have come first of all from Ethiopia beyond Egypt; and from there it fell on Egypt and Libya and on much of the King's land. It struck the city of Athens suddenly. People in the Piraeus caught it first, and so, since there were not yet any fountains there, they actually alleged that the Peloponnesians had put poison in the wells. Afterwards it arrived in the upper city too, and then deaths started to occur on a much larger scale. Every one, whether doctor or layman, may say from his own experience what the origin of it is likely to have been, and what causes he thinks had the power to bring about so great a change. I shall give a statement of what it was like, which people can study in case it should ever attack again, to equip themselves with foreknowledge so that they shall not fail to recognise it. I can give this account because I both suffered from the disease myself and saw other victims of it. *48*

2

3

It was universally agreed that this particular year was exceptionally free from disease as far as other afflictions were concerned. If people did first suffer from other illnesses, all ended in this. Others were caught with no warning, but suddenly, when they were in good health. The disease began with a strong fever in the head, and reddening and burning heat in the eyes; the *49*

2

φάρυγξ καὶ ἡ γλῶσσα, εὐθὺς αἱματώδη ἦν καὶ πνεῦμα
3 ἄτοπον καὶ δυσῶδες ἠφίει· ἔπειτα ἐξ αὐτῶν πταρμὸς καὶ
βράγχος ἐπεγίγνετο, καὶ ἐν οὐ πολλῷ χρόνῳ κατέβαινεν ἐς
τὰ στήθη ὁ πόνος μετὰ βηχὸς ἰσχυροῦ· καὶ ὁπότε ἐς τὴν
καρδίαν στηρίξειεν, ἀνέστρεφέ τε αὐτὴν καὶ ἀποκαθάρσεις 5
χολῆς πᾶσαι ὅσαι ὑπὸ ἰατρῶν ὠνομασμέναι εἰσὶν ἐπῇσαν,
4 καὶ αὗται μετὰ ταλαιπωρίας μεγάλης. λύγξ τε τοῖς πλέοσιν ἐνέπιπτε κενή, σπασμὸν ἐνδιδοῦσα ἰσχυρόν, τοῖς μὲν
5 μετὰ ταῦτα λωφήσαντα, τοῖς δὲ καὶ πολλῷ ὕστερον. καὶ
τὸ μὲν ἔξωθεν ἁπτομένῳ σῶμα οὔτ' ἄγαν θερμὸν ἦν οὔτε 10
χλωρόν, ἀλλ' ὑπέρυθρον, πελιτνόν, φλυκταίναις μικραῖς καὶ
ἕλκεσιν ἐξηνθηκός· τὰ δὲ ἐντὸς οὕτως ἐκάετο ὥστε μήτε
τῶν πάνυ λεπτῶν ἱματίων καὶ σινδόνων τὰς ἐπιβολὰς μηδ'
ἄλλο τι ἢ γυμνοὶ ἀνέχεσθαι, ἥδιστά τε ἂν ἐς ὕδωρ ψυχρὸν
σφᾶς αὐτοὺς ῥίπτειν. καὶ πολλοὶ τοῦτο τῶν ἠμελημένων 15
ἀνθρώπων καὶ ἔδρασαν ἐς φρέατα, τῇ δίψῃ ἀπαύστῳ ξυν-
εχόμενοι· καὶ ἐν τῷ ὁμοίῳ καθειστήκει τό τε πλέον καὶ
6 ἔλασσον ποτόν. καὶ ἡ ἀπορία τοῦ μὴ ἡσυχάζειν καὶ ἡ
ἀγρυπνία ἐπέκειτο διὰ παντός. καὶ τὸ σῶμα, ὅσονπερ
χρόνον καὶ ἡ νόσος ἀκμάζοι, οὐκ ἐμαραίνετο, ἀλλ' ἀντεῖχε 20
παρὰ δόξαν τῇ ταλαιπωρίᾳ, ὥστε[ἢ]διεφθείροντο οἱ πλεῖστοι
ἐναταῖοι καὶ ἑβδομαῖοι ὑπὸ τοῦ ἐντὸς καύματος, ἔτι ἔχοντές
τι δυνάμεως, ἢ εἰ διαφύγοιεν, ἐπικατιόντος τοῦ νοσήματος
ἐς τὴν κοιλίαν καὶ ἑλκώσεώς τε αὐτῇ ἰσχυρᾶς ἐγγιγνομένης
καὶ διαρροίας ἅμα ἀκράτου ἐπιπιπτούσης οἱ πολλοὶ ὕστερον 25
7 δι' αὐτὴν ἀσθενείᾳ ἀπεφθείροντο. διεξῄει γὰρ διὰ παντὸς
τοῦ σώματος ἄνωθεν ἀρξάμενον τὸ ἐν τῇ κεφαλῇ πρῶτον
ἱδρυθὲν κακόν, καὶ εἴ τις ἐκ τῶν μεγίστων περιγένοιτο, τῶν
8 γε ἀκρωτηρίων ἀντίληψις αὐτοῦ ἐπεσήμαινεν. κατέσκηπτε
γὰρ ἐς αἰδοῖα καὶ ἐς ἄκρας χεῖρας καὶ πόδας, καὶ πολλοὶ 30
στερισκόμενοι τούτων διέφευγον, εἰσὶ δ' οἳ καὶ τῶν ὀφθαλμῶν. τοὺς δὲ καὶ λήθη ἐλάμβανε παραυτίκα ἀναστάντας
τῶν πάντων ὁμοίως, καὶ ἠγνόησαν σφᾶς τε αὐτοὺς καὶ τοὺς

---

21. ἢ secl. Gomme.
26. ἀπεφθείροντο cett.: διεφθείροντο C <G>.

first internal symptoms were that the throat and tongue became bloody and the breath unnatural and malodorous. This was followed by sneezing and hoarseness, and in a short time the affliction descended to the chest, producing violent coughing. When it became established in the heart, it convulsed that and produced every kind of evacuation of bile known to the doctors, accompanied by great discomfort. Most victims then suffered from empty retching, which induced violent convulsions: they abated after this for some sufferers, but only much later for others.

3

4

The exterior of the body was not particularly hot to the touch or yellow, but was reddish, livid, and burst out in small blisters and sores. But inside the burning was so strong that the victims could not bear to put on even the lightest clothes and linens, but had to go naked, and gained the greatest relief by plunging into cold water. Many who had no one to keep watch on them even plunged into wells, under the pressure of insatiable thirst; but it made no difference whether they drank a large quantity or a small. Throughout the course of the disease people suffered from sleeplessness and inability to rest. For as long as the disease was raging, the body did not waste away, but held out unexpectedly against its suffering. Most died about the seventh or the ninth day from the beginning of the internal burning, while they still had some strength. If they escaped then, the disease descended to the belly: there violent ulceration and totally fluid diarrhoea occurred, and most people then died from the weakness caused by that.

5

6

The disease worked its way right through the body from the top, beginning with the affliction which first settled in the head. If any one survived the worst symptoms, the disease left its mark by catching his extremities. It attacked the privy parts, and the fingers and toes, and many people survived but lost these, while others lost their eyes. Others on first recovering suffered total loss of memory, and were unable to recognise themselves and their relatives.

7

8

50 ἐπιτηδείους. γενόμενον γὰρ κρεῖσσον λόγου τὸ εἶδος τῆς νόσου τά τε ἄλλα χαλεπωτέρως ἢ κατὰ τὴν ἀνθρωπείαν φύσιν προσέπιπτεν ἑκάστῳ καὶ ἐν τῷδε ἐδήλωσε μάλιστα ἄλλο τι ὂν ἢ τῶν ξυντρόφων τι· τὰ γὰρ ὄρνεα καὶ τετράποδα ὅσα ἀνθρώπων ἅπτεται, πολλῶν ἀτάφων γιγνομένων ἢ οὐ 2 προσῄει ἢ γευσάμενα διεφθείρετο. τεκμήριον δέ· τῶν μὲν τοιούτων ὀρνίθων ἐπίλειψις σαφὴς ἐγένετο, καὶ οὐχ ἑωρῶντο οὔτε ἄλλως οὔτε περὶ τοιοῦτον οὐδέν· οἱ δὲ κύνες μᾶλλον αἴσθησιν παρεῖχον τοῦ ἀποβαίνοντος διὰ τὸ ξυνδιαιτᾶσθαι.

51 Τὸ μὲν οὖν νόσημα, πολλὰ καὶ ἄλλα παραλιπόντι ἀτοπίας, ὡς ἑκάστῳ ἐτύγχανέ τι διαφερόντως ἑτέρῳ πρὸς ἕτερον γιγνόμενον, τοιοῦτον ἦν ἐπὶ πᾶν τὴν ἰδέαν. καὶ ἄλλο παρελύπει κατ' ἐκεῖνον τὸν χρόνον οὐδὲν τῶν εἰωθότων· ὃ 2 δὲ καὶ γένοιτο, ἐς τοῦτο ἐτελεύτα. ἔθνῃσκον δὲ οἱ μὲν ἀμελείᾳ, οἱ δὲ καὶ πάνυ θεραπευόμενοι. ἕν τε οὐδὲ ἓν κατέστη ἴαμα ὡς εἰπεῖν ὅτι χρῆν προσφέροντας ὠφελεῖν· 3 τὸ γάρ τῳ ξυνενεγκὸν ἄλλον τοῦτο ἔβλαπτεν. σῶμά τε αὔταρκες ὂν οὐδὲν διεφάνη πρὸς αὐτὸ ἰσχύος πέρι ἢ ἀσθενείας, ἀλλὰ πάντα ξυνῄρει καὶ τὰ πάσῃ διαίτῃ θεραπευόμενα. 4 δεινότατον δὲ παντὸς ἦν τοῦ κακοῦ ἥ τε ἀθυμία ὁπότε τις αἴσθοιτο κάμνων (πρὸς γὰρ τὸ ἀνέλπιστον εὐθὺς τραπόμενοι τῇ γνώμῃ πολλῷ μᾶλλον προΐεντο σφᾶς αὐτοὺς καὶ οὐκ ἀντεῖχον), καὶ ὅτι ἕτερος ἀφ' ἑτέρου θεραπείας ἀναπιμπλάμενοι ὥσπερ τὰ πρόβατα ἔθνῃσκον· καὶ τὸν πλεῖστον 5 φθόρον τοῦτο ἐνεποίει. εἴτε γὰρ μὴ 'θέλοιεν δεδιότες ἀλλήλοις προσιέναι, ἀπώλλυντο ἔρημοι, καὶ οἰκίαι πολλαὶ ἐκενώθησαν ἀπορίᾳ τοῦ θεραπεύσοντος· εἴτε προσίοιεν, διεφθείροντο, καὶ μάλιστα οἱ ἀρετῆς τι μεταποιούμενοι· αἰσχύνῃ γὰρ ἠφείδουν σφῶν αὐτῶν ἐσιόντες παρὰ τοὺς φίλους, ἐπεὶ καὶ τὰς ὀλοφύρσεις τῶν ἀπογιγνομένων τελευτῶντες καὶ οἱ οἰκεῖοι ἐξέκαμον ὑπὸ τοῦ πολλοῦ κακοῦ

---

31. ἐξέκαμον cett.: ἐξέκαμινον C G.

The nature of the disease was beyond description, and the sufferings that it brought to each victim were greater than human nature can bear. There is one particular point in which it showed that it was unlike the usual run of illnesses: the birds and animals which feed on human flesh either kept away from the bodies, although there were many unburied, or if they did taste them it proved fatal. To confirm this, there was an evident shortage of birds of that kind, which were not to be seen either near the victims or anywhere else. What happened was particularly noticeable in the case of dogs, since they live with human beings.

Apart from the various unusual features in the different effects which it had on different people, that was the general nature of the disease. None of the other common afflictions occurred at that time; or any that did ended in this.

Some victims were neglected and died; others died despite a great deal of care. There was not a single remedy, you might say, which ought to be applied to give relief, for what helped one sufferer harmed another. No kind of constitution, whether strong or weak, proved sufficient against the plague, but it killed off all, whatever regime was used to care for them. The most terrifying aspect of the whole affliction was the despair which resulted when some one realised that he had the disease: people immediately lost hope, and so through their attitude of mind were much more likely to let themselves go and not hold out. In addition, one person caught the disease through caring for another, and so they died like sheep: this was the greatest cause of loss of life. If people were afraid and unwilling to go near to others, they died in isolation, and many houses lost all their occupants through the lack of any one to care for them. Those who did go near to others died, especially those with any claim to virtue, who from a sense of honour did not spare themselves in going to visit their friends, persisting when in the end even the members of the family were overcome by the scale of the disaster and gave up

6 νικώμενοι. ἐπὶ πλέον δ' ὅμως οἱ διαπεφευγότες τόν τε
θνῄσκοντα καὶ τὸν πονούμενον ᾠκτίζοντο διὰ τὸ προειδέναι
τε καὶ αὐτοὶ ἤδη ἐν τῷ θαρσαλέῳ εἶναι· δὶς γὰρ τὸν αὐτόν,
ὥστε καὶ κτείνειν, οὐκ ἐπελάμβανεν. καὶ ἐμακαρίζοντό τε
ὑπὸ τῶν ἄλλων, καὶ αὐτοὶ τῷ παραχρῆμα περιχαρεῖ καὶ ἐς
τὸν ἔπειτα χρόνον ἐλπίδος τι εἶχον κούφης μηδ' ἂν ὑπ'
ἄλλου νοσήματός ποτε ἔτι διαφθαρῆναι.

52 Ἐπίεσε δ' αὐτοὺς μᾶλλον πρὸς τῷ ὑπάρχοντι πόνῳ καὶ
ἡ ξυγκομιδὴ ἐκ τῶν ἀγρῶν ἐς τὸ ἄστυ, καὶ οὐχ ἧσσον τοὺς
2 ἐπελθόντας. οἰκιῶν γὰρ οὐχ ὑπαρχουσῶν, ἀλλ' ἐν καλύβαις
πνιγηραῖς ὥρᾳ ἔτους διαιτωμένων ὁ φθόρος ἐγίγνετο οὐδενὶ
κόσμῳ, ἀλλὰ καὶ νεκροὶ ἐπ' ἀλλήλοις *ἀποθνῄσκοντες ἔκειντο
καὶ ἐν ταῖς ὁδοῖς ἐκαλινδοῦντο καὶ περὶ τὰς κρήνας ἁπάσας
3 ἡμιθνῆτες τοῦ ὕδατος ἐπιθυμίᾳ. τά τε ἱερὰ ἐν οἷς ἐσκήνηντο
νεκρῶν πλέα ἦν, αὐτοῦ ἐναποθνῃσκόντων· ὑπερβιαζομένου
γὰρ τοῦ κακοῦ οἱ ἄνθρωποι, οὐκ ἔχοντες ὅτι γένωνται, ἐς
4 ὀλιγωρίαν ἐτράποντο καὶ ἱερῶν καὶ ὁσίων ὁμοίως. νόμοι
τε πάντες ξυνεταράχθησαν οἷς ἐχρῶντο πρότερον περὶ τὰς
ταφάς, ἔθαπτον δὲ ὡς ἕκαστος ἐδύνατο. καὶ πολλοὶ ἐς
ἀναισχύντους θήκας ἐτράποντο σπάνει τῶν ἐπιτηδείων διὰ
τὸ συχνοὺς ἤδη προτεθνάναι σφίσιν· ἐπὶ πυρὰς γὰρ ἀλλο-
τρίας φθάσαντες τοὺς νήσαντας οἱ μὲν ἐπιθέντες τὸν ἑαυτῶν
νεκρὸν ὑφῆπτον, οἱ δὲ καιομένου ἄλλου ἐπιβαλόντες ἄνωθεν
ὃν φέροιεν ἀπῇσαν.

53 Πρῶτόν τε ἦρξε καὶ ἐς τἆλλα τῇ πόλει ἐπὶ πλέον ἀνομίας
τὸ νόσημα. ῥᾷον γὰρ ἐτόλμα τις ἃ πρότερον ἀπεκρύπτετο
μὴ καθ' ἡδονὴν ποιεῖν, ἀγχίστροφον τὴν μεταβολὴν ὁρῶντες
τῶν τε εὐδαιμόνων καὶ αἰφνιδίως θνῃσκόντων καὶ τῶν οὐδὲν
2 πρότερον κεκτημένων, εὐθὺς δὲ τἀκείνων ἐχόντων. ὥστε

---

*12. ἀποθνήσκοντες: <καὶ> ἀποθνήσκοντες Gomme, recte ut opinor, ἀποθνήσκοντές <τε> Steup, ἀποθνήσκοντες post ἔκειντο καὶ transposuit Oncken.

their dirges for the dead.

 Those who had come through the disease had the greatest pity for the suffering and the dying, since they had previous experience of it and were now feeling confident for themselves, as the disease did not attack the same person a second time, or at any rate not fatally. Those who recovered were congratulated by the others, and in their immediate elation cherished the vain hope that for the the future they would be immune to death from any other disease. *6*

 The distress was aggravated by the migration from the country into the city, especially in the case of those who had themselves made the move. There were no houses for them, so they had to live in stifling huts in the hot season of the year, and destruction raged unchecked. The bodies of the dead and dying were piled on one another, and people at the point of death reeled about the streets and around all the springs in their passion to find water. The sanctuaries in which people were camping were filled with corpses, as deaths took place even there: the disaster was overpowering, and as people did not know what would become of them they tended to neglect the sacred and the secular alike. All the funeral customs which had previously been observed were thrown into confusion, and the dead were buried in any way possible. Many who lacked friends because so many had died before them turned to shameless forms of disposal: some would put their own dead on some one else's pyre, and set light to it before those who had prepared it could do so themselves; others threw the body they were carrying on to the top of another's pyre when it was already alight, and slipped away. *52* *2* *3* *4*

 In other respects too the plague marked the beginning of a decline to greater lawlessness in the city. People were more willing to dare to do things which they would not previously have admitted to enjoying, when they saw the sudden changes of fortune, as some who were prosperous suddenly died, and their property was immediately acquired by others who had previously been destitute. So *53* *2*

ταχείας τὰς ἐπαυρέσεις καὶ πρὸς τὸ τερπνὸν ἠξίουν ποιεῖσθαι, ἐφήμερα τά τε σώματα καὶ τὰ χρήματα ὁμοίως ἡγούμενοι. 3 καὶ τὸ μὲν προσταλαιπωρεῖν τῷ δόξαντι καλῷ οὐδεὶς πρόθυμος ἦν, ἄδηλον νομίζων εἰ πρὶν ἐπ' αὐτὸ ἐλθεῖν διαφθαρήσεται· ὅτι δὲ ἤδη τε ἡδὺ πανταχόθεν τε ἐς αὐτὸ κερδαλέον, 4 τοῦτο καὶ καλὸν καὶ χρήσιμον κατέστη. θεῶν δὲ φόβος ἢ ἀνθρώπων νόμος οὐδεὶς ἀπεῖργε, τὸ μὲν κρίνοντες ἐν ὁμοίῳ καὶ σέβειν καὶ μὴ ἐκ τοῦ πάντας ὁρᾶν ἐν ἴσῳ ἀπολλυμένους, τῶν δὲ ἁμαρτημάτων οὐδεὶς ἐλπίζων μέχρι τοῦ δίκην γενέσθαι βιοὺς ἂν τὴν τιμωρίαν ἀντιδοῦναι, πολὺ δὲ μείζω τὴν ἤδη κατεψηφισμένην σφῶν ἐπικρεμασθῆναι, ἣν πρὶν ἐμπεσεῖν εἰκὸς εἶναι τοῦ βίου τι ἀπολαῦσαι.

54 Τοιούτῳ μὲν πάθει οἱ Ἀθηναῖοι περιπεσόντες ἐπιέζοντο, 2 ἀνθρώπων τ' ἔνδον θνῃσκόντων καὶ γῆς ἔξω δῃουμένης. ἐν δὲ τῷ κακῷ οἷα εἰκὸς ἀνεμνήσθησαν καὶ τοῦδε τοῦ ἔπους, φάσκοντες οἱ πρεσβύτεροι πάλαι ᾄδεσθαι "ἥξει Δωριακὸς 3 πόλεμος καὶ λοιμὸς ἅμ' αὐτῷ." ἐγένετο μὲν οὖν ἔρις τοῖς ἀνθρώποις μὴ λοιμὸν ὠνομάσθαι ἐν τῷ ἔπει ὑπὸ τῶν παλαιῶν, ἀλλὰ λιμόν, ἐνίκησε δὲ ἐπὶ τοῦ παρόντος εἰκότως λοιμὸν εἰρῆσθαι· οἱ γὰρ ἄνθρωποι πρὸς ἃ ἔπασχον τὴν μνήμην ἐποιοῦντο. ἢν δέ γε οἶμαί ποτε ἄλλος πόλεμος καταλάβῃ Δωρικὸς τοῦδε ὕστερος καὶ ξυμβῇ γενέσθαι λιμόν, κατὰ τὸ 4 εἰκὸς οὕτως ᾄσονται. μνήμη δὲ ἐγένετο καὶ τοῦ Λακεδαιμονίων χρηστηρίου τοῖς εἰδόσιν, ὅτε ἐπερωτῶσιν αὐτοῖς τὸν θεὸν εἰ χρὴ πολεμεῖν ἀνεῖλε κατὰ κράτος πολεμοῦσι νίκην 5 ἔσεσθαι, καὶ αὐτὸς ἔφη ξυλλήψεσθαι. περὶ μὲν οὖν τοῦ χρηστηρίου τὰ γιγνόμενα ἤκαζον ὁμοῖα εἶναι· ἐσβεβληκότων δὲ τῶν Πελοποννησίων ἡ νόσος ἤρξατο εὐθύς, καὶ ἐς μὲν Πελοπόννησον οὐκ ἐσῆλθεν, ὅτι καὶ ἄξιον εἰπεῖν, ἐπενείματο δὲ Ἀθήνας μὲν μάλιστα, ἔπειτα δὲ καὶ τῶν ἄλλων

---

3. προσταλαιπωρεῖν cett.: προταλαιπωρεῖν C E.

they thought it reasonable to concentrate on immediate profit and pleasure, believing that their bodies and their possessions alike would be short-lived. No one was willing to persevere in struggling for what was considered an honourable result, since he could not be sure that he would not perish before he achieved it. What was pleasant in the short term, and what was in any way conducive to that, came to be accepted as honourable and useful. No fear of the gods or law of men had any restraining power, since it was judged to make no difference whether one was pious or not as all alike could be seen dying. No one expected to live long enough to have to pay the penalty for his misdeeds: people tended much more to think that a sentence already decided was hanging over them, and that before it was executed they might reasonably get some enjoyment out of life.

So the Athenians had fallen into this great misfortune and were being ground down by it, with people dying inside the city and the land being laid waste outside. It is not surprising that in this calamity they remembered a verse which the older people said had been recited long before: "There will come a Dorian war, and with it a plague." Arguments arose as to whether the original version of the verse had referred to *loimos*, "plague", or *limos*, "famine"; but as one would expect in the circumstances the view which prevailed was that it was plague that had been mentioned. People adjusted their memories in the light of their experience; and I think that if we were involved in another Dorian war after this one and a famine were to coincide with it we might expect the other form of the verse to be used.

Those who knew about it remembered the oracle given to the Spartans, when they asked the god if they ought to go to war, and he replied that if they fought valiantly victory would be theirs, and he would join in. It was reckoned that what was happening was in accordance with the oracle. At any rate, the plague began as soon as the Peloponnesians had invaded, and it did not reach the Peloponnese to a significant extent, but spread over Ath-

χωρίων τὰ πολυανθρωπότατα. ταῦτα μὲν τὰ κατὰ τὴν νόσον γενόμενα.

55 Οἱ δὲ Πελοποννήσιοι ἐπειδὴ ἔτεμον τὸ πεδίον, παρῆλθον ἐς τὴν Πάραλον γῆν καλουμένην μέχρι Λαυρείου, οὗ τὰ ἀργύρεια μέταλλά ἐστιν Ἀθηναίοις. καὶ πρῶτον μὲν ἔτεμον ταύτην ᾗ πρὸς Πελοπόννησον ὁρᾷ, ἔπειτα δὲ τὴν πρὸς
2 Εὔβοιάν τε καὶ Ἄνδρον τετραμμένην. Περικλῆς δὲ στρατηγὸς ὢν καὶ τότε περὶ μὲν τοῦ μὴ ἐπεξιέναι τοὺς Ἀθηναίους τὴν
56 αὐτὴν γνώμην εἶχεν ὥσπερ καὶ ἐν τῇ προτέρᾳ ἐσβολῇ. ἔτι δ' αὐτῶν ἐν τῷ πεδίῳ ὄντων, πρὶν ἐς τὴν παραλίαν ἐλθεῖν, ἑκατὸν νεῶν ἐπίπλουν τῇ Πελοποννήσῳ παρεσκευάζετο, καὶ
2 ἐπειδὴ ἑτοῖμα ἦν, ἀνήγετο. ἦγε δ' ἐπὶ τῶν νεῶν ὁπλίτας Ἀθηναίων τετρακισχιλίους καὶ ἱππέας τριακοσίους ἐν ναυσὶν ἱππαγωγοῖς πρῶτον τότε ἐκ τῶν παλαιῶν νεῶν ποιηθείσαις· ξυνεστρατεύοντο δὲ καὶ Χῖοι καὶ Λέσβιοι πεντήκοντα ναυσίν.
3 ὅτε δὲ ἀνήγετο ἡ στρατιὰ αὕτη Ἀθηναίων, Πελοποννησίους
4 κατέλιπον τῆς Ἀττικῆς ὄντας ἐν τῇ παραλίᾳ. ἀφικόμενοι δὲ ἐς Ἐπίδαυρον τῆς Πελοποννήσου ἔτεμον τῆς γῆς τὴν πολλήν, καὶ πρὸς τὴν πόλιν προσβαλόντες ἐς ἐλπίδα μὲν
5 ἦλθον τοῦ ἑλεῖν, οὐ μέντοι προυχώρησέ γε. ἀναγαγόμενοι δὲ ἐκ τῆς Ἐπιδαύρου ἔτεμον τήν τε Τροιζηνίδα γῆν καὶ Ἁλιάδα καὶ Ἑρμιονίδα· ἔστι δὲ ταῦτα πάντα ἐπιθαλάσσια
6 τῆς Πελοποννήσου. ἄραντες δὲ ἀπ' αὐτῶν ἀφίκοντο ἐς Πρασιὰς τῆς Λακωνικῆς πόλισμα ἐπιθαλάσσιον, καὶ τῆς τε γῆς ἔτεμον καὶ αὐτὸ τὸ πόλισμα εἷλον καὶ ἐπόρθησαν. ταῦτα δὲ ποιήσαντες ἐπ' οἴκου ἀνεχώρησαν. τοὺς δὲ Πελοποννησίους οὐκέτι κατέλαβον ἐν τῇ Ἀττικῇ ὄντας, ἀλλ' ἀνακεχωρηκότας.

57 Ὅσον δὲ χρόνον οἵ τε Πελοποννήσιοι ἦσαν ἐν τῇ γῇ τῇ Ἀθηναίων καὶ οἱ Ἀθηναῖοι ἐστράτευον ἐπὶ τῶν νεῶν, ἡ νόσος ἔν τε τῇ στρατιᾷ τοὺς Ἀθηναίους ἔφθειρε καὶ ἐν τῇ πόλει, ὥστε καὶ ἐλέχθη τοὺς Πελοποννησίους δείσαντας τὸ νόσημα, ὡς ἐπυνθάνοντο τῶν αὐτομόλων ὅτι ἐν τῇ πόλει

ens particularly and the most thickly populated of the other places. That is what happened when the plague struck.

The Peloponnesians, after laying waste the plain, moved on to what is called the Coastal Territory, going as far as Laurium, where the Athenians have their silver mines. They ravaged first the part which faces the Peloponnese, and then the part which is turned towards Euboea and Andros. Pericles was general, and held the same view as he had during the first invasion, that the Athenians ought not to go outside.

While the enemy were still in the plain, before they moved to the coast, he prepared an expedition of a hundred ships against the Peloponnese, and when they were ready he took them out. He had four thousand Athenian hoplites on board the ships, and three hundred cavalry in horse-transports, which had been constructed for the first time out of old ships. The Chians and Lesbians joined the expedition with fifty ships. At the time when this force set out from Athens, the Peloponnesians were in the coastal part of Attica. When they arrived at Epidaurus, in the Peloponnese, they laid waste the greater part of its territory. They also made an attack on the city, and they came within sight of capturing it, but in fact did not manage to do so. After putting out from Epidaurus, they ravaged the land of Troezen, Halieis and Hermione (these are all coastal sites in the Peloponnese). When they had left there, they came to Prasiae, a coastal township in Laconia. They ravaged the land, and also captured and sacked the town. After this they returned home. By then the Peloponnesians were no longer in Attica, but had withdrawn.

Throughout the time when the Peloponnesians were in the Athenians' territory, and the Athenians were on their naval expedition, the plague continued killing both the Athenians on the expedition and those in the city. So it was even alleged that the Peloponnesians left the country sooner than they would otherwise have done, through fear of the disease, when they learned from the deserters that

εἴη καὶ θάπτοντας ἅμα ᾐσθάνοντο, θᾶσσον ἐκ τῆς γῆς ἐξελ-
2 θεῖν. τῇ δὲ ἐσβολῇ ταύτῃ πλεῖστόν τε χρόνον ἐνέμειναν
καὶ τὴν γῆν πᾶσαν ἔτεμον· ἡμέρας γὰρ τεσσαράκοντα μάλιστα
ἐν τῇ γῇ τῇ Ἀττικῇ ἐγένοντο.

58 Τοῦ δ' αὐτοῦ θέρους Ἅγνων ὁ Νικίου καὶ Κλεόπομπος
ὁ Κλεινίου, ξυστράτηγοι ὄντες Περικλέους, λαβόντες τὴν
στρατιὰν ἥπερ ἐκεῖνος ἐχρήσατο ἐστράτευσαν εὐθὺς ἐπὶ
Χαλκιδέας τοὺς ἐπὶ Θρᾴκης καὶ Ποτείδαιαν ἔτι πολιορκου-
μένην, ἀφικόμενοι δὲ μηχανάς τε τῇ Ποτειδαίᾳ προσέφερον
2 καὶ παντὶ τρόπῳ ἐπειρῶντο ἑλεῖν. προυχώρει δὲ αὐτοῖς
οὔτε ἡ αἵρεσις τῆς πόλεως οὔτε τἆλλα τῆς παρασκευῆς
ἀξίως· ἐπιγενομένη γὰρ ἡ νόσος ἐνταῦθα δὴ πάνυ ἐπίεσε
τοὺς Ἀθηναίους, φθείρουσα τὴν στρατιάν, ὥστε καὶ τοὺς
προτέρους στρατιώτας νοσῆσαι τῶν Ἀθηναίων ἀπὸ τῆς ξὺν
Ἅγνωνι στρατιᾶς, ἐν τῷ πρὸ τοῦ χρόνῳ ὑγιαίνοντας. Φορμίων δὲ καὶ οἱ ἑξακόσιοι καὶ χίλιοι οὐκέτι ἦσαν περὶ Χαλκι-
3 δέας. ὁ μὲν οὖν Ἅγνων ἀνεχώρησε ταῖς ναυσὶν ἐς τὰς
Ἀθήνας, ἀπὸ τετρακισχιλίων ὁπλιτῶν χιλίους καὶ πεντήκοντα τῇ νόσῳ ἀπολέσας ἐν τεσσαράκοντα μάλιστα ἡμέραις·
οἱ δὲ πρότεροι στρατιῶται κατὰ χώραν μένοντες ἐπολιόρκουν
τὴν Ποτείδαιαν.

59 Μετὰ δὲ τὴν δευτέραν ἐσβολὴν τῶν Πελοποννησίων οἱ
Ἀθηναῖοι, ὡς ἥ τε γῆ αὐτῶν ἐτέτμητο τὸ δεύτερον καὶ ἡ
νόσος ἐπέκειτο ἅμα καὶ ὁ πόλεμος, ἠλλοίωντο τὰς γνώμας,
2 καὶ τὸν μὲν Περικλέα ἐν αἰτίᾳ εἶχον ὡς πείσαντα σφᾶς
πολεμεῖν καὶ δι' ἐκεῖνον ταῖς ξυμφοραῖς περιπεπτωκότες,
πρὸς δὲ τοὺς Λακεδαιμονίους ὥρμηντο ξυγχωρεῖν· καὶ
πρέσβεις τινὰς πέμψαντες ὡς αὐτοὺς ἄπρακτοι ἐγένοντο.
πανταχόθεν τε τῇ γνώμῃ ἄποροι καθεστηκότες ἐνέκειντο
3 τῷ Περικλεῖ. ὁ δὲ ὁρῶν αὐτοὺς πρὸς τὰ παρόντα χαλεπαίνοντας καὶ πάντα ποιοῦντας ἅπερ αὐτὸς ἤλπιζε, ξύλλογον ποιήσας (ἔτι δ' ἐστρατήγει) ἐβούλετο θαρσῦναί τε
καὶ ἀπαγαγὼν τὸ ὀργιζόμενον τῆς γνώμης πρὸς τὸ ἠπιώ-
τερον καὶ ἀδεέστερον καταστῆσαι· παρελθὼν δὲ ἔλεξε
τοιάδε.

60 "Καὶ προσδεχομένῳ μοι τὰ τῆς ὀργῆς ὑμῶν ἔς με γεγέ-

it was present in the city, and also they could observe the funerals. But in fact this was their longest-lasting 2 invasion, and they ravaged the whole of the country: they were in the land of Attica for about forty days.

In the same summer Hagnon son of Nicias and Cleo- 58 pompus son of Clinias, fellow generals of Pericles, took over the force which he had commanded, and immediately went on a campaign against the Thraceward Chalcidians and against Potidaea, which was still under siege. On arrival they brought up machines against Potidaea and tried in every way possible to capture it. However, they did not 2 achieve either the capture of the city or anything else worthy of their efforts, since the plague broke out there, causing great suffering among the Athenians and destroying the expedition. Even the previous contingent of Athenian soldiers, who up to that time had remained healthy, caught the disease from Hagnon's force; but Phormio and his sixteen hundred were no longer in the region of Chalcidice. Hagnon returned to Athens with 3 his ships, after losing a thousand and fifty from the disease out of four thousand hoplites in about forty days. The previous contingent of soldiers remained in the country and continued the siege of Potidaea.

After the second Peloponnesian invasion the Atheni- 59 ans underwent a change of mind, since their land had been laid waste a second time and they were suffering from the plague as well as the war. They held Pericles to blame 2 for persuading them to go to war, and thought he was responsible for the misfortunes that had fallen on them. They therefore attempted to reach an agreement with the Spartans, and sent envoys to them, but they achieved nothing. They were dejected in every respect, and so they attacked Pericles. Seeing that they were complaining 3 about the situation and in every respect behaving as he had expected, he called a meeting (since he was still in office as general), intending to encourage them, to quell their anger and to make them calmer and more confident. He came forward and spoke on these lines.

"I am not surprised that your anger is directed 60

νηται (αἰσθάνομαι γὰρ τὰς αἰτίας) καὶ ἐκκλησίαν τούτου
ἕνεκα ξυνήγαγον, ὅπως ὑπομνήσω καὶ μέμψωμαι εἴ τι μὴ
2 ὀρθῶς ἢ ἐμοὶ χαλεπαίνετε ἢ ταῖς ξυμφοραῖς εἴκετε. ἐγὼ
γὰρ ἡγοῦμαι πόλιν πλείω ξύμπασαν ὀρθουμένην ὠφελεῖν
τοὺς ἰδιώτας ἢ καθ' ἕκαστον τῶν πολιτῶν εὐπραγοῦσαν, 5
3 ἁθρόαν δὲ σφαλλομένην. καλῶς μὲν γὰρ φερόμενος ἀνὴρ
τὸ καθ' ἑαυτὸν διαφθειρομένης τῆς πατρίδος οὐδὲν ἧσσον
ξυναπόλλυται, κακοτυχῶν δὲ ἐν εὐτυχούσῃ πολλῷ μᾶλλον
4 διασῴζεται. ὁπότε οὖν πόλις μὲν τὰς ἰδίας ξυμφορὰς οἵα
τε φέρειν, εἷς δ' ἕκαστος τὰς ἐκείνης ἀδύνατος, πῶς οὐ χρὴ 10
πάντας ἀμύνειν αὐτῇ, καὶ μὴ ὃ νῦν ὑμεῖς δρᾶτε· ταῖς κατ'
οἶκον κακοπραγίαις ἐκπεπληγμένοι τοῦ κοινοῦ τῆς σωτηρίας
ἀφίεσθε, καὶ ἐμέ τε τὸν παραινέσαντα πολεμεῖν καὶ ὑμᾶς
5 αὐτοὺς οἳ ξυνέγνωτε δι' αἰτίας ἔχετε. καίτοι ἐμοὶ τοιούτῳ
ἀνδρὶ ὀργίζεσθε ὃς οὐδενὸς ἥσσων οἴομαι εἶναι γνῶναί τε 15
τὰ δέοντα καὶ ἑρμηνεῦσαι ταῦτα, φιλόπολίς τε καὶ χρημάτων
6 κρείσσων. ὅ τε γὰρ γνοὺς καὶ μὴ σαφῶς διδάξας ἐν ἴσῳ
καὶ εἰ μὴ ἐνεθυμήθη· ὅ τε ἔχων ἀμφότερα, τῇ δὲ πόλει
δύσνους, οὐκ ἂν ὁμοίως τι οἰκείως φράζοι· προσόντος δὲ
καὶ τοῦδε, χρήμασι δὲ νικωμένου, τὰ ξύμπαντα τούτου ἑνὸς 20
7 ἂν πωλοῖτο. ὥστ' εἴ μοι καὶ μέσως ἡγούμενοι μᾶλλον ἑτέρων
προσεῖναι αὐτὰ πολεμεῖν ἐπείσθητε, οὐκ ἂν εἰκότως νῦν τοῦ
γε ἀδικεῖν αἰτίαν φεροίμην.
61 "Καὶ γὰρ οἷς μὲν αἵρεσις γεγένηται τἆλλα εὐτυχοῦσι,
πολλὴ ἄνοια πολεμῆσαι· εἰ δ' ἀναγκαῖον ἦν ἢ εἴξαντας 25
εὐθὺς τοῖς πέλας ὑπακοῦσαι ἢ κινδυνεύσαντας περιγενέσθαι,

against me: I understand the reason for it. I have called this assembly in order to remind you of certain things, and to rebuke you for any unjustified complaints against me or unjustified submission to your misfortunes.

"I believe it is far more advantageous to its individual members that a whole city should be on the right lines than that the citizens separately should be prosperous but the city as a whole be in trouble. If a man's own situation is good but his country is destroyed, he still cannot escape the general ruin, but if he suffers bad fortune in a country which enjoys good, he is much more likely to come through safely. Since the city is able to bear individuals' misfortunes, but the separate members are unable to bear those of the city, surely you ought all to come to the city's defence, and not behave as you are doing now: in consternation at your household ills you are neglecting the safety of the community, and so you are finding fault with me for urging you to war, and with yourselves for joining in the decision.

"Yet I believe that I, the man with whom you are angry, am inferior to no one either at determining or at expounding what is needed, and in addition I am devoted to the city and am not to be bought for money. A man who can determine what is needed but not give clear instruction is on the same level as one who has never had the ideas in the first place; one who has both these abilities but is not well disposed towards the city will still not be able to speak appropriately; if good will is present also but he can be had for money, all the rest could be sold for this one fault. So, if you thought that I had these qualifications more than others, even to a moderate extent, and for that reason accepted my advice to go to war, it is not reasonable that I should now be accused of wrongdoing.

"If in other respects you are enjoying good fortune, and you can choose whether or not to go to war, war is enormous folly; but if you have to choose either to give way, and promptly become subject to your neighbours, or to confront the risks and prevail, it is shirking the

2 ὁ φυγὼν τὸν κίνδυνον τοῦ ὑποστάντος μεμπτότερος. καὶ ἐγὼ μὲν ὁ αὐτός εἰμι καὶ οὐκ ἐξίσταμαι· ὑμεῖς δὲ μεταβάλλετε, ἐπειδὴ ξυνέβη ὑμῖν πεισθῆναι μὲν ἀκεραίοις, μεταμέλειν δὲ κακουμένοις, καὶ τὸν ἐμὸν λόγον ἐν τῷ ὑμετέρῳ ἀσθενεῖ τῆς γνώμης μὴ ὀρθὸν φαίνεσθαι, διότι τὸ μὲν λυποῦν ἔχει ἤδη τὴν αἴσθησιν ἑκάστῳ, τῆς δὲ ὠφελίας ἄπεστιν ἔτι ἡ δήλωσις ἅπασι, καὶ μεταβολῆς μεγάλης, καὶ ταύτης ἐξ ὀλίγου, ἐμπεσούσης ταπεινὴ ὑμῶν
3 ἡ διάνοια ἐγκαρτερεῖν ἃ ἔγνωτε. δουλοῖ γὰρ φρόνημα τὸ αἰφνίδιον καὶ ἀπροσδόκητον καὶ τὸ πλείστῳ παραλόγῳ ξυμβαῖνον· ὃ ὑμῖν πρὸς τοῖς ἄλλοις οὐχ ἥκιστα καὶ κατὰ τὴν
4 νόσον γεγένηται. ὅμως δὲ πόλιν μεγάλην οἰκοῦντας καὶ ἐν ἤθεσιν ἀντιπάλοις αὐτῇ τεθραμμένους χρεὼν καὶ ξυμφοραῖς ταῖς μεγίσταις ἐθέλειν ὑφίστασθαι καὶ τὴν ἀξίωσιν μὴ ἀφανίζειν (ἐν ἴσῳ γὰρ οἱ ἄνθρωποι δικαιοῦσι τῆς τε ὑπαρχούσης δόξης αἰτιᾶσθαι ὅστις μαλακίᾳ ἐλλείπει καὶ τῆς μὴ προσηκούσης μισεῖν τὸν θρασύτητι ὀρεγόμενον), ἀπαλγήσαντας δὲ τὰ ἴδια τοῦ κοινοῦ τῆς σωτηρίας ἀντιλαμβάνεσθαι.

62 "Τὸν δὲ πόνον τὸν κατὰ τὸν πόλεμον, μὴ γένηταί τε πολὺς καὶ οὐδὲν μᾶλλον περιγενώμεθα, ἀρκείτω μὲν ὑμῖν καὶ ἐκεῖνα ἐν οἷς ἄλλοτε πολλάκις γε δὴ ἀπέδειξα οὐκ ὀρθῶς αὐτὸν ὑποπτευόμενον, δηλώσω δὲ καὶ τόδε, ὅ μοι δοκεῖτε οὔτ' αὐτοὶ πώποτε ἐνθυμηθῆναι ὑπάρχον ὑμῖν μεγέθους πέρι ἐς τὴν ἀρχὴν οὔτ' ἐγὼ ἐν τοῖς πρὶν λόγοις· οὐδ' ἂν νῦν ἐχρησάμην κομπωδεστέραν ἔχοντι τὴν προσποίησιν,
2 εἰ μὴ καταπεπληγμένους ὑμᾶς παρὰ τὸ εἰκὸς ἑώρων. οἴεσθε μὲν γὰρ τῶν ξυμμάχων μόνων ἄρχειν, ἐγὼ δὲ ἀποφαίνω δύο μερῶν τῶν ἐς χρῆσιν φανερῶν, γῆς καὶ θαλάσσης, τοῦ ἑτέρου ὑμᾶς παντὸς κυριωτάτους ὄντας, ἐφ' ὅσον τε νῦν νέμεσθε καὶ ἢν ἐπὶ πλέον βουληθῆτε· καὶ οὐκ ἔστιν ὅστις τῇ ὑπαρχούσῃ παρασκευῇ τοῦ ναυτικοῦ πλέοντας ὑμᾶς οὔτε βασιλεὺς οὔτε ἄλλο οὐδὲν ἔθνος τῶν ἐν τῷ παρόντι κωλύσει.

danger rather than withstanding it that is blameworthy. I 2
am not changing my position, but remain the same as I
was. It is you who are changing. What has happened is
that you accepted my argument when you were unharmed but
are regretting it now that you are suffering. In your
weakened state of mind you think that argument mistaken,
because each individual is conscious of the distress here
and now but the benefit for all of us is not yet apparent. You have been struck by a great change of fortune,
and moreover a sudden one, and so your will to persevere
in the decision you have made is weak. Happenings 3
which are sudden, unforeseen and contrary to all reasonable expectation enslave the spirit. This has happened to
you for various reasons, and particularly because of the
plague. Nevertheless, as people living in a great city, 4
brought up in a correspondingly great way of life, you
must be prepared to stand up against the greatest disasters, and not obliterate your reputation; for men think
it equally right to blame those who through cowardice
fall short of the distinction they already have and to
resent those who through arrogance aspire to a distinction they do not deserve. You must put away your private
sorrows and work for the safety of the community.

"Your suspicion that the burden of the war will be 62
heavy and will not improve our chances of survival is
mistaken. The points I have often made in previous explanations should be sufficient, but I will add this
point, concerning the greatness brought by our empire: I
think you have never taken it to heart, and I have
not emphasised it in my previous speeches. I should not
dwell on it now, since it involves a claim of a rather
boastful kind, if I did not see that you are downcast beyond reason. You think that you are rulers simply over 2
the allies. I shall demonstrate, however, that of the two
elements available for men's use, land and sea, you have
total mastery of the whole of the second, both as far as
you already possess it and as much further as you wish.
No one, neither the King nor any other race that now ex-
ists, can prevent you from sailing with the naval force

111

3 ὥστε οὐ κατὰ τὴν τῶν οἰκιῶν καὶ τῆς γῆς χρείαν, ὧν μεγάλων νομίζετε ἐστερῆσθαι, αὕτη ἡ δύναμις φαίνεται· οὐδ' εἰκὸς χαλεπῶς φέρειν αὐτῶν μᾶλλον ἢ οὐ κηπίον καὶ ἐγκαλλώπισμα πλούτου πρὸς ταύτην νομίσαντας ὀλιγωρῆσαι, καὶ γνῶναι ἐλευθερίαν μέν, ἢν ἀντιλαμβανόμενοι αὐτῆς διασώσωμεν, ῥᾳδίως ταῦτα ἀναληψομένην, ἄλλων δὲ ὑπακούσασι καὶ τὰ προκεκτημένα φιλεῖν ἐλασσοῦσθαι. τῶν τε πατέρων μὴ χείρους κατ' ἀμφότερα φανῆναι, οἳ μετὰ πόνων καὶ οὐ παρ' ἄλλων δεξάμενοι κατέσχον τε καὶ προσέτι διασώσαντες παρέδοσαν ὑμῖν αὐτά (αἴσχιον δὲ ἔχοντας ἀφαιρεθῆναι ἢ κτωμένους ἀτυχῆσαι), ἰέναι δὲ τοῖς ἐχθροῖς ὁμόσε μὴ φρονήματι μόνον, ἀλλὰ καὶ καταφρονήματι. αὔχημα μὲν γὰρ καὶ
4 ἀπὸ ἀμαθίας εὐτυχοῦς καὶ δειλῷ τινι ἐγγίγνεται, καταφρόνησις δὲ ὃς ἂν καὶ γνώμῃ πιστεύῃ τῶν ἐναντίων προύχειν,
5 ὃ ἡμῖν ὑπάρχει. καὶ τὴν τόλμαν ἀπὸ τῆς ὁμοίας τύχης ἡ ξύνεσις ἐκ τοῦ ὑπέρφρονος ἐχυρωτέραν παρέχεται, ἐλπίδι τε ἧσσον πιστεύει, ἧς ἐν τῷ ἀπόρῳ ἡ ἰσχύς, γνώμῃ δὲ ἀπὸ
63 τῶν ὑπαρχόντων, ἧς βεβαιοτέρα ἡ πρόνοια. τῆς τε πόλεως ὑμᾶς εἰκὸς τῷ τιμωμένῳ ἀπὸ τοῦ ἄρχειν, ᾧπερ ἅπαντες ἀγάλλεσθε, βοηθεῖν, καὶ μὴ φεύγειν τοὺς πόνους ἢ μηδὲ τὰς τιμὰς διώκειν· μηδὲ νομίσαι περὶ ἑνὸς μόνου, δουλείας ἀντ' ἐλευθερίας, ἀγωνίζεσθαι, ἀλλὰ καὶ ἀρχῆς στερήσεως
2 καὶ κινδύνου ὧν ἐν τῇ ἀρχῇ ἀπήχθεσθε. ἧς οὐδ' ἐκστῆναι ἔτι ὑμῖν ἔστιν, εἴ τις καὶ τόδε ἐν τῷ παρόντι δεδιὼς ἀπραγμοσύνῃ ἀνδραγαθίζεται· ὡς τυραννίδα γὰρ ἤδη ἔχετε αὐτήν, ἣν

at your disposal. This power is not on the same scale as 3
the use of your houses and land, the loss of which you
regard as a great blow. It is not reasonable to take that
deprivation to heart: you should rather think of those
possessions as a pleasure-garden or adornment of your
wealth in contrast to your naval power, and should reckon
that if we strive for our freedom and win through we
shall then easily recover them, whereas those who become
subject to others are apt to lose even what they had before.

"Your fathers secured this empire not by inheritance
from others but by their own efforts, and furthermore
they preserved it and handed it on to you (losing what
they had would have been more shameful than failing in
the attempt to acquire it). You must show that you are as
good as them in both these respects, and must go against
the enemy not merely with spirit but with a spirit of
confident superiority. Boasting may be indulged in even 4
by a coward, if though ignorant he enjoys good fortune;
but confident superiority is the right of those who have
a rational trust that they are stronger than their opponents, as is the case with us. Intelligence based on 5
confident superiority makes boldness more secure when the
balance of fortune is equal: it trusts not in hope, which
is a source of strength in desperate straits, but in
reason grounded in the facts, which allows more reliable
forethought.

"It is right that you should rally to the support of 63
the honour which the empire brings to our city, in which
you all delight. You cannot avoid the burden unless you
are prepared not to seek the honour. Do not suppose that
your struggle is about one thing only, slavery or freedom
for yourselves: it is also about the loss of the empire
and the danger from those whose hatred you have incurred
through the empire. It is no longer possible for you to 2
abdicate from it (I must say this in case in the present
circumstances any of you are frightened and to avoid
trouble propose this as a virtuous course). You now possess the empire like a tyranny, and, though it may be

3 λαβεῖν μὲν ἄδικον δοκεῖ εἶναι, ἀφεῖναι δὲ ἐπικίνδυνον. τάχιστ᾽ ἄν τε πόλιν οἱ τοιοῦτοι ἑτέρους τε πείσαντες ἀπολέσειαν καὶ εἴ που ἐπὶ σφῶν αὐτῶν αὐτόνομοι οἰκήσειαν· τὸ γὰρ ἄπραγμον οὐ σῴζεται μὴ μετὰ τοῦ δραστηρίου τεταγμένον, οὐδὲ ἐν ἀρχούσῃ πόλει ξυμφέρει, ἀλλ᾽ ἐν ὑπηκόῳ, ἀσφαλῶς δουλεύειν.

64 "Ὑμεῖς δὲ μήτε ὑπὸ τῶν τοιῶνδε πολιτῶν παράγεσθε μήτε ἐμὲ δι᾽ ὀργῆς ἔχετε, ᾧ καὶ αὐτοὶ ξυνδιέγνωτε πολεμεῖν, εἰ καὶ ἐπελθόντες οἱ ἐναντίοι ἔδρασαν ἅπερ εἰκὸς ἦν μὴ ἐθελησάντων ὑμῶν ὑπακούειν, ἐπιγεγένηταί τε πέρα ὧν προσεδεχόμεθα ἡ νόσος ἥδε, πρᾶγμα μόνον δὴ τῶν πάντων ἐλπίδος κρεῖσσον γεγενημένον. καὶ δι᾽ αὐτὴν οἶδ᾽ ὅτι μέρος τι μᾶλλον ἔτι μισοῦμαι, οὐ δικαίως, εἰ μὴ καὶ ὅταν παρὰ
2 λόγον τι εὖ πράξητε ἐμοὶ ἀναθήσετε. φέρειν δὲ χρὴ τά τε δαιμόνια ἀναγκαίως τά τε ἀπὸ τῶν πολεμίων ἀνδρείως· ταῦτα γὰρ ἐν ἔθει τῇδε τῇ πόλει πρότερόν τε ἦν νῦν τε μὴ
3 ἐν ὑμῖν κωλυθῇ. γνῶτε δὲ ὄνομα μέγιστον αὐτὴν ἔχουσαν ἐν ἅπασιν ἀνθρώποις διὰ τὸ ταῖς ξυμφοραῖς μὴ εἴκειν, πλεῖστα δὲ σώματα καὶ πόνους ἀνηλωκέναι πολέμῳ, καὶ δύναμιν μεγίστην δὴ μέχρι τοῦδε κεκτημένην, ἧς ἐς ἀίδιον τοῖς ἐπιγιγνομένοις, ἢν καὶ νῦν ὑπενδῶμέν ποτε (πάντα γὰρ πέφυκε καὶ ἐλασσοῦσθαι), μνήμη καταλελείψεται, Ἑλλήνων τε ὅτι Ἕλληνες πλείστων δὴ ἤρξαμεν, καὶ πολέμοις μεγίστοις ἀντέσχομεν πρός τε ξύμπαντας καὶ καθ᾽ ἑκάστους, πόλιν τε
4 τοῖς πᾶσιν εὐπορωτάτην καὶ μεγίστην ᾠκήσαμεν. καίτοι ταῦτα ὁ μὲν ἀπράγμων μέμψαιτ᾽ ἄν, ὁ δὲ δρᾶν τι καὶ αὐτὸς

24–5. καὶ <τὰ> τοιαῦτα Reifferscheid, fortasse recte.

considered unjust to have acquired it, to renounce it would be dangerous. If men who thought like that persuaded the rest, they would very quickly ruin their city, even if they lived on their own somewhere and had no ties with others. Avoiders of trouble are not safe unless ranked alongside men willing to act. That is a policy fitting not for an imperial city but for a subject city, which through this policy is enabled to live safely in slavery.

"Do not be led astray by citizens of that kind; and do not be angry with me, in whose decision to go to war you yourselves joined, even though the enemy have attacked and have acted as was to be expected when you refused to submit, and though in addition to what we were prepared for we have been struck by the plague, the only one of all our afflictions which goes beyond what could be foreseen. I know that the plague has increased my unpopularity to a considerable extent, but that is not fair, unless when you enjoy some unpredictable success you are prepared to give me the credit for that too. We must bear blows from heaven with resignation, and blows from the enemy with manliness: that has been characteristic of our city in the past, and must not be undermined by your action now. You must recognise that Athens has the greatest renown among all men because she does not give in to disasters, but has sacrificed the largest number of lives and has undertaken the heaviest burdens in war, and has built up the greatest power of any city up to the present time. Even if in our present condition we do some time give way (for it is part of the nature of all things to decline), all posterity will be able to recall that we ruled over a larger number of Greeks than any other Greeks have ruled, that we held out against the Greeks, separately and all together, in the greatest wars, that we lived in the city that was greatest and best provided in all respects.

"Those who prefer to avoid trouble might find this objectionable, but those who want to achieve something themselves will be spurred to emulate it, while those who

5 βουλόμενος ζηλώσει· εἰ δέ τις μὴ κέκτηται, φθονήσει. τὸ
δὲ μισεῖσθαι καὶ λυπηροὺς εἶναι ἐν τῷ παρόντι πᾶσι μὲν
ὑπῆρξε δὴ ὅσοι ἕτεροι ἑτέρων ἠξίωσαν ἄρχειν· ὅστις δὲ ἐπὶ
μεγίστοις τὸ ἐπίφθονον λαμβάνει, ὀρθῶς βουλεύεται. μῖσος
μὲν γὰρ οὐκ ἐπὶ πολὺ ἀντέχει, ἡ δὲ παραυτίκα [τε] λαμπρότης
6 καὶ ἐς τὸ ἔπειτα δόξα αἰείμνηστος καταλείπεται. ὑμεῖς δὲ
ἔς τε τὸ μέλλον καλὸν προγνόντες ἔς τε τὸ αὐτίκα μὴ
αἰσχρὸν τῷ ἤδη προθύμῳ ἀμφότερα κτήσασθε, καὶ Λακεδαιμονίοις μήτε ἐπικηρυκεύεσθε μήτε ἔνδηλοι ἔστε τοῖς
παροῦσι πόνοις βαρυνόμενοι, ὡς οἵτινες πρὸς τὰς ξυμφορὰς
γνώμῃ μὲν ἥκιστα λυποῦνται, ἔργῳ δὲ μάλιστα ἀντέχουσιν,
οὗτοι καὶ πόλεων καὶ ἰδιωτῶν κράτιστοί εἰσιν."

65 Τοιαῦτα ὁ Περικλῆς λέγων ἐπειρᾶτο τοὺς Ἀθηναίους τῆς
τε ἐς αὑτὸν ὀργῆς παραλύειν καὶ ἀπὸ τῶν παρόντων δεινῶν
2 ἀπάγειν τὴν γνώμην. οἱ δὲ δημοσίᾳ μὲν τοῖς λόγοις ἀνε-
πείθοντο καὶ οὔτε πρὸς τοὺς Λακεδαιμονίους ἔτι ἔπεμπον ἔς
τε τὸν πόλεμον μᾶλλον ὥρμηντο, ἰδίᾳ δὲ τοῖς παθήμασιν
ἐλυποῦντο, ὁ μὲν δῆμος ὅτι ἀπ' ἐλασσόνων ὁρμώμενος
ἐστέρητο καὶ τούτων, οἱ δὲ δυνατοὶ καλὰ κτήματα κατὰ
τὴν χώραν οἰκοδομίαις τε καὶ πολυτελέσι κατασκευαῖς ἀπο-
λωλεκότες, τὸ δὲ μέγιστον, πόλεμον ἀντ' εἰρήνης ἔχοντες.
3 οὐ μέντοι πρότερόν γε οἱ ξύμπαντες ἐπαύσαντο ἐν ὀργῇ
4 ἔχοντες αὐτὸν πρὶν ἐζημίωσαν χρήμασιν. ὕστερον δ' αὖθις
οὐ πολλῷ, ὅπερ φιλεῖ ὅμιλος ποιεῖν, στρατηγὸν εἵλοντο καὶ
πάντα τὰ πράγματα ἐπέτρεψαν, ὧν μὲν περὶ τὰ οἰκεῖα
ἕκαστος ἤλγει ἀμβλύτεροι ἤδη ὄντες, ὧν δὲ ἡ ξύμπασα
5 πόλις προσεδεῖτο πλείστου ἄξιον νομίζοντες εἶναι. ὅσον
τε γὰρ χρόνον προύστη τῆς πόλεως ἐν τῇ εἰρήνῃ, μετρίως
ἐξηγεῖτο καὶ ἀσφαλῶς διεφύλαξεν αὐτήν, καὶ ἐγένετο ἐπ'
ἐκείνου μεγίστη, ἐπειδή τε ὁ πόλεμος κατέστη, ὁ δὲ
6 φαίνεται καὶ ἐν τούτῳ προγνοὺς τὴν δύναμιν. ἐπεβίω δὲ

---

5. τε secl. Stahl.

have failed to build up their power will be envious. Short-term hatred and unpopularity have always been the lot of those who have claimed the right to rule over others, but those who incur such jealousy in pursuit of the highest objectives are following the right policy. Hatred does not persist for long, but distinction here and now survives into the future as undying glory. You, then, must decide for honour in the future and for the avoidance of disgrace in the present, and you must achieve both by your enthusiasm now. Do not negotiate with the Spartans; do not let it appear that you are weighed down by your present burdens. The best cities and the best individuals are those who in the face of disaster suffer least distress in their minds and hold out most valiantly in their actions."

Pericles spoke on those lines, to try to dispel the Athenians' anger against himself and lead their thoughts away from their current misfortunes. Collectively, they were persuaded by what he said, and instead of continuing their approaches to Sparta they rather turned their energies to the war. Individually, however, they were still distressed by their sufferings. The common people had started out from a poor base and had lost even that. The rich had been deprived of handsome possessions in the country, with houses and expensive furnishings. Above all, the Athenians were not at peace but at war. The community's anger against Pericles did not subside until he had been sentenced to a fine. Not long afterwards, as the masses are apt to do, they elected him general and entrusted the whole conduct of affairs to him, since by then they were less sensitive to their individual domestic miseries and they judged him most able to meet the needs of the whole city.

Throughout the time he had presided over the city in peace, he had led it modestly and so had preserved it safely, and under his guidance it had risen to its greatest height. Moreover, it is clear that, when the war came, he foresaw the strong position that Athens would have in it. He lived on for two years and six months;

δύο ἔτη καὶ ἓξ μῆνας· καὶ ἐπειδὴ ἀπέθανεν, ἐπὶ πλέον ἔτι
7 ἐγνώσθη ἡ πρόνοια αὐτοῦ ἡ ἐς τὸν πόλεμον. ὁ μὲν γὰρ
ἡσυχάζοντάς τε καὶ τὸ ναυτικὸν θεραπεύοντας καὶ ἀρχὴν μὴ
ἐπικτωμένους ἐν τῷ πολέμῳ μηδὲ τῇ πόλει κινδυνεύοντας ἔφη
περιέσεσθαι· οἱ δὲ ταῦτά τε πάντα ἐς τοὐναντίον ἔπραξαν
καὶ ἄλλα ἔξω τοῦ πολέμου δοκοῦντα εἶναι κατὰ τὰς ἰδίας
φιλοτιμίας καὶ ἴδια κέρδη κακῶς ἔς τε σφᾶς αὐτοὺς καὶ
τοὺς ξυμμάχους ἐπολίτευσαν, ἃ κατορθούμενα μὲν τοῖς ἰδιώταις τιμὴ καὶ ὠφελία μᾶλλον ἦν, σφαλέντα δὲ τῇ πόλει ἐς
8 τὸν πόλεμον βλάβη καθίστατο. αἴτιον δ' ἦν ὅτι ἐκεῖνος
μὲν δυνατὸς ὢν τῷ τε ἀξιώματι καὶ τῇ γνώμῃ χρημάτων
τε διαφανῶς ἀδωρότατος γενόμενος κατεῖχε τὸ πλῆθος ἐλευθέρως, καὶ οὐκ ἤγετο μᾶλλον ὑπ' αὐτοῦ ἢ αὐτὸς ἦγε, διὰ τὸ
μὴ κτώμενος ἐξ οὐ προσηκόντων τὴν δύναμιν πρὸς ἡδονήν τι
λέγειν, ἀλλ' ἔχων ἐπ' ἀξιώσει καὶ πρὸς ὀργήν τι ἀντειπεῖν.
9 ὁπότε γοῦν αἴσθοιτό τι αὐτοὺς παρὰ καιρὸν ὕβρει θαρσοῦντας,
λέγων κατέπλησσεν ἐπὶ τὸ φοβεῖσθαι, καὶ δεδιότας αὖ ἀλό-
γως ἀντικαθίστη πάλιν ἐπὶ τὸ θαρσεῖν. ἐγίγνετό τε λόγῳ
10 μὲν δημοκρατία, ἔργῳ δὲ ὑπὸ τοῦ πρώτου ἀνδρὸς ἀρχή. οἱ
δὲ ὕστερον ἴσοι μᾶλλον αὐτοὶ πρὸς ἀλλήλους ὄντες καὶ
ὀρεγόμενοι τοῦ πρῶτος ἕκαστος γίγνεσθαι ἐτράποντο καθ'
11 ἡδονὰς τῷ δήμῳ καὶ τὰ πράγματα ἐνδιδόναι. ἐξ ὧν ἄλλα
τε πολλά, ὡς ἐν μεγάλῃ πόλει καὶ ἀρχὴν ἐχούσῃ, ἡμαρτήθη
καὶ ὁ ἐς Σικελίαν πλοῦς, ὃς οὐ τοσοῦτον γνώμης ἁμάρτημα
ἦν πρὸς οὓς ἐπῇσαν, ὅσον οἱ ἐκπέμψαντες οὐ τὰ πρόσφορα
τοῖς οἰχομένοις ἐπιγιγνώσκοντες, ἀλλὰ κατὰ τὰς ἰδίας δια-
βολὰς περὶ τῆς τοῦ δήμου προστασίας τά τε ἐν τῷ στρατο-
πέδῳ ἀμβλύτερα ἐποίουν καὶ τὰ περὶ τὴν πόλιν πρῶτον ἐν
12 ἀλλήλοις ἐταράχθησαν. σφαλέντες δὲ ἐν Σικελίᾳ ἄλλῃ τε

---

3. ἡσυχάζοντάς τε <τῷ ὁπλιτικῷ> Gomme, fortasse recte.
8–9. τοῖς ἰδιώταις codd.: αὐτοῖς ἰδίᾳ Gomme.

and after his death his foresight with regard to the war could be recognised even more clearly. He had said that 7 the Athenians would prevail if they kept quiet, looked after their fleet, and did not try to add to their empire during the war or put the city at risk. But they did the opposite of all these things, and did still other things which appeared irrelevant to the war. For the sake of private ambition and private profit they pursued policies which were bad for themselves and for the allies, from which the honour and advantage accrued rather to private individuals when they succeeded, but which when they failed brought damage to the city with regard to the war. The reason was that Pericles, since he was strong in both 8 repute and intellect and was conspicuously incorruptible, held the masses on a light rein, and led them rather than let them lead him. This was because he did not have to adapt what he said in order to please his hearers, in an attempt to gain power by improper means, but his standing allowed him even to speak against them and provoke their anger. Whenever he saw that they were arrogant and un- 9 deservedly confident, he would speak to strike terror into them; and when he saw them unreasonably afraid he would restore their confidence once more. The result was in theory democracy but in fact rule by the first man.

The leaders who followed Pericles were more on a 10 level with one another, and as each strove to become first they tended to abandon affairs to the people to gratify their whims. As was to be expected in a great 11 city at the head of an empire, various mistakes were made, in particular the Sicilian expedition. That involved not so much an error of judgment about the people against whom it was sent as the failure by those who sent out the expedition to make the right decisions in support of the men who had gone. Instead, through the accusations made against individuals in the struggle for political supremacy they made the expeditionary force less effective, and for the first time they brought affairs inside the city to a state of upheaval. Even so, 12 after failing in Sicily with the greater part of their

παρασκευῇ καὶ τοῦ ναυτικοῦ τῷ πλέονι μορίῳ καὶ κατὰ τὴν πόλιν ἤδη ἐν στάσει ὄντες ὅμως ὀκτὼ πολεμοῦντες ἔτη ἀντεῖχον τοῖς τε πρότερον ὑπάρχουσι πολεμίοις καὶ τοῖς ἀπὸ Σικελίας μετ' αὐτῶν, καὶ τῶν ξυμμάχων ἔτι τοῖς πλέοσιν ἀφεστηκόσι, Κύρῳ τε ὑστερον βασιλέως παιδὶ προσγενομένῳ, ὃς παρεῖχε χρήματα Πελοποννησίοις ἐς τὸ ναυτικόν, καὶ οὐ πρότερον ἐνέδοσαν ἢ αὐτοὶ [ἐν] σφίσι κατὰ τὰς ἰδίας διαφορὰς περιπεσόντες ἐσφάλησαν. τοσοῦτον τῷ Περικλεῖ ἐπερίσσευσε τότε ἀφ' ὧν [αὐτὸς] προέγνω καὶ πάνυ ἂν ῥᾳδίως περιγενέσθαι τὴν πόλιν Πελοποννησίων αὐτῶν τῷ πολέμῳ.

66 Οἱ δὲ Λακεδαιμόνιοι καὶ οἱ ξύμμαχοι τοῦ αὐτοῦ θέρους ἐστράτευσαν ναυσὶν ἑκατὸν ἐς Ζάκυνθον τὴν νῆσον, ἣ κεῖται ἀντιπέρας Ἤλιδος· εἰσὶ δὲ Ἀχαιῶν τῶν ἐκ Πελοποννήσου ἄποικοι καὶ Ἀθηναίοις ξυνεμάχουν. ἐπέπλεον δὲ Λακεδαιμονίων χίλιοι ὁπλῖται καὶ Κνῆμος Σπαρτιάτης ναύαρχος. ἀποβάντες δὲ ἐς τὴν γῆν ἐδῄωσαν τὰ πολλά. καὶ ἐπειδὴ οὐ ξυνεχώρουν, ἀπέπλευσαν ἐπ' οἴκου.

67 Καὶ τοῦ αὐτοῦ θέρους τελευτῶντος Ἀριστεὺς Κορίνθιος καὶ Λακεδαιμονίων πρέσβεις Ἀνήριστος καὶ Νικόλαος καὶ Πρατόδαμος καὶ Τεγεάτης Τιμαγόρας καὶ Ἀργεῖος ἰδίᾳ Πόλλις, πορευόμενοι ἐς τὴν Ἀσίαν ὡς βασιλέα, εἴ πως πείσειαν αὐτὸν χρήματά τε παρέχειν καὶ ξυμπολεμεῖν, ἀφικνοῦνται ὡς Σιτάλκην πρῶτον τὸν Τήρεω ἐς Θρᾴκην, βουλόμενοι πεῖσαί τε αὐτόν, εἰ δύναιτο, μεταστάντα τῆς Ἀθηναίων ξυμμαχίας στρατεῦσαι ἐπὶ τὴν Ποτείδαιαν, οὗ ἦν στράτευμα τῶν Ἀθηναίων πολιορκοῦν, καὶ ᾗπερ ὥρμηντο, δι' ἐκείνου πορευθῆναι πέραν τοῦ Ἑλλησπόντου ὡς Φαρνάκην τὸν Φαρναβάζου, ὃς αὐτοὺς ἔμελλεν ὡς βασιλέα ἀναπέμψειν. παρατυχόντες δὲ Ἀθηναίων πρέσβεις Λέαρχος Καλλιμάχου καὶ Ἀμεινιάδης Φιλήμονος παρὰ τῷ Σιτάλκῃ πείθουσι τὸν Σάδοκον τὸν γεγενημένον Ἀθηναῖον, Σιτάλκου υἱόν, τοὺς ἄνδρας ἐγχειρίσαι σφίσιν, ὅπως μὴ διαβάντες ὡς βασιλέα τὴν ἐκείνου πόλιν τὸ μέρος βλάψωσιν. ὁ δὲ

---

2. ὀκτὼ Shilleto: τρία codd., def. Bury (= 411/0−408/7), δέκα Haacke.
   πολεμοῦντες Gomme: μὲν codd., τρυχόμενοι vel τριβόμενοι Shilleto, ὅμως τετρυχωμένοι ἔτι sine numero Connor.
7. ἐν secl. Herwerden.
9. αὐτὸς secl. Gomme: αὐτοὺς Classen.
10. τὴν πόλιν C G Π²¹ Aristid. XLVI. *Quattuor* (ii. 163 Dindorf): τῶν cett.
22. παρέχειν cett. (in rasura B pc) Π²¹ (?): παρασχεῖν C G.

fleet and with the other forces that they sent, and falling into a state of dissension in the city, the Athenians still held out for eight years of war against both the enemies they already had and those from Sicily who joined them, and, in addition, against the majority of their allies, who revolted against them, and later the King's son Cyrus too, who gave the Peloponnesians money for their navy. They did not give in until they stumbled over themselves in their internal disputes and in that way came to ruin. So ample were the grounds which Pericles had at this time for predicting that the city would very easily prevail over the Peloponnesians on their own in the war. 13

In the same summer the Spartans and their allies mounted an expedition with a hundred ships against the island of Zacynthus, which lies opposite Elis. Its inhabitants are colonists from Achaea in the Peloponnese, and were allied to Athens. The force included a thousand Spartan hoplites, and the Spartiate Cnemus as navarch. They descended on the land and laid most of it waste; and, when the Zacynthians refused to come to terms with them, they returned home. 66 2

At the end of the same summer Aristeus of Corinth, Aneristus, Nicolaus and Pratodamus as envoys from Sparta, Timagoras of Tegea and, going as a private individual, Pollis of Argos, set out to the King in Asia, to see if they could persuade him to provide money and join in the war on their side. They first called on Sitalces son of Teres in Thrace, intending if they could to persuade him to desert his alliance with Athens and go on campaign to Potidaea, which was being besieged by Athenian forces. Then they planned with his help to go across the Hellespont to Pharnaces son of Pharnabazus, who would send them on to the King. However, with Sitalces there were Athenian envoys, Learchus son of Callimachus and Aminiades son of Philemon, and they tried to persuade Sitalces' son Sadocus, who had been made an Athenian citizen, to hand over the men to them, and prevent them from going across to the King and doing their best to harm what was Sadocus' city. He agreed. He sent men with 67 2 3

πεισθεὶς πορευομένους αὐτοὺς διὰ τῆς Θρᾴκης ἐπὶ τὸ πλοῖον ᾧ ἔμελλον τὸν Ἑλλήσποντον περαιώσειν, πρὶν ἐσβαίνειν ξυλλαμβάνει, ἄλλους ξυμπέμψας μετὰ τοῦ Λεάρχου καὶ Ἀμειινιάδου, καὶ ἐκέλευσεν ἐκείνοις παραδοῦναι. οἱ δὲ λα-
4 βόντες ἐκόμισαν ἐς τὰς Ἀθήνας. ἀφικομένων δὲ αὐτῶν δείσαντες οἱ Ἀθηναῖοι τὸν Ἀριστέα μὴ αὖθις σφᾶς ἔτι πλείω κακουργῇ διαφυγών, ὅτι καὶ πρὸ τούτων τὰ τῆς Ποτειδαίας καὶ τῶν ἐπὶ Θρᾴκης πάντα ἐφαίνετο πράξας, ἀκρίτους καὶ βουλομένους ἔστιν ἃ εἰπεῖν αὐθημερὸν ἀπέκτειναν πάντας καὶ ἐς φάραγγα ἐσέβαλον, δικαιοῦντες τοῖς αὐτοῖς ἀμύνεσθαι οἷσπερ καὶ οἱ Λακεδαιμόνιοι ὑπῆρξαν, τοὺς ἐμπόρους οὓς ἔλαβον Ἀθηναίων καὶ τῶν ξυμμάχων ἐν ὁλκάσι περὶ Πελοπόννησον πλέοντας ἀποκτείναντες καὶ ἐς φάραγγας ἐσβαλόντες. πάντας γὰρ δὴ κατ' ἀρχὰς τοῦ πολέμου Λακεδαιμόνιοι ὅσους λάβοιεν ἐν τῇ θαλάσσῃ ὡς πολεμίους διέφθειρον, καὶ τοὺς μετὰ Ἀθηναίων ξυμπολεμοῦντας καὶ τοὺς μηδὲ μεθ' ἑτέρων.

68 Κατὰ δὲ τοὺς αὐτοὺς χρόνους, τοῦ θέρους τελευτῶντος, καὶ Ἀμπρακιῶται αὐτοί τε καὶ τῶν βαρβάρων πολλοὺς ἀναστήσαντες ἐστράτευσαν ἐπ' Ἄργος τὸ Ἀμφιλοχικὸν καὶ
2 τὴν ἄλλην Ἀμφιλοχίαν. ἔχθρα δὲ πρὸς τοὺς Ἀργείους
3 ἀπὸ τοῦδε αὐτοῖς ἤρξατο πρῶτον γενέσθαι. Ἄργος τὸ Ἀμφιλοχικὸν καὶ Ἀμφιλοχίαν τὴν ἄλλην ἔκτισε μὲν μετὰ τὰ Τρωικὰ οἴκαδε ἀναχωρήσας καὶ οὐκ ἀρεσκόμενος τῇ ἐν Ἄργει καταστάσει Ἀμφίλοχος ὁ Ἀμφιάρεω ἐν τῷ Ἀμπρακικῷ κόλπῳ, ὁμώνυμον τῇ ἑαυτοῦ πατρίδι Ἄργος ὀνομάσας
4 (καὶ ἦν ἡ πόλις αὕτη μεγίστη τῆς Ἀμφιλοχίας καὶ τοὺς
5 δυνατωτάτους εἶχεν οἰκήτορας), ὑπὸ ξυμφορῶν δὲ πολλαῖς γενεαῖς ὕστερον πιεζόμενοι Ἀμπρακιώτας ὁμόρους ὄντας τῇ Ἀμφιλοχικῇ ξυνοίκους ἐπηγάγοντο, καὶ ἡλληνίσθησαν τὴν νῦν γλῶσσαν τότε πρῶτον ἀπὸ τῶν Ἀμπρακιωτῶν ξυνοικη-
6 σάντων· οἱ δὲ ἄλλοι Ἀμφίλοχοι βάρβαροί εἰσιν. ἐκβάλ-

Learchus and Aminiades, with instructions to hand over the envoys to them, and they arrested the envoys while they were travelling through Thrace towards the boat in which he was to send them across the Hellespont, before they could embark.

Learchus and Aminiades took the men and conveyed them to Athens. On their arrival, the Athenians were *4* afraid that Aristeus would get away and do them still further mischief, since it was clear that earlier he had been responsible for everything to do with Potidaea and the Thraceward region. So, without holding a trial, and in spite of the men's wish to make a speech, they put them all to death that same day and threw them into a pit. In justification they claimed that they were taking the same kind of measures to protect themselves as the Spartans had done previously, when they had killed and thrown into pits the Athenian and allied traders whom they had caught sailing round the Peloponnese in merchant ships. At the beginning of the war the Spartans put to death as enemies every single man whom they caught at sea, both those who were allies of Athens and those who did not belong to either side.

At the same time, at the end of the summer, the Am- *68* braciots, with many of the barbarians whom they incited to join them, undertook a campaign against Amphilochian Argos and the rest of Amphilochia. The origin of their *2* enmity with Argos was as follows. Amphilochian Argos and *3* the rest of Amphilochia were founded on the Ambracian Gulf by Amphilochus son of Amphiaraus, when he returned home after the Trojan War and did not like the state of affairs which he found in Argos. He gave the foundation the same name as his own country, Argos, and this became *4* the greatest city in Amphilochia and the one with the most powerful inhabitants. Many generations later, under *5* the pressure of misfortune, they brought in as fellow settlers Ambraciots, who lived on the borders of Amphilochia. It was from the Ambraciot settlers that the Argives learned to speak Greek, as they do now: the rest of the Amphilochians are barbarians. In time the Argives *6*

λουσιν οὖν τοὺς Ἀργείους οἱ Ἀμπρακιῶται χρόνῳ καὶ αὐτοὶ
7 ἴσχουσι τὴν πόλιν. οἱ δ' Ἀμφίλοχοι γενομένου τούτου
διδόασιν ἑαυτοὺς Ἀκαρνᾶσι, καὶ προσπαρακαλέσαντες ἀμφότεροι Ἀθηναίους, οἳ αὐτοῖς Φορμίωνά τε στρατηγὸν ἔπεμψαν
καὶ ναῦς τριάκοντα, ἀφικομένου [δὲ] τοῦ Φορμίωνος αἱροῦσι
κατὰ κράτος Ἄργος καὶ τοὺς Ἀμπρακιώτας ἠνδραπόδισαν,
8 κοινῇ τε ᾤκισαν αὐτὸ Ἀμφίλοχοι καὶ Ἀκαρνᾶνες. μετὰ δὲ
τοῦτο ἡ ξυμμαχία πρῶτον ἐγένετο Ἀθηναίοις καὶ Ἀκαρνᾶσιν.
9 οἱ δὲ Ἀμπρακιῶται τὴν μὲν ἔχθραν ἐς τοὺς Ἀργείους
ἀπὸ τοῦ ἀνδραποδισμοῦ σφῶν αὐτῶν πρῶτον ἐποιήσαντο.
ὕστερον δὲ ἐν τῷ πολέμῳ τήνδε τὴν στρατείαν ποιοῦνται
αὐτῶν τε καὶ Χαόνων καὶ ἄλλων τινῶν τῶν πλησιοχώρων
βαρβάρων· ἐλθόντες τε πρὸς τὸ Ἄργος τῆς μὲν χώρας
ἐκράτουν, τὴν δὲ πόλιν ὡς οὐκ ἐδύναντο ἑλεῖν προσβαλόντες,
ἀπεχώρησαν ἐπ' οἴκου καὶ διελύθησαν κατὰ ἔθνη. τοσαῦτα
μὲν ἐν τῷ θέρει ἐγένετο.
69 Τοῦ δ' ἐπιγιγνομένου χειμῶνος Ἀθηναῖοι ναῦς ἔστειλαν
εἴκοσι μὲν περὶ Πελοπόννησον καὶ Φορμίωνα στρατηγόν, ὃς
ὁρμώμενος ἐκ Ναυπάκτου φυλακὴν εἶχε μήτ' ἐκπλεῖν ἐκ
Κορίνθου καὶ τοῦ Κρισαίου κόλπου μηδένα μήτ' ἐσπλεῖν,
ἑτέρας δὲ ἓξ ἐπὶ Καρίας καὶ Λυκίας καὶ Μελήσανδρον
στρατηγόν, ὅπως ταῦτά τε ἀργυρολογῶσι καὶ τὸ λῃστικὸν
τῶν Πελοποννησίων μὴ ἐῶσιν αὐτόθεν ὁρμώμενον βλάπτειν
τὸν πλοῦν τῶν ὁλκάδων τῶν ἀπὸ Φασήλιδος καὶ Φοινίκης
2 καὶ τῆς ἐκεῖθεν ἠπείρου. ἀναβὰς δὲ στρατιᾷ Ἀθηναίων τε
τῶν ἀπὸ τῶν νεῶν καὶ τῶν ξυμμάχων ἐς τὴν Λυκίαν ὁ
Μελήσανδρος ἀποθνῄσκει καὶ τῆς στρατιᾶς μέρος τι διέφθειρε
νικηθεὶς μάχῃ.
70 Τοῦ δ' αὐτοῦ χειμῶνος οἱ Ποτειδεᾶται ἐπειδὴ οὐκέτι
ἐδύναντο πολιορκούμενοι ἀντέχειν, ἀλλ' αἵ τε ἐς τὴν Ἀττικὴν
ἐσβολαὶ Πελοποννησίων οὐδὲν μᾶλλον ἀπανίστασαν τοὺς
Ἀθηναίους ὅ τε σῖτος ἐπελελοίπει, καὶ ἄλλα τε πολλὰ
ἐπεγεγένητο αὐτόθι ἤδη βρώσεως πέρι ἀναγκαίας καί τινες
καὶ ἀλλήλων ἐγέγευντο, οὕτω δὴ λόγους προσφέρουσι περὶ

---

5. δὲ secl. Krüger.
33. αὐτόθι codd.: ἄτοπα Reiske, <καὶ> ἄτοπα Gomme, fortasse recte.

were driven out by the Ambraciots, who occupied the city themselves. When this happened, the Amphilochians entrusted themselves to the Acarnanians, and together they sent an appeal to the Athenians, who sent them thirty ships and Phormio as general. When Phormio arrived, they took Argos by force and enslaved the Ambraciots, and Argos was settled jointly by the Amphilochians and the Acarnanians. It was after this that the alliance was first made between Athens and the Acarnanians. The Ambraciots first became enemies of Argos as a result of this enslavement of their people. *7*

8
9

On this later occasion, during the war, the Ambraciots mounted this expedition of themselves, the Chaonians and some of the other neighbouring barbarians. They went to Argos, and got control of the countryside, but although they attacked the city they did not succeed in taking it, and so they returned home and dispersed among their separate peoples. Those were the events of the summer.

In the following winter the Athenians sent twenty ships round the Peloponnese with Phormio as general, to be based on Naupactus and to prevent any one from sailing out of or into Corinth and the Gulf of Crisa. They sent another six ships to Caria and Lycia, with Melesandrus as general, to raise money there, and to prevent raiders from the Peloponnese from using the region as a base to interfere with merchant shipping from Phaselis, Phoenicia and that part of the mainland. Melesandrus went inland into Lycia with a force of Athenians from the ships and of the allies, but he was defeated in battle, part of his force was lost and he himself was killed. **69**

2

In the same winter the people of Potidaea were unable to hold out any longer against the siege. The Peloponnesians' invasions of Attica showed no sign of making the Athenians withdraw. In addition, their food supplies had run out, and they had already had to resort for a minimum of nourishment to various things that could be found locally, including in some cases their fellow human beings. So they put forward an offer to come to terms **70**

125

ξυμβάσεως τοῖς στρατηγοῖς τῶν Ἀθηναίων τοῖς ἐπὶ σφίσι τεταγμένοις, Ξενοφῶντί τε τῷ Εὐριπίδου καὶ Ἑστιοδώρῳ
2 τῷ Ἀριστοκλείδου καὶ Φανομάχῳ τῷ Καλλιμάχου. οἱ δὲ προσεδέξαντο, ὁρῶντες μὲν τῆς στρατιᾶς τὴν ταλαιπωρίαν ἐν χωρίῳ χειμερινῷ, ἀνηλωκυίας δὲ ἤδη τῆς πόλεως δισχίλια
3 τάλαντα ἐς τὴν πολιορκίαν. ἐπὶ τοῖσδε οὖν ξυνέβησαν, ἐξελθεῖν αὐτοὺς καὶ παῖδας καὶ γυναῖκας καὶ τοὺς ἐπικούρους ξὺν ἑνὶ ἱματίῳ, γυναῖκας δὲ ξὺν δυοῖν, καὶ ἀργύριόν τι
4 ῥητὸν ἔχοντας ἐφόδιον. καὶ οἱ μὲν ὑπόσπονδοι ἐξῆλθον ἔς τε τὴν Χαλκιδικὴν καὶ ᾗ ἕκαστος ἐδύνατο· Ἀθηναῖοι δὲ τούς τε στρατηγοὺς ἐπῃτιάσαντο ὅτι ἄνευ αὐτῶν ξυνέβησαν (ἐνόμιζον γὰρ ἂν κρατῆσαι τῆς πόλεως ᾗ ἐβούλοντο), καὶ ὕστερον ἐποίκους ἔπεμψαν ἑαυτῶν ἐς τὴν Ποτείδαιαν καὶ κατῴκισαν. ταῦτα μὲν ἐν τῷ χειμῶνι ἐγένετο, καὶ [τὸ] δεύτερον ἔτος ἐτελεύτα τῷ πολέμῳ τῷδε ὃν Θουκυδίδης ξυνέγραψεν.

71 Τοῦ δ' ἐπιγιγνομένου θέρους οἱ Πελοποννήσιοι καὶ οἱ ξύμμαχοι ἐς μὲν τὴν Ἀττικὴν οὐκ ἐσέβαλον, ἐστράτευσαν δὲ ἐπὶ Πλάταιαν· ἡγεῖτο δὲ Ἀρχίδαμος ὁ Ζευξιδάμου Λακεδαιμονίων βασιλεύς. καὶ καθίσας τὸν στρατὸν ἔμελλε δῃώσειν τὴν γῆν· οἱ δὲ Πλαταιῆς εὐθὺς πρέσβεις πέμψαντες
2 πρὸς αὐτὸν ἔλεγον τοιάδε. " Ἀρχίδαμε καὶ Λακεδαιμόνιοι, οὐ δίκαια ποιεῖτε οὐδ' ἄξια οὔτε ὑμῶν οὔτε πατέρων ὧν ἐστέ, ἐς γῆν τὴν Πλαταιῶν στρατεύοντες. Παυσανίας γὰρ ὁ Κλεομβρότου Λακεδαιμόνιος ἐλευθερώσας τὴν Ἑλλάδα ἀπὸ τῶν Μήδων μετὰ Ἑλλήνων τῶν ἐθελησάντων ξυνάρασθαι τὸν κίνδυνον τῆς μάχης ἣ παρ' ἡμῖν ἐγένετο, θύσας ἐν τῇ Πλαταιῶν ἀγορᾷ ἱερὰ Διὶ ἐλευθερίῳ καὶ ξυγκαλέσας πάντας τοὺς ξυμμάχους ἀπεδίδου Πλαταιεῦσι γῆν καὶ πόλιν τὴν σφετέραν ἔχοντας αὐτονόμους οἰκεῖν, στρατεῦσαί τε μηδένα ποτὲ ἀδίκως ἐπ' αὐτοὺς μηδ' ἐπὶ δουλείᾳ· εἰ δὲ μή,

---

14. τὸ secl. Poppo.

with the Athenian generals appointed against them, Xenophon son of Euripides, Hestiodorus son of Aristoclides and Phanomachus son of Callimachus. They accepted the offer, taking into account the sufferings of their own force in a locality exposed to the winter, and the fact that Athens had already spent two thousand talents on the siege. The terms of the agreement were that the men, children, women and mercenaries should leave the city, with one outer garment each (but two for the women), and with a fixed sum of money for their journey. So the people departed under truce, to Chalcidice and wherever each of them could go. The Athenians found fault with the generals for making the agreement without their permission, since they thought they could have got control of the city on whatever terms they liked. Subsequently they sent some of their own people to occupy Potidaea, and settled them there. That is what happened in the winter; and so ended the second year of this war of which Thucydides wrote the history.

In the following summer the Peloponnesians and their allies did not invade Attica, but mounted a campaign against Plataea. They were commanded by Archidamus son of Zeuxidamus, king of Sparta. When he had taken up position with his army, and was preparing to lay waste the countryside, the Plataeans immediately sent envoys to him to speak as follows.

"Archidamus and Spartans, in campaigning against the land of Plataea you are acting wrongly, and in a manner unworthy of yourselves and the fathers from whom you are descended. When Pausanias son of Cleombrotus, of Sparta, together with the Greeks who were willing to join in the dangerous battle fought in our territory, had liberated Greece from the Medes, he made sacrifice to Zeus the god of freedom in the main square of Plataea, called together all the allies, and gave back to the Plataeans the right to occupy their own land and city and live there in independence; no one was ever to campaign against them unjustly, or in order to subject them, and if any one did so the allies who were present were to defend them with

3 ἀμύνειν τοὺς παρόντας ξυμμάχους κατὰ δύναμιν. τάδε μὲν ἡμῖν πατέρες οἱ ὑμέτεροι ἔδοσαν ἀρετῆς ἕνεκα καὶ προθυμίας τῆς ἐν ἐκείνοις τοῖς κινδύνοις γενομένης, ὑμεῖς δὲ τἀναντία δρᾶτε· μετὰ γὰρ Θηβαίων τῶν ἡμῖν ἐχθίστων ἐπὶ δουλείᾳ
4 τῇ ἡμετέρᾳ ἥκετε. μάρτυρας δὲ θεοὺς τούς τε ὁρκίους τότε γενομένους ποιούμενοι καὶ τοὺς ὑμετέρους πατρῴους καὶ ἡμετέρους ἐγχωρίους, λέγομεν ὑμῖν γῆν τὴν Πλαταιίδα μὴ ἀδικεῖν μηδὲ παραβαίνειν τοὺς ὅρκους, ἐᾶν δὲ οἰκεῖν αὐτονόμους καθάπερ Παυσανίας ἐδικαίωσεν."

72 Τοσαῦτα εἰπόντων τῶν Πλαταιῶν Ἀρχίδαμος ὑπολαβὼν εἶπεν. " δίκαια λέγετε, ὦ ἄνδρες Πλαταιῆς, ἢν ποιῆτε ὁμοῖα τοῖς λόγοις. καθάπερ γὰρ Παυσανίας ὑμῖν παρέδωκεν, αὐτοί τε αὐτονομεῖσθε καὶ τοὺς ἄλλους ξυνελευθεροῦτε, ὅσοι μετασχόντες τῶν τότε κινδύνων ὑμῖν τε ξυνώμοσαν καὶ εἰσὶ νῦν ὑπ' Ἀθηναίοις, παρασκευή τε τοσήδε καὶ πόλεμος γεγένηται αὐτῶν ἕνεκα καὶ τῶν ἄλλων ἐλευθερώσεως. ἧς μάλιστα μὲν μετασχόντες καὶ αὐτοὶ ἐμμείνατε τοῖς ὅρκοις· εἰ δὲ μή, ἅπερ καὶ πρότερον ἤδη προυκαλεσάμεθα, ἡσυχίαν ἄγετε νεμόμενοι τὰ ὑμέτερα αὐτῶν, καὶ ἔστε μηδὲ μεθ' ἑτέρων, δέχεσθε δὲ ἀμφοτέρους φίλους, ἐπὶ πολέμῳ δὲ
2 μηδετέρους. καὶ τάδε ἡμῖν ἀρκέσει." ὁ μὲν Ἀρχίδαμος τοσαῦτα εἶπεν· οἱ δὲ Πλαταιῶν πρέσβεις ἀκούσαντες ταῦτα ἐσῆλθον ἐς τὴν πόλιν, καὶ τῷ πλήθει τὰ ῥηθέντα κοινώσαντες ἀπεκρίναντο αὐτῷ ὅτι ἀδύνατα σφίσιν εἴη ποιεῖν ἃ προκαλεῖται ἄνευ Ἀθηναίων (παῖδες γὰρ σφῶν καὶ γυναῖκες παρ' ἐκείνοις εἶεν), δεδιέναι δὲ καὶ περὶ τῇ πάσῃ πόλει μὴ ἐκείνων ἀποχωρησάντων Ἀθηναῖοι ἐλθόντες σφίσιν οὐκ ἐπιτρέπωσιν, ἢ Θηβαῖοι, ὡς ἔνορκοι ὄντες κατὰ τὸ ἀμφοτέρους δέχεσθαι, αὖθις σφῶν τὴν πόλιν πειράσωσι καταλα-
3 βεῖν. ὁ δὲ θαρσύνων αὐτοὺς πρὸς ταῦτα ἔφη· "ὑμεῖς δὲ πόλιν μὲν καὶ οἰκίας ἡμῖν παράδοτε τοῖς Λακεδαιμονίοις, καὶ γῆς ὅρους ἀποδείξατε καὶ δένδρα ἀριθμῷ τὰ ὑμέτερα

all their strength. This is what your fathers granted to us on account of the courage and spirit which we showed at that moment of danger, but what you are doing now is the opposite: you have come against us with the Thebans, our greatest enemies, in order to subject us. We call to witness the gods who were invoked in the oaths then, your ancestral gods and our local gods, and we call on you not to do wrong against the land of Plataea, and not to break your oaths, but to allow us to live in independence as Pausanias judged right." 3

4

When the Plataeans had said that, Archidamus spoke in reply. 72

"What you say is right, men of Plataea, if your actions match your words. As Pausanias granted to you, enjoy independence yourselves, and join in liberating the others who on that occasion shared in the danger and joined in swearing the oaths to you, and who are now in the power of Athens. It is to liberate them and the others that we have assembled this great force and gone to war. The best policy for you is to join with us and abide by your oaths. Or, if you will not do that, act as we have already called on you to do: remain neutral, attending to your own affairs and not joining either side; receive both as friends, but neither for purposes of war. Even that will satisfy us."

That is what Archidamus said. When the Plataean envoys had heard it, they entered the city and communicated what had been said to the people. They replied that they were unable to act as Archidamus demanded without the approval of Athens, since their children and women were there. Also they were afraid for their whole city: after the Spartans had withdrawn, the Athenians might come and not allow them to remain neutral; or else the Thebans, who would be covered by the oath to receive both sides, might again try to get possession of their city. 2

To reassure them Archidamus said in answer to those points, "You must entrust your city and your houses to us Spartans, and indicate the boundaries of your territory and the number of your trees and anything else that can 3

καὶ ἄλλο εἴ τι δυνατὸν ἐς ἀριθμὸν ἐλθεῖν· αὐτοὶ δὲ μεταχωρήσατε ὅποι βούλεσθε, ἕως ἂν ὁ πόλεμος ᾖ· ἐπειδὰν δὲ παρέλθῃ, ἀποδώσομεν ὑμῖν ἃ ἂν παραλάβωμεν. μέχρι δὲ τοῦδε ἕξομεν παρακαταθήκην, ἐργαζόμενοι καὶ φορὰν 73 φέροντες ἣ ἂν ὑμῖν μέλλῃ ἱκανὴ ἔσεσθαι." οἱ δ' ἀκούσαντες ἐσῆλθον αὖθις ἐς τὴν πόλιν, καὶ βουλευσάμενοι μετὰ τοῦ πλήθους ἔλεξαν ὅτι βούλονται ἃ προκαλεῖται Ἀθηναίοις κοινῶσαι πρῶτον, καὶ ἢν πείθωσιν αὐτούς, ποιεῖν ταῦτα· μέχρι δὲ τούτου σπείσασθαι σφίσιν ἐκέλευον καὶ τὴν γῆν μὴ δῃοῦν. ὁ δὲ ἡμέρας τε ἐσπείσατο ἐν αἷς εἰκὸς ἦν 2 κομισθῆναι, καὶ τὴν γῆν οὐκέτι ἔτεμνεν. ἐλθόντες δὲ οἱ [Πλαταιῆς] πρέσβεις ὡς τοὺς Ἀθηναίους καὶ βουλευσάμενοι μετ' αὐτῶν πάλιν ἦλθον ἀπαγγέλλοντες τοῖς ἐν τῇ πόλει 3 τοιάδε. " οὔτ' ἐν τῷ πρὸ τοῦ χρόνῳ, ὦ ἄνδρες Πλαταιῆς, ἀφ' οὗ ξύμμαχοι ἐγενόμεθα, Ἀθηναῖοί φασιν ἐν οὐδενὶ ὑμᾶς προέσθαι ἀδικουμένους οὔτε νῦν περιόψεσθαι, βοηθήσειν δὲ κατὰ δύναμιν. ἐπισκήπτουσί τε ὑμῖν πρὸς τῶν ὅρκων οὓς οἱ πατέρες ὤμοσαν μηδὲν νεωτερίζειν περὶ τὴν 74 ξυμμαχίαν." τοιαῦτα τῶν πρέσβεων ἀπαγγειλάντων οἱ Πλαταιῆς ἐβουλεύσαντο Ἀθηναίους μὴ προδιδόναι, ἀλλ' ἀνέχεσθαι καὶ γῆν τεμνομένην, εἰ δεῖ, ὁρῶντας καὶ ἄλλο πάσχοντας ὅτι ἂν ξυμβαίνῃ· ἐξελθεῖν τε μηδένα ἔτι, ἀλλ' ἀπὸ τοῦ τείχους ἀποκρίνασθαι ὅτι ἀδύνατα σφίσι ποιεῖν 2 ἐστὶν ἃ Λακεδαιμόνιοι προκαλοῦνται. ὡς δὲ ἀπεκρίναντο, ἐντεῦθεν δὴ πρῶτον μὲν ἐς ἐπιμαρτυρίαν καὶ θεῶν καὶ ἡρώων τῶν ἐγχωρίων Ἀρχίδαμος ὁ βασιλεὺς κατέστη, λέγων ὧδε· 3 "θεοὶ ὅσοι γῆν τὴν Πλαταιίδα ἔχετε καὶ ἥρωες, ξυνίστορες ἔστε ὅτι οὔτε τὴν ἀρχὴν ἀδίκως, ἐκλιπόντων δὲ τῶνδε προτέρων τὸ ξυνώμοτον, ἐπὶ γῆν τήνδε ἤλθομεν, ἐν ᾗ οἱ πατέρες ἡμῶν εὐξάμενοι ὑμῖν Μήδων ἐκράτησαν καὶ παρέσχετε αὐτὴν εὐμενῆ ἐναγωνίσασθαι τοῖς Ἕλλησιν, οὔτε νῦν, ἤν τι ποιῶμεν, ἀδικήσομεν· προκαλεσάμενοι γὰρ πολλὰ καὶ εἰκότα οὐ τυγχάνομεν. ξυγγνώμονες δὲ ἔστε τῆς μὲν ἀδικίας κολάζεσθαι τοῖς ὑπάρχουσι προτέροις, τῆς δὲ τιμω-

---

11. οὐκέτι Π³⁴: οὐκ codd., Dion. Hal. 904. *Thuc.* 36.
12. Πλαταιῆς secl. Stuart Jones.
16. ὑμᾶς codd., Dion. Hal.: ἡμᾶς rec., Π³⁴.
27–8. ξυνίστορες ἔστε M F, cf. ξυγγνώμονες ἔστε infra: ξυνίστορές ἐστε cett., Dion. Hal. 905. *Thuc.* 36.

be quantified. You yourselves must withdraw, wherever you like, for the duration of the war. When the war is over, we shall give back to you whatever we have received: until then we shall hold it in trust, working it, and handing over such revenue as shall be sufficient for you."

On hearing this, the men went inside the city again and discussed the matter with the people. They replied that they wished first to communicate his demands to the Athenians, and they would act in that way if the Athenians agreed; until then, they urged the Spartans to make a truce with them and not ravage their land. He made a truce for the number of days the journey should take, and discontinued ravaging the land. The envoys went to the Athenians, discussed the matter with them, and came back with the following message to the men in the city.

"Men of Plataea, the Athenians say that in time past, since we became allies, they have never abandoned you to injustice; and they will not look on now, but will help you with all their might. They charge you, by the oaths which your fathers swore, not to depart in any respect from the alliance."

When the envoys brought back this message, the Plataeans decided not to let the Athenians down, but to hold out, and if necessary watch their land being ravaged and suffer whatever else might happen to them. No one would now go outside, but they would reply from the wall that they were unable to act as the Spartans demanded.

When they had replied, Archidamus' first move was to call the local gods and heroes to witness. He said, "You gods and heroes who possess the land of Plataea, be my witnesses that we did not at first come unjustly against this land in which our fathers made their prayers to you and defeated the Medes, this land which you made auspicious for the Greeks to contend in, but these men were the first to break the oath. Neither shall we be doing wrong if we take action now, for we have put forward many fair proposals and have not obtained what we asked. Grant that those who were the first to commit wrong may be punished for it, and that those who lawfully seek to exact

ρίας τυγχάνειν τοῖς ἐπιφέρουσι νομίμως."

75 Τοσαῦτα ἐπιθειάσας καθίστη ἐς πόλεμον τὸν στρατόν, καὶ πρῶτον μὲν περιεσταύρωσαν αὐτοὺς τοῖς δένδρεσιν ἃ ἔκοψαν, τοῦ μηδένα ἐπεξιέναι, ἔπειτα χῶμα ἔχουν πρὸς τὴν πόλιν, ἐλπίζοντες ταχίστην αἵρεσιν ἔσεσθαι αὐτῶν
2 στρατεύματος τοσούτου ἐργαζομένου. ξύλα μὲν οὖν τέμνοντες ἐκ τοῦ Κιθαιρῶνος παρῳκοδόμουν ἑκατέρωθεν, φορμηδὸν ἀντὶ τοίχων τιθέντες, ὅπως μὴ διαχέοιτο ἐπὶ πολὺ τὸ χῶμα· ἐφόρουν δὲ ὕλην ἐς αὐτὸ καὶ λίθους καὶ γῆν καὶ
3 εἴ τι ἄλλο ἀνύτειν μέλλοι ἐπιβαλλόμενον. ἡμέρας δὲ ἔχουν †ἑβδομήκοντα† καὶ νύκτας ξυνεχῶς, διῃρημένοι κατ᾽ ἀναπαύλας, ὥστε τοὺς μὲν φέρειν, τοὺς δὲ ὕπνον τε καὶ σῖτον αἱρεῖσθαι· Λακεδαιμονίων τε οἱ ξεναγοὶ ἑκάστης
4 πόλεως ξυνεφεστῶτες ἠνάγκαζον ἐς τὸ ἔργον. οἱ δὲ Πλαταιῆς ὁρῶντες τὸ χῶμα αἱρόμενον, ξύλινον τεῖχος ξυνθέντες καὶ ἐπιστήσαντες τῷ ἑαυτῶν τείχει ᾗ προσεχοῦτο, ἐσῳκοδόμουν ἐς αὐτὸ πλίνθους ἐκ τῶν ἐγγὺς οἰκιῶν καθαι-
5 ροῦντες. ξύνδεσμος δ᾽ ἦν αὐτοῖς τὰ ξύλα, τοῦ μὴ ὑψηλὸν γιγνόμενον ἀσθενὲς εἶναι τὸ οἰκοδόμημα, καὶ προκαλύμματα εἶχε δέρσεις καὶ διφθέρας, ὥστε τοὺς ἐργαζομένους καὶ τὰ ξύλα μήτε πυρφόροις οἰστοῖς βάλλεσθαι ἐν ἀσφαλείᾳ τε
6 εἶναι. ἤρετο δὲ τὸ ὕψος τοῦ τείχους μέγα, καὶ τὸ χῶμα οὐ σχολαίτερον ἀντανῄει αὐτῷ. καὶ οἱ Πλαταιῆς τοιόνδε τι ἐπινοοῦσιν· διελόντες τοῦ τείχους ᾗ προσέπιπτε τὸ χῶμα
76 ἐσεφόρουν τὴν γῆν. οἱ δὲ Πελοποννήσιοι αἰσθόμενοι ἐν ταρσοῖς καλάμου πηλὸν ἐνίλλοντες ἐσέβαλλον ἐς τὸ διῃρη-
2 μένον, ὅπως μὴ διαχεόμενον ὥσπερ ἡ γῆ φοροῖτο. οἱ δὲ ταύτῃ ἀποκληόμενοι τοῦτο μὲν ἐπέσχον, ὑπόνομον δὲ ἐκ τῆς πόλεως ὀρύξαντες καὶ ξυντεκμηράμενοι ὑπὸ τὸ χῶμα

---

4. ἐπεξιέναι C: ἔτι ἐπεξιέναι G ac, ἔτι ἐξιέναι cett., [ἔτι] ἐξιέναι Gomme.
13. ξεναγοὶ cett.: ξεναγοὶ καὶ C G.
14. ξυνεφεστῶτες cett.: ἐφεστῶτες C G P, ‹οἱ› ἐφεστῶτες Hude.

vengeance may obtain it."

After this invocation of the gods, he set the army to prosecuting the war. First they erected a stockade round the Plataeans with the trees which they cut down, so that no one could come out to attack them. Then they built up a mound against the city, hoping that with so large a force employed on the work they would capture it very quickly. They cut down timber from Mount Cithaeron and built this up against the mound on each side, laying it in a lattice-pattern, to serve as a containing-wall and prevent the mound from spreading out to a great distance. In it they incorporated brushwood, stones, earth and anything else which would help them to finish the job. They continued to heap up the mound without interruption for †seventy† days and nights, dividing the work to give men a break, so that some were working while others were sleeping and eating. The Spartans' *xenagoi* placed in charge of each city compelled the men to persevere in the work.

When the Plataeans saw the mound rising, they put together a wooden wall, which they placed on top of their own wall where the mound was being raised against it, and they built into it bricks which they tore down from the houses nearby. They used the timber as a framework, so that the structure should not become weak as it grew in height, and in front they put a screen of skins and hides to protect the workmen and the timber against harm from flaming arrows. The wall was carried up to a great height, and the mound was built up no less energetically opposite it.

The Plataeans also thought of a clever device: they made a breach in their wall where the mound fell against it, and carried the earth inside. The Peloponnesians discovered this, and they worked clay into a framework of reeds and inserted that into the gap, so that it could not be loosened and removed as the earth had been. The Plataeans abandoned that device when they were frustrated in this way, but instead they dug a tunnel out from the city, calculating where it should go under the mound, and

133

ὑφεῖλκον αὖθις παρὰ σφᾶς τὸν χοῦν· καὶ ἐλάνθανον ἐπὶ πολὺ τοὺς ἔξω, ὥστε ἐπιβάλλοντας ἧσσον ἀνύτειν ὑπαγομένου αὐτοῖς κάτωθεν τοῦ χώματος καὶ ἱζάνοντος αἰεὶ ἐπὶ τὸ κενούμενον. δεδιότες δὲ μὴ οὐδ' οὕτω δύνωνται ὀλίγοι πρὸς πολλοὺς ἀντέχειν, προσεπεξηῦρον τόδε· τὸ μὲν μέγα οἰκοδόμημα ἐπαύσαντο ἐργαζόμενοι τὸ κατὰ τὸ χῶμα, ἔνθεν δὲ καὶ ἔνθεν αὐτοῦ ἀρξάμενοι ἀπὸ τοῦ βραχέος τείχους ἐκ τοῦ ἐντὸς μηνοειδὲς ἐς τὴν πόλιν ἐσῳκοδόμουν, ὅπως, εἰ τὸ μέγα τεῖχος ἁλίσκοιτο, τοῦτ' ἀντέχοι, καὶ δέοι τοὺς ἐναντίους αὖθις πρὸς αὐτὸ χοῦν καὶ προχωροῦντας ἔσω διπλάσιόν τε πόνον ἔχειν καὶ ἐν ἀμφιβόλῳ μᾶλλον γίγνεσθαι. ἅμα δὲ τῇ χώσει καὶ μηχανὰς προσῆγον οἱ Πελοποννήσιοι τῇ πόλει, μίαν μὲν ἣ τοῦ μεγάλου οἰκοδομήματος κατὰ τὸ χῶμα προσαχθεῖσα ἐπὶ μέγα τε κατέσεισε καὶ τοὺς Πλαταιᾶς ἐφόβησεν, ἄλλας δὲ ἄλλῃ τοῦ τείχους, ἃς βρόχους τε περιβάλλοντες ἀνέκλων οἱ Πλαταιῆς, καὶ δοκοὺς μεγάλας ἀρτήσαντες ἁλύσεσι μακραῖς σιδηραῖς ἀπὸ τῆς τομῆς ἑκατέρωθεν ἀπὸ κεραιῶν δύο ἐπικεκλιμένων καὶ ὑπερτεινουσῶν ὑπὲρ τοῦ τείχους ἀνελκύσαντες ἐγκαρσίας, ὁπότε προσπεσεῖσθαί πῃ μέλλοι ἡ μηχανή, ἀφίεσαν τὴν δοκὸν χαλαραῖς ταῖς ἁλύσεσι καὶ οὐ διὰ χειρὸς ἔχοντες, ἡ δὲ ῥύμη ἐμπίπτουσα ἀπεκαύλιζε τὸ προῦχον τῆς ἐμβολῆς.

77 Μετὰ δὲ τοῦτο οἱ Πελοποννήσιοι, ὡς αἵ τε μηχαναὶ οὐδὲν ὠφέλουν καὶ τῷ χώματι τὸ ἀντιτείχισμα ἐγίγνετο, νομίσαντες ἄπορον εἶναι ἀπὸ τῶν παρόντων δεινῶν ἑλεῖν τὴν πόλιν πρὸς τὴν περιτείχισιν παρεσκευάζοντο. πρότερον δὲ πυρὶ ἔδοξεν αὐτοῖς πειρᾶσαι εἰ δύναιντο πνεύματος γενο-

---

8. ἐσῳκοδόμουν C G P: προσῳκοδόμουν cett.

once more proceeded to steal away the material into the city. For a long time the men outside failed to detect this tunnel, and so they continued to pile earth on but made no progress, since the mound was being eroded from below and kept settling into the space that was being emptied.

Even so, the Plataeans were afraid that, as a small number opposed to a large, they would be unable to hold out, and so in addition they resorted to another device. They stopped building their large structure opposite the mound, and beginning from each side of that they built a crescent-shaped wall projecting into the city on the inner side of the low wall, so that if the high wall were taken this one would hold. The enemy would then have to build up a mound once more against this wall, and because they were pushing inwards they would have twice as much work to do and would now be open to attack from both sides.

As well as building the mound, the Peloponnesians brought up machines against the city. One was brought up by the mound against the large structure and shook down a large part of it, terrifying the Plataeans. Others were used against other parts of the wall. The Plataeans fastened nooses round these to deflect them; and also they fitted large beams with long iron chains at each of their sawn ends, and hung these at right angles to the rams from two yard-arms resting on the wall and reaching out over it. Whenever a machine was about to strike anywhere they let the beam fall, with the chains not held in their hands but free, and it descended with great force and broke off the projecting part of the ram. Since they were achieving nothing with their machines, and their mound was being matched by the counter-fortification, the Peloponnesians reckoned that in the present difficult circumstances it would be impossible to take the city by force, and they turned to constructing a circumvallation.

First, however, they resolved on an attempt by fire, to see if, since the city was not large, they could set

μένου ἐπιφλέξαι τὴν πόλιν οὖσαν οὐ μεγάλην· πᾶσαν γὰρ
δὴ ἰδέαν ἐπενόουν, εἴ πως σφίσιν ἄνευ δαπάνης καὶ πολιορ-
3 κίας προσαχθείη. φοροῦντες δὲ ὕλης φακέλους παρέβαλον
ἀπὸ τοῦ χώματος ἐς τὸ μεταξὺ πρῶτον τοῦ τείχους καὶ τῆς
προσχώσεως, ταχὺ δὲ πλήρους γενομένου διὰ πολυχειρίαν
ἐπιπαρένησαν καὶ τῆς ἄλλης πόλεως ὅσον ἐδύναντο ἀπὸ
τοῦ μετεώρου πλεῖστον ἐπισχεῖν, ἐμβαλόντες δὲ πῦρ ξὺν
4 θείῳ καὶ πίσσῃ ἧψαν τὴν ὕλην. καὶ ἐγένετο φλὸξ τοσαύτη
ὅσην οὐδείς πω ἔς γε ἐκεῖνον τὸν χρόνον χειροποίητον
εἶδεν· ἤδη γὰρ ἐν ὄρεσιν ὕλη τριφθεῖσα ὑπ' ἀνέμων πρὸς
αὐτὴν ἀπὸ ταὐτομάτου πῦρ καὶ φλόγα ἀπ' αὐτοῦ ἀνῆκεν.
5 τοῦτο δὲ μέγα τε ἦν καὶ τοὺς Πλαταιᾶς τἆλλα διαφυγόντας
ἐλαχίστου ἐδέησε διαφθεῖραι· ἐντὸς γὰρ πολλοῦ χωρίου
τῆς πόλεως οὐκ ἦν πελάσαι, πνεῦμά τε εἰ ἐπεγένετο αὐτῇ
ἐπίφορον, ὅπερ καὶ ἤλπιζον οἱ ἐναντίοι, οὐκ ἂν διέφυγον.
6 νῦν δὲ καὶ τόδε λέγεται ξυμβῆναι, ὕδωρ ἐξ οὐρανοῦ πολὺ καὶ
βροντὰς γενομένας σβέσαι τὴν φλόγα καὶ οὕτω παυσθῆναι
τὸν κίνδυνον.

78 Οἱ δὲ Πελοποννήσιοι ἐπειδὴ καὶ τούτου διήμαρτον, μέρος
μέν τι καταλιπόντες τοῦ στρατοῦ, τὸ δὲ πλέον ἀφέντες
περιετείχιζον τὴν πόλιν κύκλῳ, διελόμενοι κατὰ πόλεις τὸ
χωρίον· τάφρος δὲ ἐντός τε ἦν καὶ ἔξωθεν ἐξ ἧς ἐπλινθεύ-
2 σαντο. καὶ ἐπειδὴ πᾶν ἐξείργαστο περὶ ἀρκτούρου ἐπιτολάς,
καταλιπόντες φυλακὰς τοῦ ἡμίσεος τείχους (τὸ δὲ ἥμισυ
Βοιωτοὶ ἐφύλασσον) ἀνεχώρησαν τῷ στρατῷ καὶ διελύθησαν
3 κατὰ πόλεις. Πλαταιῆς δὲ παῖδας μὲν καὶ γυναῖκας καὶ
τοὺς πρεσβυτάτους τε καὶ πλῆθος τὸ ἀχρεῖον τῶν ἀνθρώπων
πρότερον ἐκκεκομισμένοι ἦσαν ἐς τὰς Ἀθήνας, αὐτοὶ δὲ
ἐπολιορκοῦντο ἐγκαταλελειμμένοι τετρακόσιοι, Ἀθηναίων δὲ
4 ὀγδοήκοντα, γυναῖκες δὲ δέκα καὶ ἑκατὸν σιτοποιοί. τοσοῦτοι
ἦσαν οἱ ξύμπαντες ὅτε ἐς τὴν πολιορκίαν καθίσταντο, καὶ

---

16. ἐξ οὐρανοῦ om. C P, def. Gomme.

fire to it when a wind arose. For they contrived every kind of device in the hope of getting control of the city without the expense of a blockade. They brought bundles of brushwood, and started by throwing these from the mound into the gap between the wall and the heap of earth against it: since many men were engaged in the work, the gap was soon filled, and then they piled up the bundles against the rest of the city as far as they could reach from the top of the mound. Then they applied fire with sulphur and pitch, and set light to the wood. The result was the largest man-made conflagration that any one had ever seen up to that time (but previously in the mountains, when friction had been caused in timber by the winds, that had spontaneously produced a fire and flames rising from it). This was an enormous fire, and it should almost certainly have destroyed the Plataeans, though they had escaped the rest: a large part of the city became inaccessible, and if a wind had arisen to drive the fire on, as the enemy hoped, they would have been unable to escape. Yet it is said that what happened was that a thunderstorm brought a great deluge of rain from the heavens, so that the flames were quenched and the danger was removed.

When they had failed in this too, the Peloponnesians kept a small part of their army and dismissed the rest. They proceeded to build a circumvallation round the city, dividing up the territory by cities, and digging ditches both inside and outside from which they took the clay to make bricks. When it was all complete, about the time of the rising of Arcturus, the Peloponnesians left guards on half the wall, while the Boeotians mounted guard on the other half, and they withdrew with their army and dispersed among their separate cities. The Plataeans had already transported to Athens the children, the women, the oldest men and the large number of unfit in their population, and those left behind to withstand the blockade amounted to four hundred Plataeans, eighty Athenians, and a hundred and ten women to act as bakers. That was the total number when the blockade was set up,

137

ἄλλος οὐδεὶς ἦν ἐν τῷ τείχει οὔτε δοῦλος οὔτ' ἐλεύθερος. τοιαύτη μὲν ἡ Πλαταιῶν πολιορκία κατεσκευάσθη.

79 Τοῦ δ' αὐτοῦ θέρους καὶ ἅμα τῇ τῶν Πλαταιῶν ἐπιστρατείᾳ Ἀθηναῖοι δισχιλίοις ὁπλίταις ἑαυτῶν καὶ ἱππεῦσι διακοσίοις ἐπεστράτευσαν ἐπὶ Χαλκιδέας τοὺς ἐπὶ Θρᾴκης καὶ Βοττιαίους ἀκμάζοντος τοῦ σίτου· ἐστρατήγει δὲ Ξενοφῶν 2 ὁ Εὐριπίδου τρίτος αὐτός. ἐλθόντες δὲ ὑπὸ Σπάρτωλον τὴν Βοττικὴν τὸν σῖτον διέφθειρον. ἐδόκει δὲ καὶ προσχωρήσειν ἡ πόλις ὑπό τινων ἔνδοθεν πρασσόντων. προσπεμψάντων δὲ ἐς Ὄλυνθον τῶν οὐ ταῦτα βουλομένων ὁπλῖταί τε ἦλθον καὶ στρατιὰ ἐς φυλακήν· ἧς ἐπεξελθούσης ἐκ τῆς Σπαρτώλου 3 ἐς μάχην καθίστανται οἱ Ἀθηναῖοι ὑπ' αὐτῇ τῇ πόλει. καὶ οἱ μὲν ὁπλῖται τῶν Χαλκιδέων καὶ ἐπίκουροί τινες μετ' αὐτῶν νικῶνται ὑπὸ τῶν Ἀθηναίων καὶ ἀναχωροῦσιν ἐς τὴν Σπάρτωλον, οἱ δὲ ἱππῆς τῶν Χαλκιδέων καὶ ψιλοὶ νικῶσι 4 τοὺς τῶν Ἀθηναίων ἱππέας καὶ ψιλούς· εἶχον δέ τινας οὐ πολλοὺς πελταστὰς ἐκ τῆς Κρουσίδος γῆς καλουμένης. ἄρτι δὲ τῆς μάχης γεγενημένης ἐπιβοηθοῦσιν ἄλλοι πελτασταὶ 5 ἐκ τῆς Ὀλύνθου. καὶ οἱ ἐκ τῆς Σπαρτώλου ψιλοὶ ὡς εἶδον, θαρσήσαντες τοῖς τε προσγιγνομένοις καὶ ὅτι πρότερον οὐχ ἥσσηντο, ἐπιτίθενται αὖθις μετὰ τῶν Χαλκιδέων ἱππέων καὶ τῶν προσβοηθησάντων τοῖς Ἀθηναίοις· καὶ ἀναχωροῦσι πρὸς 6 τὰς δύο τάξεις ἃς κατέλιπον παρὰ τοῖς σκευοφόροις. καὶ ὁπότε μὲν ἐπίοιεν οἱ Ἀθηναῖοι, ἐνεδίδοσαν, ἀναχωροῦσι δ' ἐνέκειντο καὶ ἐσηκόντιζον. οἵ τε ἱππῆς τῶν Χαλκιδέων προσιππεύοντες ᾗ δοκοίη προσέβαλλον, καὶ οὐχ ἥκιστα φοβήσαντες ἔτρεψαν τοὺς Ἀθηναίους καὶ ἐπεδίωξαν ἐπὶ 7 πολύ. καὶ οἱ μὲν Ἀθηναῖοι ἐς τὴν Ποτείδαιαν καταφεύγουσι, καὶ ὕστερον τοὺς νεκροὺς ὑποσπόνδους κομισάμενοι ἐς τὰς Ἀθήνας ἀναχωροῦσι τῷ περιόντι τοῦ στρατοῦ· ἀπ-

---

8. διέφθειρον E F A B: διέφθειραν cett.
22. Ἀθηναίοις <κεκμηκόσι τε τῇ μάχῃ vel sim.> καὶ ἀναχωροῦσι Gomme, fortasse recte.
24. ἀναχωροῦσι B: ἀποχωροῦσι cett., Π²⁵.

and there was no one else, either slave or free, inside the city wall. Those were the arrangements for the blockade of Plataea.

79 In the same summer, and at the same time as the campaign against Plataea, when the corn was growing ripe, the Athenians sent out an expedition of two thousand of their own hoplites and two hundred cavalry against the Thraceward Chalcidians and the Bottiaeans; Xenophon son of Euripides and two others were the generals. On arriv- 2 ing before Spartolus, in the Bottiaeans' territory, they proceeded to destroy the standing corn, and it seemed likely that through the agency of certain men inside the city it would actually go over to them. However, those who took the opposite line sent to Olynthus, and obtained hoplites and a garrison force. When these came out from Spartolus to attack, the Athenians joined battle with them directly outside the city. The Chalcidian hoplites, 3 and some mercenaries with them, were defeated by the Athenians and withdrew into Spartolus; but the Chalcidian cavalry and light-armed defeated the Athenian cavalry and light-armed. (The Athenians had a small force of peltasts 4 from the land called Crusis.)

Just after the battle had ended, more peltasts arrived from Olynthus to help. On seeing them, the light- 5 armed from Spartolus were encouraged both by this addition to their strength and by the fact that they had not been defeated before. They therefore joined the Chalcidian cavalry and the new arrivals in a fresh attack on the Athenians, and the Athenians withdrew towards the two regiments which they had left by the baggage-carriers. Whenever the Athenians attacked, the Chalcidians gave 6 ground, but when the Athenians withdrew, the Chalcidians pressed on them and hurled javelins at them. The Chalcidian cavalry rode up and attacked the Athenians whenever they wished, and this particularly terrified the Athenians, who were routed and pursued for a considerable distance. They took refuge in Potidaea, and afterwards they 7 recovered their dead under a truce and returned to Athens with what remained of their force: they had lost four

ἔθανον δὲ αὐτῶν τριάκοντα καὶ τετρακόσιοι καὶ οἱ στρατηγοὶ πάντες. οἱ δὲ Χαλκιδῆς καὶ Βοττιαῖοι τροπαῖόν τε ἔστησαν καὶ τοὺς νεκροὺς τοὺς αὑτῶν ἀνελόμενοι διελύθησαν κατὰ πόλεις.

80 Τοῦ δ' αὐτοῦ θέρους, οὐ πολλῷ ὕστερον τούτων, Ἀμπρακιῶται καὶ Χάονες βουλόμενοι Ἀκαρνανίαν τὴν πᾶσαν καταστρέψασθαι καὶ Ἀθηναίων ἀποστῆσαι πείθουσι Λακεδαιμονίους ναυτικόν τε παρασκευάσασθαι ἐκ τῆς ξυμμαχίδος καὶ ὁπλίτας χιλίους πέμψαι ἐπ' Ἀκαρνανίαν, λέγοντες ὅτι, ἢν ναυσὶ καὶ πεζῷ ἅμα μετὰ σφῶν ἔλθωσιν, ἀδυνάτων ὄντων ξυμβοηθεῖν τῶν ἀπὸ θαλάσσης Ἀκαρνάνων ῥᾳδίως Ἀκαρνανίαν σχόντες καὶ τῆς Ζακύνθου καὶ Κεφαλληνίας κρατήσουσι, καὶ ὁ περίπλους οὐκέτι ἔσοιτο Ἀθηναίοις ὁμοίως περὶ Πελοπόννησον· ἐλπίδα δ' εἶναι καὶ Ναύπακ-
2 τον λαβεῖν. οἱ δὲ Λακεδαιμόνιοι πεισθέντες Κνῆμον μὲν ναύαρχον ἔτι ὄντα καὶ τοὺς ὁπλίτας ἐπὶ ναυσὶν ὀλίγαις εὐθὺς πέμπουσι, τῷ δὲ ναυτικῷ περιήγγειλαν παρασκευα-
3 σαμένῳ ὡς τάχιστα πλεῖν ἐς Λευκάδα. ἦσαν δὲ Κορίνθιοι ξυμπροθυμούμενοι μάλιστα τοῖς Ἀμπρακιώταις ἀποίκοις οὖσιν. καὶ τὸ μὲν ναυτικὸν ἔκ τε Κορίνθου καὶ Σικυῶνος καὶ τῶν ταύτῃ χωρίων ἐν παρασκευῇ ἦν, τὸ δ' ἐκ Λευκάδος καὶ Ἀνακτορίου καὶ Ἀμπρακίας πρότερον ἀφικόμενον ἐν
4 Λευκάδι περιέμενεν. Κνῆμος δὲ καὶ οἱ μετ' αὐτοῦ χίλιοι ὁπλῖται ἐπειδὴ ἐπεραιώθησαν λαθόντες Φορμίωνα, ὃς ἦρχε τῶν εἴκοσι νεῶν τῶν Ἀττικῶν αἳ περὶ Ναύπακτον ἐφρού-
5 ρουν, εὐθὺς παρεσκευάζοντο τὴν κατὰ γῆν στρατείαν. καὶ αὐτῷ παρῆσαν Ἑλλήνων μὲν Ἀμπρακιῶται καὶ Λευκάδιοι καὶ Ἀνακτόριοι καὶ οὓς αὐτὸς ἔχων ἦλθε χίλιοι Πελοποννησίων, βάρβαροι δὲ Χάονες χίλιοι ἀβασίλευτοι, ὧν ἡγοῦντο ἐπετησίῳ προστατείᾳ ἐκ τοῦ ἀρχικοῦ γένους Φώτυος καὶ Νικάνωρ. ξυνεστρατεύοντο δὲ μετὰ Χαόνων καὶ Θεσπρωτοὶ
6 ἀβασίλευτοι. Μολοσσοὺς δὲ ἦγε καὶ Ἀτιντᾶνας Σαβύλινθος ἐπίτροπος ὢν Θάρυπος τοῦ βασιλέως ἔτι παιδὸς ὄντος, καὶ Παραναίους Ὄροιδος βασιλεύων. Ὀρέσται δὲ χίλιοι, ὧν ἐβασίλευεν Ἀντίοχος, μετὰ Παραναίων ξυνεστρατεύοντο

---

30. Φώτυος codd.: Φώτιος C pc G pc, edd. plerique.

hundred and thirty men, and all their generals. The Chalcidians and Bottiaeans set up a trophy, recovered their own dead, and dispersed to their separate cities.

In the same summer, not long afterwards, the Ambraciots and Chaonians, who wanted to get control of the whole of Acarnania and detach it from Athens, persuaded the Spartans to prepare a fleet from their alliance and send a thousand hoplites against Acarnania. They argued that if the Spartans joined them, with ships and a land force simultaneously, the coastal Acarnanians would be unable to rally to the defence: they could easily hold Acarnania and then capture Zacynthus and Cephallenia, and it would no longer be easy for the Athenians to sail round the Peloponnese as it was at present. There was a hope that they might also take Naupactus. The Spartans agreed. They immediately sent a few ships with Cnemus, still in office as navarch, and the hoplites, and they gave orders for the fleet to be prepared and to sail to Leucas as soon as possible. Corinth, as the state from which Ambracia had been settled, was particularly enthusiastic in support. While the ships from Corinth, Sicyon and that region were being made ready, those of Leucas, Anactorium and Ambracia assembled first at Leucas and waited there. 80

2

3

Cnemus and the thousand hoplites with him made their voyage without being detected by Phormio, who was in command of the twenty Athenian ships on guard at Naupactus. They immediately began preparations for the campaign on land. The Greeks in Cnemus' force comprised Ambraciots, Leucadians, Anactorians and the thousand Peloponnesians whom he had brought. Of the barbarians, there were a thousand Chaonians (these have no king: their commanders were Photyus and Nicanor, men of the ruling clan to whom the annual presidency had fallen); Thesprotians joining with the Chaonians (these have no king); Molossians and Atintanians (commanded by Sabylinthus, guardian of king Tharyps, who was still a boy); Paravaeans (commanded by king Oroedus); and a thousand Orestians, who came with the Paravaeans as their king Antiochus had entrusted them 4

5

6

7 Ὀροίδῳ Ἀντιόχου ἐπιτρέψαντος. ἔπεμψε δὲ καὶ Περδίκκας κρύφα τῶν Ἀθηναίων χιλίους Μακεδόνων, οἳ ὕστερον
8 ἦλθον. τούτῳ τῷ στρατῷ ἐπορεύετο Κνῆμος οὐ περιμείνας
τὸ ἀπὸ Κορίνθου ναυτικόν, καὶ διὰ τῆς Ἀργείας ἰόντες
Λιμναίαν, κώμην ἀτείχιστον, ἐπόρθησαν. ἀφικνοῦνταί τε
ἐπὶ Στράτον, πόλιν μεγίστην τῆς Ἀκαρνανίας, νομίζοντες,
εἰ ταύτην πρώτην λάβοιεν, ῥᾳδίως ἂν σφίσι τἆλλα προσχωρῆσαι.

81 Ἀκαρνᾶνες δὲ αἰσθόμενοι κατά τε γῆν πολλὴν στρατιὰν
ἐσβεβληκυῖαν ἔκ τε θαλάσσης ναυσὶν ἅμα τοὺς πολεμίους
παρεσομένους, οὔτε ξυνεβοήθουν ἐφύλασσόν τε τὰ αὑτῶν
ἕκαστοι, παρά τε Φορμίωνα ἔπεμπον κελεύοντες ἀμύνειν·
ὁ δὲ ἀδύνατος ἔφη εἶναι ναυτικοῦ ἐκ Κορίνθου μέλλοντος
2 ἐκπλεῖν Ναύπακτον ἐρήμην ἀπολιπεῖν. οἱ δὲ Πελοποννήσιοι
καὶ οἱ ξύμμαχοι τρία τέλη ποιήσαντες σφῶν αὐτῶν ἐχώρουν
πρὸς τὴν τῶν Στρατίων πόλιν, ὅπως ἐγγὺς στρατοπεδευσά-
μενοι, εἰ μὴ λόγοις πείθοιεν, ἔργῳ πειρῷντο τοῦ τείχους.
3 καὶ μέσον μὲν ἔχοντες προσῇσαν Χάονες καὶ οἱ ἄλλοι
βάρβαροι, ἐκ δεξιᾶς δ' αὐτῶν Λευκάδιοι καὶ Ἀνακτόριοι
καὶ οἱ μετὰ τούτων, ἐν ἀριστερᾷ δὲ Κνῆμος καὶ οἱ Πελοποννήσιοι καὶ Ἀμπρακιῶται· διεῖχον δὲ πολὺ ἀπ' ἀλλήλων
4 καὶ ἔστιν ὅτε οὐδὲ ἑωρῶντο. καὶ οἱ μὲν Ἕλληνες τεταγμένοι τε προσῇσαν καὶ διὰ φυλακῆς ἔχοντες, ἕως ἐστρατο-
πεδεύσαντο ἐν ἐπιτηδείῳ· οἱ δὲ Χάονες σφίσι τε αὐτοῖς
πιστεύοντες καὶ ἀξιούμενοι ὑπὸ τῶν ἐκείνῃ ἠπειρωτῶν
μαχιμώτατοι εἶναι οὔτε ἐπέσχον τοῦ στρατοπέδον καταλαβεῖν, χωρήσαντές τε ῥύμῃ μετὰ τῶν ἄλλων βαρβάρων
ἐνόμισαν αὐτοβοεὶ ἂν τὴν πόλιν ἑλεῖν καὶ αὐτῶν τὸ ἔργον
5 γενέσθαι. γνόντες δ' αὐτοὺς οἱ Στράτιοι ἔτι προσιόντας
καὶ ἡγησάμενοι, μεμονωμένων εἰ κρατήσειαν, οὐκ ἂν ἔτι
σφίσι τοὺς Ἕλληνας ὁμοίως προσελθεῖν, προλοχίζουσι [δὴ]
τὰ περὶ τὴν πόλιν ἐνέδραις, καὶ ἐπειδὴ ἐγγὺς ἦσαν, ἔκ τε
τῆς πόλεως ὁμόσε χωρήσαντες καὶ ἐκ τῶν ἐνέδρων προσ-

---

7. ἂν om. C.
7—8. προσχωρῆσαι G pc rec. pc: προσχωρήσειν codd.
26. τοῦ Steup: τὸ codd.
31. δὴ C pc G (δὲ C ac?): om. cett.

to the command of Oroedus. In addition, Perdiccas sent a thousand Macedonians without letting the Athenians know, but these arrived too late. Without waiting for the fleet from Corinth, Cnemus set out with this force. They proceeded through the territory of Argos, and sacked Limnaea, an unfortified village. Then they went to Stratus, the largest city in Acarnania, thinking that if they could capture this first they would easily get possession of the rest. When the Acarnanians learned that a large army had invaded by land, and that also the enemy fleet was going to arrive by sea, they did not rally to support Stratus, but each community kept guard on its own territory. They sent to Phormio and urged him to come to their defence, but he replied that he could not abandon Naupactus while a fleet was planning to sail out from Corinth.

The Peloponnesians and their allies organised themselves in three divisions and advanced towards the city of Stratus, in order to camp near it and, if they could not win the people over by negotiation, act by making an attempt on the city wall. As they marched, the centre was occupied by the Chaonians and the other barbarians; on their right were the Leucadians, the Anactorians and the men with them; and on the left were Cnemus and the Peloponnesians, and also the Ambraciots. The three columns were some distance apart, at times not even within sight of one another. The Greeks marched in good order, keeping a look-out, and eventually pitched camp in a suitable position. The Chaonians, however, were full of self-confidence: they had the most warlike reputation in that part of the mainland, and they had no intention of making a camp, but advanced at a rush with the rest of the barbarians, thinking that they could capture the city instantly and claim the credit for the achievement.

The men of Stratus, realising that the Chaonians were still advancing, reckoned that if they could defeat them while they were isolated the Greeks would no longer be so eager to advance against them. They therefore set up ambushes around the city, and when the Chaonians were near they simultaneously advanced out of the city and at-

6 πίπτουσιν. καὶ ἐς φόβον καταστάντων διαφθείρονταί τε πολλοὶ τῶν Χαόνων, καὶ οἱ ἄλλοι βάρβαροι ὡς εἶδον αὐτοὺς 7 ἐνδόντας, οὐκέτι ὑπέμειναν, ἀλλ' ἐς φυγὴν κατέστησαν. τῶν δὲ Ἑλληνικῶν στρατοπέδων οὐδέτερον ᾔσθετο τῆς μάχης διὰ τὸ πολὺ προελθεῖν αὐτοὺς καὶ στρατόπεδον οἰηθῆναι 8 καταληψομένους ἐπείγεσθαι. ἐπεὶ δ' ἐνέκειντο φεύγοντες οἱ βάρβαροι, ἀνελάμβανόν τε αὐτοὺς καὶ ξυναγαγόντες τὰ στρατόπεδα ἡσύχαζον αὐτοῦ τὴν ἡμέραν, ἐς χεῖρας μὲν οὐκ ἰόντων σφίσι τῶν Στρατίων διὰ τὸ μήπω τοὺς ἄλλους Ἀκαρνᾶνας ξυμβεβοηθηκέναι, ἄπωθεν δὲ σφενδονώντων καὶ ἐς ἀπορίαν καθιστάντων· οὐ γὰρ ἦν ἄνευ ὅπλων κινηθῆναι. δοκοῦσι δὲ οἱ Ἀκαρνᾶνες κράτιστοι εἶναι τοῦτο ποιεῖν.

82 ἐπειδὴ δὲ νὺξ ἐγένετο, ἀναχωρήσας ὁ Κνῆμος τῇ στρατιᾷ κατὰ τάχος ἐπὶ τὸν Ἄναπον ποταμόν, ὃς ἀπέχει σταδίους ὀγδοήκοντα Στράτου, τούς τε νεκροὺς κομίζεται τῇ ὑστεραίᾳ ὑποσπόνδους, καὶ Οἰνιαδῶν ξυμπαραγενομένων κατὰ φιλίαν ἀναχωρεῖ παρ' αὐτοὺς πρὶν τὴν ξυμβοήθειαν ἐλθεῖν. κἀκεῖθεν ἐπ' οἴκου ἀπῆλθον ἕκαστοι. οἱ δὲ Στράτιοι τροπαῖον ἔστησαν τῆς μάχης τῆς πρὸς τοὺς βαρβάρους.

83 Τὸ δ' ἐκ τῆς Κορίνθου καὶ τῶν ἄλλων ξυμμάχων τῶν ἐκ τοῦ Κρισαίου κόλπου ναυτικόν, ὃ ἔδει παραγενέσθαι τῷ Κνήμῳ, ὅπως μὴ ξυμβοηθῶσιν οἱ ἀπὸ θαλάσσης ἄνω Ἀκαρνᾶνες, οὐ παραγίγνεται, ἀλλ' ἠναγκάσθησαν περὶ τὰς αὐτὰς ἡμέρας τῆς ἐν Στράτῳ μάχης ναυμαχῆσαι πρὸς Φορμίωνα καὶ τὰς εἴκοσι ναῦς τῶν Ἀθηναίων αἳ ἐφρούρουν ἐν 2 Ναυπάκτῳ. ὁ γὰρ Φορμίων παραπλέοντας αὐτοὺς ἔξω τοῦ 3 κόλπου ἐτήρει, βουλόμενος ἐν τῇ εὐρυχωρίᾳ ἐπιθέσθαι. οἱ δὲ Κορίνθιοι καὶ οἱ ξύμμαχοι ἔπλεον μὲν οὐχ ὡς ἐπὶ ναυμαχίᾳ, ἀλλὰ στρατιωτικώτερον παρεσκευασμένοι ἐς τὴν Ἀκαρνανίαν καὶ οὐκ ἂν οἰόμενοι πρὸς ἑπτὰ καὶ τεσσαράκοντα ναῦς τὰς σφετέρας τολμῆσαι τοὺς Ἀθηναίους εἴκοσι ταῖς ἑαυτῶν ναυμαχίαν ποιήσασθαι· ἐπειδὴ μέντοι ἀντιπαραπλέοντάς τε ἑώρων αὐτούς, παρὰ γῆν σφῶν κομιζομένων,

tacked them from the ambushes. The Chaonians were struck with terror, and many of them were killed; and when the rest of the barbarians witnessed their failure they did not stay but turned to flight. 6

Neither of the Greek camps knew about the battle, since the barbarians had gone a long way ahead: the Greeks imagined that they had pressed on to make a camp. When the fleeing barbarians descended on them, the Greeks took them in, amalgamated their two camps, and for that day stayed where they were without further action. The Stratians did not attack them at close quarters, since the rest of the Acarnanians had not yet come to support them, but they used their slings from a distance, and this caused great difficulty, since it made it impossible to move without armour. (The Acarnanians seem to be the most proficient at this kind of warfare.) When night fell, Cnemus withdrew rapidly with his army to the River Anapus, which is about eighty stades from Stratus. The next day he recovered his dead under a truce, and when in accordance with their friendship the men of Oeniadae joined him he retired into their territory before the enemy's reinforcements could arrive. From there they all returned to their own homes. The Stratians set up a trophy for their battle with the barbarians. 7 8

82

The naval force from Corinth and the other allies in the Gulf of Crisa, which was supposed to join Cnemus and prevent the Acarnanians on the coast from giving support inland, never arrived. About the same time as the battle at Stratus, this force was obliged to fight a naval battle against Phormio and the twenty Athenian ships keeping guard at Naupactus. Phormio wanted to make his attack in an open space, and watched as they sailed out of the gulf. The Corinthians and their allies were sailing with no expectation of a battle, but had equipped their ships more as transports for the voyage to Acarnania, not thinking that the Athenians with their twenty ships would dare to engage in battle against their own forty-seven. However, as they sailed along the Peloponnesian coast they saw the Athenians keeping pace with them; and when 83 2 3

καὶ ἐκ Πατρῶν τῆς Ἀχαΐας πρὸς τὴν ἀντιπέρας ἤπειρον διαβάλλοντες ἐπ' Ἀκαρνανίας κατεῖδον τοὺς Ἀθηναίους ἀπὸ τῆς Χαλκίδος καὶ τοῦ Εὐήνου ποταμοῦ προσπλέοντας σφίσι καὶ οὐκ ἔλαθον νυκτὸς ἀφορμισάμενοι, οὕτω δὴ ἀναγκάζονται 4 ναυμαχεῖν κατὰ μέσον τὸν πορθμόν. στρατηγοὶ δὲ ἦσαν μὲν καὶ κατὰ πόλεις ἑκάστων οἳ παρεσκευάζοντο, Κορινθίων 5 δὲ Μαχάων καὶ Ἰσοκράτης καὶ Ἀγαθαρχίδας. καὶ οἱ μὲν Πελοποννήσιοι ἐτάξαντο κύκλον τῶν νεῶν ὡς μέγιστον οἷοί τ' ἦσαν μὴ διδόντες διέκπλουν, τὰς πρῴρας μὲν ἔξω, ἔσω δὲ τὰς πρύμνας, καὶ τά τε λεπτὰ πλοῖα ἃ ξυνέπλει ἐντὸς ποιοῦνται καὶ πέντε ναῦς τὰς ἄριστα πλεούσας, ὅπως ἐκπλέοιεν διὰ βραχέος παραγιγνόμενοι, εἴ πη προσπίπτοιεν 84 οἱ ἐναντίοι. οἱ δ' Ἀθηναῖοι κατὰ μίαν ναῦν τεταγμένοι περιέπλεον αὐτοὺς κύκλῳ καὶ ξυνῆγον ἐς ὀλίγον, ἐν χρῷ αἰεὶ παραπλέοντες καὶ δόκησιν παρέχοντες αὐτίκα ἐμβαλεῖν· προείρητο δ' αὐτοῖς ὑπὸ Φορμίωνος μὴ ἐπιχειρεῖν πρὶν ἂν 2 αὐτὸς σημήνῃ. ἤλπιζε γὰρ αὐτῶν οὐ μενεῖν τὴν τάξιν, ὥσπερ ἐν γῇ πεζῇν, ἀλλὰ ξυμπεσεῖσθαι πρὸς ἀλλήλας τὰς ναῦς καὶ τὰ πλοῖα ταραχὴν παρέξειν, εἴ τ' ἐκπνεύσειεν ἐκ τοῦ κόλπου τὸ πνεῦμα, ὅπερ ἀναμένων τε περιέπλει καὶ εἰώθει γίγνεσθαι ἐπὶ τὴν ἕω, οὐδένα χρόνον ἡσυχάσειν αὐτούς· καὶ τὴν ἐπιχείρησιν ἐφ' ἑαυτῷ τε ἐνόμιζεν εἶναι, ὁπόταν βούληται, τῶν νεῶν ἄμεινον πλεουσῶν, καὶ τότε 3 καλλίστην γίγνεσθαι. ὡς δὲ τό τε πνεῦμα κατῄει καὶ αἱ νῆες ἐν ὀλίγῳ ἤδη οὖσαι ὑπ' ἀμφοτέρων, τοῦ τε ἀνέμου τῶν τε πλοίων, ἅμα προσκειμένων ἐταράσσοντο, καὶ ναῦς τε νηὶ προσέπιπτε καὶ τοῖς κοντοῖς διεωθοῦντο, βοῇ τε χρώμενοι καὶ πρὸς ἀλλήλους ἀντιφυλακῇ τε καὶ λοιδορίᾳ οὐδὲν κατήκουον οὔτε τῶν παραγγελλομένων οὔτε τῶν κελευστῶν, καὶ τὰς κώπας ἀδύνατοι ὄντες ἐν κλύδωνι ἀναφέρειν ἄνθρωποι

they crossed from Patrae in Achaea to the mainland opposite, on their way to Acarnania, they saw the Athenians coming out towards them from Chalcis and the River Evenus. Although they slipped their moorings during the night, the Athenians noticed them; and so they were compelled to fight in the middle of the channel. Each city 4 which contributed to the fleet had its own generals: the Corinthian generals were Machaon, Isocrates and Agatharchidas.

The Peloponnesians deployed their ships in as large 5 a circle as they could without leaving room to sail through, with their prows facing outwards and their sterns inwards; and inside the circle they placed the small boats which were accompanying them, and also their five best-sailing ships, which were to be available to sail out at close range wherever the enemy attacked. The 84 Athenians, on the other hand, formed a single line with their ships, and sailed round the Peloponnesians in a circle, confining them in a limited space, and constantly grazing past them and leading them to expect an immediate attack. However, Phormio had ordered the Athenians not to make the attempt until he signalled. He hoped that the 2 Peloponnesians would not stay in formation like infantry on land, but that the ships would fall foul of one another and the small boats would cause confusion; if, as normally happened towards dawn, the wind were to blow out of the gulf (it was in the expectation of this that he was sailing round them), they would not remain still for any time at all. He thought that as his ships were the better sailers he could attack whenever he chose, and that would be the best opportunity.

When the wind arose, the Peloponnesian ships, al- 3 ready confined in a tight space, were caught by the wind and the boats simultaneously and were thrown into confusion. As one ship collided with another, the crews pushed them apart with their poles. They shouted, warded one another off and cursed, and took no notice of the orders passed on to them or of their officers; and through their lack of experience they were unable to raise their

ἄπειροι τοῖς κυβερνήταις ἀπειθεστέρας τὰς ναῦς παρεῖχον. τότε δὴ κατὰ τὸν καιρὸν τοῦτον σημαίνει, καὶ οἱ Ἀθηναῖοι προσπεσόντες πρῶτον μὲν καταδύουσι τῶν στρατηγίδων νεῶν μίαν, ἔπειτα δὲ καὶ τὰς ἄλλας ᾗ χωρήσειαν διέφθειρον, καὶ κατέστησαν ἐς ἀλκὴν μὲν μηδένα τρέπεσθαι αὐτῶν ὑπὸ τῆς ταραχῆς, φεύγειν δὲ ἐς Πάτρας καὶ Δύμην τῆς Ἀχαΐας. 4 οἱ δὲ Ἀθηναῖοι καταδιώξαντες καὶ ναῦς δώδεκα λαβόντες τούς τε ἄνδρας ἐξ αὐτῶν τοὺς πλείστους ἀνελόμενοι ἐς Μολύκρειον ἀπέπλεον, καὶ τροπαῖον στήσαντες ἐπὶ τῷ Ῥίῳ καὶ ναῦν ἀναθέντες τῷ Ποσειδῶνι ἀνεχώρησαν ἐς Ναύ- 5 πακτον. παρέπλευσαν δὲ καὶ οἱ Πελοποννήσιοι εὐθὺς ταῖς περιλοίποις τῶν νεῶν ἐκ τῆς Δύμης καὶ Πατρῶν ἐς Κυλ-λήνην τὸ Ἠλείων ἐπίνειον· καὶ ἀπὸ Λευκάδος Κνῆμος καὶ αἱ ἐκείνων νῆες, ἃς ἔδει ταύταις ξυμμεῖξαι, ἀφικνοῦνται μετὰ τὴν ἐν Στράτῳ μάχην ἐς τὴν Κυλλήνην.

85 Πέμπουσι δὲ καὶ οἱ Λακεδαιμόνιοι τῷ Κνήμῳ ξυμβούλους ἐπὶ τὰς ναῦς Τιμοκράτη καὶ Βρασίδαν καὶ Λυκόφρονα, κελεύ-οντες ἄλλην ναυμαχίαν βελτίω παρασκευάζεσθαι καὶ μὴ 2 ὑπ' ὀλίγων νεῶν εἴργεσθαι τῆς θαλάσσης. ἐδόκει γὰρ αὐτοῖς ἄλλως τε καὶ πρῶτον ναυμαχίας πειρασαμένοις πολὺς ὁ παράλογος εἶναι, καὶ οὐ τοσούτῳ ᾤοντο σφῶν τὸ ναυτικὸν λείπεσθαι, γεγενῆσθαι δέ τινα μαλακίαν, οὐκ ἀντιτιθέντες τὴν Ἀθηναίων ἐκ πολλοῦ ἐμπειρίαν τῆς σφετέρας δι' ὀλίγου 3 μελέτης. ὀργῇ οὖν ἀπέστελλον. οἱ δὲ ἀφικόμενοι μετὰ τοῦ Κνήμου ναῦς τε προσπεριήγγειλαν κατὰ πόλεις καὶ τὰς 4 προϋπαρχούσας ἐξηρτύοντο ὡς ἐπὶ ναυμαχίαν. πέμπει δὲ καὶ ὁ Φορμίων ἐς τὰς Ἀθήνας τήν τε παρασκευὴν αὐτῶν ἀγγελοῦντας καὶ περὶ τῆς ναυμαχίας ἣν ἐνίκησαν φράσοντας, καὶ κελεύων αὐτῷ ναῦς ὅτι πλείστας διὰ τάχους ἀποστεῖλαι, ὡς καθ' ἡμέραν ἑκάστην ἐλπίδος οὔσης αἰεὶ ναυμαχήσειν. 5 οἱ δὲ ἀποπέμπουσιν εἴκοσι ναῦς αὐτῷ, τῷ δὲ κομίζοντι αὐτὰς προσεπέστειλαν ἐς Κρήτην πρῶτον ἀφικέσθαι. Νικίας γὰρ Κρὴς Γορτύνιος πρόξενος ὢν πείθει αὐτοὺς ἐπὶ Κυδωνίαν

---

20. πρῶτον <μετὰ πολὺν χρόνον> Classen, πρῶτον <ἐν τῷδε τῷ πολέμῳ> Gomme.
33. Κρὴς Γορτύνιος defendit Karavites: [Κρὴς] Γορτυνίων Connor.

oars in the rough water, and so made it harder for the helmsmen to control the ships.

At that point Phormio gave the signal, and the Athenians fell on the **enemy**. First they holed one of the generals' ships, **and** then they proceeded to cripple the others wherever they went, so that in their confusion none of the enemy thought of resistance but fled to Patrae and Dyme in Achaea. The Athenians pursued them, captured twelve ships and took most of the men from them. Then they sailed off to Molycrium, set up a trophy at Rhium and dedicated a ship to Poseidon, and returned to Naupactus. The Peloponnesians immediately sailed round with their surviving ships from Dyme and Patrae to Cyllene, the harbour of Elis. Cnemus and the ships in his force which had been supposed to join this fleet came to Cyllene from Leucas after the battle at Stratus.

Consequently the Spartans sent Timocrates, Brasidas and Lycophron to Cnemus as advisers for the fleet, with orders to make better preparations for another battle and not allow the sea to be closed to them by a small number of ships. They were greatly surprised by the outcome, particularly as this was the first time they had attempted a naval battle, and they could not believe that their fleet was so greatly inferior: failing to acknowledge the contrast between the Athenians' long experience and their own short period of training, they imagined there had been some lack of determination. The sending of the advisers was therefore an expression of anger. When the men reached Cnemus, they sent round to the cities for additional ships, and fitted out for battle the ones they already had.

At the same time Phormio sent to Athens, giving news of the preparations which the enemy were making, reporting the victory which he had won, and urging that he should quickly be sent as many ships as possible, since he was in constant daily expectation of a battle. The Athenians sent him twenty ships, but added to the commander's instructions that they were first to go to Crete. Nicias, a Cretan from Gortyn who was a *proxenos* of Ath-

πλεῦσαι, φάσκων προσποιήσειν αὐτὴν οὖσαν πολεμίαν· ἐπῆγε δὲ Πολιχνίταις χαριζόμενος ὁμόροις τῶν Κυδωνιατῶν. 6 καὶ ὁ μὲν λαβὼν τὰς ναῦς ᾤχετο ἐς Κρήτην, καὶ μετὰ τῶν Πολιχνιτῶν ἐδῄου τὴν γῆν τῶν Κυδωνιατῶν, καὶ ὑπ' ἀνέμων 86 καὶ ἀπλοίας ἐνδιέτριψεν οὐκ ὀλίγον χρόνον. οἱ δ' ἐν τῇ Κυλλήνῃ Πελοποννήσιοι, ἐν τούτῳ ἐν ᾧ οἱ Ἀθηναῖοι περὶ Κρήτην κατείχοντο, παρεσκευασμένοι ὡς ἐπὶ ναυμαχίαν παρέπλευσαν ἐς Πάνορμον τὸν Ἀχαϊκόν, οὗπερ αὐτοῖς ὁ κατὰ γῆν στρατὸς τῶν Πελοποννησίων προσεβεβοηθήκει. 2 παρέπλευσε δὲ καὶ ὁ Φορμίων ἐπὶ τὸ Ῥίον τὸ Μολυκρικὸν καὶ ὡρμίσατο ἔξω αὐτοῦ ναυσὶν εἴκοσιν, αἷσπερ καὶ ἐναυ- 3 μάχησεν. ἦν δὲ τοῦτο μὲν τὸ Ῥίον φίλιον τοῖς Ἀθηναίοις, τὸ δ' ἕτερον Ῥίον ἐστὶν ἀντιπέρας, τὸ ἐν τῇ Πελοποννήσῳ· διέχετον δὲ ἀπ' ἀλλήλων σταδίους μάλιστα ἑπτὰ τῆς θα- 4 λάσσης, τοῦ δὲ Κρισαίου κόλπου στόμα τοῦτό ἐστιν. ἐπὶ οὖν τῷ Ῥίῳ τῷ Ἀχαϊκῷ οἱ Πελοποννήσιοι, ἀπέχοντι οὐ πολὺ τοῦ Πανόρμου, ἐν ᾧ αὐτοῖς ὁ πεζὸς ἦν, ὡρμίσαντο καὶ αὐτοὶ ναυσὶν ἑπτὰ καὶ ἑβδομήκοντα, ἐπειδὴ καὶ τοὺς 5 Ἀθηναίους εἶδον. καὶ ἐπὶ μὲν ἓξ ἢ ἑπτὰ ἡμέρας ἀνθώρμουν ἀλλήλοις μελετῶντές τε καὶ παρασκευαζόμενοι τὴν ναυμα- χίαν, γνώμην ἔχοντες οἱ μὲν μὴ ἐκπλεῖν ἔξω τῶν Ῥίων ἐς τὴν εὐρυχωρίαν, φοβούμενοι τὸ πρότερον πάθος, οἱ δὲ μὴ ἐσπλεῖν ἐς τὰ στενά, νομίζοντες πρὸς ἐκείνων εἶναι τὴν ἐν 6 ὀλίγῳ ναυμαχίαν. ἔπειτα ὁ Κνῆμος καὶ ὁ Βρασίδας καὶ οἱ ἄλλοι τῶν Πελοποννησίων στρατηγοί, βουλόμενοι ἐν τάχει τὴν ναυμαχίαν ποιῆσαι πρίν τι καὶ ἀπὸ τῶν Ἀθηναίων ἐπιβοη- θῆσαι, ξυνεκάλεσαν τοὺς στρατιώτας πρῶτον, καὶ ὁρῶντες αὐτῶν τοὺς πολλοὺς διὰ τὴν προτέραν ἧσσαν φοβουμένους καὶ οὐ προθύμους ὄντας παρεκελεύσαντο καὶ ἔλεξαν τοιάδε. 87 "Ἡ μὲν γενομένη ναυμαχία, ὦ ἄνδρες Πελοποννήσιοι, εἴ τις ἄρα δι' αὐτὴν ὑμῶν φοβεῖται τὴν μέλλουσαν, οὐχὶ 2 δικαίαν ἔχει τέκμαρσιν τὸ ἐκφοβῆσαι. τῇ τε γὰρ παρα- σκευῇ ἐνδεὴς ἐγένετο, ὥσπερ ἴστε, καὶ οὐχὶ ἐς ναυμαχίαν μᾶλλον ἢ ἐπὶ στρατείαν ἐπλέομεν· ξυνέβη δὲ καὶ τὰ ἀπὸ τῆς τύχης οὐκ ὀλίγα ἐναντιωθῆναι, καί πού τι καὶ ἡ ἀπειρία

4–5. ὑπ' ἀνέμων καὶ secl. Krüger.

ens, persuaded them to sail against Cydonia: he alleged that it was hostile to them and they could win it over, but in fact he took them to oblige Cydonia's neighbour Polichna. So the commander took the ships and went to Crete. He joined Polichna in ravaging the territory of Cydonia, and was delayed for some considerable time by the wind and rough weather.

While the Athenians were being detained in Crete, the Peloponnesians at Cyllene completed their preparations for battle, and sailed round to Panormus in Achaea, where their own land forces had come to support them. Phormio sailed along to Molycrian Rhium with the twenty ships with which he had fought the battle, and anchored outside. (This Rhium was friendly to the Athenians. The other Rhium, in the Peloponnese, lies opposite: they are separated from each other by about seven stades of sea, and this gap forms the mouth of the Gulf of Crisa.) When the Peloponnesians saw the Athenians, they too anchored, with seventy-seven ships, at Achaean Rhium, not far from Panormus, where their army was.

For six or seven days the two fleets remained in position opposite each other, practising and preparing for battle. The Peloponnesians, fearing a repetition of the previous disaster, did not want to sail out from the Rhia into open water; and the Athenians, thinking that a battle in a confined space would be to the enemy's advantage, did not want to sail into the narrows. However, Cnemus, Brasidas and the other Peloponnesian commanders wanted to engage in battle quickly, before any help could reach their opponents from Athens, so they first called their men together and, seeing that on account of their previous defeat the majority were afraid and not eager to fight, they spoke as follows to encourage them.

"Peloponnesians, some of you may be afraid of the battle ahead of us because of the one we have already fought, but there are no good reasons for fear. As you know, we were not properly prepared, and were sailing not so much to fight a battle as to make a journey. In addition, it happened that we had considerable bad luck, and

3 πρῶτον ναυμαχοῦντας ἔσφηλεν. ὥστε οὐ κατὰ τὴν ἡμετέραν κακίαν τὸ ἡσσᾶσθαι προσεγένετο, οὐδὲ δίκαιον τῆς γνώμης τὸ μὴ κατὰ κράτος νικηθέν, ἔχον δέ τινα ἐν αὑτῷ ἀντιλογίαν, τῆς γε ξυμφορᾶς τῷ ἀποβάντι ἀμβλύνεσθαι, νομίσαι δὲ ταῖς μὲν τύχαις ἐνδέχεσθαι σφάλλεσθαι τοὺς ἀνθρώπους, ταῖς δὲ γνώμαις τοὺς αὐτοὺς αἰεὶ ὀρθῶς ἀνδρείους εἶναι, καὶ μὴ ἀπειρίαν τοῦ ἀνδρείου παρόντος προβαλλομένους
4 εἰκότως ἄν ἔν τινι κακοὺς γενέσθαι. ὑμῶν δὲ οὐδ' ἡ ἀπειρία τοσοῦτον λείπεται ὅσον τόλμῃ προύχετε· τῶνδε δὲ ἡ ἐπιστήμη, ἣν μάλιστα φοβεῖσθε, ἀνδρείαν μὲν ἔχουσα καὶ μνήμην ἕξει ἐν τῷ δεινῷ ἐπιτελεῖν ἃ ἔμαθεν, ἄνευ δὲ εὐψυχίας οὐδεμία τέχνη πρὸς τοὺς κινδύνους ἰσχύει. φόβος γὰρ μνήμην ἐκπλήσσει, τέχνη δὲ ἄνευ ἀλκῆς οὐδὲν ὠφελεῖ.
5 πρὸς μὲν οὖν τὸ ἐμπειρότερον αὐτῶν τὸ τολμηρότερον ἀντιτάξασθε, πρὸς δὲ τὸ διὰ τὴν ἧσσαν δεδιέναι τὸ ἀπαράσκευοι
6 τότε τυχεῖν. περιγίγνεται δὲ ὑμῖν πλῆθός τε νεῶν καὶ πρὸς τῇ γῇ οἰκείᾳ οὔσῃ ὁπλιτῶν παρόντων ναυμαχεῖν· τὰ δὲ πολλὰ τῶν πλεόνων καὶ ἄμεινον παρεσκευασμένων τὸ κρά-
7 τος ἐστίν. ὥστε οὐδὲ καθ' ἓν εὑρίσκομεν εἰκότως ἂν ἡμᾶς σφαλλομένους· καὶ ὅσα ἡμάρτομεν πρότερον, νῦν αὐτὰ
8 ταῦτα προσγενόμενα διδασκαλίαν παρέξει. θαρσοῦντες οὖν καὶ κυβερνῆται καὶ ναῦται τὸ καθ' ἑαυτὸν ἕκαστος ἕπεσθε,
9 χώραν μὴ προλείποντες ᾗ ἄν τις προσταχθῇ. τῶν δὲ προτέρων ἡγεμόνων οὐ χεῖρον τὴν ἐπιχείρησιν ἡμεῖς παρασκευάσομεν, καὶ οὐκ ἐνδώσομεν πρόφασιν οὐδενὶ κακῷ γενέσθαι· ἢν δέ τις ἄρα καὶ βουληθῇ, κολασθήσεται τῇ πρεπούσῃ ζημίᾳ, οἱ δὲ ἀγαθοὶ τιμήσονται τοῖς προσήκουσιν ἄθλοις τῆς ἀρετῆς."

88 Τοιαῦτα μὲν τοῖς Πελοποννησίοις οἱ ἄρχοντες παρεκελεύσαντο. ὁ δὲ Φορμίων δεδιὼς καὶ αὐτὸς τὴν τῶν στρατιωτῶν ὀρρωδίαν καὶ αἰσθόμενος ὅτι τὸ πλῆθος τῶν νεῶν κατὰ σφᾶς αὐτοὺς ξυνιστάμενοι ἐφοβοῦντο, ἐβούλετο ξυγκαλέσας θαρσῦναί τε καὶ παραίνεσιν ἐν τῷ παρόντι

---

5. ἀνθρώπους codd.: ἀνδρείους Cobet.
6. ὀρθῶς ἀνδρείους C G: ἀνδρείους ὀρθῶς cett., ὀρθοὺς [ἀνδρείους] Badham, Cobet, αἰεὶ <τοὺς> ὀρθῶς vel <καὶ> αἰεὶ ὀρθῶς Gomme, fortasse recte.

this was our first naval battle and we perhaps suffered from inexperience. Our defeat was not due to cowardice on *3* our part; and since our spirit was not forcibly defeated but still has some power of reply we must not allow it to be blunted by the outcome of that event. We must admit that men are sometimes caught out by chance; but, when it comes to spirit, it is always the same men who are truly brave, and if they are brave they can never fairly put forward inexperience as an excuse for cowardly behaviour on any occasion. In any case, your inferiority *4* in experience is not as great as your superiority in boldness. You are particularly afraid of the enemy's skill: in a desperate situation skill would provide the memory needed to accomplish what had been learned, but without a good spirit no ability is of use against danger. Fear drives memory out, and ability without valour is useless. Against the enemy's greater experience set *5* your greater boldness; against the fear caused by your previous defeat set the fact that then you were caught unprepared.

"You have the advantage of a large number of ships, *6* and of fighting in front of friendly territory with hoplites present: in most cases those who have the larger numbers and are better prepared succeed. We believe there *7* is no respect in which we are likely to fail: even our previous mistakes will now be an additional advantage, because we have learned from them. Helmsmen and sailors, *8* attend to your duties with confidence. Do not abandon the position to which each of you is assigned. We shall prepare *9* pare for the engagement better than the previous commanders, and we shall not give any one an excuse for cowardice: any one who is remiss will be appropriately punished, while those who do well will be honoured with the rewards that their courage deserves."

That was the exhortation delivered to the Pelopon- *88* nesians by their commanders. Phormio was afraid for the courage of his men, and noticed that they were coming together in groups and taking fright at the number of the enemy ships, so he decided to call a meeting to encourage

2 ποιήσασθαι. πρότερον μὲν γὰρ αἰεὶ αὐτοῖς ἔλεγε καὶ προ-
παρεσκεύαζε τὰς γνώμας ὡς οὐδὲν αὐτοῖς πλῆθος νεῶν
τοσοῦτον, ἢν ἐπιπλέῃ, ὅτι οὐχ ὑπομενετέον ἐστί, καὶ οἱ
στρατιῶται ἐκ πολλοῦ ἐν σφίσιν αὐτοῖς τὴν ἀξίωσιν ταύτην
εἰλήφεσαν, μηδένα ὄχλον Ἀθηναῖοι ὄντες Πελοποννησίων 5
3 νεῶν ὑποχωρεῖν· τότε δὲ πρὸς τὴν παροῦσαν ὄψιν ὁρῶν
αὐτοὺς ἀθυμοῦντας ἐβούλετο ὑπόμνησιν ποιήσασθαι τοῦ
θαρσεῖν, καὶ ξυγκαλέσας τοὺς Ἀθηναίους ἔλεγε τοιάδε.
89 "Ὁρῶν ὑμᾶς, ὦ ἄνδρες στρατιῶται, πεφοβημένους τὸ
πλῆθος τῶν ἐναντίων ξυνεκάλεσα, οὐκ ἀξιῶν τὰ μὴ δεινὰ 10
2 ἐν ὀρρωδίᾳ ἔχειν. οὗτοι γὰρ πρῶτον μὲν διὰ τὸ προνενική-
σθαι καὶ μηδ' αὐτοὶ οἴεσθαι ὁμοῖοι ἡμῖν εἶναι τὸ πλῆθος
τῶν νεῶν καὶ οὐκ ἀπὸ τοῦ ἴσου παρεσκευάσαντο· ἔπειτα
ᾧ μάλιστα πιστεύοντες προσέρχονται, ὡς προσῆκον σφίσιν
ἀνδρείοις εἶναι, οὐ δι' ἄλλο τι θαρσοῦσιν ἢ διὰ τὴν ἐν τῷ 15
πεζῷ ἐμπειρίαν τὰ πλείω κατορθοῦντες, καὶ οἴονται σφίσι
3 καὶ ἐν τῷ ναυτικῷ ποιήσειν τὸ αὐτό. τὸ δ' ἐκ τοῦ δικαίου
ἡμῖν μᾶλλον νῦν περιέσται, εἴπερ καὶ τούτοις ἐν ἐκείνῳ,
ἐπεὶ εὐψυχίᾳ γε οὐδὲν προφέρουσι, τῷ δὲ ἑκάτεροί τι εἶναι
4 ἐμπειρότεροι θρασύτεροί ἐσμεν. Λακεδαιμόνιοί τε ἡγού- 20
μενοι αὐτῶν διὰ τὴν σφετέραν δόξαν ἄκοντας προσάγουσι
τοὺς πολλοὺς ἐς τὸν κίνδυνον, ἐπεὶ οὐκ ἄν ποτε ἐνεχείρησαν
5 ἡσσηθέντες παρὰ πολὺ αὖθις ναυμαχεῖν. μὴ δὴ αὐτῶν τὴν
τόλμαν δείσητε. πολὺ δὲ ὑμεῖς ἐκείνοις πλείω φόβον
παρέχετε καὶ πιστότερον κατά τε τὸ προνενικηκέναι καὶ ὅτι 25
οὐκ ἂν ἡγοῦνται μὴ μέλλοντάς τι ἄξιον τοῦ παραλόγου
6 πράξειν ἀνθίστασθαι ὑμᾶς. ἀντίπαλοι μὲν γὰρ οἱ πλείους,
ὥσπερ οὗτοι, τῇ δυνάμει τὸ πλέον πίσυνοι ἢ τῇ γνώμῃ
ἐπέρχονται· οἱ δὲ ἐκ πολλῷ ὑποδεεστέρων, καὶ ἅμα οὐκ
ἀναγκαζόμενοι, μέγα τι τῆς διανοίας τὸ βέβαιον ἔχοντες 30

---

26. τοῦ παραλόγου Steup: τοῦ παρὰ πολὺ codd., locum corruptum Gomme, qui τῆς δόξης desideravit.

them and give appropriate advice in their present situation. He had always told them before, and had trained their minds to think, that there was no force of ships so large that they could not face an attack by it, and the men themselves had for a long time accepted this claim that as Athenians they need never retire before a collection of Peloponnesian ships. However, he realised that on this occasion they were dismayed at the sight before their eyes, and, wanting to revive their confidence, he called the Athenians together and spoke as follows.

"I have called you together, my men, because I see you are frightened at the enemy's numbers, and I do not want you to be afraid where there is no cause for fear. First of all, because they have been beaten before, these men do not even themselves believe that they are equal to us, and that is why they have prepared such a large number of ships and have not kept to the same scale as us. Next, although they place most trust in the reputation for courage which they have to live up to, their confidence is based only on the fact that their experience on land has normally brought them success, and they suppose that the same will apply to their navy too. But we deserve to enjoy the advantage of confidence now, if they have it for actions on land, for they have no greater allowance of courage, but each of us is bolder in the element where we are more experienced. The Spartans who are their leaders have brought the majority into danger against their will, for the sake of Sparta's reputation: they would not otherwise have attempted another battle after their overwhelming defeat. Do not be afraid of their courage. You are a far greater object of fear to them, and more justifiably, because you were victorious before, and they would not expect you to face them unless you were going to bring off a success worthy of the surprising confrontation.

"Opponents who have the superior numbers, as these have, usually trust in their size rather than their intelligence: those whose numbers are far inferior, and who do not have to fight, must have a great consciousness of

ἀντιτολμῶσιν. ἃ λογιζόμενοι οὗτοι τῷ οὐκ εἰκότι πλέον
7 πεφόβηνται ἡμᾶς ἢ τῇ κατὰ λόγον παρασκευῇ. πολλὰ δὲ
καὶ στρατόπεδα ἤδη ἔπεσεν ὑπ' ἐλασσόνων τῇ ἀπειρίᾳ, ἔστι
δὲ ἃ καὶ τῇ ἀτολμίᾳ· ὧν οὐδετέρου ἡμεῖς νῦν μετέχομεν.
8 τὸν δὲ ἀγῶνα οὐκ ἐν τῷ κόλπῳ ἑκὼν εἶναι ποιήσομαι οὐδ'
ἐσπλεύσομαι ἐς αὐτόν. ὁρῶ γὰρ ὅτι πρὸς πολλὰς ναῦς
ἀνεπιστήμονας ὀλίγαις ναυσὶν ἐμπείροις καὶ ἄμεινον πλεού-
σαις ἡ στενοχωρία οὐ ξυμφέρει. οὔτε γὰρ ἂν ἐπιπλεύσειέ
τις ὡς χρὴ ἐς ἐμβολήν, μὴ ἔχων τὴν πρόσοψιν τῶν πολεμίων ἐκ πολλοῦ, οὔτ' ἂν ἀποχωρήσειεν ἐν δέοντι πιεζό-
μενος· διέκπλοι τε οὐκ εἰσὶν οὐδ' ἀναστροφαί, ἅπερ νεῶν
ἄμεινον πλεουσῶν ἔργα ἐστίν, ἀλλὰ ἀνάγκη ἂν εἴη τὴν
ναυμαχίαν πεζομαχίαν καθίστασθαι, καὶ ἐν τούτῳ αἱ πλείους
9 νῆες κρείσσους γίγνονται. τούτων μὲν οὖν ἐγὼ ἕξω τὴν
πρόνοιαν κατὰ τὸ δυνατόν. ὑμεῖς δὲ εὔτακτοι παρὰ ταῖς
ναυσὶ μένοντες τά τε παραγγελλόμενα ὀξέως δέχεσθε,
ἄλλως τε καὶ δι' ὀλίγου τῆς ἐφορμήσεως οὔσης, καὶ ἐν τῷ
ἔργῳ κόσμον καὶ σιγὴν περὶ πλείστου ἡγεῖσθε, ὃ ἔς τε τὰ
πολλὰ τῶν πολεμικῶν ξυμφέρει καὶ ναυμαχίᾳ οὐχ ἥκιστα,
10 ἀμύνεσθέ τε τούσδε ἀξίως τῶν προειργασμένων. ὁ δὲ
ἀγὼν μέγας ὑμῖν, ἢ καταλῦσαι Πελοποννησίων τὴν ἐλπίδα
τοῦ ναυτικοῦ ἢ ἐγγυτέρω καταστῆσαι Ἀθηναίοις τὸν φόβον
11 περὶ τῆς θαλάσσης. ἀναμιμνήσκω δ' αὖ ὑμᾶς ὅτι νενική-
κατε αὐτῶν τοὺς πολλούς· ἡσσημένων δὲ ἀνδρῶν οὐκ
ἐθέλουσιν αἱ γνῶμαι πρὸς τοὺς αὐτοὺς κινδύνους ὁμοῖαι
εἶναι."

90   Τοιαῦτα δὲ καὶ ὁ Φορμίων παρεκελεύσατο. οἱ δὲ Πελοποννήσιοι, ἐπειδὴ αὐτοῖς οἱ Ἀθηναῖοι οὐκ ἐπέπλεον ἐς τὸν
κόλπον καὶ τὰ στενά, βουλόμενοι ἄκοντας ἔσω προαγαγεῖν
αὐτούς, ἀναγαγόμενοι ἅμα ἕῳ ἔπλεον, ἐπὶ τεσσάρων ταξά-
μενοι τὰς ναῦς, παρὰ τὴν ἑαυτῶν γῆν, ἔσω ἐπὶ τοῦ κόλπου,

---

19. πολεμικῶν cett.: πολεμίων C.
31. παρὰ τὴν C G: ἐπὶ τὴν cett.

security if they dare to risk a confrontation. If the enemy are taking this into account, they will be more frightened of our paradoxical response than they would be of sensible preparations. Many forces in the past have been defeated by inferior numbers through their lack of experience, and sometimes lack of courage; and we now are not deficient in either of those qualities. *7*

"As far as possible, I shall avoid fighting the battle in the gulf or sailing into it, since I realise that a confined space will not be to our advantage, fighting with a small number of experienced and better-sailing ships against a large number of inexperienced. We cannot sail up to ram as we need to unless we can get a sight of the enemy from a distance; nor can we withdraw if we have to when under pressure; nor can we sail through the line and turn on the enemy, as the better-sailing ships expect to do. Instead we should have to turn the naval battle into an infantry battle, and in that kind of encounter the larger number of ships has the advantage. I shall bear these considerations in mind as far as I can. *8* *9*

"You must stay in good order by your ships, respond promptly to commands, especially as our two forces are only a short distance apart, and when you are in action set the highest value on discipline and silence, which are advantageous in most aspects of warfare, and not least in a naval battle. Fight against the enemy in a manner worthy of your previous achievements. The stakes are high: either you will extinguish the Peloponnesians' hopes for their navy or you will bring closer to Athens the fear of losing control of the sea. Let me remind you again that you have already defeated most of these men; and when men have been beaten before they do not face the same danger with the same spirit." *10* *12*

Such was Phormio's speech of encouragement. Since the Athenians refused to sail into the narrows of the gulf to meet them, the Peloponnesians wanted to draw them in against their will. They therefore set out at dawn, deployed their ships in four columns, and sailed along their own shore towards the interior of the gulf, led by *90*

157

2 δεξιῷ κέρᾳ ἡγουμένῳ, ὥσπερ καὶ ὥρμουν· ἐπὶ δ' αὐτῷ
εἴκοσιν ἔταξαν τὰς ἄριστα πλεούσας, ὅπως, εἰ ἄρα νομίσας
ἐπὶ τὴν Ναύπακτον αὐτοὺς πλεῖν ὁ Φορμίων καὶ αὐτὸς
ἐπιβοηθῶν ταύτῃ παραπλέοι, μὴ διαφύγοιεν [πλέοντα] τὸν
ἐπίπλουν σφῶν οἱ Ἀθηναῖοι ἔξω τοῦ ἑαυτῶν κέρως, ἀλλ' 5
3 αὗται αἱ νῆες περικλῄσειαν. ὁ δέ, ὅπερ ἐκεῖνοι προσ-
εδέχοντο, φοβηθεὶς περὶ τῷ χωρίῳ ἐρήμῳ ὄντι, ὡς ἑώρα
ἀναγομένους αὐτούς, ἄκων καὶ κατὰ σπουδὴν ἐμβιβάσας
ἔπλει παρὰ τὴν γῆν· καὶ ὁ πεζὸς ἅμα τῶν Μεσσηνίων
4 παρεβοήθει. ἰδόντες δὲ οἱ Πελοποννήσιοι κατὰ μίαν ἐπὶ 10
κέρως παραπλέοντας καὶ ἤδη ὄντας ἐντὸς τοῦ κόλπου τε καὶ
πρὸς τῇ γῇ, ὅπερ ἐβούλοντο μάλιστα, ἀπὸ σημείου ἑνὸς
ἄφνω ἐπιστρέψαντες τὰς ναῦς μετωπηδὸν ἔπλεον, ὡς εἶχε
τάχους ἕκαστος, ἐπὶ τοὺς Ἀθηναίους, καὶ ἤλπιζον πάσας
5 τὰς ναῦς ἀπολήψεσθαι. τῶν δὲ ἕνδεκα μέν τινες αἵπερ 15
ἡγοῦντο ὑπεκφεύγουσι τὸ κέρας τῶν Πελοποννησίων καὶ
τὴν ἐπιστροφὴν ἐς τὴν εὐρυχωρίαν· τὰς δ' ἄλλας ἐπικατα-
λαβόντες ἐξέωσάν τε πρὸς τὴν γῆν ὑποφευγούσας καὶ
διέφθειραν, ἄνδρας τε τῶν Ἀθηναίων ἀπέκτειναν ὅσοι μὴ
6 ἐξένευσαν αὐτῶν. καὶ τῶν νεῶν τινὰς ἀναδούμενοι εἷλκον 20
κενάς (μίαν δὲ αὐτοῖς ἀνδράσιν εἷλον ἤδη), τὰς δέ τινας οἱ
Μεσσήνιοι παραβοηθήσαντες καὶ ἐπεσβαίνοντες ξὺν τοῖς
ὅπλοις ἐς τὴν θάλασσαν καὶ ἐπιβάντες ἀπὸ τῶν καταστρω-
μάτων μαχόμενοι ἀφείλοντο ἑλκομένας ἤδη.

91 Ταύτῃ μὲν οὖν οἱ Πελοποννήσιοι ἐκράτουν τε καὶ 25
διέφθειρον τὰς Ἀττικὰς ναῦς· αἱ δὲ εἴκοσι νῆες αὐτῶν αἱ
ἀπὸ τοῦ δεξιοῦ κέρως ἐδίωκον τὰς ἕνδεκα ναῦς τῶν Ἀθηναίων
αἵπερ ὑπεξέφυγον τὴν ἐπιστροφὴν ἐς τὴν εὐρυχωρίαν. καὶ
φθάνουσιν αὐτοὺς πλὴν μιᾶς νεὼς προκαταφυγοῦσαι ἐς τὴν
Ναύπακτον, καὶ σχοῦσαι ἀντίπρῳροι κατὰ τὸ Ἀπολλώνιον 30
παρεσκευάζοντο ἀμυνούμενοι, ἢν ἐς τὴν γῆν ἐπὶ σφᾶς
2 πλέωσιν. οἱ δὲ παραγενόμενοι ὕστερον ἐπαιάνιζόν τε ἅμα
πλέοντες ὡς νενικηκότες, καὶ τὴν μίαν ναῦν τῶν Ἀθηναίων
τὴν ὑπόλοιπον ἐδίωκε Λευκαδία ναῦς μία πολὺ πρὸ τῶν
3 ἄλλων. ἔτυχε δὲ ὁλκὰς ὁρμοῦσα μετέωρος, περὶ ἣν ἡ

---

4. πλέοντα secl. Croiset.
26. διεφθειρον C pc G pc: διεφθειραν C ac,
 ἐφθειρον cett., ἐφθειραν γρ. G pc.

what had been the right wing when they were at anchor. The twenty best-sailing ships were positioned there, so that, if Phormio thought they were sailing against Naupactus, and himself sailed back to defend it, the Athenians should not excape the enemy's attack by getting beyond their wing, but should be hemmed in by these ships.

2

As they expected, when Phormio saw them put to sea he was afraid for Naupactus, which was unguarded, and, reluctant as he was, he quickly embarked and sailed along the coast; and the Messenians' infantry marched in support. When the Peloponnesians saw that the Athenians were sailing in a single column, and were now inside the gulf and close to the shore, as they particularly wanted, then suddenly, in response to a single command, they turned their ships and sailed in line, as quickly as each of them could, against the Athenians, hoping to catch all their ships. In fact, the eleven ships in the lead outran the turn into the open sea performed by the Peloponnesians' wing; but the Peloponnesians caught the remainder, drove them in flight to the shore and crippled them, killing those Athenians who did not swim away. Some of the ships they attached ropes to and towed away empty; one they captured with its crew; others were saved from them when they were already being towed away, as the Messenians came to the rescue, went into the sea with their weapons, and boarded the ships and fought from the decks.

3

4

5

6

Up to that point the Peloponnesians were victorious and able to cripple the Athenian ships. The twenty ships from the Peloponnesians' right wing pursued the eleven Athenian ships which had escaped their turn into the open sea. With the exception of one ship the Athenians made good their escape and reached Naupactus first, and they took up a position by the temple of Apollo, with prows outwards, preparing to resist if the Peloponnesians sailed against their territory. The Peloponnesians arrived afterwards, singing a paean of victory as they sailed. The one Athenian ship which was left behind was pursued by a ship of Leucas a long way ahead of the others. There happened to be a merchant vessel anchored out

91

2

3

Ἀττικὴ ναῦς φθάσασα καὶ περιπλεύσασα τῇ Λευκαδίᾳ
4 διωκούσῃ ἐμβάλλει μέσῃ καὶ καταδύει. τοῖς μὲν οὖν Πελοποννησίοις γενομένου τούτου ἀπροσδοκήτου τε καὶ παρὰ λόγον φόβος ἐμπίπτει, καὶ ἅμα ἀτάκτως διώκοντες διὰ τὸ κρατεῖν αἱ μέν τινες τῶν νεῶν καθεῖσαι τὰς κώπας ἐπέστησαν τοῦ πλοῦ, ἀξύμφορον δρῶντες πρὸς τὴν ἐξ ὀλίγου ἀντεφόρμησιν, βουλόμενοι τὰς πλείους περιμεῖναι, αἱ δὲ καὶ
92 ἐς βράχεα ἀπειρίᾳ χωρίων ὤκειλαν. τοὺς δ' Ἀθηναίους ἰδόντας ταῦτα γιγνόμενα θάρσος τε ἔλαβε, καὶ ἀπὸ ἑνὸς κελεύσματος ἐμβοήσαντες ἐπ' αὐτοὺς ὥρμησαν. οἱ δὲ διὰ τὰ ὑπάρχοντα ἁμαρτήματα καὶ τὴν παροῦσαν ἀταξίαν ὀλίγον μὲν χρόνον ὑπέμειναν, ἔπειτα δὲ ἐτράποντο ἐς τὸν Πάνορμον,
2 ὅθενπερ ἀνηγάγοντο. ἐπιδιώκοντες δὲ οἱ Ἀθηναῖοι τάς τε ἐγγὺς οὔσας μάλιστα ναῦς ἔλαβον ἓξ καὶ τὰς ἑαυτῶν ἀφείλοντο, ἃς ἐκεῖνοι πρὸς τῇ γῇ διαφθείραντες τὸ πρῶτον ἀνεδήσαντο· ἄνδρας τε τοὺς μὲν ἀπέκτειναν, τινὰς δὲ καὶ
3 ἐζώγρησαν. ἐπὶ δὲ τῆς Λευκαδίας νεώς, ἣ περὶ τὴν ὁλκάδα κατέδυ, Τιμοκράτης ὁ Λακεδαιμόνιος πλέων, ὡς ἡ ναῦς διεφθείρετο, ἔσφαξεν ἑαυτόν, καὶ ἐξέπεσεν ἐς τὸν
4 Ναυπακτίων λιμένα. ἀναχωρήσαντες δὲ οἱ Ἀθηναῖοι τροπαῖον ἔστησαν, ὅθεν ἀναγαγόμενοι ἐκράτησαν, καὶ τοὺς νεκροὺς καὶ τὰ ναυάγια ὅσα πρὸς τῇ ἑαυτῶν ἦν ἀνείλοντο,
5 καὶ τοῖς ἐναντίοις τὰ ἐκείνων ὑπόσπονδα ἀπέδοσαν. ἔστησαν δὲ καὶ οἱ Πελοποννήσιοι τροπαῖον ὡς νενικηκότες τῆς τροπῆς, ἃς πρὸς τῇ γῇ διέφθειραν ναῦς· καὶ ἥνπερ ἔλαβον ναῦν, ἀνέθεσαν ἐπὶ τὸ Ῥίον τὸ Ἀχαϊκὸν παρὰ τὸ τροπαῖον.
6 μετὰ δὲ ταῦτα φοβούμενοι τὴν ἀπὸ τῶν Ἀθηναίων βοήθειαν ὑπὸ νύκτα ἐσέπλευσαν ἐς τὸν κόλπον τὸν Κρισαῖον καὶ
7 Κόρινθον ἅπαντες πλὴν Λευκαδίων. καὶ οἱ ἐκ τῆς Κρήτης Ἀθηναῖοι ταῖς εἴκοσι ναυσίν, αἷς ἔδει πρὸ τῆς ναυμαχίας τῷ Φορμίωνι παραγενέσθαι, οὐ πολλῷ ὕστερον τῆς ἀναχωρήσεως τῶν νεῶν ἀφικνοῦνται ἐς τὴν Ναύπακτον. καὶ τὸ θέρος ἐτελεύτα.

at sea, and the Athenian ship was in time to sail round this, ram in the middle the Leucadian ship which was pursuing it, and hole it. The Peloponnesians were terror-struck at this unexpected and amazing occurrence. Moreover, because they were victorious, they had fallen into disorder in their pursuit: some ships had lowered their oars and stopped their advance, in order to wait for the others, which was a dangerous thing to do when the enemy were positioned a short distance away; and others, not knowing the locality, had run aground in the shallows.

When the Athenians saw this happening, they were filled with confidence, and at a single command they shouted and attacked the Peloponnesians. Owing to the mistakes they had made and the disorder into which they had fallen, the Peloponnesians held out only for a short time, and then fled to Panormus, the place from which they had started. The Athenians pursued them, catching the six nearest ships and recovering those of their own which at the beginning had been crippled near the shore and taken in tow. They killed some of the men, and took others alive. The Spartan Timocrates, who was sailing on the Leucadian ship which was holed near the merchant vessel, killed himself when the ship was disabled; and his body was washed up in the harbour of Naupactus.

The Athenians on their return set up a trophy at the point from which they had put out to obtain their victory. They took up the bodies and wrecks which were by their own shore, and returned under truce those belonging to the enemy. The Peloponnesians also set up a trophy, for the victory they had obtained when they crippled the ships by the shore: they dedicated the ship which they had captured at Achaean Rhium beside the trophy. After that, afraid of the reinforcements coming from Athens, all of them except the Leucadians sailed by night into the Gulf of Crisa and to Corinth. The Athenians from Crete, with the twenty ships which ought to have reached Phormio before the battle, arrived at Naupactus shortly after the Peloponnesians had retired. So the summer ended.

161

Πρὶν δὲ διαλῦσαι τὸ ἐς Κόρινθόν τε καὶ τὸν Κρισαῖον
93 κόλπον ἀναχωρῆσαν ναυτικόν, ὁ Κνῆμος καὶ ὁ Βρασίδας καὶ
οἱ ἄλλοι ἄρχοντες τῶν Πελοποννησίων ἀρχομένου τοῦ
χειμῶνος ἐβούλοντο διδαξάντων Μεγαρέων ἀποπειρᾶσαι τοῦ
Πειραιῶς τοῦ λιμένος τῶν Ἀθηναίων· ἦν δὲ ἀφύλακτος καὶ 5
ἄκλῃστος εἰκότως διὰ τὸ ἐπικρατεῖν πολὺ τῷ ναυτικῷ.
ἐδόκει δὲ λαβόντα τῶν ναυτῶν ἕκαστον τὴν κώπην καὶ τὸ
2 ὑπηρέσιον καὶ τὸν τροπωτῆρα πεζῇ ἰέναι ἐκ Κορίνθου ἐπὶ
τὴν πρὸς Ἀθήνας θάλασσαν καὶ ἀφικομένους κατὰ τάχος
ἐς Μέγαρα καθελκύσαντας ἐκ Νισαίας τοῦ νεωρίου αὐτῶν 10
τεσσαράκοντα ναῦς, αἳ ἔτυχον αὐτόθι οὖσαι, πλεῦσαι εὐθὺς
ἐπὶ τὸν Πειραιᾶ· οὔτε γὰρ ναυτικὸν ἦν προφυλάσσον ἐν
3 αὐτῷ οὐδὲν οὔτε προσδοκία οὐδεμία μὴ ἄν ποτε οἱ πολέμιοι
ἐξαπιναίως οὕτως ἐπιπλεύσειαν, ἐπεὶ οὐδ' ἀπὸ τοῦ προφα-
νοῦς τολμῆσαι ἂν καθ' ἡσυχίαν, οὐδ' εἰ διενοοῦντο, μὴ οὐκ 15
ἂν προαισθέσθαι. ὡς δὲ ἔδοξεν αὐτοῖς, καὶ ἐχώρουν εὐθύς·
4 καὶ ἀφικόμενοι νυκτὸς καὶ καθελκύσαντες ἐκ τῆς Νισαίας
τὰς ναῦς ἔπλεον ἐπὶ μὲν τὸν Πειραιᾶ οὐκέτι, ὥσπερ διενοοῦντο, καταδείσαντες τὸν κίνδυνον (καί τις καὶ ἄνεμος
αὐτοὺς λέγεται κωλῦσαι), ἐπὶ δὲ τῆς Σαλαμῖνος τὸ ἀκρωτή- 20
ριον τὸ πρὸς Μέγαρα ὁρῶν· καὶ φρούριον ἐπ' αὐτοῦ ἦν
καὶ νεῶν τριῶν φυλακὴ τοῦ μὴ ἐσπλεῖν Μεγαρεῦσι μηδὲ
ἐκπλεῖν μηδέν. τῷ τε φρουρίῳ προσέβαλον καὶ τὰς τριήρεις
ἀφείλκυσαν κενάς, τήν τε ἄλλην Σαλαμῖνα ἀπροσδόκητοι
94 ἐπιπεσόντες ἐπόρθουν. ἐς δὲ τὰς Ἀθήνας φρυκτοί τε ᾔροντο 25
πολέμιοι καὶ ἔκπληξις ἐγένετο οὐδεμιᾶς τῶν κατὰ τὸν
πόλεμον ἐλάσσων. οἱ μὲν γὰρ ἐν τῷ ἄστει ἐς τὸν Πειραιᾶ
ᾤοντο τοὺς πολεμίους ἐσπεπλευκέναι ἤδη, οἱ δ' ἐν τῷ
Πειραιεῖ τήν τε Σαλαμῖνα ᾑρῆσθαι καὶ παρὰ σφᾶς ὅσον οὐκ
ἐσπλεῖν αὐτούς· ὅπερ ἄν, εἰ ἐβουλήθησαν μὴ κατοκνῆσαι, 30
2 ῥᾳδίως ἐγένετο, καὶ οὐκ ἂν ἄνεμος ἐκώλυσεν. βοηθήσαντες
δὲ ἅμ' ἡμέρᾳ πανδημεὶ οἱ Ἀθηναῖοι ἐς τὸν Πειραιᾶ ναῦς τε

---

24. ἀπροσδόκητοι Gomme: ἀπροσδοκήτοις codd.,
ἀπροσδοκήτως Hude.

At the beginning of winter, before disbanding the fleet which had retired to Corinth and the Gulf of Crisa, Cnemus, Brasidas and the other Peloponnesian commanders wanted to act on a suggestion of the Megarians, and make an attempt on Athens' harbour, the Piraeus. The harbour was not guarded or closed — reasonably enough, in view of the Athenians' great naval superiority. It was decided that each of the sailors should take his oar, cushion and strap, go on foot from Corinth to the sea on the Athenian side, then go as quickly as possible to Megara, launch from Megara's harbour Nisaea forty ships which happened to be there, and immediately sail for the Piraeus. There were no ships on guard there, and there was no expectation that the enemy would ever make so sudden an attack: the Athenians did not expect them to risk it even openly, after preparing at leisure, and in any case they were sure that they would find out in advance if plans were being made.

As soon as the decision had been taken, the Peloponnesians set out. They arrived at night, launched the ships from Nisaea and set sail — but not after all against the Piraeus, as they had originally intended. They were afraid of the danger, and it is alleged that they were prevented by wind, so they made for the headland of Salamis facing Megara. There was a garrison post there, and three ships stationed to prevent any one from sailing into or out of Megara. They attacked the fort, captured the ships without their equipment, and, catching the rest of Salamis unprepared, proceeded to ravage the land.

News of the enemy action was transmitted by torch-signals to Athens, and the result was a panic as great as any in the war. The people in the city thought that the enemy had already sailed into the Piraeus; those in the Piraeus thought that Salamis had been captured and the enemy were on the point of attacking them. Indeed, that could easily have happened if the Peloponnesians had not lost their nerve, and no wind would have stopped them. At daybreak the Athenians went in full force to defend the

καθεῖλκον καὶ ἐσβάντες κατὰ σπουδὴν καὶ πολλῷ θορύβῳ
ταῖς μὲν ναυσὶν ἐπὶ τὴν Σαλαμῖνα ἔπλεον, τῷ πεζῷ δὲ
3 φυλακὰς τοῦ Πειραιῶς καθίσταντο. οἱ δὲ Πελοποννήσιοι
ὡς ᾔσθοντο τὴν βοήθειαν, καταδραμόντες τῆς Σαλαμῖνος τὰ
πολλὰ καὶ ἀνθρώπους καὶ λείαν λαβόντες καὶ τὰς τρεῖς
ναῦς ἐκ τοῦ Βουδόρου τοῦ φρουρίου κατὰ τάχος ἐπὶ τῆς
Νισαίας ἀπέπλεον· ἔστι γὰρ ὅτι καὶ αἱ νῆες αὐτοὺς διὰ
χρόνου καθελκυσθεῖσαι καὶ οὐδὲν στέγουσαι ἐφόβουν. ἀφικόμενοι δὲ ἐς τὰ Μέγαρα πάλιν ἐπὶ τῆς Κορίνθου ἀπεχώρησαν
4 πεζῇ· οἱ δ' Ἀθηναῖοι οὐκέτι καταλαβόντες πρὸς τῇ Σαλαμῖνι
ἀπέπλευσαν καὶ αὐτοί, καὶ μετὰ τοῦτο φυλακὴν ἤδη τοῦ
Πειραιῶς μᾶλλον τὸ λοιπὸν ἐποιοῦντο λιμένων τε κλῄσει καὶ
τῇ ἄλλῃ ἐπιμελείᾳ.

95 Ὑπὸ δὲ τοὺς αὐτοὺς χρόνους, τοῦ χειμῶνος τούτου ἀρχομένου, Σιτάλκης ὁ Τήρεω Ὀδρύσης Θρᾳκῶν βασιλεὺς
ἐστράτευσεν ἐπὶ Περδίκκαν τὸν Ἀλεξάνδρου Μακεδονίας
βασιλέα καὶ ἐπὶ Χαλκιδέας τοὺς ἐπὶ Θρᾴκης, δύο ὑποσχέ-
σεις τὴν μὲν βουλόμενος ἀναπρᾶξαι, τὴν δὲ αὐτὸς ἀποδοῦναι.
2 ὅ τε γὰρ Περδίκκας αὐτῷ ὑποσχόμενος, εἰ Ἀθηναίοις τε
διαλλάξειεν ἑαυτὸν κατ' ἀρχὰς τῷ πολέμῳ πιεζόμενον καὶ
Φίλιππον τὸν ἀδελφὸν αὐτοῦ πολέμιον ὄντα μὴ καταγάγοι
ἐπὶ βασιλείᾳ, ἃ ὑπεδέξατο οὐκ ἐπετέλει· τοῖς τε Ἀθηναίοις
αὐτὸς ὡμολογήκει, ὅτε τὴν ξυμμαχίαν ἐποιεῖτο, τὸν ἐπὶ
3 Θρᾴκης Χαλκιδικὸν πόλεμον καταλύσειν. ἀμφοτέρων οὖν
ἕνεκα τὴν ἔφοδον ἐποιεῖτο καὶ τόν τε Φιλίππου υἱὸν
Ἀμύνταν ὡς ἐπὶ βασιλείᾳ τῶν Μακεδόνων ἦγε καὶ τῶν
Ἀθηναίων πρέσβεις, οἳ ἔτυχον παρόντες τούτων ἕνεκα, καὶ
ἡγεμόνα Ἅγνωνα· ἔδει γὰρ καὶ τοὺς Ἀθηναίους ναυσί τε
καὶ στρατιᾷ ὡς πλείστῃ ἐπὶ τοὺς Χαλκιδέας παραγενέσθαι.
96 ἀνίστησιν οὖν ἐκ τῶν Ὀδρυσῶν ὁρμώμενος πρῶτον μὲν τοὺς
ἐντὸς τοῦ Αἵμου τε ὄρους καὶ τῆς Ῥοδόπης Θρᾷκας, ὅσων
ἦρχε μέχρι θαλάσσης ἐς τὸν Εὔξεινόν τε πόντον καὶ τὸν
Ἑλλήσποντον, ἔπειτα τοὺς ὑπερβάντι Αἷμον Γέτας καὶ ὅσα

32–3. ἐς ... Ἑλλήσποντον secl. Krüger.

Piraeus, launched ships and embarked on them in haste and great uproar. The ships sailed to Salamis while the army mounted guard on the Piraeus. The Peloponnesians had 3 overrun most of the island, and had taken men and booty as well as the three ships from the fort at Budorum, but when they learned of the Athenians' reaction they rapidly sailed back to Nisaea. One factor contributing to their fear was that their ships had been in the water for a long time and were not water-tight. After reaching Megara, they went back to Corinth on foot. The Athenians 4 sailed back themselves when they found that the enemy were no longer at Salamis. After this, they at last took the guarding of the Piraeus more seriously, closing the harbours and taking other precautions.

About the same time, at the beginning of this winter, Sitalces the Odrysian, son of Teres and king of the Thracians, campaigned against Perdiccas son of Alexander, king of Macedon, and against the Thraceward Chalcidians. Sitalces' intention was to enforce one promise made to him and keep a second made by him. Perdiccas, when he 2 was under pressure at the beginning of the war, had made a promise on condition that Sitalces should arrange a reconciliation between him and the Athenians, and should not restore his brother Philip, who was hostile to him, with a view to making him king; but he showed no sign of keeping his promise. Sitalces himself had undertaken to the Athenians, when he made his alliance with them, that he would put an end to their war with the Thraceward Chalcidians. He went on this expedition on account of 3 those two promises, taking with him Philip's son Amyntas, in order to make him king of Macedon, and Athenian envoys who were at his court on this business, with Hagnon as commander, since the Athenians were meant to join him against the Chalcidians with ships and as large an army as possible.

Setting out from the Odrysians, Sitalces called out 96 first the Thracians who were subject to him in the region between Mount Haemus and Rhodope as far as the sea in the direction of the Black Sea and the Hellespont, and

ἄλλα μέρη ἐντὸς τοῦ Ἴστρου ποταμοῦ πρὸς θάλασσαν μᾶλλον τὴν τοῦ Εὐξείνου πόντου κατῴκητο· εἰσὶ δ' οἱ Γέται καὶ οἱ ταύτῃ ὅμοροί τε τοῖς Σκύθαις καὶ ὁμόσκευοι, πάντες ἱππο-
2 τοξόται. παρεκάλει δὲ καὶ τῶν ὀρεινῶν Θρᾳκῶν πολλοὺς τῶν αὐτονόμων καὶ μαχαιροφόρων, οἳ Δῖοι καλοῦνται, τὴν Ῥοδόπην οἱ πλεῖστοι οἰκοῦντες· καὶ τοὺς μὲν μισθῷ ἔπειθεν,
3 οἱ δ' ἐθελονταὶ ξυνηκολούθουν. ἀνίστη δὲ καὶ Ἀγριᾶνας καὶ Λαιαίους καὶ ἄλλα ὅσα ἔθνη Παιονικὰ ὧν ἦρχε καὶ ἔσχατοι τῆς ἀρχῆς οὗτοι ἦσαν· μέχρι γὰρ Λαιαίων Παιόνων καὶ τοῦ Στρυμόνος ποταμοῦ, ὃς ἐκ τοῦ Σκόμβρου ὄρους δι' Ἀγριάνων καὶ Λαιαίων ῥεῖ, [οὗ] ὡρίζετο ἡ ἀρχὴ τὰ πρὸς
4 Παίονας αὐτονόμους ἤδη. τὰ δὲ πρὸς Τριβαλλούς, καὶ τούτους αὐτονόμους, Τρῆρες ὥριζον καὶ Τιλαταῖοι· οἰκοῦσι δ' οὗτοι πρὸς βορέαν τοῦ Σκόμβρου ὄρους καὶ παρήκουσι πρὸς ἡλίου δύσιν μέχρι τοῦ Ὀσκίου ποταμοῦ. ῥεῖ δ' οὗτος ἐκ τοῦ ὄρους ὅθενπερ καὶ ὁ Νέστος καὶ ὁ Ἕβρος· ἔστι δὲ ἐρῆμον τὸ ὄρος καὶ μέγα, ἐχόμενον τῆς Ῥοδόπης.

97 Ἐγένετο δὲ ἡ ἀρχὴ ἡ Ὀδρυσῶν μέγεθος ἐπὶ μὲν θάλασσαν καθήκουσα ἀπὸ Ἀβδήρων πόλεως ἐς τὸν Εὔξεινον πόντον μέχρι Ἴστρου ποταμοῦ· αὕτη περίπλους ἐστὶν ἡ γῆ τὰ ξυντομώτατα, ἢν αἰεὶ κατὰ πρύμναν ἱστῆται τὸ πνεῦμα, νηὶ στρογγύλῃ τεσσάρων ἡμερῶν καὶ ἴσων νυκτῶν· ὁδῷ δὲ τὰ ξυντομώτατα ἐξ Ἀβδήρων ἐς Ἴστρον ἀνὴρ εὔζωνος ἑνδεκα-
2 ταῖος τελεῖ. τὰ μὲν πρὸς θάλασσαν τοσαύτη ἦν, ἐς ἤπειρον δὲ ἀπὸ Βυζαντίου ἐς Λαιαίους καὶ ἐπὶ τὸν Στρυμόνα (ταύτῃ γὰρ διὰ πλείστου ἀπὸ θαλάσσης ἄνω ἐγίγνετο)
3 ἡμερῶν ἀνδρὶ εὐζώνῳ τριῶν καὶ δέκα ἀνύσαι. φόρος τε ἐκ πάσης τῆς βαρβάρου καὶ τῶν Ἑλληνίδων πόλεων, ὅσων-περ ἦρξαν ἐπὶ Σεύθου, ὃς ὕστερον Σιτάλκου βασιλεύσας πλεῖστον δὴ ἐποίησε, τετρακοσίων ταλάντων ἀργυρίου μά-λιστα δύναμις, ἃ χρυσὸς καὶ ἄργυρος ᾔει· καὶ δῶρα οὐκ ἐλάσσω τούτων χρυσοῦ τε καὶ ἀργύρου προσεφέρετο, χωρὶς δὲ ὅσα ὑφαντά τε καὶ λεῖα καὶ ἡ ἄλλη κατασκευή, καὶ οὐ μόνον αὐτῷ, ἀλλὰ καὶ τοῖς παραδυναστεύουσί τε καὶ γενναίοις

10–11. οὗ secl. Arnold: ποταμοῦ <ἦρχεν> Gomme.
12. Παίονας <τοὺς> Gomme, fortasse recte.
28–9. ὅσωνπερ ἦρξαν Dobree: ὅσων προσῆξαν codd., ὅσον προσῆξαν rec., edd. plerique.

then the Getae beyond Haemus and the peoples living in the other regions south of the River Danube in the direction of the Black Sea. (The Getae and the peoples in this area are neighbours of the Scythians and are armed in the same way as them, all being mounted archers.) He summoned 2 also many of the mountain Thracians who are independent and armed with daggers, men called Dians, most of whom live in Rhodope: some he hired as mercenaries, others came as volunteers. He called up also the Agrianians and 3 Laeaeans, and the other Paeonian tribes subject to him. These were the remotest of his subjects: his kingdom reached as far as the Laeaean Paeonians and the River Strymon, which flows from Mount Scombrus through the territory of the Agrianians and Laeaeans and forms the frontier with those Paeonians who are fully independent. Bordering on the Triballians, who themselves are independent, are the Treres and the Tilataeans: these live to the north of Mount Scombrus and extend in the direction of the sun's setting as far as the River Oscius, which rises in the same mountain as the Nestus and the Hebrus, a large uninhabited mountain connected with Rhodope.

The extent of the Odrysian kingdom along the sea 97 reaches from the city of Abdera to the Black Sea as far as the River Danube: the shortest time for the voyage along the coast, for a merchant ship with a following wind all the way, is four days and four nights; the shortest journey by land from Abdera for a man travelling light is eleven days. That is the length of the coastline. Inland, the greatest distance up-country from the sea is from Byzantium to the Laeaeans and the Strymon, and that takes a man travelling light thirteen days.

The tribute from all the barbarian territory and the 3 Greek cities which they ruled in the time of Seuthes (who reigned after Sitalces and enlarged the kingdom to its greatest extent) was the equivalent of about four hundred talents of silver, paid in gold and silver; there were also gifts of gold and silver worth as much as that, and brocaded and plain cloth and other goods, given not only to the king but also to the Odrysian princes and nobles.

4 Ὀδρυσῶν. κατεστήσαντο γὰρ τοὐναντίον τῆς Περσῶν βασιλείας τὸν νόμον, ὄντα μὲν καὶ τοῖς ἄλλοις Θραξί, λαμβάνειν μᾶλλον ἢ διδόναι (καὶ αἴσχιον ἦν αἰτηθέντα μὴ δοῦναι ἢ αἰτήσαντα μὴ τυχεῖν), ὅμως δὲ κατὰ τὸ δύνασθαι ἐπὶ πλέον αὐτῷ ἐχρήσαντο· οὐ γὰρ ἦν πρᾶξαι οὐδὲν μὴ διδόντα δῶρα. ὥστε ἐπὶ μέγα ἡ βασιλεία ἦλθεν ἰσχύος.
5 τῶν γὰρ ἐν τῇ Εὐρώπῃ ὅσαι μεταξὺ τοῦ Ἰονίου κόλπου καὶ τοῦ Εὐξείνου πόντου μεγίστη ἐγένετο χρημάτων προσόδῳ καὶ τῇ ἄλλῃ εὐδαιμονίᾳ, ἰσχύι δὲ μάχης καὶ στρατοῦ πλήθει
6 πολὺ δευτέρα μετὰ τὴν Σκυθῶν. ταύτῃ δὲ ἀδύνατα ἐξισοῦσθαι οὐχ ὅτι τὰ ἐν τῇ Εὐρώπῃ, ἀλλ᾽ οὐδ᾽ ἐν τῇ Ἀσίᾳ ἔθνος ἓν πρὸς ἓν οὐκ ἔστιν ὅτι δυνατὸν Σκύθαις ὁμογνωμονοῦσι πᾶσιν ἀντιστῆναι. οὐ μὴν οὐδ᾽ ἐς τὴν ἄλλην εὐβουλίαν καὶ ξύνεσιν περὶ τῶν παρόντων ἐς τὸν βίον ἄλλοις ὁμοιοῦνται.

98 Σιτάλκης μὲν οὖν χώρας τοσαύτης βασιλεύων παρεσκευάζετο τὸν στρατόν. καὶ ἐπειδὴ αὐτῷ ἑτοῖμα ἦν, ἄρας ἐπορεύετο ἐπὶ τὴν Μακεδονίαν πρῶτον μὲν διὰ τῆς αὑτοῦ ἀρχῆς, ἔπειτα διὰ Κερκίνης ἐρήμου ὄρους, ὅ ἐστι μεθόριον Σιντῶν καὶ Παιόνων· ἐπορεύετο δὲ δι᾽ αὐτοῦ τῇ ὁδῷ ἣν πρότερον αὐτὸς ἐποιήσατο τεμὼν τὴν ὕλην, ὅτε ἐπὶ Παίονας
2 ἐστράτευσεν. τὸ δὲ ὄρος ἐξ Ὀδρυσῶν διιόντες ἐν δεξιᾷ μὲν εἶχον Παίονας, ἐν ἀριστερᾷ δὲ Σιντοὺς καὶ Μαιδούς. διελθόντες δὲ αὐτὸ ἀφίκοντο ἐς Δόβηρον τὴν Παιονικήν.
3 πορευομένῳ δὲ αὐτῷ ἀπεγίγνετο μὲν οὐδὲν τοῦ στρατοῦ εἰ μή τι νόσῳ, προσεγίγνετο δέ· πολλοὶ γὰρ τῶν αὐτονόμων Θρᾳκῶν ἀπαράκλητοι ἐφ᾽ ἁρπαγὴν ἠκολούθουν, ὥστε τὸ πᾶν πλῆθος λέγεται οὐκ ἔλασσον πέντε καὶ δέκα μυριάδων
4 γενέσθαι· καὶ τούτου τὸ μὲν πλέον πεζὸν ἦν, τριτημόριον δὲ μάλιστα ἱππικόν. τοῦ δ᾽ ἱππικοῦ τὸ πλεῖστον αὐτοὶ Ὀδρύσαι παρείχοντο καὶ μετ᾽ αὐτοὺς Γέται. τοῦ δὲ πεζοῦ [οἱ μαχαιροφόροι] μαχιμώτατοι μὲν ἦσαν οἱ ἐκ τῆς Ῥοδόπης

---

32. οἱ μαχαιροφόροι secl. de Romilly.

They had adopted the opposite custom to that of the Persian empire, a custom of taking rather than giving, and it was more disgraceful to be asked and not to give than to ask and not to obtain. They shared this custom with the other Thracians, but their power enabled them to practise it to a greater extent, and it was impossible to achieve anything without giving presents. So the kingdom was able to rise to great heights of strength. Of all the nations in Europe between the Ionic Gulf and the Black Sea, this was the greatest in terms of the revenue it received and general prosperity, though for strength in battle and the size of its army it fell a long way short of the Scythians. In that respect, not only in Europe but in Asia as well, if one single people is to be compared with another there is none that could match the Scythians when they were all united. However, with regard to good policy and intelligent use of their natural resources the Scythians are not on the same level as others. That is the territory over which Sitalces ruled.

He prepared his army, and when he was ready he set out for Macedonia. He proceeded first through his own kingdom, then through the uninhabited Mount Cercina, which marks the boundary between the Sintians and the Paeonians. He made this journey along the road which he had built, by felling the timber, on a previous occasion when he had campaigned against the Paeonians. As they passed through the mountain from the land of the Odrysians, they had the Paeonians on their right and the Sintians and Maedians on their left. On completing their passage they arrived at Doberus in Paeonia. During the march the army suffered no losses except from illness, but it received additions, since many of the independent Thracians joined it spontaneously in the hope of booty. The whole force was said to number not less than a hundred and fifty thousand, of whom the majority were infantry but about a third were cavalry. The largest number of cavalry were provided by the Odrysians themselves, and next to them by the Getae. The most warlike infantry were the independent men who had come down from Rhodope, while

αὐτόνομοι καταβάντες, ὁ δὲ ἄλλος ὅμιλος ξύμμεικτος πλήθει
99 φοβερώτατος ἠκολούθει. ξυνηθροίζοντο οὖν ἐν τῇ Δοβήρῳ
καὶ παρεσκευάζοντο, ὅπως κατὰ κορυφὴν ἐσβαλοῦσιν ἐς τὴν
2 κάτω Μακεδονίαν, ἧς ὁ Περδίκκας ἦρχεν. τῶν γὰρ Μακεδόνων εἰσὶ καὶ Λυγκησταὶ καὶ Ἐλιμιῶται καὶ ἄλλα ἔθνη 5
ἐπάνωθεν, ἃ ξύμμαχα μέν ἐστι τούτοις καὶ ὑπήκοα, βασιλείας
3 δ᾽ ἔχει καθ᾽ αὑτά. τὴν δὲ παρὰ θάλασσαν νῦν Μακεδονίαν
Ἀλέξανδρος ὁ Περδίκκου πατὴρ καὶ οἱ πρόγονοι αὐτοῦ,
Τημενίδαι τὸ ἀρχαῖον ὄντες ἐξ Ἄργους, πρῶτοι ἐκτήσαντο
καὶ ἐβασίλευσαν ἀναστήσαντες μάχῃ ἐκ μὲν Πιερίας Πίερας, 10
οἳ ὕστερον ὑπὸ τὸ Πάγγαιον πέραν Στρυμόνος ᾤκησαν
Φάγρητα καὶ ἄλλα χωρία (καὶ ἔτι καὶ νῦν Πιερικὸς κόλπος
καλεῖται ἡ ὑπὸ τῷ Παγγαίῳ πρὸς θάλασσαν γῆ), ἐκ δὲ τῆς
Βοττίας καλουμένης Βοττιαίους, οἳ νῦν ὅμοροι Χαλκιδέων
4 οἰκοῦσιν· τῆς δὲ Παιονίας παρὰ τὸν Ἀξιὸν ποταμὸν 15
στενήν τινα καθήκουσαν ἄνωθεν μέχρι Πέλλης καὶ θαλάσσης ἐκτήσαντο, καὶ πέραν Ἀξιοῦ μέχρι Στρυμόνος τὴν
Μυγδονίαν καλουμένην Ἠδῶνας ἐξελάσαντες νέμονται.
5 ἀνέστησαν δὲ καὶ ἐκ τῆς νῦν Ἐορδίας καλουμένης Ἐορδούς,
ὧν οἱ μὲν πολλοὶ ἐφθάρησαν, βραχὺ δέ τι αὐτῶν περὶ 20
6 Φύσκαν κατῴκηται, καὶ ἐξ Ἀλμωπίας Ἄλμωπας. ἐκράτησαν
δὲ καὶ τῶν ἄλλων ἐθνῶν οἱ Μακεδόνες οὗτοι, ἃ καὶ νῦν ἔτι
ἔχουσι, τόν τε Ἀνθεμοῦντα καὶ Γρηστωνίαν καὶ Βισαλτίαν
καὶ Μακεδόνων αὐτῶν πολλήν. τὸ δὲ ξύμπαν Μακεδονία
καλεῖται, καὶ Περδίκκας Ἀλεξάνδρου βασιλεὺς αὐτῶν ἦν 25
ὅτε Σιτάλκης ἐπῄει.
100 Καὶ οἱ μὲν Μακεδόνες οὗτοι ἐπιόντος πολλοῦ στρατοῦ
ἀδύνατοι ὄντες ἀμύνεσθαι ἔς τε τὰ καρτερὰ καὶ τὰ τείχη,
2 ὅσα ἦν ἐν τῇ χώρᾳ, ἐσεκομίσθησαν. ἦν δὲ οὐ πολλά, ἀλλὰ
ὕστερον Ἀρχέλαος ὁ Περδίκκου υἱὸς βασιλεὺς γενόμενος 30
τὰ νῦν ὄντα ἐν τῇ χώρᾳ ᾠκοδόμησε καὶ ὁδοὺς εὐθείας ἔτεμε
καὶ τἆλλα διεκόσμησε τά [τε] κατὰ τὸν πόλεμον ἵπποις καὶ
ὅπλοις καὶ τῇ ἄλλῃ παρασκευῇ κρείσσονι ἢ ξύμπαντες οἱ
3 ἄλλοι βασιλῆς ὀκτὼ οἱ πρὸ αὐτοῦ γενόμενοι. ὁ δὲ στρατὸς
τῶν Θρᾳκῶν ἐκ τῆς Δοβήρου ἐσέβαλε πρῶτον μὲν ἐς τὴν

the rest of the crowd was a mixture terrifying mostly for its size.

This force assembled in Doberus and made its preparations, in order to descend from the heights on to Lower Macedonia, over which Perdiccas ruled. The Macedonians include also the Lyncestians, Elimiotians and other upland tribes, which are allies and subjects of Lower Macedonia but have their own royal houses. What is now coastal Macedonia was first obtained by Perdiccas' father Alexander and his forebears, who were Temenids originating from Argos. They established the kingdom by defeating in battle and expelling the Pierians from Pieria (they subsequently settled in Phagres and other places below Pangaeum beyond the Strymon, on account of which the coastal stretch below Pangaeum is still called the Pierian Gulf) and the Bottiaeans, who are now neighbours of the Chalcidians, from what is called Bottia. The Macedonians also acquired a narrow stretch of Paeonia running down along the River Axius as far as Pella and the sea; and by driving out the Edonians they occupied what is called Mygdonia, beyond the Axius as far as the Strymon. They also expelled the Eordians from what is now called Eordia (most of these were killed, but a small number were settled near Physca), and the Almopians from Almopia. These Macedonians conquered other peoples too, and still control them: Anthemus, Grestonia, Bisaltia and much of Macedonia also. The whole of this is known as Macedonia, and Perdiccas son of Alexander was its king when Sitalces attacked.

These Macedonians were unable to withstand the attack of a large army, so they migrated into such strong points and fortresses as there were in the country. There were not many of these. It was Perdiccas' son Archelaus, who reigned afterwards, who constructed those which now exist in the country, built straight roads, and organised other military matters so as to obtain stronger cavalry, infantry and other forces than any of the eight kings who reigned before him had possessed. The Thracian army on leaving Doberus first invaded what had previously been

Φιλίππου πρότερον οὖσαν ἀρχήν, καὶ εἷλεν Εἰδομενὴν μὲν κατὰ κράτος, Γορτυνίαν δὲ καὶ Ἀταλάντην καὶ ἄλλα ἄττα χωρία ὁμολογίᾳ διὰ τὴν Ἀμύντου φιλίαν προσχωροῦντα τοῦ Φιλίππου υἱέος παρόντος· Εὐρωπὸν δὲ ἐπολιόρκησαν 4 μέν, ἑλεῖν δὲ οὐκ ἐδύναντο. ἔπειτα δὲ καὶ ἐς τὴν ἄλλην Μακεδονίαν προυχώρει τὴν ἐν ἀριστερᾷ Πέλλης καὶ Κύρρου. ἔσω δὲ τούτων ἐς τὴν Βοττίαν καὶ Πιερίαν οὐκ ἀφίκοντο, ἀλλὰ τήν τε Μυγδονίαν καὶ Γρηστωνίαν καὶ Ἀνθεμοῦντα 5 ἐδῄουν. οἱ δὲ Μακεδόνες πεζῷ μὲν οὐδὲ διενοοῦντο ἀμύνεσθαι, ἵππους δὲ προσμεταπεμψάμενοι ἀπὸ τῶν ἄνω ξυμμάχων, ὅπῃ δοκοίη, ὀλίγοι πρὸς πολλοὺς ἐσέβαλλον ἐς τὸ στράτευμα τῶν Θρᾳκῶν. καὶ ᾗ μὲν προσπέσοιεν, οὐδεὶς ὑπέμενεν ἄνδρας ἱππέας τε ἀγαθοὺς καὶ τεθωρακισμένους, ὑπὸ δὲ πλήθους περικλῃόμενοι αὑτοὺς πολλαπλασίῳ τῷ ὁμίλῳ ἐς κίνδυνον καθίστασαν, ὥστε τέλος ἡσυχίαν ἦγον, 101 οὐ νομίζοντες ἱκανοὶ εἶναι πρὸς τὸ πλέον κινδυνεύειν. ὁ δὲ Σιτάλκης πρός τε τὸν Περδίκκαν λόγους ἐποιεῖτο ὧν ἕνεκα ἐστράτευσε, καὶ ἐπειδὴ οἱ Ἀθηναῖοι οὐ παρῆσαν ταῖς ναυσίν, ἀπιστοῦντες αὐτὸν μὴ ἥξειν, δῶρα δὲ καὶ πρέσβεις ἔπεμψαν αὐτῷ, ἔς τε τοὺς Χαλκιδέας καὶ Βοττιαίους μέρος τι τοῦ στρατοῦ πέμπει, καὶ τειχήρεις ποιήσας ἐδῄου τὴν γῆν. 2 καθημένου δ' αὐτοῦ περὶ τοὺς χώρους τούτους οἱ πρὸς νότον οἰκοῦντες Θεσσαλοὶ καὶ Μάγνητες καὶ οἱ ἄλλοι ὑπήκοοι Θεσσαλῶν καὶ οἱ μέχρι Θερμοπυλῶν Ἕλληνες ἐφοβήθησαν μὴ καὶ ἐπὶ σφᾶς ὁ στρατὸς χωρήσῃ, καὶ ἐν παρασκευῇ 3 ἦσαν. ἐφοβήθησαν δὲ καὶ οἱ πέραν Στρυμόνος πρὸς βορέαν Θρᾷκες, ὅσοι πεδία εἶχον, Παναῖοι καὶ Ὀδόμαντοι καὶ Δρῶοι καὶ Δερσαῖοι· αὐτόνομοι δ' εἰσὶ πάντες. 4 παρέσχε δὲ λόγον καὶ ἐπὶ τοὺς τῶν Ἀθηναίων πολεμίους Ἕλληνας, μὴ ὑπ' αὐτῶν ἀγόμενοι κατὰ τὸ ξυμμαχικὸν καὶ

---

7. Βοττίαν scripsi, cf. 99 § 3: Βοττιαίαν codd.

Philip's kingdom: Eidomene was taken by force, while Gortynia, Atalante and some other places went over to the Thracians by voluntary agreement, because of their friendship with Philip's son Amyntas, who was accompanying the Thracians. They attempted to take Europus by siege, but were unsuccessful. Then they advanced into the 4 rest of Macedonia, on the left of Pella and Cyrrhus. They did not continue beyond there to Bottia and Pieria, but proceeded to lay waste Mygdonia, Grestonia and Anthemus.

The Macedonians did not even think of resisting with 5 infantry, but they sent for additional cavalry from those of their allies in the interior to whom they decided to appeal, and, few against many though they were, they attacked the Thracian army. At the point where their attack was made, no one could withstand them, since they were good horsemen and were protected by corslets; but they were encircled by the large forces of the enemy, and were in danger through confronting numbers many times their own, so in the end they gave up their attempt, thinking that the danger from the enemy's larger forces was too great for them.

Sitalces began negotiations with Perdiccas about the 101 objects of his campaign; and, since the Athenians, not believing that he would come, had not arrived with their ships but had merely sent him presents and envoys, he sent part of his army against the Chalcidians and Bottiaeans, forced them to stay inside their walls and proceeded to lay waste their land. When he was established 2 in that region the peoples to the south — the Thessalians, the Magnesians, the other subjects of the Thessalians and the Greeks as far as Thermopylae — grew afraid that the army might move against them, and began to make preparations. The same fear was felt by the Thracians to 3 the north beyond the Strymon who occupied the plains — that is, by the Panaeans, the Odomantians, the Droans and the Dersaeans, who are all independent. Sitalces aroused 4 speculation even among the Greeks who were opposed to Athens, that the Thracians might be invoked by Athens in accordance with their alliance and might move against

5 ἐπὶ σφᾶς χωρήσωσιν. ὁ δὲ τήν τε Χαλκιδικὴν καὶ Βοττικὴν καὶ Μακεδονίαν ἅμα ἐπέχων ἔφθειρε, καὶ ἐπειδὴ αὐτῷ οὐδὲν ἐπράσσετο ὧν ἕνεκα ἐσέβαλε καὶ ἡ στρατιὰ σῖτόν τε οὐκ εἶχεν αὐτῷ καὶ ὑπὸ χειμῶνος ἐταλαιπώρει, ἀναπείθεται ὑπὸ Σεύθου τοῦ Σπαραδόκου, ἀδελφιδοῦ ὄντος καὶ μέγιστον μεθ' ἑαυτὸν δυναμένου, ὥστ' ἐν τάχει ἀπελθεῖν. τὸν δὲ Σεύθην κρύφα Περδίκκας ὑποσχόμενος ἀδελφὴν ἑαυτοῦ δώσειν καὶ 6 χρήματα ἐπ' αὐτῇ προσποιεῖται. καὶ ὁ μὲν πεισθεὶς καὶ μείνας τριάκοντα τὰς πάσας ἡμέρας, τούτων δὲ ὀκτὼ ἐν Χαλκιδεῦσιν, ἀνεχώρησε τῷ στρατῷ κατὰ τάχος ἐπ' οἴκου· Περδίκκας δὲ ὕστερον Στρατονίκην τὴν ἑαυτοῦ ἀδελφὴν δίδωσι Σεύθῃ, ὥσπερ ὑπέσχετο. τὰ μὲν οὖν κατὰ τὴν Σιτάλκου στρατείαν οὕτως ἐγένετο.

102 Οἱ δὲ ἐν Ναυπάκτῳ Ἀθηναῖοι τοῦ αὐτοῦ χειμῶνος, ἐπειδὴ τὸ τῶν Πελοποννησίων ναυτικὸν διελύθη, Φορμίωνος ἡγουμένου ἐστράτευσαν, παραπλεύσαντες ἐπ' Ἀστακοῦ καὶ ἀποβάντες, ἐς τὴν μεσόγειαν τῆς Ἀκαρνανίας τετρακοσίοις μὲν ὁπλίταις Ἀθηναίων τῶν ἀπὸ τῶν νεῶν, τετρακοσίοις δὲ Μεσσηνίων, καὶ ἔκ τε Στράτου καὶ Κορόντων καὶ ἄλλων χωρίων ἄνδρας οὐ δοκοῦντας βεβαίους εἶναι ἐξήλασαν, καὶ Κύνητα τὸν Θεολύτου ἐς Κόροντα καταγαγόντες ἀνεχώρησαν 2 πάλιν ἐπὶ τὰς ναῦς. ἐς γὰρ Οἰνιάδας αἰεί ποτε πολεμίους ὄντας μόνους Ἀκαρνάνων οὐκ ἐδόκει δυνατὸν εἶναι χειμῶνος ὄντος στρατεύειν. ὁ γὰρ Ἀχελῷος ποταμὸς ῥέων ἐκ Πίνδου ὄρους διὰ Δολοπίας καὶ Ἀγραίων καὶ Ἀμφιλόχων καὶ διὰ τοῦ Ἀκαρνανικοῦ πεδίου, ἄνωθεν μὲν παρὰ Στράτον πόλιν, ἐς θάλασσαν δ' ἐξιεὶς παρ' Οἰνιάδας καὶ τὴν πόλιν αὐτοῖς περιλιμνάζων, ἄπορον ποιεῖ ὑπὸ τοῦ ὕδατος ἐν χειμῶνι 3 στρατεύειν. κεῖνται δὲ καὶ τῶν νήσων τῶν Ἐχινάδων αἱ πολλαὶ καταντικρὺ Οἰνιαδῶν τοῦ Ἀχελῴου τῶν ἐκβολῶν οὐδὲν ἀπέχουσαι, ὥστε μέγας ὢν ὁ ποταμὸς προσχοῖ αἰεὶ καὶ εἰσὶ τῶν νήσων αἳ ἠπείρωνται, ἐλπὶς δὲ καὶ πάσας οὐκ

them.

However, after holding and ravaging Chalcidice, the 5
land of the Bottiaeans and also Macedonia, when he found
that he could not achieve any of the objects of his invasion, and his army was running out of food and was suffering from the wintry conditions, he was persuaded to
make a speedy withdrawal by Seuthes son of Sparadocus,
who was his nephew and had the greatest authority after
himself. Perdiccas had won over Seuthes by secretly promising to give him his sister in marriage and a dowry
with her. Sitalces accepted Seuthes' advice, and returned 6
home quickly with his army. He had stayed thirty days in
all, eight of them in Chalcidian territory. Afterwards
Perdiccas kept his promise, and gave his sister Strato-
nice in marriage to Seuthes. That is how Sitalces' campaign turned out.

In the same winter, after the Peloponnesian fleet 102
had been disbanded, the Athenians at Naupactus went on a
campaign under the command of Phormio. They sailed along
the coast to Astacus, disembarked there, and went inland
with four hundred Athenian hoplites from the crews of
their ships and four hundred Messenians. They expelled
from Stratus, Coronta and other places men whom they considered unreliable, reinstated Cynes son of Theolytus in
Coronta, and went back to their ships. As it was winter, 2
they decided that they could not campaign against Oeniadae, the one place in Acarnania which had always been
hostile to them.

The reason for this decision was that the River
Achelous, which flows from Mount Pindus through the territory of the Dolopians, Agraeans and Amphilochians and
through the plain of Acarnania, and passes the city of
Stratus as it descends from the hills, flows into the sea
by Oeniadae and forms a lake around the city, so that in
winter the level of the water makes an attack impossible.
Most of the Echinades Islands lie opposite Oeniadae, not 3
far from the mouths of the Achelous, so that the river
with its strong current is always forming deposits against them: some of the islands have already been joined

4 ἐν πολλῷ τινὶ ἂν χρόνῳ τοῦτο παθεῖν· τό τε γὰρ ῥεῦμά ἐστι μέγα καὶ πολὺ καὶ θολερόν, αἵ τε νῆσοι πυκναί, καὶ ἀλλήλαις τῆς προσχώσεως τοῦ μὴ σκεδάννυσθαι ξύνδεσμοι γίγνονται, παραλλὰξ καὶ οὐ κατὰ στοῖχον κείμεναι, οὐδ'
5 ἔχουσαι εὐθείας διόδους τοῦ ὕδατος ἐς τὸ πέλαγος. ἐρῆμοι δ' εἰσὶ καὶ οὐ μεγάλαι. λέγεται δὲ καὶ Ἀλκμέωνι τῷ Ἀμφιάρεω, ὅτε δὴ ἀλᾶσθαι αὐτὸν μετὰ τὸν φόνον τῆς μητρός, τὸν Ἀπόλλω ταύτην τὴν γῆν χρῆσαι οἰκεῖν, ὑπειπόντα οὐκ εἶναι λύσιν τῶν δειμάτων πρὶν ἂν εὑρὼν ἐν ταύτῃ τῇ χώρᾳ κατοικίσηται ἥτις ὅτε ἔκτεινε τὴν μητέρα μήπω ὑπὸ ἡλίου ἑωρᾶτο μηδὲ γῆ ἦν, ὡς τῆς γε ἄλλης αὐτῷ
6 μεμιασμένης. ὁ δ' ἀπορῶν, ὥς φασι, μόλις κατενόησε τὴν πρόσχωσιν ταύτην τοῦ Ἀχελῴου, καὶ ἐδόκει αὐτῷ ἱκανὴ ἂν ἰεχῶσθαι δίαιτα τῷ σώματι ἀφ' οὗπερ κτείνας τὴν μητέρα οὐκ ὀλίγον χρόνον ἐπλανᾶτο. καὶ κατοικισθεὶς ἐς τοὺς περὶ Οἰνιάδας τόπους ἐδυνάστευσέ τε καὶ ἀπὸ Ἀκαρνᾶνος παιδὸς ἑαυτοῦ τῆς χώρας τὴν ἐπωνυμίαν ἐγκατέλιπεν. τὰ μὲν περὶ Ἀλκμέωνα τοιαῦτα λεγόμενα παρελάβομεν.
103 Οἱ δὲ Ἀθηναῖοι καὶ ὁ Φορμίων ἄραντες ἐκ τῆς Ἀκαρνανίας καὶ ἀφικόμενοι ἐς τὴν Ναύπακτον ἅμα ἦρι κατέπλευσαν ἐς τὰς Ἀθήνας, τούς τε ἐλευθέρους τῶν αἰχμαλώτων ἐκ τῶν ναυμαχιῶν ἄγοντες, οἳ ἀνὴρ ἀντ' ἀνδρὸς ἐλύθησαν,
2 καὶ τὰς ναῦς ἃς εἷλον. καὶ ὁ χειμὼν ἐτελεύτα οὗτος, καὶ τρίτον ἔτος τῷ πολέμῳ ἐτελεύτα τῷδε ὃν Θουκυδίδης ξυνέγραψεν.

3. τοῦ μὴ σκεδάννυσθαι Poppo: τὸ μὴ σκεδάννυσθαι C E, τῷ μὴ σκεδάννυσθαι cett., non legit schol., secl. Stahl.

to the mainland, and it is to be expected that this will happen to all of them within a short time, since the current is strong, deep and muddy, and the islands are close together and form a framework to hold the deposit and prevent it from being dispersed. The islands are situated not in lines but across the current, so that they do not leave the water straight routes out into the sea. They are small and uninhabited.

It is said that Alcmeon son of Amphiaraus, when he became a fugitive after the murder of his mother, received an oracle from Apollo that he was to live in this land: it was indicated that he would not be released from his fears until he found somewhere in this country to occupy which had not yet been seen by the sun or existed as land at the time when he killed his mother, since all other land was unclean for him. He was at a loss, they say, but he eventually discovered this deposit of the Achelous and decided that a sufficient amount had accumulated to sustain his life during the considerable period of his wanderings after killing his mother. So he settled in the district around Oeniadae, became its ruler, and gave the land its name from his son Acarnan. That is the tradition which has come down to us about Acarnan.

Phormio and the Athenians set out from Acarnania and arrived at Naupactus. At the beginning of spring they sailed back to Athens, taking with them the free men from the prisoners whom they had taken in the naval battles, who were released in a one-for-one exchange, and the ships which they had captured. That was the end of the winter, and of the third year of this war of which Thucydides wrote the history.

COMMENTARY

1. Formal Beginning of War

1. Here we reach the starting-point: Book I was concerned with the causes of the war and the preliminary incidents, up to the final diplomatic exchanges of winter 432/1. Thucydides regards the attack on Plataea, though made "while the peace still held", as the first incident of the war proper. It would be possible to regard this as the last preliminary incident and Sparta's invasion of Attica, preceded by a final herald (10-12, 18-23) as the formal beginning of the war (cf. 19. 1 n., where there is a second introduction): V. 20. 1 seems at first sight to treat the invasion of Attica as the beginning of the war, but its chronology takes the attack on Plataea to be the beginning, and many emend the text there to eliminate the alternative view.

the Athenians and Peloponnesians: The reverse order was used in I. 1. 1. We adopt an Athenian viewpoint and write of the Peloponnesian War, but on this formal matter Thucydides achieves neutrality.

without a herald: Heralds, sent to make formal proclamations, were recognised as inviolate, and so could enter enemy territory even during a state of war. Until this point normal contacts had continued, but uneasily (I. 146).

state of continuous war: The war of 431 - 421 is thus described in V. 24. 2, VI. 26. 2.

I have recorded the events: Some have seen in the Greek wording the implication that Thucydides recorded all of the events (cf. Marcellin. *Vit. Thuc.* 47 and Hornblower, *Thucydides*, 37), but this view seems to me mistaken. In III. 91 Thucydides admits to being selective on Sicilian events in the 420s.

by summers and winters: Since each state had its own calendar, and many including Athens began their new year in the summer, i.e. in the middle of the campaigning season, Thucydides adopts a natural calendar of summers and winters, and identifies points within summer or winter by natural phenomena (cf. 2. 1 n., 19. 1 n., 1. 1, 78. 2 n.). In V. 20. 2-3 he claims that this is more accurate than the use of official years; in I. 97. 2 he complains of the chronological inaccuracy of Hellanicus of Lesbos (but makes the complaint in the course of a survey of Athens' growth before the Peloponnesian War which is itself lacking in chronological precision, and does not indicate in what respects Hellanicus was inaccurate). It may be partly because the attack on Plataea occurred "at the beginning of spring" (2. 1) that he has decided to treat this as the beginning of the war.

2 - 32. First Summer (431)

2. Thebes' Attempt to Seize Plataea

2. 1. <u>The thirty-year truce</u>: Euboea revolted against Athens; Sparta invaded Attica, but turned back without reaching Athens; the Athenians recovered Euboea; and then a thirty-year peace treaty was made, by which Athens gave up the possessions which she had acquired in mainland Greece since c. 460 but had her control of the Delian League recognised by Sparta and her allies (I. 114 - 115. 1). Counting with ordinal numbers is inclusive: Euboea revolted and Sparta invaded Attica in 446, and the peace was made in 446/5; the Peloponnesian War began in 432/1 (for events before the summer of 431 Thucydides probably uses Athenian official years).

<u>Chrysis</u>: Although Thucydides proposes to use natural years (1), he identifies the year in which the war began by reference to the eponymous officials of three leading states, Argos (neutral in the first phase of the war), Sparta and Athens. Similarly the Spartan ephor and the Athenian archon of 421/0 are named in V. 25. 1, where Thucydides records the continuation of the war after the Peace of Nicias (as well as in the preamble of the treaty, with precise dates, V. 19. 1). The multiple dating adds emphasis and solemnity to the formal record of the beginning of the war, and establishes the history as one written not just for an Athenian audience. Argos dated by priestesses of Hera (a work on whom was written by Hellanicus: *FGrH* 4 FF 74-84); Chrysis fled into exile when the temple of Hera was burned in summer 423 (IV. 133. 2-3); Sparta dated by one of the five annual ephors; Athens dated by that one of the annual board of nine archons whose title was simply archon. Herodotus once dates by an Athenian archon, for the Persian King Xerxes' arrival at Athens in 480/79 (VIII. 51. 1).

<u>four months</u>: The manuscripts have "two", but since the Athenian year ended after the summer solstice "the beginning of spring" should be more than two months earlier: δ = 4 and δ as initial of δύo = 2 were easily confused.

<u>tenth month</u>: The battle at Potidaea, a city founded by and friendly with Corinth but in the Delian League and subjected to

pressure by Athens, was fought in the summer of 432 (I. 56 - 66). It cannot be dated precisely, but the manuscripts' "sixth" is too small a figure, and Hude's "tenth" is both plausible and palaeographically close (δεκάτῳ corrupted to ἕκτῳ).

at the beginning of spring: Cf. 1 n.: "the beginning of spring" is the beginning of Thucydides' summer (IV. 117. 1). It is disputed whether he uses such terms in a common-sense way (e.g. Meritt, *Athenian Calendar*, 108-9) or has in mind precise astronomical definitions (e.g. Gomme, iii. 699 - 721). In favour of the first view is the fact that some of his expressions do not suggest a precise definition (e.g. "when the corn was growing ripe", 19. 1); in favour of the second are the facts that others do (e.g. "about the time of the <heliacal> rising of Arcturus", 78. 2), and that V. 20. 1, stating that the first phase of the war lasted ten years and a few days, seems to imply a fixed point for the beginning of spring. 19. 1 suggests that Thucydides had a more precise date than he gives his readers for the attack on Plataea, but I nevertheless prefer to believe that the only expressions which have a precise astronomical definition are those in which it is explicit. In our calendar, the attack on Plataea is best dated *c*. 10 March 431.

However, G. Busolt, *Griechische Geschichte*, III. ii. 907-15, is followed by W. E. Thompson, *Hermes* 96 (1968), 216-32, and J. D. Smart, in I. S. Moxon *et al.* (edd.), *Past Perspectives*, 19 - 35, in arguing that this attack took place *c*. 8 April, that Pythodorus' archonship ended two months later, *c*. 10 June, and that the Peloponnesian invasion of Attica (19. 1 n.) occurred *c*. 20 June, in the year 431/0 (cf. Diod. Sic. XII. 38. 1). Thompson and Smart leave "sixth month" unemended also, to date the battle at Potidaea to October 432, and Smart believes that "spring" began precisely at the vernal equinox.

at the time of the first watch: A vivid detail. Connor, *Thucydides*, 52-3, points out that this attack is a surprise to the reader as well as to the Plataeans: Thebes and Plataea have not been prominent in book I.

slightly more than three hundred: Four hundred according to Herodotus, wo briefly mentions the episode (VII. 233. 2).

Plataea was situated in Boeotia: Since 519 (Hdt. V. 39 - 42 with Thuc. III. 68. 5; but some emend Thuc. to obtain a later date) Plataea, on the north slope of the Cithaeron - Parnes range which separates Attica from Boeotia, had resisted incorporation in a Boeotian federation dominated by Thebes, and had been an ally of Athens; while she remained pro-Athenian, communication between Thebes and the Peloponnesians would be difficult. At the beginning of the fourth century Boeotia was divided into eleven units, each supplying one of the federal officials called boeotarchs, and Thebes controlled two units in her own right and two on behalf of the suppressed Plataea (*Hell. Oxy.* 16. 2-4): presumably before the destruction of Plataea there were nine units of which Thebes controlled two, and the two boeotarchs mentioned here (of whom nothing is known) were the two from Thebes.

2. 2. Nauclides and his party: In III. 65. 2 the Thebans call them "the leading men by wealth and by family": contrast "the majority of the Plataeans", 3. 2. Nauclides again is unknown. It was common for leaders of minority parties to hope that with support from an outside power they could acquire a ruling position in their state: cf. next note.

2. 3. Eurymachus: His father was the man who brought Thebes on to the Persian side in 480 (Hdt. VII. 233); his son, another Leontiades, as the leader of a minority party brought Spartan occupying forces into Thebes in 382 (Xen. *Hell.* V. 2. 24 - 36, Diod. Sic. XV. 20, etc.).

no guard had yet been set: We learn only from speeches in book III (56. 2, 65. 1) that the Theban attack was made at a time of sacred truce.

2. 4. to be an ally in accordance with the tradition of the whole of Boeotia: συμμαχεῖν with genitive is not attested, but perhaps we should emend to the dative and translate, "to be an ally of all the Boeotians in accordance with tradition". Since 519 Plataea had refused to be "an ally of all the Boeotians", but it belonged to Boeotia geographically (2. 1 n.), and is included in Boeotia in the Homeric catalogue of ships (*Il.* II. 494 - 510). It suited Thebes' purpose to claim that "traditionally" Plataea belonged to Boeotia: later the Thebans are made to claim that they had founded Plataea yet the Plataeans refused to accept Theban leadership (III. 61. 2), and that the invitation from right-thinking Plataeans justified their intervention (65. 1 - 66. 1).

3. 3. to serve as a barricade: The placing of the carts in the streets could not be kept secret, but if activity in the streets was kept to a minimum the Plataeans presumably hoped that this placing of the carts would not be recognised immediately as part of an anti-Theban strategy.

4. 2. attackers: The present participle προσβαλλόντων is needed, to match χρωμένων and βαλλόντων.

at the end of the month: So there was no moon.

and so most of them were killed: Some editors delete, comparing 4. 5 and 5. 7, but it is not incredible that Thucydides wrote

this.
4. 4. a woman: T. E. J. Wiedemann, *G&R*² 31 (1983), 163-70, remarks that women appear very rarely in Thucydides (much more rarely than in Herodotus), and that when they do influence the course of history they are among the irrational influences on events.
undetected: The transposition of λαθόντες is required by the sense.
formed part of the wall: The building had been erected against the inner face of the city wall, which was used as one of its own walls.

5. 2. seventy stades: In fact, 12½ km. or 7¾ miles, equivalent to 71 Athenian stades of 176 metres or 193 yards.
the rain: Plataea allegedly benefits again from rain in 77. 6.
5. 4. there were men in the fields: It was common Greek practice to have one's home in the city (or in a village which formed part of the state) and to go out from there by day to work on the land; but there would often be huts in the fields, and at busy times not every man would return home every night.
5. 6. This is what the Thebans say: Cf. III. 66. 2-3. Thucydides normally records what he believes to be the truth, without mentioning alternative versions (contrast Herodotus, e.g. III. 9. 2, VI. 84); but here, uniquely, he reports two conflicting accounts without deciding between them. Cf. Introduction, p. 5.
5. 7. killed the men: Probably Nauclides and his supporters were put to death too. However, "if the Plataeans had soberly considered what was to their interest instead of acting in anger, . . . Thebes would have been paralysed by having so many citizens held hostage in Plataea" (Kitto, *Poiesis*, 317).

6. 2. arrested: Athens prided itself on being an open society (39. 1), but must nevertheless have kept a close eye on visiting foreigners if these arrests were to be possible.
6. 4. left a garrison: A small one, of eighty men (78. 3). The story of Plataea is continued in 71. 8 (summer 429).

Thucydides does not treat on the same scale all the events of the war which he reports. Militarily the eventual capture of Plataea by the Peloponnesians did not turn out to be of great importance, but Thucydides has chosen this as an episode worthy of full treatment, with a detailed and vivid narrative (see also 71. 1 n.). Various considerations help to explain this. The nearness of Plataea to Athens and their long-standing alliance made the fate of Plataea particularly interesting to an Athenian writer. In addition, moral and political lessons could be drawn from the episode: Plataea was a small state dragged into the conflict between the great powers, and not in the end saved by her long-standing alliance with one of them; Sparta had no direct reason for hostility to Plataea, and because of the battle fought there in 479 might have been expected to leave her alone (III. 54, 58), but to oblige Thebes she captured and destroyed Plataea. A further reason for interest in Plataea may be that in 427 Sparta was not persuaded to relent, but in the same year Athens did (to some extent) modify the savage treatment which she originally intended to inflict on Mytilene. The story of Plataea is repeated in [Dem.] LIX. *Against Neaera*, 98 - 106 (this episode, 98 - 101).

7 - 17. *Final Preparations and Resources*

7. 1. an open breach of the treaty: Cf. 2. 3.
the Persian King: The King, without further specification, is regularly the Persian King. After the Greek defeat of a Persian invasion in 480 - 479, Athens formed the Delian League in 478/7 to continue fighting against Persia, but (whether or not there was a formal treaty, the Peace of Callias) she had not prosecuted the war since *c*. 450 (cf. Introduction, pp. 21-2). Persian help represented Sparta's best chance of matching Athens' superior financial resources, and from 412 to 404 enabled Sparta to confront the Athenians at sea and eventually win the war. Athens needed at least to prevent Persian help from being given to Sparta, and was not averse to trying to obtain it for herself: Ar. *Ach*. 61 - 127 suggests that by 425 she had tried to obtain it for herself. For a Peloponnesian deputation to Persia see 67.
7. 2. in Italy and Sicily: The Greeks of southern Italy and Sicily divided on racial lines. Sparta was nominally supported by all the Dorians in Sicily except Camarina (III. 86. 2), and in Italy by her colony Taras and by Locri (VI. 34. 4, 44. 2); but in 427 "they were reckoned as part of the Spartan alliance but had not joined in the war" (III. 86. 2), and in fact no forces came from the west to fight in Greece until 412, when twenty-two ships came from Syracuse and Selinus to support Sparta (VIII. 26. 1). Athens had alliances with Egesta and Leontini in Sicily and Rhegium in Italy (M&L 37, 64, 63 = *IG* i³ 11, 54, 53): in 427 she responded to an invitation to support Leontini against Syracuse, but she had to withdraw in 424 when the Sicilian Greeks agreed to manage without outside intervention; an invitation from Egesta led to the large-scale Athenian

expedition of 415 which ended in disaster in 413.

to build ships . . . five hundred: There is no sign that this is not serious, but Corinth and her allies in a major effort had mustered 150 ships in 433 (I. 46. 1), and the largest Peloponnesian fleet mentioned in the Archidamian War is of 100 ships (II. 66. 1). Diod. Sic. XII. 41. 1 gives no size for the intended total fleet but 200 as the number of ships requested from the western Greeks: it must have been as unlikely that they would send 200 ships to the Peloponnesians as that the Peloponnesians would acquire 300 of their own. Diodorus, via his fourth-century source Ephorus, has undoubtedly made use of Thucydides (cf. Introduction, pp. 18 - 20), but he does not reproduce him slavishly, and we should not follow Herbst in inserting "to build two hundred ships" in Thucydides' text.

only if they came in a single ship: I.e. to receive their diplomatic missions but not their armed forces, a regular formula for neutrality (cf. III. 71. 1, VI. 52. 1).

7. 3. Corcyra, Cephallenia, Acarnania and Zacynthus: "Most of the Acarnanians, Corcyra and Zacynthus" are listed among Athens' allies in 9. 4; Cephallenia will be won over without fighting in the summer of 431 (30. 2). Athens made a purely defensive alliance with Corcyra when Corcyra asked for support against Corinth in 433 (I. 24 - 55, esp. 44. 1), but by 431 this must have been converted into a full alliance. According to Diod. Sic. XI. 84. 7 Tolmides in 456/5 had subjected Zacynthus and won over Cephallenia (these achievements are not mentioned in Thuc. I. 108. 5, but are credible); Phormio at an unknown date before the Peloponnesian War had taken Athenian help to the Amphilochians and Acarnanians, after which a formal alliance had been made (68. 6-8, with 6 n.).

8. 1. on this occasion: I. 1 - 21 claimed that the Peloponnesian War was greater than any previous war among the Greeks, and we read in I. 18. 3 - 19 that since the Persian Wars Athens and Sparta had reached new heights of power; cf. the claim which Pericles makes for Athens in 64. 3. On superlatives in Thucydides see Introduction, pp. 3 - 4. On Thucydides' pausing at this point, as the war is beginning, to remind us of its greatness. see Kitto, *Poiesis*, 276-7.

who had no experience of war: The Athenians and Peloponnesians had been formally at peace since 446/5 (cf. 2. 1 n.), and in fact there had been little fighting in mainland Greece since 454.

8. 2. Many oracles: Thucydides normally treats religious matters simply as phenomena to be recorded where relevant, without directly expressing disbelief but without giving any sign of belief: only in V. 26. 3-4 does he appear impressed by an oracle's prediction, and only in I. 23. 3 does he seem to entertain the possibility that there was a connection between abnormal natural phenomena and the Peloponnesian War. See Introduction, pp. 12 - 13; and for other references to oracles in book II see 17. 1-2, 54. 2-5 (both passages adopting a rationalising approach), also 21. 3.

oracle-mongers: Literally, oracle-collectors, men who collected responses said to have been given by oracles on various occasions and who tried to purvey them to those to whom they might be relevant. Cf. 21. 3.

8. 3. there had never before been an earthquake: An earlier earthquake on Delos, likewise said to be unique, is recorded by Hdt. VI. 98. 1-3; but Thucydides does not seem to be indulging in polemic against Herodotus here, as he did in I. 20. 3, and we must suppose that he and his informants have forgotten the previous earthquake.

8. 4. A large majority: The claim is repeated in Archidamus' speech, 11. 2. It is consistent with Thucydides' view that the Athenians naturally exercised the power which they could and their subjects naturally hated them for it (cf. Introduction, pp. 13 - 14), but it is not supported by the narrative: Athens does have at the beginning of the war and does acquire during the war allies which are not subjects compelled to support her, and some League cities approached by Sparta are (for whatever reason) reluctant to change sides.

they were going to liberate Greece: Cf. their final demand to Athens, I. 139. 3. They were to prove unable to do this without promising the Greeks of Asia Minor to Persia in return for her support; and other Greeks liberated from Athens were after the war subjected to Sparta.

in so far as he was not present in person: Contrast I. 141. 7, where Pericles depicts a Peloponnese in which every one relies on some one else to act for him.

9. 1. The following were the allies: There are various awkwardnesses in the catalogue which follows, and J. D. Smart, *GR&BS* 18 (1977), 33 - 42, comparing the more straightforward catalogue in Diod. Sic. XII. 42. 4-5, has suggested that what we have here is not Thucydides' own work but an interpolation derived from Ephorus. More probably we should accept that Thucydides was capable of being less than entirely complete and logical.

9. 2. all the Peloponnesians south of the Isthmus: If "Pelopon-

nesians" is taken geographically, rather than as equivalent to "the Spartan alliance", all the Peloponnesians were south of the Isthmus of Corinth; but the meaning is perfectly clear, and there is no need either to emend the text or to deny Thucydidean authorship.

Argos: Never willing to acknowledge Spartan supremacy, Argos had made a thirty-year peace treaty with Sparta in 451 (V. 14. 4), and played no part in the Peloponnesian War until that had expired. Athens may have tried to win Argos' support in 430 (cf. 56. 4 n.).

Achaea: Separated by mountains from the rest of the Peloponnesians, and not much involved with them: it had joined Athens in the 450s, and was an acquisition which Athens was required to give up by the Thirty Years' Peace of 446/5 (I. 111. 3, 115. 1).

which had friendly relations: The English like the Greek is formally ambiguous, but I take the reference to be to Achaea only: Argos did not have friendly relations with Sparta.

Pellene: The easternmost city of Achaea, and the one most ready to cooperate with its neighbours Sicyon and Corinth (e.g. V. 58. 4).

later: It is implied that they are on the Peloponnesian side in the naval campaign of 429 (83 - 92, esp. 87. 6).

Megara: Had supported Corinth in 433 (I. 46. 1), and had complained of sanctions imposed by Athens (I. 67. 4, etc.): cf. 31. 1 n.

Boeotia: Cf. 2 - 6.

Locris: North-eastern, "Opuntian" Locris (which Thucydides regularly intends when writing of Locris without qualification): south-western, "Ozolian" Locris supported Athens (III. 95. 3).

Phocis: Had been on the Athenian side in the First Peloponnesian War (I. 107. 2, 108. 3, 112. 5), and was not firmly pro-Spartan (III. 95. 3).

Ambracia: A colony of Corinth (cf. I. 26. 2), and an enemy of Athens' ally Acarnania (II. 68).

Leucas: A colony of Corinth (cf. I. 26. 2).

Anactorium: A joint colony of Corinth and Corcyra, in the territory of pro-Athenian Acarnania, over which Corinth asserted control in 433 (I. 55. 1). R. L. Beaumont, *JHS* 72 (1952), 62-3, suggested that earlier it had been won for Athens by Phormio, at the same time as Amphilochian Argos (cf. 68. 6-7 with 6 n.).

9. 3. Ships: In 433 Corinth's fleet was provided by herself and Elis, Megara, Leucas, Ambracia, and one ship from a pro-Corinthian faction in Anactorium (I. 46. 1).

9. 4. The allies of Athens were: Thucydides begins with a distinction between free allies (including two in the Delian League) and subjects; among the latter he purports to divide by race but slips into a regional division resembling, but more elaborate than, that used by Athens in the organisation of the league (the tribute quota-lists were divided into five regions from 443/2 and four from the early 430s — Caria and Ionia, Hellespont, Thraceward, Islands — and the regions appear in some other documents too).

Chios, Lesbos: The two Aegean islands which still contributed ships to the Delian League and had not had their autonomy infringed in any way (cf. III. 10. 5).

Plataea: Cf. 2 - 6.

the Messenians at Naupactus: Naupactus had been captured by Athens in 456/5 (Diod. Sic. XI. 84. 7: not mentioned in Thuc. I. 108. 5), and a home was provided there for the Messenians who in the same year agreed to leave the Peloponnese at the end of the Third Messenian War (I. 103. 3, Diod. Sic. XI. 84. 8).

most of the Acarnanians, Corcyra and Zacynthus: Cf. 7. 3 n. Of the Acarnanians Oeniadae was always at odds with the rest (102. 2 n.), and Sollium and Astacus were won during the summer of 431 (30. 1).

coastal Caria: The Carians were non-Greek but hellenised: some of the coastal cities claimed a Greek origin.

the Dorians: Grouped with the Carians in the documents.

Ionia: Which in the documents includes the Aeolians to the north. For the dark-age migration of Aeolian, Ionian and Dorian Greeks to Asia Minor (*c.* 1000 - 900) cf. Hdt. I. 142-51.

the Hellespont, the Thraceward region: Colonised by Greeks from various states in the seventh and sixth centuries.

the islands . . . and all the Cyclades: The Cyclades, the islands of the southern Aegean, are east of the Peloponnese and north of Crete (the southernmost were inhabited by Dorians, the rest by Ionians). It is not at all clear what distinction is intended here; Euboea and the more northerly islands of the Aegean do not fit obviously into either category.

Melos: Refused to join Athens in 426, despite pressure (III. 91. 1-3), was included in the optimistic tribute assessment list of 425 (M&L 69 [p. 200] = *IG* i^3 71, i. 65) but is not likely to have paid, and was finally conquered in 416 (V. 84 - 116). It is uncertain whether Melos gave positive support to Sparta: the dating of an inscription in which Melos is among contributors to a Spartan war fund is disputed between the 420s and the 390s (M&L 67, side, 1-7).

Thera: Thought to have been settled from Sparta (Hdt. IV. 147-

9). It is not mentioned again by Thucydides, but is recorded as paying tribute in 430/29 (*IG* i^3 281, ii. 54: restored) and subsequently. In view of the attention given to Melos, Thucydides' silence about Athens' acquisition of Thera is surprising.

9. 5. ships . . . infantry and money: Ships from Corcyra and other western allies are used in 431 (25. 1), and ships from Chios and Lesbos in 430 (56. 2); soldiers from tribute-paying allies are first mentioned in 425 (IV. 7, 42).

9. 6. Those were the two sides' alliances: Thucydides' lists are incomplete, omitting not only the allies of the two sides in Sicily and Italy (neither side received help from these in the Archidamian War, but Athens sent help to Sicily: cf. 7. 2 n.) but also Thessaly, which sent help to Athens in 431 (22. 2-3). Perdiccas of Macedon, hostile to Athens when the war broke out but turned into an ally during 431 (29. 4-6), changed sides so frequently that his omission here is excusable.

and resources: Only in the limited sense that we have been told which states contributed to their alliance in which way. There is a survey of Athens' own resources in 13. 3-9; for Sparta itself there is a complaint about the secrecy of the state and a review of the army which fought at Mantinea, in 418, in V. 68.

10. 1. the provisions needed: Perhaps for thirty days: cf. 23. 3 with 57. 2, and the alliance quoted in V. 47. 6. An invading force would expect to live to some extent off the enemy's crops.

10. 2. a two-thirds levy: This was normal for a major, but non-emergency, force, and was to be normal for the Peloponnesian invasions of Attica (cf. 47. 2, III. 15. 1). We are not told how many men were in this army, by Thucydides or by Diodorus (XII. 42. 3, 3); Androt. *FGrH* 324 F 39 is corrupt but appears to have had more than 100,000; Plut. *Per.* 33. 5, *An Seni* 784 E, has 60,000. Plutarch was believed by Henderson, *The Great War between Athens and Sparta*, 29, but from what we know of other Greek armies we might expect 30,000 (Busolt, *Griechische Geschichte*, III. ii. 858-61, estimated 23,000 Peloponnesians and 7,000 Boeotians).

10. 3. Archidamus the Spartan king: Given a more formal mention in 19. 1, at the point when Athenian territory is invaded, and given a similar introduction at the beginnings of the following years (47. 2, 71. 1). Sparta had two kings reigning simultaneously: Archidamus was king from the junior, Eurypontid house, perhaps from 478 in fact and from 469, when his exiled grandfather died, in name, until 427. In 432 he is given a speech urging the Spartans to take time for negotiation and prepara-

tion before going to war (I. 79 - 85).

the generals . . . office-holders and most important men: The formal distribution of office and informal distribution of influence will have differed in different states: this is a way of denoting all the leading men, whatever their formal position.

made this speech of encouragement: Only in III. 29. 2 does Thucydides state that a speaker spoke τάδε, "these things", rather than τοιάδε, "on these lines" (in I. 85. 3 he uses ὧδε, "thus"). I do not believe the two departures from his norm are significant, and I have not felt it necessary to emphasise on every occasion in my translation that Thucydides is using a relatively unspecific pronoun. On his speeches, and the balance in them of authentic reporting and free composition, see Introduction, pp. 8 - 9. The speech actually made on this occasion will certainly not have been heard by Thucydides, and is not likely to have been particularly memorable: the speech given here, which helps to focus attention on the first act of war by Sparta and the Peloponnesian League, is consonant both with Thucydides' own view of Athens' unpopularity and with the cautious attitude to Athenian power attributed to Archidamus in his speech in book I and in the narrative of this invasion.

Chs. 10 - 22 are studied by Hunter, *Thucydides, the Artful Reporter*, 11 - 21: she notes how Archidamus' speech in 11 and virtual speech in 20 are matched by the actions which follow (apart from the unexpected response of Pericles), and argues that Thucydides has inferred intentions from results.

11. 1. the older men among ourselves: Cf. 8. 1 n.
we have never set out with a greater force: Cf. 8. 1 n.
11. 2. The whole of Greece: Cf. 8. 1.
with good wishes: Cf. 8. 4 n.
11. 3. there is no danger that our opponents will risk: The main line of the Spartans' strategy was to invade Attica with a large army year after year in the hope that the Athenians would, preferably, take fright and submit to them, or, failing that, come out of the city to fight and be beaten. It was generally expected that this strategy would lead to a Spartan victory (cf. V. 14. 3, VI. 11. 5, VII. 28. 3), but in I. 81. 1-4 Archidamus considers the point that the Peloponnesians are superior in forces and can ravage Athens' territory, but doubts whether they can obtain victory in this way. For Athens' response to this strategy see especially 13. 2, 21. 2 - 22. 2.
11. 4. War is full of uncertainty: Cf. Archidamus in I. 84. 3, Pericles in II. 64. 1 on what cannot be foreseen, and other

Thucydidean speakers. Thucydides believed in chance as a factor leading to results which cannot be predicted: cf. Introduction, p. 12.

11. 6. not at all unable to defend itself: Inferior in infantry and cavalry to the Peloponnesians, so Archidamus has to warn his men against despising them, but still no mean force, so likely to resist rather than take fright and submit.

is most fully prepared in every respect: Cf. Archidamus in I. 80. 3. Pericles will give the Athenians an account of their resources in 13. 3-9.

11. 7. before their very eyes: Cf. 21. 2.

least able to reason . . . most liable to act in passion: The contrast between reason and passion is frequently made in book II. Pericles will claim that the Athenians, more than others, act not in passion but after reasoned deliberation (40. 2-3, 62. 4-5); in 22. 1 he will prevent the assembly from meeting during the Peloponnesian invasion, when it is likely to be infulenced by passion rather than reason.

11. 8. are accustomed to invade their neighbours' land: Cf. Pericles in 39. 2.

11. 9. for our ancestors and for ourselves: Pericles in his funeral speech and his final speech thinks more of posterity than of ancestors (41. 4, 64. 3).

discipline: This is a characteristic associated particularly with Sparta (cf. Archidamus in I. 84. 3), but in 89. 9 Phormio calls on the Athenian sailors to show it.

respond promptly to commands: Cf. V. 66. 3-4, on the promptness with which commands are handed down in the Spartan army.

12. 1. Melesippus: One of the three members of the final Spartan deputation to Athens in winter 432/1 (I. 139. 3); nothing else is known of him.

12. 2. meet the public authorities: The correct procedure would be for him to approach the *prytaneis*, the fifty members from one tribe in the council of five hundred who served as its standing committee for one tenth of the year; they, if they saw fit, could bring him before the council; the council could bring him before the assembly (cf. *Ath. Pol.* 43. 2-6). For the involvement of the generals in these procedures during the Peloponnesian War see 22. 1 n., 59. 3.

a proposal of Pericles had been carried: Probably as a decree of the assembly.

12. 3. the beginning of great misfortune for the Greeks: Likewise, the Peace of Nicias in 421 was to be the beginning of great benefit for the Greeks (Ar. *Pax* 435-6). The original

model for such remarks is Hom. *Od.* VIII. 81; cf. *Il.* XXII. 116, also Hdt. V. 97. 3.

12. 4. <u>advanced towards their territory</u>: But by a circuitous route, postponing the moment of invasion (cf. 18. 1, 19. 1).

13. 1. <u>Pericles . . . one of the ten Athenian generals</u>: He is formally introduced here, as Archidamus is formally introduced in 19. 1, though these are not the first appearances in Thucydides of either (Pericles has already been formally introduced once, in I. 139. 4, before his first speech, and the first mention of him is earlier than that). Pericles was born in the 490s, was active in politics from the late 460s, and died in 429: for his position as leader of the Athenian democracy see 65 nn. K. J. Dover has shown that στρατηγὸς ὢν . . . δέκατος αὐτός means simply "one of the ten generals", without ascribing any formal superiority to the one so designated (*JHS* 80 (1960), 61 - 77: rejected unconvincingly by E. F. Bloedow, *Chiron* 11 (1981), 65 - 72). When the board of ten generals was established, in 501/0, one general was elected from each tribe (*Ath. Pol.* 22. 2): this remained the norm until the second half of the fourth century, but at any rate from 441/0 (Androt. *FGrH* 324 F 38) it was possible at any rate for one tribe to supply two generals and one other to supply none. The best explanation is that this was a provision for occasions when none of the candidates in one tribe could obtain a majority vote (M. Piérart, *BCH* 98 (1974), 125-46), and that when Pericles had a colleague from his own tribe, as happened on a number of occasions, what was striking was not that fact (probably Pericles was elected to his own tribe's place, not as a substitute for a man from another tribe) but the fact that another tribe supplied no general.

<u>with whom he had relations of hospitality</u>: Archidamus' grandfather Leotychidas and Pericles' father Xanthippus commanded the Spartan and Athenian naval contingents against the Persians in 479 (Hdt. VIII. 131. 2-3). In an insecure world the best way to ensure one's comfort and safety away from home was to have a friend in the place one visited, on whose hospitality and protection one could rely; and the institution of guest-friendship is found in the Greek world from Homer onwards.

<u>to expel the accursed</u>: Cf. I. 126. 2 - 127. Pericles' mother Agariste belonged to the Alcmaeonid family, which had incurred a curse in the late seventh century through involvement in the killing, despite a promise that their lives would be spared, of men who had supported Cylon in an attempt to make himself tyrant of Athens. In 432 the Spartans had invoked this curse in

the hope of undermining Pericles' position in Athens; but the Athenians had replied by invoking a Spartan curse (I. 128. 1 – 135. 1).

did not ravage his land and houses: This presupposes that Pericles' property was sufficiently compact and clearly delimited for a large invading army to be able to spare that while damaging all around it. The presupposition may not be justified, but that is not to say that Pericles cannot have entertained the fear and have made the offer here attributed to him. The contrast between public and private concerns is frequently made in book II.

13. 2. on the same lines as before: A speech of Pericles in 432 is given in I. 140-4, with the superiority of Athens' resources for a long war emphasised in 141. 2 – 143; a summary of Pericles' strategy will be given in 65. 7. On this occasion Thucydides does not use direct speech but through indirect speech presents a factual summary of Athens' resources at the beginning of the war.

they were not to go out to battle: Which Archidamus expected them to do (11. 3 n.). The Athenians could not field an army which was a match for that of the invaders, so Pericles proposed that they should avoid battle, and rely on their sea power to keep themselves provisioned when denied access to local produce (cf. I. 143. 4-5, also II. 21. 2 – 22, 55, 62. 2-3): the city of Athens was inland, but the long walls built in the middle of the century (§7 n.) contained the city and the harbour town of the Piraeus within a single fortified area (cf. 77. 1 n.).

make ready the fleet, in which their superiority lay: This theme runs throughout the central part of Pericles' first speech; cf. 65. 7, and Archidamus in I. 80. 4. For the part to be played by the fleet in Pericles' strategy see 25. 1 n.

keep a firm hold on their allies: Cf. 63. On the other hand, they were not to run unnecessary risks through attempting to extend the empire (I. 144. 1, II. 65, 7).

the money which they received from the allies: For Athens' financial superiority cf. I. 141. 3-5, 142. 1; also Archidamus in I. 80. 3-4 and the Corinthians in I. 121. 2.

good judgment: Cf. I. 144. 4, II. 40. 2-3, 62. 4-5.

ready supplies: περιουσία is used in the same sense in I. 141. 5.

13. 3. six hundred talents tribute from the allies: The correctness of the text is confirmed by the citation in Plut. *Arist.* 24.4, but it appears from the tribute quota lists that a realistic assessment of the tribute that could be collected at

the beginning of the war would be about 430 talents (Meiggs, *The Athenian Empire*, 527). Thucydides likewise gives a surprisingly high figure, 460 talents, for the tribute at the foundation of the League (I. 96. 2: Diod. Sic. XII. 40. 1 gives that figure for the tribute at the beginning of the war). The one assessment list of which much is preserved, that of 425, was an optimistic list, including such states as Melos, which could not realistically be expected to pay (*IG* i³ 71, extracts M&L 69: cf. 9. 4 n.): a possible explanation of Thucydides' figures is that they are derived from similarly optimistic assessment lists.

apart from its other revenue: Which Thucydides does not specify. Xen. *An*. VII. 1. 27 gives Athens' total external and internal revenue at the beginning of the war as 1,000 talents, which is plausible as an approximation.

had always kept on the Acropolis six thousand talents: According to the manuscripts' text they "still at that time had on the Acropolis six thousand talents . . . ; the largest sum they had had was three hundred short of the ten thousand." Diod. Sic. XII. 40. 2 agrees with the manuscripts on this (10,000 talents reduced by 4,000), and on the 500 talents of §4, but not on other figures. The text as quoted by a scholiast on Aristophanes was championed by B. D. Meritt and his collaborators in *The Athenian Tribute Lists*, iii. 118-32; *Hesp.* 23 (1954), 185 - 231; *Hesp.* 26 (1957), 163-97 (esp. 188-97). The manuscripts' text was defended by Gomme in *Hist*. 2 (1953-4), 1 - 21; *Hist*. 3 (1954-5), 333-8; *Comm*. ii. 26 - 33. The scholiast's text seems more likely to be historically correct (cf. below), but is not acceptable Greek: I suggest a way in which an acceptable text could have been corrupted into the scholiast's text. (I do not accept the suggestion of Meritt, *Hesp.* Supp. 19 (1982), 112-21, that αἰεί ποτε means since the initiation of the policy in 434/3.) Although there was also on the Acropolis a Treasury of the Other Gods (§5 n.), I suspect that all the money specified at this point was in the Treasury of Athena. No reserve had been built up in the state treasury: in time of need the sacred treasuries were called on to support the state.

Sparta and her allies had no comparably rich sacred treasuries. The panhellenic sanctuaries of Delphi and Olympia both lay in the territory of Sparta's allies, and Delphi had declared its support for Sparta (I. 118. 3): the Corinthians suggested in I. 121. 3 that the Peloponnesians might draw on these, and Pericles in I. 143. 1 considered the possibility, but there is no evidence that they did so.

the Propylaea of the Acropolis and the other buildings: A major building programme on the Acropolis had been started with the beginning of work on the Parthenon in 447/6; the Propylaea, the elaborate gatehouse at the west end of the Acropolis, was begun in 437/6; the financial decrees of Callias in 434/3 ordered the winding-up of the programme, and the Parthenon was completed and the Propylaea was left incomplete in 433/2 (Callias M&L 58 = *IG* i³ 52; other dates from the accounts of the overseers, *IG* i³ 436-66). Heliodorus, *FGrH* 373 F 1 (corrected by J. J. Keaney, *Hist.* 17 (1968), 507-8), gave the cost of the Propylaea as 2,000 talents, but more probably that sum would have paid for all the work on the Acropolis in the Periclean period (cf. R. S. Stanier, *JHS* 73 (1953), 68 - 76). The buildings are said to have been erected at the allies' expense (Plut. *Per.* 12 - 14), and a papyrus fragment may record the transfer of 5,000 talents from League funds to Athenian funds about the middle of the century (reconstruction of H. T. Wade-Gery & B. D. Meritt, *Hesp.* 26 (1957), 163-88, reprinted in Meiggs, *The Athenian Empire*, 515). Since little of the tribute received during the building period can have been spent on fighting, it is easier to believe that the reserve remained in the region of 6,000 talents while the tribute was spent on buildings than that it declined from 9,700 to 6,000.

Potidaea: Attacked in 432 (I. 56 - 66), and besieged until winter 430/29: the siege cost 2,000 talents in all (II. 70, cf. 31).

13. 4. uncoined gold and silver . . . not less than five hundred talents: The objects mentioned in the surviving inventories published annually by the sacred tresurers account for only about 20 talents (*IG* i³ 293 - 362): presumably there were other dedications not included in these inventories.

booty from the Medes: Acquired in the Persian Wars of 490 and 480 - 479, and in the campaigns of the Greeks in 478 and of the Delian League since then. The Persians are referred to as the Medes (whom they supplanted as the dominant people in the Near East in the mid sixth century) more often than by their own name, both by Thucydides and by other Greek writers.

13. 5. the monies from the other sanctuaries: Most, but not all, of the other sacred treasuries had been amalgamated in a Treasury of the Other Gods, kept on the Acropolis with the Treasury of Athena, in 434/3 (M&L 58 = *IG* i³ 52), and I imagine that the reference is primarily to this treasury. We do not know how much it contained, but between the summer of 433 and the summer of 422 the state borrowed about 821 talents from the Other Gods and 4,778 talents from Athena (M&L 72 = *IG* i³ 369:

cf. below)

the gold plate cladding the goddess herself: According to Plut. *Per*. 31. 3 the gold plate was designed to be removable so that it could be checked that there had been no embezzlement: probably it is true that when there were charges of embezzlement the gold was removed and checked. The gold survived the Peloponnesian War, and eventually was removed in 296/5 (but Gomme suspected that the texts which assert this, *FGrH* 257a F 4 and Paus. I. 25. 7, have taken too literally Demetrius II fr. 1 (iii. 357 Kock) *ap*. Ath. IX. 405 E-F).

forty talents' weight: Diod. Sic. XII. 40. 3 has 50 talents. At this date 1 talent of gold was worth 14 talents of silver (D. M. Lewis, *Essays* . . . *S. Robinson*, 105-10).

on condition that no less was replaced afterwards: The Athenians kept careful records of the sums taken from the sacred treasuries, and calculated the interest due on these loans: M&L 72 = *IG* i^3 369 gives details for the years 426 - 422, with a summary for 433 - 426 (the programme of borrowing to finance the war was regarded as beginning with the campaign to support Corcyra in 433: M&L 61 = *IG* i^3 364). Much if not all of the sum due was repaid after the Peace of Nicias in 421 (but the statement of Andoc. III. *De Pace* 8 - 9 that the Athenians deposited 7,000 talents on the Acropolis may reflect the decision to make the payments rather than the successful completion of them); in the later years of the Peloponnesian War Athens had to draw on the sacred treasuries again; and, although there were ups as well as downs, by the end of the war she had no funds left. Uncoined treasures were first used in 409/8 (*IG* i^3 376). After the war the sacred treasuries were built up again, but the large cash debt must have been written off.

13. 6. 13,000 hoplites . . . the 16,000: For the first figure cf. 31. 2. Diod. Sic. XII. 40. 4 has 12,000 + 17,000, probably just variation for variation's sake (cf. his variation on Sitalces' army in 429/8: 98. 3-4 n.). For discussion of these figures see Appendix, pp. 271-7.

in the garrison posts: Garrison posts are attested during the Peloponnesian War at Oenoe (18. 1-2) and Panactum (V. 3. 5), in north-western Attica, and in Oropus (VIII. 60. 1); in the late fourth century inscriptions attest garrisons of second-year *epheboi* (men aged 19) at Eleusis, Phyle and Rhamnus. In the Peloponnesian War there must also have been Athenian garrisons in various places overseas (cf. 24. 1).

13. 7. those metics who were hoplites: Probably any free non-citizen who stayed in Attica longer than a specified period, perhaps a month, was required to register as a metic ("mig-

rant"), and most of those who did so will have been people who had taken up residence (cf. D. Whitehead, *PCPS* Supp. 4 (1977), 7 - 10): the obligation to serve in the army could only seriously be enforced on residents. Citizens were divided into four classes according to the produce of their land (*Ath. Pol.* 7. 3-4), and members of the three higher classes were liable for hoplite service (probably a man's own declaration was accepted unless some one challenged it, and probably a son would register in the same class as his father). Metics unless specially privileged could not own land in Attica: probably on registration they were asked whether they could serve as hoplites.

<u>The Phaleric Wall</u>: The purpose of this digression is to explain why so many men were needed for garrison duty. The city wall had been rebuilt hurriedly after the Persian War of 480 - 479 (I. 89. 3 - 94). The first long walls linking Athens to the Piraeus (cf. §2 n.), the Phaleric Wall to Phalerum and the "north wall" (the "outer wall" of this §) to the north side of the Piraeus, were built in the early 450s (I. 107. 1, 108. 3); the "middle wall" (the other of the Long Walls of this §), a short distance south of the "north wall" and parallel to it, was perhaps built in the 440s (Andoc. III. *De Pace* 7, cf. Pl. *Grg.* 455 E, Plut. *Bell. an Pace* 351 A). The Piraeus wall was built, or at any rate finished, immediately after the Persian Wars (I. 93. 3-5: I accept that work at the Piraeus began in Themistocles' archonship, 493/2, but the wall need not have been built then).

<u>thirty-five stades</u>: Just over 6 km. or just under 4 miles (for the stade cf. 5. 2 n.). The line of the Phaleric Wall is uncertain, and we are not in a position to say that Thucydides' figure is wrong. The city wall is now known to have involved more deviations from a direct line than used to be thought, and Thucydides' figure (about 7½ km. or 4¾ miles), once considered excessive, now seems acceptable (cf. Wycherley, *The Stones of Athens*, 11 - 12). The figure for the "north wall" (7 km. or just under 4½ miles) is acceptable. The Piraeus wall as rebuilt in the 390s was 78 stades long (13¾ km. or 8½ miles) rather than 60 (10½ km. or over 6½ miles), but it is possible that the fifth-century wall was shorter, omitting the peninsula of Acte. The part of the Piraeus wall exposed on land, running westwards from the end of the "north wall", was much less than half of the whole, and originally the Piraeus was not guarded against attacks from the sea (93-4): perhaps the precision of "half" should not be pressed.

13. 8. <u>1,200 cavalry . . . mounted archers</u>: Cf. *Ath. Pol.* 24. 3 (in a list of men maintained at the state's expense), Andoc.

III. *De Pace* 7: there were in fact 1,000 cavalry (Ar. *Eq*. 225) and 200 mounted archers. The cavalry had to provide their own horses, though the state helped in maintenance, so they were presumably drawn from the richest citizens: it is not known how nearly coextensive they were with the membership of the first two property-classes (the second was called *hippeis*, "cavalry").

<u>1,600 archers</u>: Cf. *Ath. Pol.* 24. 3: Andoc. III. *De Pace* 7 repeats the 1,200 of the cavalry.

<u>300 seaworthy triremes</u>: Cf. Diod. Sic. XII. 40. 4. Thuc. III. 17 alleges that 250 were in use in one summer, but 100 were set aside as a special reserve (24. 2 n.), and many editors condemn III. 17 as an interpolation. [Xen.] *Ath. Pol.* 3. 4 mentions 400 trierarchs, men responsible for funding and commanding ships, but that may be an exaggeration; according to the manuscripts of Andoc. III. *De Pace* 9 Athens had over 400 ships, but Aeschin. II. *F.L.* 175 is derived from that and there the manuscripts have 300. If 300 triremes were at sea simultaneously, they would require about 60,000 men. Oarsmen were drawn from the lowest property-class of citizens, and from non-citizens who accepted this form of employment: we do not know what proportion of the crews were citizens, but in the fifth century Athens had no difficulty in finding oarsmen (cf. Pericles in I. 143. 1-2).

<u>13. 9. These were the resources</u>: We have no reason to think Thucydides' details inaccurate, but they are frustratingly incomplete. Not all the financial items are quantified, and we are not told how much of Athens' income would be consumed by routine expenditure. We are given indications of manpower, but not total numbers of citizens or of other individuals (on which see Appendix, pp. 271-7). And no comparable figures are given for other states, either allies or enemies of Athens. The record of borrowing from the sacred treasuries between 433 and 422 (cf. 13. 5 n.) gives some idea of Athens' financial history during that period: until 428 she ran down her reserves at a rate which would have led to bankruptcy in a few more years; after that, taxation from the Athenians (III. 19. 1) and tribute from the Delian League (cf. esp. M&L 69 = *IG* i^3 71, of 425) were increased, expenditure was reduced (cf. 25. 1 n.), and if allowance is made for some income reaching the sacred treasuries the continuing drain on reserves cannot have been large.

<u>on the point of going to war</u>: Cf. 19. 1 n.

<u>14. 1. equipment . . . woodwork</u>: The first will include farm-

ing implements and domestic furniture; the second, such things as doors. As little as possible that could be reused would be left to the invaders.

<u>Euboea</u>: There were cleruchies, settlements of Athenian citizens which did not constitute an independent city state, in Euboea, and some rich Athenians had acquired land of their own there; in addition the Euboean cities, as allies, may have been called on to provide pasture for Athenians' animals. The importance of Euboea to Athens during the war is stressed in VIII. 96. 1-2.

<u>14. 2. The removal was a hard thing</u>: Thucydides writes as if the evacuation of Attica was total. It is not clear how nearly total it was, or needed to be: the invaders were present for a limited time, and in 431 they did not reach the part of Attica south-east of Pentelicon and Hymettus (23), though in 430 they did (55. 1): it would not be surprising if some poorer countrymen remained outside, intending to take to the hills if the enemy approached. Likewise we do not know what proportion returned to their homes after the invaders had left.

<u>living in the country</u>: For the most part, not in separate houses on their separate farms, but in demes (village communities: cf. 19. 2 n.) distributed throughout Attica.

<u>15. 1. of the Athenians more than of the others</u>: What distinguished Athens from other states (except Sparta) was that a single city controlled an unusually large area (about 2,600 sq. km. or 1,000 sq. miles): for that reason an unusually low proportion of the citizens lived inside the city, but Attica will have differed from neighbouring Boeotia, where a federal state was composed of cities with a measure of autonomy (cf. 2. 1 n.), in the status of the centres of habitation rather than in the pattern of settlement.

<u>In the time of Cecrops</u>: The history of Athens cannot seriously be traced back beyond the attempt by Cylon to make himself tyrant, in the 630s or 620s (cf. 13. 1 n.); but the Athenians like other Greeks had legends about the "heroic" period, were unaware of the breakdown of the bronze-age Mycenaean civilisation, and of the dark age which followed that, and gradually coordinated and elaborated the legends to provide a continuous history from the heroic period to the classical. Cecrops, born from the soil, was believed to have been the first king of Athens. Thucydides approaches the legends in a rationalising spirit, but accepts the general outlines of the legendary history: cf. I. 1 - 21, II. 29. 3, 68. 3, 102, and Introduction, pp. 6 - 7.

<u>dispersed among cities</u>: It was believed that there had been

twelve cities (Philoch. *FGrH* 328 F 94).

<u>the Eleusinians</u>: Apart from some hill country acquired in the sixth century, Eleusis seems in fact to have been the last part of Attica to be incorporated in the Athenian state. According to the legend as later systematised, Eleusis and the Thracians under Eumolpus went to war against Athens in the mid fifteenth century, and Ion, son of Erechtheus' daughter Creusa, led the Athenians to victory.

15. 2. <u>Theseus</u>: The Athenian whose exploits included killing the Minotaur on Crete: the chronographers placed his reign in the late thirteenth century.

<u>intelligent</u>: One of Thucydides' favourite words of commendation: in 34. 6 it is applied by implication to Pericles, and in 60. 5 Pericles claims exceptional ability to determine and expound what is needed.

<u>organised the land in general</u>: Theseus is said to have been a king with democratic leanings, who somehow gave up the kingship or a part of its power, created the aristocracy of the *eupatridai* ("well born"), and established a régime in which both they and the ordinary people had a recognised part to play in the running of the state (cf. Eur. *Supp.* 399 - 408, Plut. *Thes.* 24. 1 - 25. 3).

<u>brought all the people together in the present city</u>: By the process known as synoecism. Cf. Plut. *Thes.* 24. 1-4 (§3 is very close in its wording to Thucydides). If there was in fact a unification of Attica in the bronze age, it will almost certainly have been undone in the breakdown of the Mycenaean civilisation, and the unity of the classical period will have been created towards the end of the dark age.

<u>a single council-house and town hall</u>: In classical Athens these were two separate buildings, and probably Thucydides is envisaging two separate buildings.

<u>were to attend to their own affairs as before</u>: They were not forced to migrate from their homes to the neighbourhood of the city, as in the most drastic forms of synoecism.

Synoikia: Plut. *Thes.* 24. 4 (calling it *Metoikia*, "migration" rather than "unification") gives the date, 16 Hecatombaeon (i).

15. 3. <u>earlier</u>: Earlier than Thucydides, not earlier than Theseus.

<u>towards the south</u>: This may be true, but there was also early occupation of the area north-west of the Acropolis, where the Agora of classical Athens was located. However, it is clear from what follows that Thucydides is thinking of the area south-east of the Acropolis, and we should not emend "south" to "north".

15. 4. **Here is confirmation of this**: *Tekmerion* is one of the words regularly used in arguments from what is reasonable. Cf. Introduction, pp. 6 - 7.

The oldest temples both of Athena and of the other gods: The insertion "both of Athena" is certainly necessary, and "oldest" probably necessary, to make sense of the passage. On all the buildings mentioned in §§4-5 see Travlos, *Pictorial Dictionary of Ancient Athens* (which will be cited by author's name). There was a series of temples of Athena on the Acropolis, on the site of the Parthenon and on a site to the north of it (Travlos, p. 61 fig. 71 nos. 107, 108); there were other ancient sanctuaries on the site of the Erechtheum, to the north of that (Travlos, p. 71 fig. 91 no. 122).

Olympian Zeus: South-east of the Acropolis (Travlos, p. 169 fig. 219 or p. 291 fig. 379 no. 158: cf. Paus. I. 18. 6-8). The visible remains are of a temple begun in the sixth century B.C. and completed in the second century A.D.; prehistoric pottery has been found on the site.

Pythium: A sanctuary of Pythian Apollo, probably south-west of Olympian Zeus, near the River Ilissus (Travlos, p. 169 fig. 219 or p. 291 fig. 379 no. 189: cf. Paus. I. 19. 1).

Ge: Earth. Presumably Thucydides means the sanctuary by the south-west corner of Olympian Zeus (Travlos, p. 291 fig. 379 no. 187: cf. Paus. I. 18. 7) rather than the one west of the Acropolis (p. 8 fig. 5 no. 7: cf. Paus. I. 22. 3).

Dionysus in the Marshes: Said by [Dem.] LIX. *Neaer*. 76 to be the oldest temple of Dionysus: it was perhaps no longer standing in the time of Pausanias (second century A.D.), who does not mention a temple with this name and says that the oldest was near the theatre, immediately south of the east end of the Acropolis (I. 20. 3: Travlos, p. 61 fig. 71 no. 115). A possible location for Dionysus in the Marshes has been found farther south-east (but west of the buildings previously mentioned: p. 169 fig. 219 no. 184); Burkert, *Greek Religion*, 237, suggests that we should not look for a marsh in Athens but "in the marshes" was a cult title which arrived with the cult.

the oldest festival of Dionysus: Known as the Anthesteria; it was primarily a wine festival, and seems to predate the Ionian migration of *c*. 1000 B.C. Since there were two other major festivals of Dionysus, the Lenaea and the Great Dionysia, the superlative "oldest" is preferable to the comparative. See Pickard-Cambridge rev. Gould & Lewis, *The Dramatic Festivals of Athens*, 1 - 25; Parke, *Festivals of the Athenians*, 107-20.

on the twelfth of the month Anthesterion: The eighth month, corresponding approximately to February. The festival occupied the three days 11th – 13th, of which the 12th was the most important: since the date is given in the text as quoted by the papyrus commentary as well as in the manuscripts, it should not be deleted as a gloss.

the Ionians descended from the Athenians: Athens was regarded as the mother city of the Ionians in the strict sense of that name, the Greeks occupying the central stretch of western Asia Minor and the offshore islands (cf. 9. 4 n.). Evidence for celebrations of the Anthesteria outside Athens is cited by Pickard-Cambridge.

other ancient sanctuaries: We do not know which are intended.

15. 5. the tyrants: Pisistratus and his sons Hippias and Hipparchus, who ruled Athens from 546 to 510 (cf. VI. 54-9, I. 20. 2).

Enneakrounos: A majority of ancient writers agree with Thucydides in implying a location south of the city for *Kallirhoe* / *Enneakrounos*, but some imply a city-centre location. W. Dörpfeld in the 1890s placed it west of the Acropolis (and Dionysus in the Marshes in the same region: Travlos, p. 169 fig. 219 nos. 250, 248); and the Agora excavators originally identified it with the (fourth-century) South-West Fountain House (p. 21 fig. 29 no. 41); but there are now two serious candidates. There is a fountain by the Ilissus, south of Olympian Zeus, (p. 291 fig. 379 no. 155: cf. Travlos, p. 204), which is in the right area for Thucydides, and is called *Kallirhoe* ("fair-flow") by [Pl.] *Axioch*. 364 A, but no trace of Pisistratid building has been found there. Pausanias locates Pisistratus' *Enneakrounos* ("ninefold fountain") in the Agora (I. 14. 1), and apparently means what the excavators call the South-East Fountain House (p. 21 fig. 29 no. 31), which is a building of Pisistratid date. It is hard to think that Thucydides could be wrong and Pausanias right about the identity of a Pisistratid building: possibly the name *Enneakrounos* was originally given to a fountain house at *Kallirhoe*, by the Ilissus, but by the mid fourth century that building had been destroyed and the name had been transferred to the Pisistratid fountain house in the Agora (cf. E. J. Owens, *JHS* 102 (1982), 222-5).

15. 6. call the Acropolis *polis*: This is regular usage in fifth-century Athenian documents (e.g. M&L 68 = *IG* i³ 68, 25, M&L 80 = *IG* i³ 98, 15, of 426 and 411: A. S. Henry, *Chiron* 12 (1982), 91-7, argues for an official abandonment of this usage in 386); cf. Ar. *Lys*. 245 and elsewhere. In the *Iliad* we find πόλις ἄκρη (VI. 88, cf. XX. 52); the *Odyssey* has ἀκρόπολις (VIII. 494).

16. 1. So for the most part the Athenians lived in independent settlements in the country: Harking back to 14. 1 - 15. 2 after the digression on the ancient city. The discursive Herodotus is much given to the device of ring composition, by which a section of text ends with words recalling its beginning, and there can be a series of rings inside one another or in sequence within a greater ring. Thucydides is not a great user of digressions, and has less need for ring composition, but he employs the device when appropriate. Here "Even after . . . time of this war" recalls "The people were to attend to their own affairs as before" (15. 2); "So they . . . households" recalls "The removal was . . . " (14. 2); "It was a distressing hardship . . . " recalls "They brought in . . . " (14. 1). μετεῖχον is commented on by scholiasts, including the papyrus commentator, but produces an impossible sentence.

17. 1. The majority occupied the uninhabited places: Cf. 52. 2, where the overcrowding worsens the effect of the plague.
the Eleusinium: North of the west end of the Acropolis: (Travlos, p. 169 fig. 219 no. 14: cf. Paus. I. 14. 3): a temple of the Eleusinian goddesses Demeter and Core (Persephone).
the *Pelargikon*: Most probably at the north-west corner of the Acropolis (e.g. R. J. Hopper, *The Acropolis*, p. 81 fig. 6 no. 12; J. McK. Camp, *Studies . . . S. Dow* [*GR&BMon*. 10 (1984)], 37 - 41), but some have argued for a strip running round the western half of the Acropolis (e.g. Travlos, p. 61 fig. 71 no. 105). In most manuscripts the name is given as *Pelasgikon*. It was believed that in the distant past the Pelasgians (a name given to various non-Greek peoples) came to Attica, built the Acropolis wall (which in fact was built in the thirteenth century), and were allowed for a time to settle but later were expelled (Hecat. *FGrH* 1 F 127 *ap*. Hdt. VI. 137. 2). Probably the enclosure was called *Pelargikon* and was considered to be of religious significance before the Pelasgians were invoked to explain anything (*pelargos* means "stork", but the meaning of *Pelargikon* is unknown); later the Pelasgians were credited with the thirteenth-century wall and by assimilation it was called the Pelargic wall; later still scribes who had heard of the Pelasgians corrupted *Pelargikon* into *Pelasgikon*.
"The *Pelargikon* is better left alone": The jingle cannot be reproduced in translation.
17. 2. was not referring . . . but was predicting: On Thucydides' attitude to oracles cf. 8. 2 n., and Introduction, pp. 12 - 13. Here he suggests that an oracle was "fulfilled" in a way that does not involve any special foreknowledge.

17. 3. the towers of the city walls: Cf. Ar. *Eq.* 732-3.
17. 4. collecting allies: Cf. 7. 3.
an expedition of a hundred ships against the Peloponnese: Cf. 23. 2, 25, 30.

18 - 23. *The Peloponnesian Invasion of Attica*

18. 1. Oenoe: In the north-western corner of Attica: recent studies have returned to the site at Myoupolis which Gomme rejected (J. S. Traill, *Hesp.* Supp. 14 (1975), 52; E. Vanderpool, *CSCA* 11 (1978), 231-4; J. Ober, *Mnem.* Supp. 84 (1985), 154-5, 224). Hdt. V. 74. 2 puzzlingly refers to Oenoe and Hysiae (on the Boeotian side of Mt. Cithaeron) as "the last demes of Attica". Archidamus deliberately avoided the obvious route for invasion, by the coastal road from Megara to Eleusis: he will have followed the Road of the Towers of N. G. L. Hammond, *BSA* 49 (1954), 103-22 = *Studies*, 417-46 (but Hammond's site for Oenoe is west of Myoupolis). It is not clear what, apart from a further delay, he achieved or intended to achieve: in I. 82. 4 he represents the land of Attica as a hostage, and the better for that purpose the longer it is left unravaged.
with machines and in other ways: Cf. the siege of Plataea, 75-6 nn.
18. 2. had been fortified: Probably since *c*. 506, when it had been captured by Boeotian invaders (Hdt. V. 74. 2).
18. 3. feeble: Thucydides uses a great variety of words in this chapter to emphasise Archidamus' failure to begin the war energetically.
setting the war in motion: Echoes the Homeric "set Ares in motion" (ξυνάγειν Ἄρηα: e.g. *Il.* II. 381).
18. 4. the Peloponnesians thought: Thucydides' order of narrative implies that the Athenians had started moving long before the Peloponnesians reached Oenoe. Given the impossibility of a surprise invasion, it is unlikely that even with greater Peloponnesian speed they could have been caught with much of their property still outside.
18. 5. It is said: Thucydides tends to use this qualification with attributions of motive or excuse (cf. 20. 1, 93. 4) or with unverifiable claims for whose correctness he is not prepared to vouch (cf. 48. 1, 77. 6, 98. 3). H. D. Westlake, *Mnem.*⁴ 30 (1977), 345-62 at 352-3, suggests that here and in 20. 1 Thucydides is implying that Archidamus' expectations, although in fact unfulfilled, were reasonable.

19. 1. about the eightieth day . . . king of Sparta: Although Thucydides has decided to treat the Theban attack on Plataea as the first incident in the Peloponnesian War (1 - 2. 1 n.), it would be possible to treat that as the last of the preliminary incidents, and to regard as the beginning of the war the major invasion of Attica, commanded by a Spartan king and preceded by the sending of a last herald (cf. I. 125. 2, II. 13. 9). Thucydides marks this second beginning with a second date and the formal introduction of Archidamus (cf. 10. 3 n.: Archidamus will be similarly introduced at the beginnings of the following years): one effect of this is to underline the fact that technically the Peloponnesians started the war (cf. VII. 18. 2). If the attack on Plataea was $c.$ 10 March, the invasion of Attica will have been $c.$ 20 May: the harvest would begin at the end of May. The evidence cited in 23. 2-3 nn. is consistent with these dates.

19. 2. Eleusis and the Thriasian Plain: They will have used the Oenoe Road of E. Vanderpool, *CSCA* 11 (1978), 228-31, cf. J. Ober, *Mnem.* Supp. 84 (1985), 186. Eleusis is at the west end of the plain; there was a deme of Thria near the middle of the plain (J. S. Traill, *Hesp.* Supp. 14 (1975), 50).

Athenian cavalry: Cf. 22. 2.

The Streams: Believed to be the ancient boundary between Athens and Eleusis (cf. Paus. I. 38. 3): this was at the east end of the plain. A pedestrian bridge was built there in 421/0 for the procession to Eleusis for the Mysteries (*IG* i^3 79).

Cropia: Probably due west of Acharnae, near the north-east end of Mount Aegaleos (Traill, 47). For the route see Ober, 184-5.

places in Attica called demes: Thucydides is writing for all Greeks, not only for his fellow Athenians, and from time to time he gives explanations which no Athenian would need (cf. Introduction, p. 10). Cleisthenes in 508/7 had organised the citizen body in 139 demes, of which a few were subdivisions of the city but most were village communities: these were grouped together to form thirty *trittyes* ("thirds") and ten tribes. The demes were represented in the council of five hundred in proportion to their size, and Acharnae was indeed the largest, with twenty-two representatives in the fourth century (we have little or no evidence for the fifth).

20. 1. It is said: Cf. 18. 5 n.

the plain: The central plain of Attica: Athens is in the middle of it, and Acharnae is on the northern edge. In 430 the Peloponnesians do go down into the plain (55. 1).

20. 4. the Acharnians . . . †three thousand hoplites†: This figure is far too large for the number of hoplites from Acharnae, and probably rather large, though not beyond the bounds of possibility, even for the number of citizens; Whitehead's 1,200 yields a plausible number of hoplites, but cannot be regarded as certain. See Appendix, pp. 271-7. The Acharnians are depicted as bellicose, and as veterans of the battle of Marathon (fought by Athenian hoplites against the Persians in 490) in Aristophanes' play of that name, produced in 425.

21. 1. Plistoanax: Cf. I. 114. 2. In 447/6 Athens' subjects in mainland Greece and Euboea revolted, and in 446, probably after a five-year truce had expired (I. 112. 1), Plistoanax led a Peloponnesian invasion of Attica but withdrew after going no further than the Thriasian Plain; after that the Thirty Years' Peace was made (cf. 2. 1 n.). It was believed both in Sparta and in Athens that he had been bribed: Pericles was alleged to have included in his accounts for the year an item of 10 talents "for necessary expenses" (Ar. *Nub.* 859 with schol., Plut. *Per.* 23. 1-2). Plistoanax was king from the senior, Agid house (cf. 10. 3 n.) *c.* 460 - 408: he was recalled from exile in 427/6 (V. 16. 3).

21. 2. sixty stades: 10½ km. or somewhat over 6½ miles (for the stade cf. 5. 2 n.). This is correct, as the crow flies.

no longer tolerable: Cf. Archidamus in 11. 7.

had never happened before: Attica had been occupied and ravaged by the Persians in 480 and 479: on that occasion the Athenians had abandoned both countryside and city (as yet there were no long walls), and had gone to Salamis and elsewhere.

especially the young men: In Aristophanes' plays of the 420s it is the old men who are most bellicose: cf. 20. 4 n.

21. 3. Oracle-mongers: Cf. 8. 2 n.

anger against Pericles: In 430 there is even greater anger, leading to the deposition of Pericles from the generalship, but on that occasion the Athenians want not more energetic action but an end to the war (59 - 65). For 431 Plut. *Per.* 33 is based on Thucydides, but adds details, including a fragment mentioning the demagogue Cleon from the comedian Hermippus, and a remark by Pericles that when trees are cut down they quickly grow again but men are not so easy to replace.

22. 1. refused to call an assembly or any kind of meeting: In 430 Pericles "called a meeting (since he was still in office as general)" (59.3), but normally the decision to hold an assembly or not (subject to the laws which specified a minimum frequency of meetings) rested with the council of five hundred, and in particular with the *prytaneis* (cf. 12. 2 n.). Presumably the

generals could summon a "meeting" of the men under their command, and in the present circumstances such a meeting would be almost identical in personnel with a formal assembly of the citizens. There is a little evidence to suggest that during the Peloponnesian War the generals could be involved with the *prytaneis* and council in convening or not convening assemblies: see Rhodes, *The Athenian Boule*, 43-6; and, for other recent discussions of these passages, J. Christensen & M. H. Hansen, *C&M* 34 (1983), 17 - 31 (cf. Hansen, *The Athenian Assembly*, 22, 25), E. F. Bloedow, *Hist*. 36 (1987), 9 - 27.

passion rather than judgment: Cf. Archidamus in 11. 7.

22. 2. cavalry: Cf. 19. 2.

Phrygii: According to the papyrus commentator this was in the deme Athmonum, north-east of Athens and south-east of Acharnae (J. S. Traill, *Hesp*. Supp. 14 (1975), 50).

a few of them were killed: Paus. I. 29. 6 mentions the tomb of the Thessalians, and a tomb of "the cavalry who died when the Thessalians joined in facing the danger", in the cemetery of the Ceramicus, on the north-west side of Athens. However, there is no other evidence that the Athenian cavalry were buried separately from the other war casualties (cf. 34 - 46), and if Pausanias thought there was a separate tomb of these men he was probably mistaken.

without a truce . . . set up a trophy: The invaders did not remain in possession of the battlefield, so the Athenians were able to recover the bodies without a formal admission of defeat, but the next day they returned to it and set up a trophy as a sign of victory. The trophy, *tropaion*, was a dedication set up at the site of the defeated enemy's turning to flee (*trope*).

22. 3. their ancient alliance: Made *c*. 461 (I. 102. 4 cf. 107. 7); but *c*. 454 an Athenian attempt to reinstate an exiled leader in Pharsalus was unsuccessful (I. 111. 1). The Thessalians are not listed among Athens' allies in 9. 4, and are not recorded as providing troops for Athens on any later occasion in the war, but according to IV. 78. 2-4 the majority of the Thessalian people, if not all their leaders, remained pro-Athenian.

There were contingents: A scarcely necessary piece of detail, presumably included because Thucydides happened to have made a note of it. What he says is frustratingly incomplete: we should like to know which cities did not send contingents, and why. Larisa (in the north) and Pharsalus (in the centre) were the two most important cities in Thessaly; Pherae (in the east) was to be important in the first half of the fourth century.

one from each party: More information is needed: if Larisa was divided, we might have expected one party to be anti-Athenian, and not to supply a commander.

Meno: Perhaps grandson of the Meno who helped Cimon against Eïon *c.* 476 and was made an Athenian citizen (Dem. XXIII. *Arist.* 199), and father of the Thucydides who was Athenian *proxenos* in 411 (VIII. 92. 8, cf. Marcellin. *Vit. Thuc.* 28).

23. 1. Mount Brilessus: Usually called Pentelicon. The invaders did not descend into the plain of Athens (cf. 20. 1), but moved north-east from Acharnae. They did no damage in the deme of Decelea, with which Sparta claimed a special relationship dating from the heroic period (Hdt. IX. 73: cf. 57. 2 n., on the sparing of the Tetrapolis in 430).

23. 2. The Athenians sent out round the Peloponnese the hundred ships: Cf. 17. 4, 25, 30.

a thousand hoplites and four hundred archers: Presumably in addition to the soldiers, normally ten per ship, who regularly sailed with the fleet as *epibatai*. In the naval expedition of 430 four thousand hoplites were taken (56. 2).

Carcinus . . . Proteas . . . Socrates: The first was a tragic poet, often made fun of in comedy; the second had been general in 433/2 and was one of the commanders of the first expedition to support Corcyra (I. 45. 2); nothing is known about the third. An inscription records payments to them at the end of the ninth of the ten prytanies of 432/1 and the beginning of the tenth (*IG* i^3 365, 30 sqq.): presumably they set sail in the tenth prytany, some time in June (cf. next note). Inconvenient though it must have been, the Athenian generals served for the official year defined by the archon's term of duty, which began after the summer solstice, in the middle of the campaigning season: it is normally assumed that these men were generals for 432/1 who had already (cf. *Ath. Pol.* 44. 4) been reelected for 431/0.

23. 3. the time for which they had provisions: Perhaps thirty days (cf. 10. 1 n.). They finally entered Attica, after their delay at Oenoe, *c.* 20 May (19. 1 n.), and the Athenian fleet set sail, "while they were in their territory", in June (23. 2 n.). There is no reason to believe, with Diod. Sic. XII. 42. 7, that they withdrew because of the Athenian naval expedition.

Oropus: Facing Euboea, north of Mount Parnes but often in the hands of Athens. It was acquired by Boeotia in 412/1 (VIII. 60. 1-2). This sentence will have been written before then and not modified afterwards: it is the only passage in book II that is unquestionably early and unrevised. Cf. Introduction, p. 15.

Graea: The significance is unknown, but the use of the name for this region is as old as Hom. *Il.* II. 498.

24 - 32. *Athenian Counter-Measures*

24. 1. set up garrisons: These are presumably garrisons outside Attica, since Oenoe and other places in Attica were already guarded (18. 1-2, 19. 1, cf. 13. 6). One is mentioned in 32. One point which the Athenians did not yet guard was the entrance from the sea to the Piraeus (93. 1).
a separate fund of a thousand talents: They did not have to touch this until 412 (VIII. 15. 1).
any one who proposed or put to the vote a proposal: In 412 the conditions specified here were not satisfied, so the Athenians had first to vote themselves permission to override this decree. On a number of other occasions they made it harder to take a hasty decision by decreeing that a certain kind of matter could not be decided unless a previous meeting of the assembly had voted permission (cf. D. M. Lewis, Φόρος . . . *B. D. Meritt,* 81-9). Punishment for contravening such decrees could regularly be inflicted either on the author of the improper proposal or on the presiding officials (the chairman and the other *prytaneis*: cf. 12. 2 n.) who put it to the vote.
24. 2. their hundred best triremes . . . and trierarchs for them: It was sensible to set aside a final financial reserve, but to set aside the hundred best triremes, and the trierarchs (cf. 13. 8 n.) and presumably the crews for them would not have been a sensible use of Athens' resources, particularly since at the outbreak of the war it must have seemed extremely unlikely that the Peloponnesians would "sail against the city with their navy" (as they planned, but failed, to do in winter 429/8: 93-4). Gomme finds this decision "strange" and assumes that it was soon revoked. Athens began the war with 300 seaworthy triremes (13. 8): it is not until 413, the last year of the great Sicilian expedition, that we have reason to believe that more than 200 were away from Athens simultaneously (over 218: VI. 43 + 105. 2 cf. VII. 18. 3 + VII. 16. 2 + 17. 2 + 20. 1-2 + 31. 4, but the 20 ships of VII. 17. 2 probably became the 18 of 31. 4), and we may wonder how easily the crews for 300 ships could have been found. Perhaps there really was a decision to keep in the docks at least 100 ships, not necessarily the best; but in winter 429/8 "there were no ships on guard" at the Piraeus (93. 3).

25. 1. The Athenians sailing round the Peloponnese: Cf. 17. 4, 23. 2. Athens' naval activity in the first two years of the war presents problems. In these two years there was large-scale activity (for 430 see 56-8), but subsequently there was nothing comparable, even in 428, when after sending out two smaller expeditions (III. 3. 2, 7. 1-3) the Athenians sent out a hundred ships to deter the Peloponnesians from supporting Mytilene (III. 16. 1). Thucydides, however, makes little of the large-scale expeditions, and writes as he might have written of casual raiding expeditions of only a few ships. This is congruent with the picture which he gives of Pericles' strategy, that Athens should rely on her sea power for survival, but not, it appears, for attack, and should not run risks in trying to extend the empire; but it seems to trivialise campaigns involving 30,000 men. G. L. Cawkwell has written, "Thucydides would not for a second have dreamed that there was anything to explain. ... Ravaging was a normal way of fighting. ... If the purpose was merely to ravage, the more hands the better" (*YCS* 24 (1975), 53 - 70: quotations 69 - 70). Most scholars, however, agree that an explanation is needed: Pericles is respresented as a cautious leader who urged a strategy for survival in a long war, but Athens began by spending money at a rate which would have led to bankruptcy long before 421 (cf. 13. 9 n.), and began with these major naval expeditions which were discontinued after the first few years.

Plutarch saw in the large expeditions a desire to relieve the overcrowding of Athens (*Per.* 34. 4 - 35. 1), H. D. Westlake a desire to create a food shortage in the Peloponnese (*CQ* 39 (1945), 75 - 84 = *Essays*, 84 - 101). There may be truth in both of these, but it was not until winter 430/29 that ships were sent to Naupactus to close the Gulf of Corinth (69. 1), and it was not until 425 that Athens attempted, at Pylos (IV. 3 - 5, 41. 2-4), the building of a raiding-post in enemy territory (*epiteichismos*) which Pericles mentions as a possibility in I. 142. 4 (cf. 56. 6 n., on Prasiae). H. T. Wade-Gery thought that Pericles planned an offensive war but was forced by the siege of Potidaea and the plague to change, and Thucydides sided with "the defeatist officer class" and suppressed the original strategy (*O.C.D.*[2], 1069). I suspect that Pericles in his public pronouncements warned the Athenians to prepare for a long war, and Thucydides reflects this, but privately Pericles hoped that a massive demonstration of Athens' invulnerability would quickly lead the enemy to admit defeat. Similarly Archidamus warned the Spartans to expect a long war (I. 81. 6), but many thought that the invasions of Attica would quickly provoke the Atheni-

ans to risk a battle in which they would be beaten (V. 14. 3, VII. 28. 3).
fifty from Corcyra: By repairing old ships Corcyra was able to put out 120 in 435 (I. 29. 3-4) and 110 in 433 (I. 47. 1), but she lost many in 433.
other allies in that region: Cf. 7. 3, 9. 4.
in various places: Diod. Sic. XII. 43. 1 mentions Acte, the coast of the Argolid.
Methone in Laconia: In fact, on the west coast of Messenia; but politically Messenia was a part of Spartan territory and in this context it did not need to be distinguished from Laconia.
25. 2. Brasidas son of Tellis: The first appearance of the most energetic and adventurous Spartan of the Archidamian War, who was to cause trouble for Athens in the Thraceward region from 424 until he was killed in the battle outside Amphipolis in 422. He will be encountered again in 85 - 92 and 93-4, where again his enterprising nature will be apparent.
expeditionary force: φρουρά is a technical term in Sparta for a small mobile force.
the first man to win praise in Sparta: That is, to win an official vote of thanks. It is presumably no coincidence that he was elected ephor (one of the five civilian heads of state, counterbalancing the two kings) for 431/0 (Xen. *Hell.* III. 3. 10).
25. 3. Hollow Elis . . . the dependent territory: Hollow Elis is Elis proper, the valley of the River Peneus in the northern part of the region. The Alpheus valley to the south (in which Olympia lies) was inhabited by Pisatans, who were *perioikoi*, not fully incorporated in the state of Elis but dependent on it with local autonomy. The men who formed part of the three hundred will have been full citizens of Elis who lived in the south.
25. 5. to other places: See 30 for continuation.

26. 1. round Locris and to guard Euboea: Through the Euripus, into the northern part of the Gulf of Euboea, off the hostile Opuntian Locris (9. 2 n.).
Cleopompus: General again in the following year (58. 1), but otherwise unknown.
26. 2. Alope: Restored in the casualty list *Agora* xvii 17, 3; but C. Clairmont, *ZPE* 36 (1979), 123-6, shows that a longer name is needed and returns to the Sinope of *IG* i^2 944. [This inscription will become *IG* i^3 1180.] Cf. p. 228, below.

27. 1. particularly responsible: Surprising to the reader of book I, who finds Aegina's complaint that she was denied the autonomy promised in a treaty mentioned only briefly (67. 2, 139. 1, 140. 3). Aegina had been forced into the Delian League in the 450s (I. 105. 2-4, 108. 4).

close to the Peloponnese: And so a point of weakness in the Athenian empire. It is also close to Attica, and if occupied by the Peloponnesians might have been used as a base for raids on Attica, as was to happen in the early 380s (Xen. *Hell.* V. 1. 1-24), but there is no need to emend the text. Pericles is said to have urged the elimination of Aegina as the eye-sore of the Piraeus (Arist. *Rh.* III. 1411 A 15-16). The Spartan Lysander restored as many Aeginetans as possible to the island after the battle of Aegospotami in 405 (Xen. *Hell.* II. 2. 9).

colonists: Normally ἄποικοι if sent to found an independent city, or κληροῦχοι if sent out as men who remained citizens of Athens (cf. 14. 1 n.). ἔποικοι here emphasises that they were sent out "against" the Peloponnese.

27. 2. Thyrea: A region long disputed between Sparta and Argos (cf. V. 41. 2, and Prasiae, II. 56. 6 n.). The Athenians attacked and destroyed this settlement in 424 (IV. 56. 2 - 57).

because of: There is a similar note on the Aeginetans and on the location of Thyrea in IV. 56. 2, not coordinated with this passage.

benefactors of Sparta: Cf. I. 101. 2 - 103. 3 (where Aegina's help is not mentioned). Probably the earthquake was in 464 and the war lasted until the mid 450s (but the matter is controversial: for this view see D. W. Reece, *JHS* 82 (1962), 111-20).

28. at the beginning of the lunar month: On 3 August. "Lunar" is specified not because the Athenian calendar was out of step with the moon (though it may have been) but because it is needed for the point which Thuydides wishes to make. The natural explanation of eclipses was accepted by Pericles (Plut. *Per.* 35. 2), and was attributed to his friend Anaxagoras of Miletus (Plut. *Nic.* 23. 3-6, cf. *Per.* 6 on his opposition to superstition). Except in I. 23. 3 there is no indication that Thucydides himself considered eclipses to be more than natural phenomena on which some people placed a superstitious interpretation: here he mentions the eclipse simply because he was interested in eclipses as a marvel now explained. Cf. Introduction, pp. 12 - 13.

29. 1. *proxenos*: As a development out of the guest-friend relationship of *xenia* found in the Greek world from Homer onwards (13. 1 n.), Greek cities tended to appoint as their *proxenos* a citizen of another city who in his own city would look after visitors from and the interests of the city whose *proxenos* he

was.

Nymphodorus: Mentioned by Hdt. VII. 137. 3 as associated with Sitalces in the episode to be narrated in Thuc. II. 67, but not mentioned again by Thucydides. The Greek word order is hard to follow, with the identity of Sitalces and the reason for Athens' interest in him not explained until the end of the sentence, as if Thucydides realised only in the course of writing the sentence how much background information he would have to give.

29. 2. make the Odrysian kingdom powerful: Further details are given in 95-7. In Hdt. IV. 92 the Odrysians are simply a Thracian tribe.

29. 3. Tereus: As elsewhere (cf. 15. 1 n., and Introduction, pp. 6 - 7) Thucydides accepts the main lines of Greek legend as historical, and as open to a rational approach. Tereus was married to Procne, daughter of the Athenian king Pandion; pretending that she was dead, Tereus asked for her sister Philomela, raped her and cut out her tongue; Philomela, unable to speak, worked a message into her embroidery and sent that to Procne. In revenge Procne killed Itys, her son by Tereus, and served up his flesh for Tereus to eat; he pursued the women, but the gods turned him into a hoopoe, Procne into a nightingale and Philomela into a swallow. This is striking as one of the few totally irrelevant digressions in what is for the most part an austerely relevant history: Thucydides, with his Thracian connections (cf. Introduction, p. 1), was particularly interested in a Thracian topic; possibly a dramatist had connected Teres with Tereus to flatter Sitalces, and as in I. 20 Thucydides could not resist the temptation to refute error.

Daulian bird: No instance survives in Greek literature, but there are several in Latin, e.g. Catull. 65. 14.

one would expect: *Eikos* is one of the words regularly used in argument from what is reasonable. Cf. Introduction, pp. 6 - 7.

He wa͞s the first: Thucydides is all too capable of compression, and we do not need either of the insertions which have been proposed to make his line of reasoning clear.

29. 4. the Thraceward region: Cf. 9. 4 n. This was the region containing Potidaea and the community of Chalcidians centred on Olynthus, in revolt from the Delian League since 432 (I. 56 - 65).

29. 5. Athenian citizenship for . . . Sadocus: Cf. Ar. *Ach.* 145-7.

to send the Athenians a force: Cf. 95 - 101; Sitalces and Sadocus will appear in another connection in 67.

peltasts: Infantry lighter than hoplites but not as light as those without shields, known as *psiloi* (e.g. 31. 2): they are named after their shield, the *pelte* (cf. Hdt. VII. 75. 1 and Best, *Thracian Peltasts,* esp. 3 - 35).

29. 6. Therme: Captured by Athens in 432 (I. 61. 2). The editors of *The Athenian Tribute Lists* identified it with Serme, attested in some of the lists, but Gomme was right to object: Therme was never a member of the Delian League.

Phormio: One of the leading Athenian generals of the 430s and early 420s: he was one of Athens' commanders against Samos in 440 (I. 117. 2), and in 432 had been sent with reinforcements to Potidaea after the initial battle (I. 64. 2, 65. 2). He appears to have returned to Athens before the end of this summer (31. 2 n.). The story of Potidaea will be continued in 58; Phormio will reappear in 68-9, 80 - 92 and 102-3.

30. 1. The Athenians in the hundred ships: Cf. 25, where the previous part of this campaign was introduced with the same words.

Sollium . . . Palaerus . . . Astacus: All in Acarnania, though Thucydides can hardly have been confident that all would be sufficiently familiar to his readers to need no explanation (cf. 68. 1 n.). Sollium, whose site has not yet been found, was a Corinthian colony; but after this episode it remained friendly to Athens (cf. III. 95. 1, V. 30. 2).

took by force Astacus: Corinth reinstated Evarchus there in the following winter (33. 1-2), but Athens apparently recovered control after that (102. 1 n.).

30. 2 Cephallenia lies: This explanatory note should have been less necessary than one on the towns of Acarnania; and the modern reader familiar with accurate maps might think a better account could be given (cf. 56. 5 n., 66. 1 n.). Cephallenia remained an ally of Athens; Cranae is mentioned in 33. 3 and in V. 35. 7 cf. 56. 3, but the note here on the four cities is hardly necessary.

31. 1. invaded the territory of Megara: One of the episodes mentioned (but only briefly) by Thucydides among the immediate causes of the war was Athens' exclusion of Megarians from trade with Athens and the Delian league in retaliation for Megara's harbouring of runaway slaves and encroachment on sacred land near the border (I. 67. 4, 139. 1-2, 140. 3-4, 144. 2: the economic interpretation of the exclusion is challenged by de Ste Croix, *The Origins of the Peloponnesian War,* 225-89). Plut. *Per.* 29. 4 - 31. 1 mentions a series of Athenian measures, culminating in a decree of Charinus (presumably enacted in the summer of 431) that there should be total hostility between

Athens and Megara, and that the generals should attack Megara twice a year (for the frequency cf. IV. 66. 1).

31. 2. the plague: Cf. 47. 3 - 54.

no less than ten thousand hoplites . . . three thousand: Cf. 13. 6 n. The ten thousand include the one thousand who have been serving with the fleet (23. 2). The reader of book I is surprised to find that there were three thousand at Potidaea: in 432 1,000 were sent originally (I. 57. 6), then another 2,000 (I. 61. 2), and after the battle 1,600 with Phormio (I. 64. 2); only in the summer of 430 are we told directly that Phormio and his force are no longer there (II. 58. 2), but unless Thucydides has been careless here we must assume that they returned soon enough after the campaign of 29. 6 to join in this invasion of the Megarid.

metics: Presumably three thousand to compensate for the Athenians at Potidaea: for the total number of metic hoplites see 13. 6 n. and Appendix, pp. 271-7. Metic hoplites were not often used on campaigns outside Attica.

a large body of light-armed soldiers: Who were less important in conventional Greek warfare (but their value in mountainous country was to be demonstrated in this war: cf. esp. III. 94-8), and who, as a mixture of poorer citizens and various categories of non-citizens, could not easily be precisely enumerated.

31. 3. every year until they captured Nisaea: In fact, twice each year (§1 n.). Thucydides mentions none of these further invasions until 424, when a plot by dissidents to betray Megara to the Athenians fails, but they succeed in capturing the long walls and the harbour town of Nisaea (IV. 66 - 74).

32. Atalante: It lies just off Opus. In 426 the Athenian installations there were damaged by a tidal wave (III. 89. 3). Possibly (but not probably) this is the island which by the one-year truce of 423 was to remain in Athenian hands (IV. 118. 4); by the terms of the Peace of Nicias Athens had to give up Atalante to Sparta, though Sparta had no claim on it (V. 18. 7).

33 - 46. First Winter (431/0)

33. *A Corinthian Campaign in the North-West*

33. 1. Evarchus of Acarnania: This is a sequel to the Athenian naval campaign of summer 431 (30. 1 n.). The three Corinthians

are otherwise unknown.
33. 3. Cephallenia: Cf. 30. 2.
made their way home: For the next campaign in the north-west see 68 (summer 430).

34 - 46. *The Public Funeral in Athens*

34. 1. their traditional institution: The Greek word *nomos* can be used both of explicitly formulated laws and of customs based on no explicit laws: here I use "institution" as a word spanning both meanings. We have no fragments of inscribed Athenian casualty lists datable before *c*. 464, and Paus. I. 29. 4 claims that the men who died at Drabescus *c*. 464 (Thuc. I. 100. 3) were the first to be commemorated in this way (but contrast Paus. I. 29. 7, 14); Diod. Sic. XI. 33. 3 dates the institution of the funeral games (not mentioned by Thucydides) and the speech in 479. According to Demosthenes (XX. *Lept*. 141) the speech was an institution peculiar to Athens.
    F. Jacoby, *JHS* 64 (1944), 37 - 66 = *Abhandlungen*, 260 - 315 (in English), argued that the custom was introduced by a law of 465/4, but Gomme, ii. 94 - 100, inferred from Thucydes' "traditional" that it must be appreciably older. That seems fair — Thucydides ought not to be wrong about a law enacted not more than ten years before he was born — but it must be granted that Marathon (§5 n.) was not the only exception. It is possible, but cannot be proved, that Diodorus is right about the games and the speech. Stupperich, *Staatsbegräbnis und Privatgrabmal*, 206-24, attributes the original institution to Cleisthenes, in 508/7; Pritchett, *The Greek State at War*, iv. 106-24, suggests that although there were several earlier instances the regular custom of a public funeral in Athens dates from the 460s.
34. 2. the bones: The bodies will have been cremated on the battlefield, and the bones collected and brought to Athens afterwards.
34. 3. one for each tribe: The whole of Athenian public life was based on the ten tribes created by Cleisthenes: in the inscribed lists of casualties the names are commonly arranged by tribes (see *Agora* xvii: the texts will be republished as *IG* i^3 1144-93).
34. 5. the most beautiful suburb: The outer Ceramicus, immediately outside the Sacred Gate in the north-west of the city: the public tombs lined the road running NNW from the gate to the Academy.

given a tomb on the spot: This was the normal practice of other Greek states, and was followed by Athens not only after the battle of Marathon against the Persians in 490: for instance, those who died fighting against the Persians at Plataea in 479 were buried on the spot also (Hdt. IX. 85. 2).

34. 6. appropriate words of praise are spoken: We possess a fragment of a funeral speech by Gorgias of Leontini (fr. 5 Sauppe), a speech attributed to Lysias (II), one attributed to Demosthenes (LX), and the speech made by Hyperides (VI) over those who died fighting against Macedon in 323; Plato's *Menexenus* contains a parody of the Thucydidean speech, purporting to be the work of Pericles' mistress Aspasia. For a comparison of this speech, the others and the pronouncements of the later critics see Ziolkowski, *Thucydides and the Tradition of Funeral Speeches at Athens*. Either because this speech immediately became a classic or, more probably, because it follows what had already become a standard pattern, it exhibits the same main elements and many of the same motifs within those elements as the other funeral speeches: after a brief introduction, approving the custom and remarking on the difficulty of the speaker's task, the first main element is the praise of the dead, which tends to range over their ancestry, their city and their own achievements, and within which, inevitably, a number of commonplace motifs tend to recur from one speech to another; the second main element is the consolation of the survivors, within which there are again recurrent commonplace motifs, and a brief conclusion refers to the *nomos* again and to the mourners' lamentation, and directs the mourners to leave. What is most unusual about this speech is that praise is bestowed at length on the way of life of contemporary Athens rather than on the glorious achievements of previous generations of Athenians.

intelligence: Cf. 15. 2 n.

34. 8. Pericles . . . was chosen: He had delivered the funeral speech at least once before, over those who died in the Samian war of 440 - 439 (I. 115. 2 - 117): Plut. *Per.* 8. 9, 28. 4-7; the quotation of Arist. *Rh.* I. 1365 A 30-3, III. 1411 A 2-4, is probably from that speech.

he spoke on these lines: On Thucydides' speeches and the formulae with which he introduces them see 10. 3 n. and Introduction, pp. 8 - 9. In this case it is likely that Thucydides heard the speech actually made by Pericles; and, since the Peloponnesian War was seen as a conflict between different kinds of state, standing for different ways of life, it is not incredible that Pericles should have chosen to praise the dead by praising the kind of city they fought for. However, the view that the speech was simply a free composition by Thucydides was already held in antiquity: Dionysius of Halicarnassus criticises him for placing it here, so that it can be delivered by Pericles, rather than after one of the great episodes in the war (849-53. *Thuc.* 18).

35. 1. The majority . . . have claimed that it is good: It was normal in funeral speeches to express approval of the custom and to comment on the difficulty of the speaker's task (cf. 34. 6 n.): here Pericles is made to carry awareness of the difficulty to the point of doubting the desirability of the custom.

35. 2. It is hard to speak appropriately: Cf. above. In writing these words Thucydides may well have been conscious that this difficulty attends the history of great achievements, as well as funeral speeches.

36. 1. I shall begin . . . with our ancestors: This was normal: what is abnormal about this funeral speech is that it devotes so little attention to that theme, and concentrates on "the way of life which has enabled us to pursue these objectives" (§4 n.). For Pericles this way of life, as much as victories in battle, is Athens' achievement (cf. 41. 5 - 42. 2).
the same race of men: Cf. I. 2. 5-6, II. 14 - 16: this was generally believed, and it seems at any rate to be true that there was more continuity between the Mycenaean period and the classical in Athens than in most places in Greece.

36. 2. our own fathers . . . the present generation: Pericles was born in the 490s; the Delian League, the Athenian-led alliance which became an Athenian empire, was founded in the 470s by men of his father's generation; Pericles himself had become a leading figure by the time Athens tried to acquire a dominant position within Greece (in the 450s) and decided to keep the Delian League in being for her own purposes after giving up the league's original objective of waging war against Persia (in the 440s). Pericles returns to this theme in his last speech, in 62. 3, and in 65. 5 Athenian power is said to have reached its greatest height "under his guidance".

36. 3. most ample in all respects: Not self-sufficient, but able to supply all that she needed, whether from her own resources or by importing (cf. 38. 2). Cf. 64. 3, in Pericles' last speech, and his review of Athens' resources in 13. 2-9.

36. 4. I shall pass them over: Cf. §1 n. Brief (or not so brief) allusion to a topic which one says one will pass over is a common rhetorical device. Whether or not Pericles did pass this topic over, the omission suits Thucydides: the Persian

Wars had been narrated by Herodotus, and the growth of Athens' power after the Persian Wars has been sketched by Thucydides in I. 89 – 118 to explain why Sparta was sufficiently afraid of Athens to go to war against her.

the way of life: Praise of the city for which the dead had fought was a regular ingredient in funeral speeches, but it was normally treated in terms of the city's military achievements: what we are given from this point to 42. 1 is an unexpected interpretation of the expected theme.

37. 1. an example to others: As far as we know, the Athenian constitution resulting from Ephialtes' reforms in 462/1 was more democratic than any earlier Greek constitution; and within ten years we have the first known instance (M&L 40 = *IG* i³ 14, for Erythrae) of Athens' setting up a democratic constitution in a state which had tried to revolt from the Delian League, and so compelling others to follow her example.

democracy: *Demokratia*, "people-power". The first political distinction of which the Greeks became conscious was that between absolute rule and constitutional government of any kind; the word democracy seems to have been coined about the middle of the fifth century, and although in some of its first occurrences it seems to have denoted no more than constitutional government (e.g. Hdt. IV. 137. 2, VI. 43. 3) it soon came to be contrasted with oligarchy (*oligarchia*), the rule of a few. The word *demos*, "people", could be used either of the whole citizen body or of the mass of poor and unprivileged citizens: so Aristotle begins by defining democracy (or rather, his good version of democracy, "polity") as the rule of the many, but goes on to redefine it as the rule of the poor (*Pol*. III. 1279 A 22 – 1280 A 6). I have not accepted the argument of some scholars (e.g. J. R. Grant, *Phoen*. 25 (1971), 104-7) that the use of μέν and δέ here shows that Pericles is praising the Athenian constitution despite the attachment to it of the label democracy.

This speech points to many contrasts between Athens and Sparta. Sparta was not a typical oligarchy, in that the body of full citizens (Spartiates) was a small proportion of the total population, but nevertheless numbered some thousands, among whom there was a measure of equality; but Sparta came to be regarded as the champion of oligarchy, and encouraged oligarchy among her allies, as Athens came to be regarded as the champion of democracy (cf. I. 19). In VII. 55 Thucydides will consider it a point worthy of note that the cities in Sicily which Athens attacked in 415 (in particular, Syracuse) were democratic like Athens.

what matters is not rotation but merit: This is one of many passages in the speech where scholars have found it hard to reach agreement on the meaning. Here the problem centres on the word *meros*. For "rotation" cf. Eur. *Supp.* 406-8, where Theseus says, "The people rule in rotation (ἐν μέρει) by annual succession, and do not give the lion's share to the rich, but the poor man has an equal share"; and *Heracl.* 181-3, where Iolaus says that in Athens one can speak and listen in turn (ἐν μέρει). Many have supposed the reference to be to one part, i.e. one class within the population of the state, as at Sparta, but Gomme rightly remarks that that does not suit the sentence in which the assertion is made. On either interpretation the statement is false: though military appointments at Athens were made by election, and so on merit (of whatever kind the voters thought relevant), most civilian appointments were made by lot and were unrepeatable, so that what mattered was not merit but rotation; and men belonging to the lowest of the four property classes, the thetes, were ineligible for office in law (*Ath. Pol.* 7. 4), and in the time of Pericles almost certainly in practice too.

As for poverty: Another claim which is untrue of contemporary Athens. The thetes were not eligible to hold office (cf. above); and, although from the middle of the fifth century stipends had been paid to compensate men for earnings lost through public service, these were not lavish, and the poorest of those who were eligible to hold office would not have found an active political career easy. Leading political figures were rich men, usually the sons of rich fathers.

It is striking that Pericles should have said and/or that Thucydides should have represented him as saying things about the Athenian constitution which many of Pericles' hearers and Thucydides' readers will have known to be false. Thucydides does not of course vouch for the truth of statements made by his speakers (cf. Introduction, p. 9), but even so we should not have expected the admirer of Pericles to attribute to him an easily detected lie.

37. 2. we live as free men: A claim which could be made by all Greeks, including the Spartans (cf. Hdt. VII. 104. 4), in contrast to the subjects of a despotic régime like the Persian empire.

suspicion of one another: The Spartans' way of life encouraged supervision of one another and uniformity to an unusual extent. Even in Athens, tolerance was limited. The rich, aristocratic and ambitious Alcibiades was accused of unpatriotic selfishness (by Nicias, in VI. 12. 2: he replies in VI. 16); and after Athens' defeat in the Peloponnesian War Socrates was put to death for exercising a bad influence over Alcibiades and men like him.

37. 3. we are obedient . . . to the laws: Cf. again the claim made for Sparta in Hdt. VII. 104. 4; also Archidamus' speech, Thuc. I. 84. 3.

<u>those which have not been written down</u>: Those moral principles which, it was thought, were shared by all right-thinking people and did not need to be incorporated in codes of law. In Soph. *Ant.* 449-61 the unwritten laws are the laws of the gods, contrasted with the wicked laws which king Creon has imposed on Thebes, cf. *O.T.* 863-72; but of course no such contrast is intended here.

38. 1. <u>the greatest number of relaxations</u>: In Athens nearly 150 festival days in the year are attested, and a further allowance must be made for festivals whose dates are unknown (Mikalson, *The Sacred and Civil Calendar of the Athenian Year*, 201); in addition there were festivals which concerned not the whole state but a single deme or some other body within the state. We lack similar evidence for other states, but Strabo (280. VI. 3. 4) alleges that Sparta's colony Taras at the height of its prosperity had more festival than non-festival days in the year.

The festivals are described not as occasions of religious significance but simply as relaxations (on the other hand, despite the mention of toil, "relaxations . . . for the spirit" implies more than the mere rest from labour which is given as the secular aspect of festivals in Pl. *Leg.* II 653 C 9 - D 5, cf. Arist. *Eth. Nic.* VIII. 1160 A 21-8: Thucydides will pass to the subject of physical toil in ch. 39). As usual, we cannot be sure that this passage reflects Pericles' actual speech, though we know that he did not accept the whole of traditional religious belief (Plut. *Per.* 6, but contrast 8. 6); but what is said here is certainly consonant with Thucydides' own attitude (cf. Introduction, pp. 12 - 13).

<u>tasteful private provisions</u>: Cf. 65. 2. According to *Hell. Oxy.* 17. 5 "the land of Athens was at that time the most expensively furnished in Greece."

38. 2. <u>everything can be imported</u>: This was due not simply to the size of Athens, but to her control of the Aegean (cf. [Xen.] *Ath. Pol.* 2. 7, 12). The sanctions imposed on Megara before the war (cf. 31. 1 n.), and the privilege of importing Black Sea corn granted in the 420s to a Delian League member, Methone (M&L 65 = *IG* i³ 61, 34-41), show that the Athenians were aware of the corollary, that they could deny imports to others. The full citizens of Sparta, provided with allotments of land worked for them by helots and living in a society which frowned on imported luxuries, had less need for trade than most Greeks.

39. 1. <u>expulsions of foreigners</u>: Sparta did this from time to time (I. 144. 2), and Thucydides remarks that because of the secrecy of the Spartan state it was hard to obtain information about the Spartan army (V. 68. 2). Before the Persian invasion of 480 King Xerxes is said to have allowed Greek spies to see his large forces and return home to report (Hdt. VII. 145-7); Athens after the Persian Wars allowed Spartans to see the rebuilding of her walls, but not to return home and report what they had seen until the walls had reached a safe height (Thuc. I. 91. 2-4). Athens may not have been in the habit of expelling foreigners, but 6. 2 suggests that she kept them under surveillance. For the presence of foreigners at the state funeral see 34. 4, 36. 4.

<u>not so much in our preparations and deceit</u>: As Gomme remarks, this might have been a Spartan boast.

<u>they start right from their youth</u>: Male Spartiates were taken from their mothers at the age of seven to enter on the *agoge*, a system of training in military skills and endurance, and since their land was worked by helots they were able to devote much of their adult life to military training. Archidamus defends this stern way of life in I. 84. 4. A compulsory two-year training programme for Athenian *epheboi* (young men aged eighteen and nineteen: cf. 13. 6 n., and Appendix, p. 271) was introduced in the 330s; before then, it seems, they had opportunities for voluntary training. There is no direct evidence for the training of adult Athenian soldiers, but it is hard to believe that they never joined their regiments except to face the enemy.

<u>the dangers to which we are equal</u>: Pericles goes on to claim that there are dangers to which even the Spartans on their own are not equal; and he is not made to claim that the Athenian army was as good as the Spartan and could face any danger which the Spartan could face.

39. 2. <u>invade our territory</u>: See 10 - 12, 18 - 23; 47. 1-2, 55-7. The Spartans did require their allies to join in the invasions of Attica, and an additional invasion proposed for the autumn of 428 was prevented by the allies' refusal to join in (III. 15 - 16. 2).

<u>we attack our neighbours' territory</u>: In autumn 431 Athens began

twice-yearly attacks on Megara (31 nn.), but these did not lead to victory.

39. 3. our whole force: The first attack on Megara involved nearly all the Athenian army, but there was a detachment besieging Potidaea (31. 2), and the navy's oarsmen were not converted into soldiers to assist in the attack.

39. 4. daring: In book I the Athenians have been credited with daring at the time of the Persian Wars (74. 2, 4, 90. 1, 91. 5, 144. 4) and subsequently.

40. 1. We are lovers of beauty without extravagance: It is hard to produce an English rendering which does not jar, though the Greek original presumably did not jar on the original readers. In the twenty years before the war Athens had spent what would seem to most Greeks to be very large sums of money on public buildings, but this was more than covered by revenue (including the tribute from the Delian League), and she began the war with substantial reserves (cf. 13. 3-5 nn.). 38. 1 has mentioned numerous public festivals and tasteful private provisions. It may be that most rich Athenians did not flaunt their riches: [Xen.] *Ath. Pol.* 1. 10 alleges that citizens are no better dressed than slaves or metics, but contrast *Hell. Oxy.*, cited in n. on 38. 1. Sparta was not an impressive city (I. 10. 2): her self-conscious austerity avoided beauty as well as extravagance.

In each sentence of §1 and the first sentence of §2 τε is followed by καί. It is argued by J. S. Rusten, *CQ²* 35 (1985), 14 - 19, that Thucydides is not using τε to anticipate καί but is using the three instances of τε to link the three themes of philosophy, wealth and (last and most important) politics.

wisdom without softness: The travelling teachers of the late fifth century, called sophists, were welcome in Athens but not in Sparta. Not all Athenians approved of the new cleverness which they brought: cf. Aristophanes' *Clouds* and the eventual condemnation of Socrates; also Cleon's criticisms of clever men in III. 37. 3-4. For Sparta's contempt for cleverness cf. the speeches of Archidamus and Sthenelaidas in I. 84. 3-4, 86.

40. 2. both for their own affairs and for the state's: Pericles is in fact represented as arranging his own affairs efficiently but not taking the normal interest in them: Plut. *Per.* 7. 5, 16. 3-6.

not as non-interfering but as useless: In I. 70 the Corinthians represent the Athenians as active and interfering, "whose nature is neither to have leisure themselves nor to allow it to other people". Athens' political machinery depended on the willingness of a high proportion of the citizens to play their part in working it, by holding offices and attending meetings. *Apragmosyne* as a policy for the city as a whole is condemned in Pericles' last speech, 65. 2-3.

expound policy in speech: Cf. the claim which Pericles makes for himself in 60. 5-7. The importance of public discussion is considered again in the debate on Mytilene, III. 37-8, 42-3.

40. 3. combine boldness with reasoning: Cf. 13. 2, 62. 4-5; and contrast, again, Archidamus and Sthenelaidas in I. 84, 86; in I. 144. 4 Pericles claims that the Athenians had defeated the Persians by judgment rather than good fortune. In I. 138 Themistocles combines intelligence with practical ability — and it was to become a standard rhetorical *topos* that great leaders possess both qualities.

40. 4. displays of goodness: *Arete* normally denotes good qualities in a person's character, particularly those which are needed by a soldier; but here it is clear from the context that Thucydides is referring to generous behaviour towards others. For giving in this spirit cf. Hes. *Op.* 353-62.

40. 5. not calculating the advantage: Contrast Pericles' last speech, 60-4, and the other non-idealistic speeches in which the Athenians claim that they are realistically and unashamedly pursuing their own advantage: the most direct counterpart to this passage is Euphemus' speech, VI. 83-7.

confident in our freedom: Ziolkowski, *Thucydides and the Tradition of Funeral Speeches*, 107 n. 11, suggests that the genitive is objective: the Athenians are confident in freedom and fight for it.

41. 1. an education to Greece: Flashar, *Der Epitaphios Des Perikles*, 25 n. 48, suggests that this is a reply to a claim made by Sparta. Isocrates was to allege that Athens was the teacher of others especially in thinking and making speeches (IV. *Paneg.* 47 - 50), and the allegation, and in particular that version of it, is attacked by P. E. Harding, *LCM* 11 (1986), 134-6.

keep his person: There are verbal echoes of Hdt. l. 32. 8-9 (cf. 43. 5 n.). Cf. also 51. 3 n.

43. 3. an enemy attacker: Classen was perhaps right to delete "attacker": the Athens depicted in this speech did not limit its warfare to defence against the attacks of others (cf. 39. 2).

41. 4. the admiration: Cf. 63. 1.

whose impression of the facts: For Thucydides' attitude to Homer and other poets dee I. 10, 3-5, 21. 1, and Introduction,

pp. 6 - 7.
<u>sea and land</u>: A favourite pairing: cf. e.g. I. 2. 2.
<u>undying memorials</u>: The theme recurs at greater length in 43. 2-3.
<u>both of our failures and of our successes</u>: Athens has not succeeded in every venture, but she has been tirelessly eager to embark on ventures.

42. 1. <u>That is why . . . about our city</u>: Rounding off the section begun in 36. 4.
42. 4. <u>poor man's hope</u>: Cf. what is said of poverty in 40. 1.
<u>forsake wealth</u>: The manuscripts' ἐφίεσθαι ("covet") gives a paradoxical sense.
<u>They thought that safety</u>: This last sentence is very difficult. Earlier attempts to make sense of it are discussed by Gomme; J. S. Rusten, *HSCP* 90 (1986), 49 - 76, arguing from the pattern of polarities used by Thucydides, retains τὸ ἀμύνεσθαι ("thinking that in it, i.e. the task, were defence and death rather than survival by suffering"), and takes the last clause to mean, "Through the fortune of the briefest instant, at the height of glory rather than fear, they departed." The verb ἀπαλλάττειν normally refers to escaping from something undesirable, and both on Rusten's interpretation and on mine the point must be that these men came to the moment of death in a spirit of glorious hope for Athens, not selfish fear for their own lives; if, with Gomme, we transpose fear and glory, we have the more commonplace remark that death put an end to their fear but not to their glory.

43. 1. <u>The rest</u>: Thucydides completes the first of the main elements in the funeral speech, praise of the dead, and proceeds to the second, exhortation to the survivors (cf. 34. 6 n.). This is handled in such a way as to continue the theme of the greatness of Athens.
<u>become lovers of it</u>: An awkward conclusion to reach from the earlier emphasis on the enjoyment of private life (E. L. Hussey, *Crux . . . G. E. M. de Ste Croix*, 125). If it is something actually said by Pericles, that may explain the use of the expression in Ar. *Eq.* 732, 1341.
<u>by daring, by recognising</u>: Cf. 40. 3 n.
<u>free contribution</u>: An *eranos* is a voluntary contribution by a member of an association, or an interest-free loan.
43. 2. <u>remains recorded for ever</u>: Cf. 64. 3, in Pericles' last speech.
43. 3. <u>of their purpose rather than their accomplishment</u>: Cf. the last n. on 41. 4.

43. 5. those who risk a great downfall: Happiness and prosperity are not lasting, and the best life is one that ends at a high point, before they have been lost: cf. Solon's sermon to Croesus in Hdt. I. 29 - 33 (but that depicts a more passive view of success: Macleod, *Collected Essays*, 151-2). In 42. 4 it was stated that neither the prosperous who hoped their prosperity would continue nor the poor who hoped to win prosperity were deflected by these hopes from doing their duty.

44. 1. encouragement rather than sympathy: Pericles' words to the bereaved in 44-5 strike the modern reader as extremely bleak, after the enthusiasm for Athens displayed in what has gone before. It is hard to be sure that the original readers would have reacted similarly, but Pericles does seem to have been regarded by contemporaries as inhumanly aloof (cf. Plut. *Per.* 5, 7).

44. 3. still of an age to have children: For this theme R. S. P. Beekes, *Mnem.*⁴ 39 (1986), 225-39, compares Hdt. III. 119, Soph. *Ant.* 909-12, Eur. *Alc.* 290-4, Lucian *Toxaris* 61, and passages in non-Greek literature. In fact it is unlikely that many old enough to be the parents of sons who had died in battle could expect to have more sons afterwards; on the other hand, many of them would already have other sons who were still alive.

contribute children: A good citizen was expected to have a stake in the city by owning property in its territory and by producing children to ensure its continued existence. The requirement is found in the spurious constitution of Draco, *Ath. Pol.* 4. 2 (generals and hipparchs), the inscribed decree of Themistocles, M&L 23, 18 - 22 (trierarchs), and Din. I. *Dem.* 71 (politicians and generals).

44. 4. the life still to come will be short: Life is full of misery and one should not want it to be prolonged: Ziolkowski, *Thucydides and the Tradition of Funeral Speeches*, 147, cites other fifth-century uses of this theme.

45. 2. a wife: Translated thus, because this sentence is addressed specifically to widows (Gomme).
the least possible talk: Study of speeches made in Athens suggests that a respectable woman was not mentioned in public by name but, if she had to be mentioned, as her father's daughter or her husband's wife. Women were not necessarily oppressed, unless their exclusion from certain activities is itself regarded as oppression, but their field of activity was family life, not public life. See D. Schaps, CQ^2 27 (1977), 323-30; and, for Thucydides' own attitude to women, 4. 4 n.

46. 1. in accordance with our institution: It was normal for the conclusion of a funeral speech to refer once more to the *nomos*: cf. 34. 6 n.

the city will undertake: The upbringing of war orphans at public expense is attributed to Solon by Diog. Laert. I. 55, but Solon (archon and reformer of the Athenian state, 594/3) was credited with many later institutions; according to Arist. *Pol.* II. 1268 A 8-11 Hippodamus claimed to be creating something without precedent when he provided for this in Miletus, perhaps in the second quarter of the fifth century.

46. 2. make your lament: Ziolkowski, *Thucydides and the Tradition of Funeral Speeches*, 166-7, argues that the reference is to lamentation made earlier, before this speech concludes the ceremonies: either interpretation is grammatically possible.

47. 1. Such was the funeral: From Thucydides' account of the first year's fighting, it does not seem likely that those who had died were very numerous, or had died particularly gloriously. Yet Thucydides has given us this speech, with its proclamation of an Athenian ideal (and has not given us a comparable Peloponnesian speech). He was criticised by Dionysius of Halicarnassus for choosing to insert a funeral speech at this point: see 34. 8 n.

It is in many ways a difficult speech. Even more than in other speeches, the Greek is hard to penetrate: the language is compressed, it is often difficult to make out what is meant, and there are passages which we must assume were expected to make a favourable impact when first heard or read but from which it is hard for the modern reader to derive a favourable impression. In particular, the consolation addressed to the survivors seems very unsatisfying. Also statements are made about the Athenian constitution which are untrue, and which must have been known to be untrue by the original hearers of Pericles or readers of Thucydides. In its basic structure, and in many of the individual motifs used, the speech conforms to what we know of the tradition for funeral speeches, but the use which is made of the traditional pattern and material is unusual.

Presumably Pericles did make the funeral speech this year (and Thucydides has incorporated a speech here because this was the first year of the war and because the speech was made by Pericles), and I am prepared to believe that he did use it to praise the Athenian way of life, more or less as this speech does (cf. 34. 8 n.). Thucydides was an Athenian, admired Pericles, and in some sense admired the achievements of imperial

Athens, if he could not make up his mind on the morality of them; he was no lover of extreme democracy, but would perhaps have been happier with a state where "what matters is not rotation but merit" (37. 1) than with Athens as it actually was in the late fifth century (cf. Introduction, pp. 1 - 2, 13 - 14). Book I gives, I believe, an Athenian view, and a Periclean view, of why the Peloponnesians went to war against Athens (cf. pp. 23-4): here Thucydides lays aside his worries about Athenian power, and the cynical attitudes which he portrays elsewhere, and depicts with enthusiasm the way of life for which Athens was fighting, the way of life which had produced Thucydides.

Some have thought that the name Alope could be restored in a fragmentary casualty list, and that the list could therefore be identified as that of this year, but the most recent study shows that that restoration is unfounded (cf. 26. 2 n.).

47 - 68. Second Summer (430)

47 - 54. The Plague in Athens

<u>47. 2. as on the first occasion</u>: Cf. 10, and 19. 1 (where Archidamus is given a formal introdcution, as here, at the moment of invading Attica); also 71. 1, at the beginning of the campaign of 429. The account of this invasion is continued in 55-7.

<u>47. 3. the plague</u>: Thucydides passes almost immediately, and no doubt designedly (cf. 54. 5 n., and notes on particular parallels) from the funeral oration of Pericles depicting an ideal Athens to the suffering and demoralisation of the plague. The account of the plague, like the account of the war, is detailed and overtly matter-of-fact, but that is not inconsistent with Thucydides' using his austere account to create an atmosphere and make a point.

The view that he is indebted to contemporary medical writers, argued most strongly by D. L. Page, CQ^2 3 (1953), 97 - 119, and widely held, was attacked by A. Parry, $BICS$ 16 (1969), 106-18, who stressed that Thucydides inevitably uses some medical terms, but not technical terms which would be known only to a specialist, and who considered Thucydides' treatment not factual in the manner of the medical writers but dramatic and imaginative. Thucydides' prose is indeed not the prose of a medical writer, but his medical vocabulary is extensive if not arcane, and if contemporary medical writings had not existed it is doubtful whether it would have occurred to him to give the details which he does give in 48-9: he is in that sense indebted to them, even if he has not copied them.

There have been a great many attempts to identify the disease (Page's preference was measles; Gomme, 150-3, opted for typhus, and was confident enough to consider the problem solved; new suggestions continue to be advanced); but it is persuasively argued by J. C. F. Poole & A. J. Holladay, *CQ*² 29 (1979), 282 - 300 (cf. 32 (1982), 235-6; 34 (1984), 483-5), that, in view of the evolution of human beings and of viruses, by now the disease is likely either to be extinct or to be so changed that it could not be recognised from the symptoms described by Thucydides.

47. 4. The doctors . . . No other device: Thucydides anticipates points which he will make in detail below.

supplication . . . divination: Cf. 53. 1 n. A sanctuary of Heracles averter of evil (ἀλεξίκακος) was established in Melite, one of the demes inside the city walls (schol. Ar. *Ran.* 501); and in 420/19, when the Peace of Nicias made Epidaurus accessible, the cult of Asclepius was brought from there to Athens (*IG* ii² 4960: see W. S. Ferguson, *HTR* 37 (1944), 86 - 91; Dodds, *The Greeks and the Irrational*, 193 with 203 nn. 83-6). According to Paus. VIII. 41. 7-9 the temple of Apollo at Bassae, in Arcadia, celebrates Phigalea's deliverance from the plague; but not all archaeologists are happy with this dating (see Dinsmoor, *The Architecture of Ancient Greece*, 154; F. A. Cooper, *AJA*² 72 (1968), 103-11), and according to 54. 5 this plague did not reach the Peloponnese. J. D. Mikalson, *Studies . . . S. Dow* (*GR&BMon.* 10 [1984]), 217-25, finds little evidence for religious activity in Athens from 430/29 to 426/5, but renewed activity after that; he nevertheless suspects that the Athenians were as demoralised as Thucydides indicates only in the worst period of the plague, probably late summer 430.

48. 1-2. from Ethiopia . . . the Piraeus: In view of the clear contrasts later between Thucydides' account of the plague and Pericles' funeral speech, it is likely that he was conscious of the contrast between the boast that Athens could import whatever she wished from all over the earth (38. 2) and this deadly import.

48. 2. there were not yet any fountains there: This comment was presumably written at a time when aqueducts and fountains had been provided to improve the water supply of the Piraeus, but we have no information on what was done, or how soon. The word φρέατα covers both wells and cisterns.

48. 3. Every one, whether doctor or layman, may say: Presumably many explanations were advanced, none of them convincing to Thucydides. Diod. Sic. XII. 45. 2 regards the air as polluted because of the overcrowding in Athens (Thuc. 52. 1-2 uses the overcrowding to make a different point), and 58. 3-5 blames stagnant water and inferior crops resulting from heavy rain in the previous winter, and the failure in 430 of the "etesian" winds which normally blew from the north-west from June to August. We cannot be sure whether that is authentic memory, omitted by Thucydides but picked up by Ephorus, or later speculation.

in case it should ever attack again: For the view that, human nature being what it is, the like of what has happened in the past will happen in the future, cf. I. 22. 4, III. 82. 2; but this does not mean that all that happens is predictable (cf. 11. 4 n., 64. 1 n.). Thucydides' account of the plague, like his account of the war, is intended to be useful; but the foreknowledge which he offers here is limited to a description of the symptoms and the bleak message that the disease is not fatal in every case but there is no reliable cure.

suffered from the disease myself: Thucydides does not say whether the plague left its mark on him in any of the ways mentioned in 49. 7-8: we can say only that he recovered sufficiently to be able to serve as general in 424/3, and to live until 404 or slightly later (cf. Introduction, p. 1).

49. 1. free from disease . . . all ended in this: To be repeated in 51. 1, where it closes the ring before Thucydides proceeds from his description of the symptoms to a discussion of wider issues.

50. 2. birds . . . dogs: Birds of prey kept away from the plague-ridden; dogs, presumably, stayed with their masters and died.

51. 3. sufficient: The same Greek word (αὐτάρκης) is used in Pericles' funeral speech at 41. 1: "Each individual man among us can keep his person ready to profit from the greatest variety in life."

51. 4. caught the disease through caring for another: The disease was contagious (cf. 58. 2, where we learn that the men sent to reinforce the army outside Potidaea took the disease with them). This observation may have been general, or may be peculiar to Thucydides; but the medical writers do not show much understanding of contagion.

51. 6. did not attack . . . cherished the vain hope: It is again a medically significant observation that the disease gave survivors limited immunity against this disease but none against others.

52. 1. The distress was aggravated: The point is not that the overcrowding and inadequate housing hastened the spread of the disease (although that must be true, and is the point made by Diod. Sic. XII. 45. 2: see 48. 3 n.), but simply that they worsened the suffering of those who caught the disease.

52. 2. There were no houses for them: On the living conditions of those who moved in from the country cf. 17.
the dead and dying: Gomme's is the best way to restore sense.
in their passion to find water: Cf. 49. 5.

52. 3. deaths took place even there: Because of the associated pollution, deaths in sacred precincts were avoided if possible: cf. I. 134. 3.
to neglect the sacred and the secular alike: Cf. 53; and on the inefficacy of religion against the plague 47. 4 n.

52. 4. Many who lacked friends: And who therefore had no one to help them organise a proper funeral.

53. 1. the beginning of a decline: Thucydides believes not only that there was a collapse of standards during the plague but also that the Athenians did not return to the old standards afterwards. Cf. III. 82-3 on the collapse of standards in public life which resulted from the war and from the opportunity which it provided for rivalry in cities between pro-Athenian democrats and pro-Spartan oligarchs; also II. 65. 8-13, contrasting the statesmanlike Pericles with the short-sighted and self-seeking politicians who competed for supremacy in Athens after his death. This degenerate Athens stands out in sharp contrast to the ideal Athens of Pericles' funeral speech.

Belief that one lives in degenerate times and that one's forebears lived simpler and more virtuous lives is often to be found in developed civilisations: the fact that such a belief is hard to justify does not prove that it can never be correct. It is an observable phenomenon today that some people misbehave in the wake of a natural disaster as they would not at other times (though others rise to heights of heroism); and it does seem that realisation of the different possibilities of democracy and oligarchy, and the outbreak of the war between an Athens associated with democracy and a Sparta associated with oligarchy, led to a polarisation in attitudes and an increase in political violence within the cities.

Also the intellectual climate was changing: the sophists, the travelling teachers of the late fifth century, were prepared to challenge all the traditional certainties. including the existence of gods, of an anthropomorphic kind or indeed of any kind, and the existence of any absolute standards of conduct. Thucydides himself was affected by this change: it is clear from passages like this that he believed in high standards of conduct for individuals, however he would have justified them; it is arguable that he could not make up his mind whether comparable standards shoul' govern the behaviour of states; except in I. 23. 3 (where the plague forms the climax of his list) and V. 26. 3-4 there is no sign that he believed in gods, or in oracles, or in any connection between abnormal natural phenomena and human conduct. Cf. Introduction, pp. 12 - 14.

53. 1-2. changes of fortune . . . immediate profit and pleasure: Contrast what is said of wealth and poverty in Pericles' funeral speech, 40. 1, 42. 4.

53. 3. No one was willing: It is clear from 51. 2-5 that Thucydides is exaggerating here and that some Athenians did behave unselfishly.

an honourable result: Contrast 44. 4.

53. 4. No fear of the gods or law of men: The gods are not prominent in the funeral speech, and festivals are mentioned without reference to their religious dimension (38. 1), but Pericles does allude to the Athenians' respect for both written and unwritten laws (37. 3).

54. 2. they remembered a verse: For Thucydides' rationalising approach to the verse cf. his treatment of the oracle on the *Pelargikon*, 17. 1-2.

54. 3. *loimos* . . . or *limos*: In modern Greek *oi* and *i* are pronounced alike; but it does not appear that they were in classical Greek, and it is certainly not necessary that they should have been for this argument to have arisen. The words first appear together in Hes. *Op*. 243.

and I think that if . . . a famine: It is arguable, but by no means certain, that Thucydides would not have left this sentence as it stands if he had been conscious of it after the blockade of Athens by Sparta in 405/4 (cf. Introduction, p. 15).

54. 4. the oracle given to the Spartans: At Delphi. It is reported in I. 118. 3, in almost the same words but with the addition that Apollo would join in "whether invited or not".

54. 5. as soon as the Peloponnesians had invaded: Cf. 47. 3.

That is what happened: Further information is to be given later: we learn from 58. 2-3 that 1,050 died out of a force of

4,000 taken to Potidaea this year; and from III. 87 that the plague originally persisted for two years and returned for one year in winter 427/6, and that in all 4,400 hoplites of the field army (cf. 13. 6 n.), 300 cavalry (cf. 13. 8 n.) and an incalculable number of the others (presumably about a third again) lost their lives.

It is remarkable that Thucydides, whose criteria of relevance are for most of the time so narrow, should have included this detailed account of the plague in his history of the Peloponnesian War. He is influenced by the medical writers, at least in the sense that, but for their existence, it would probably not have occurred to him to write a detailed account of the symptoms and progress of a disease (cf. 47. 3 n.); he is surely conscious that there was a plague in the course of the Trojan War, with which he compares the Peloponnesian War (I. 9 - 10), though in the *Iliad* that receives only a brief mention, not a detailed account (I. 43 - 61); and probably here as on some topics of general history (e.g. I. 20, 23. 5-6) he has yielded to a temptation to show that he can give a better account than others. He is to give another detailed technical account in book II, of the siege of Plataea (71-8: see especially 71. 1 n.). In addition the plague enables him to draw attention to contrasts — between the ideal Athens of Pericles' funeral speech and the actual Athens where in a calamity standards broke down; between the Athens which was well prepared for the war both in manpower and other resources and in planning (13, 40. 2-3) and the Athens which lost a third of its manpower through a chance misfortune which could not have been predicted or prevented (61. 2-3).

Lucretius ends his *De Rerum Natura* with a section on epidemics, blaming them on an accumulation of noxious atoms in the atmosphere of a particular place, and proceeding to an account of the plague at Athens (VI. 1090 - 1286). This is closely based on Thucydides' account, but it omits a few of the details which he gives, and inserts some details which he does not give (notably the signs of death in 1182-98).

55 - 58. *The Summer's Campaigns (i)*

55. 1. the Peloponnesians: Continued from 47. 2.
what is called the Coastal Territory: "Is called" because Thucydides is using not an ordinary adjective but an established name. It denotes the south-west-facing coast from the plain of Athens to Cape Sunium, and the east-facing coast running north

from Sunium: Laurium is on and inland from the latter coast, a few miles north of Sunium. Of the three regions into which Cleisthenes divided Attica in 508/7 (*Ath. Pol.* 21. 4), the coastal comprised these stretches and the whole of western Attica.

55. 2. Pericles was general, and held the same view: Cf. 13. 1-2, 21. 4 - 22.

56. 1. While the enemy were still in the plain . . . he prepared an expedition: Cf. 17. 4, 23. 2 (431). Thucydides is meticulous over the relative chronology of the Peloponnesian invasion and the Athenian expedition, but he gives no indication of absolute chronology apart from "the very beginning of summer" (47. 2) and the forty days' duration of the invasion (57. 2); and for this year we have no other evidence (contr. 23. 2 n.). The treatment of this expedition is as perfunctory as that of the expedition sent round the Peloponnese in 431 (cf. 25. 1 n.).

56. 2. four thousand Athenian hoplites on board: I.e. forty per trireme: in 431 one thousand hoplites and four hundred archers were taken on a hundred ships (23. 2).

which had been constructed for the first time out of old ships: The Persians had used horse-transports in 490 and 480 (Hdt. VI. 48. 2, VII. 97), so what happened for the first time in 430 was probably the use of horse-transports by Greeks, possibly the conversion of old triremes into horse-transports. For a possible reconstruction see Morrison & Coates, *The Athenian Trireme*, 157, 226-8.

The Chians and Lesbians: Cf. 9. 5 n. They had not joined in the expedition of 431, which went to the west side of Greece; Athens' western allies did not join in this expedition.

56. 4. Epidaurus: On the side of the Argolid facing the Saronic Gulf and Athens. It was the strongest city in the Argolid after Argos, and was often hostile to Argos. If it had been captured by Athens it might have been used to put pressure on Argos (technically neutral: 9. 2 n.), but nothing is said by Thucydides to suggest that the capture of Epidaurus might have served that or any other further purpose.

56. 5. Troezen, Halieis and Hermione: At the south-east end of the Argolid; Hermione will in fact have been reached before Halieis. It is a little surprising that Thucydides thinks it necessary to explain their location (though he does not do it very helpfully): cf. 30 nn. During the First Peloponnesian War, in the 450s, the Athenians lost a battle at Halieis (I. 105. 1); they made an alliance with Hermione (*IG* i^3 31); they acquired Troezen, and gave it up in the Thirty Years' Peace (115. 1). They were to make another raid in this region in 425 (IV. 45. 2), and were to make an alliance with Halieis in 424/3 (*IG* i³ 75).

56. 6. Prasiae: On the east coast of Laconia, south of Thyrea (27. 2 n.), and like Thyrea disputed between Sparta and Argos. There seems to have been no attempt to occupy it for an *epiteichismos* against Sparta (cf. 25. 1 n., 65. 7 n., and Introduction, pp. 26-7), but Aristophanes refers to its sufferings (*Pax* 242-5), and Thucydides mentions another raid, in 414 (VI. 105. 2, cf. VII. 18. 3).

57. 1. the deserters: With the article because desertion, especially by slaves, was a regular phenomenon in wartime.

57. 2. their longest-lasting invasion: Of the (almost) annual invasions from 431 to 425. Sparta's occupation of Decelea (cf. next note) lasted without interruption from 413 until the end of the war.

they ravaged the whole of the country: They are not likely to have overrun non-cultivable land very thoroughly. According to Diod. Sic. XII. 45. 1 they spared the Tetrapolis (Marathon and its neighbours in north-east Attica) because of a special relationship dating from the heroic period (cf. 23. 1 n., on the sparing of Decelea in 431): Gomme on 55. 1 was prepared to trust Thucydides' silence, perhaps unwisely.

In III. 26. 2 Thucydides says that this was the most damaging invasion, as well as the longest-lasting. It is hard to tell how much damage was done: certainly much more harm was done by the Peloponnesians' permanent presence at Decelea from 413 to 404 (VII. 19. 1-3, 27. 3 - 28. 2), and according to *Hell. Oxy.* 17. 4-5 these earlier invasions were not very damaging. The total destruction of olives and vines would be very hard work, and it seems likely that the invaders did considerable short-term but little long-term damage to Athenian agriculture (see Hanson, *Warfare and Agriculture in Ancient Greece*; P. Harvey, *Ath.*² 64 (1986), 205-18). The working of the silver mines does not seem to have been brought to a halt in the 420s.

58. 1. Hagnon son of Nicias and Cleopompus son of Clinias: Hagnon was a distinguished man, attested first as general in 440/39 (I. 117. 2) and as a supporter of Pericles (cf. Plut. *Per.* 32. 3-4), and last as one of the ten *probouloi* elected as an emergency cabinet in 413 (VIII. 1. 3): his father is not known, but the oligarch Theramenes was Hagnon's son (VIII. 68. 4). Hagnon appears again in book II as a general (?) in 429/8 (95. 3 n.). For Cleopompus cf. 26. 1 n.

the Thraceward Chalcidians: Cf. 29. 4 n. Thucydides regularly identifies them as "Thraceward" to distinguish them from the Chalcidians of Chalcis in Euboea (in ch. 29 "Chalcidians" in §6 is preceded by "Thraceward" in §4).
Potidaea: Cf. 29. 6, 31. 2 nn.
58. 2. Phormio and his sixteen hundred: They had probably been at Potidaea only for a short time in 431. Presumably the reason for mentioning them here is to make it clear that they are not included among the men exposed to the plague at Potidaea. The story of Potidaea will be continued in 67.

59 - 65. Pericles under Attack

59. 1. underwent a change of mind: Gomme presses the pluperfect tense of the Greek verb, to make the change of mind coincide with Hagnon's departure from Athens after Pericles' return from "a not very successful expedition" (56); but the change was presumably a gradual process rather than a sudden event. Connor, *Thucydides*, 58 n. 19, suggests that Thucydides is using medical language, and for the verb compares Hippocr. *Praec.* 9.
59. 2. attempted to reach an agreement with the Spartans: de Romilly, Budé ed. of book II, p. xx, notes that whereas in 431 Pericles was in trouble for not being sufficiently belligerent (21. 2 - 22. 1) in 430 he was in trouble for being too belligerent. Thucydides does not say what line the negotiations took, or how far they were pursued; and Dion. Hal. 842-3. *Thuc.* 14 criticises him for not saying who was responsible or what the arguments were. The reader of this chapter would assume that the talks broke down, but 65. 2 implies that, when their mood changed again, the Athenians withdrew from talks in which they could have persevered. At this stage there were probably limits to the terms which the Athenians would accept, even in their despairing mood, and the Spartans might well have thought that if they kept up their pressure Athens could be brought to a more abject surrender.
59. 3. complaining . . . behaving as he had expected: Cf. I. 140. 1.
he called a meeting: Cf. 22. 1 n., on Pericles' refusal "to call an assembly or any kind of meeting" when men objected in 431 to his policy of not going out to meet the Peloponnesian invaders. Thucydides does not always use technical language where he might do so, and we cannot be sure whether we are dealing with a "meeting" of the armed forces called by a general or an "assembly" of the citizens summoned by the *prytaneis*

at the request of or with the agreement of a general: what is called a meeting here is called an assembly by Pericles in 60. 1.
he was still in office as general: But after this he was deposed (cf. 65. 3 n.).

60. 2. a whole city should be on the right lines: Cf. Creon in Soph. *Ant*. 184-90; also Eur. fr. 360, 16-21 (ed. Nauck).
60. 4. joining in the decision: This reminder is repeated in 61. 2 and 64. 1, and Thucydides remarks in VIII. 1. 1 on the people's tendency to forget their responsibility for decisions.
60. 5. I . . . am inferior to no one: Gomme found §§5-6 "perhaps the most artificial thing in all Thucydides' speeches", but shrank from the conclusion that the passage is Thucydides' own invention. Certainly it rivals the bleak consolation to the bereaved at the end of the funeral speech as a passage which seems unnatural to the twentieth-century reader (44-5 with 44. 1 n.). §6 is acceptable as a piece of late-fifth-century rhetoric; what shocks about §5 is that Pericles is represented as saying about himself what would be unremarkable if said about a third person, and we cannot tell whether this is an authentic touch.

In Greek and Latin "inferior to no one" is regularly qualified with an expression of respect, as here (E. D. Rawson, *Hist*. 26 (1977), 345-6; A. J. Woodman, commentary on Vell. Pat. II. 76. 1).
determining . . . expounding: Cf. 65. 8-9; also what is said of Themistocles in I. 138. 3 and of Antiphon in VIII. 68. 1. In II. 15. 2 intelligence is ascribed to Theseus; in 34. 6 it is made one of the criteria for the choice of the man to deliver the funeral speech; in 40. 2 Pericles credits the Athenians collectively with understanding and discussion of political issues.
devoted to the city: In VI. 92. 2-4 Alcibiades defends himself sophistically against the charge that previously he seemed devoted to the city but now he is joining its greatest enemies in attacking it.
not to be bought for money: Cf. 65. 8; and notice the allegations in 65. 7 that after his death the Athenians were motivated by considerations of private gain, and in VI. 12. 2, 15. 2, that Alcibiades in particular hoped to enrich himself through political success. The claim is perhaps polemical: Aristophanes was prepared to allege that Pericles led Athens into the Peloponnesian War for disreputable private reasons (*Ach*. 514-38, *Pax* 605-9), and the story was current that Pericles had given a

bribe to the Spartan king Plistoanax in 446 (21. 1 n.).

60. 7. more than others, even to a moderate extent: The litotes is the first-person counterpart of the claim made directly of Themistocles in I. 138. 3, "outstandingly more than others".

61. 1. war is enormous folly: Cf. Hermocrates of Syracuse in IV. 62. 2, Croesus in Hdt. I. 87. 4.

61. 2. remain the same as I was: Cf. Pericles in I. 140. 1, Cleon in III. 38. 1.

61. 3. enslave the spirit: Cf. the references in IV. 34. 1, VII. 71. 3, to men's being enslaved in their mind (*gnome*).

61. 4. brought up in a correspondingly great way of life: Cf. the funeral speech, 37 - 42.

aspire to a distinction they do not deserve: Included for the sake of the antithesis, but not required by the argument of the speech. M. H. B. Marshall, *G&R*² 31 (1984), 27, suspects an allusion to Cleon, but that is not necessary.

62. 1. rather boastful: In 41. 2, in the funeral speech, Pericles states that what he says of Athens is no mere boast but the truth — but nevertheless he goes on to claim in 41. 4 that Athens "has compelled the whole of sea and land to make itself accessible to her daring." What he is about to say here of Athens' sea power is similarly extravagant and boastful.

62. 2. you have total mastery of the whole of the second: Cf. [Xen.] *Ath. Pol.* 2. 5, 11-12 (probably written in the mid 420s: W. G. Forrest, *Klio* 52 (1970), 107-16).

neither the King nor any other race: Since the King, without further specification, is regularly the Persian King (cf. 7. 1 n.), this is not as inconsequential in thought as it appears in expression. The question of prevention by Greeks does not arise, since Athens already does control (most) Greek waters.

62. 3. a great blow: Cf. especially 14. 2.

a pleasure-garden or adornment of your wealth: Only a few sayings of Pericles are preserved, but it is at any rate possible that this vivid expression is authentically Periclean.

even what they had before: The reference appears to be to Attica itself, in contrast to the recently acquired naval power.

Your fathers: Cf. 36. 2, in the funeral speech.

62. 4. a rational trust that they are stronger: Cf. 13. 2, 40. 2-3.

62. 5. reason grounded in the facts: In IV. 18. 2 the Spartans plead that they are in trouble because their reasoning from the facts has misled them.

63. 1. the honour which the empire brings: Cf. 41. 4.

slavery or freedom . . . the loss of the empire: For lesser states freedom from "slavery", i.e. outright subjection, was the most that could be hoped for (cf. V. 9. 9), and often the only serious choice was between one master and another (Brasidas in IV. 85-7 has to insist that he has not come to the Thraceward region to substitute Spartan rule for Athenian), but Athens claims the fullest kind of freedom, not merely from obeying the rule of others but to impose her own rule on others (cf. Diodotus in III. 45. 6).

those whose hatred you have incurred: Primarily Athens' subjects, but also others who feared and resented her power (cf. 64. 5 n.).

63. 2. **to avoid trouble**: In the funeral speech Pericles condemns avoiders of trouble (*apragmones*) within the city, men who opt out of political activity (40. 2), and says that those who have died in the war did not let private considerations lead them to cowardice (42. 4). His theme here is taken up by Alcibiades in VI. 18. 3-7; and cf. the Corinthians' depiction of Athens in I. 70. 8-9.

propose this as a virtuous course: In III. 40. 4 Cleon says that Athens must either punish Mytilene or give up the empire and make a virtue of avoiding danger.

like a tyranny: Cf. the Corinthians in I. 122. 3, 124. 3, Cleon in III. 37. 2, and Euphemus in VI. 85. 1; also, showing that the comparison is not of Thucydides' own devising, Ar. *Eq.* 1110-20.

it may be considered unjust to have acquired it: In book I, both in the Athenian speech at Sparta (76. 2) and in the narrative (95. 1-2, 96. 1), the emphasis is on Athens' acceptance of a position offered to her by the allies; Athens became more despotic in the course of insisting on the allies' obligations. Pericles would hardly have admitted that the acquisition was unjust: perhaps the analogy with tyranny is being pressed dangerously far.

to renounce it would be dangerous: Cf. the Athenian speech at Sparta in 432 (I. 75. 3 - 76. 2).

63. 3. **are not safe unless**: They are a luxury which can be afforded only by a community consisting largely of people unlike them.

64. 1. **acted as was to be expected . . . beyond what could be foreseen**: Though the wise use reason and foresight as far as they can, and not only the Peloponnesians' strategy but also the Athenians' reaction was as Pericles had expected (59. 3), not everything that happens in human affairs can be foreseen:

cf. 11. 4 n. Opponents of Pericles might have claimed that the crowding of the citizens in the city invited trouble (cf. 52. 1 n.), but it was correct to say that the arrival of a particularly deadly virus in Athens could not have been predicted.

64. 2. <u>blows from heaven</u>: Cf. Soph. *Phil*. 1316-7, Eur. *Phoen*. 382, 1763. Like my English rendering, the Greek expression need not have a strong theological content. For Pericles' religious views see 38. 1 n.

64. 3. <u>does not give in to disasters</u>: To be repeated in the final sentence of the speech (§6). Cf. the Corinthians' depiction of Athens in I. 70. 5, 7.

<u>has sacrificed . . . has undertaken</u>: Cf. I. 70. 6, 8.

<u>Even if . . . we do some time give way</u>: It is often, but unjustifiably, alleged that this could not have been written until after 404.

<u>all posterity will be able to recall</u>: Cf. 41. 4, 43. 2-3, in the funeral speech.

<u>we ruled over a larger number</u>: Cf. 8. 1 n.

<u>best provided in all respects</u>: Cf. 36. 3, in the funeral speech, and the review of Athens' resources in 13. 2-9.

64. 4. <u>Those who prefer to avoid trouble</u>: Cf. 63. 2-3.

64. 5. <u>hatred and unpopularity have always been the lot</u>: Cf. I. 76, in the Athenian speech at Sparta (Athens has naturally incurred hatred, and Sparta or any other state which took her place would do likewise). The view that the Athenians naturally wielded power as far as they could, and naturally were hated for it, permeates Thuydides: in book II notice 8. 4-5, 11. 2 (Archidamus), 63. 1 (earlier in this speech); and cf. Introduction, pp. 13 - 14.

<u>in pursuit of the highest objectives</u>: In Eur. *Phoen*. 499 - 525 Eteocles begins by saying that there is no agreement on right and wrong but they are mere names, and ends, "If one must do wrong, it is noblest to do so for tyranny and to be upright otherwise." That is close to the view of such sophists as Polus in Pl. *Grg*. 461 B - 481 B, that right and wrong are mere human conventions and it is finest to do "wrong" on a grand scale and get away with it, as a tyrant. Pericles would probably not have been prepared to call Athens' empire "wrong" (cf. 63. 2 n.): like other Thucydidean speakers he discusses the empire without questioning the morality of power as such, but he adds that if one is to exercise power and arouse unpopularity, in accordance with nature, one should do so in ways that are admirable by the criteria of ch. 41.

65. 1. <u>Pericles spoke on those lines</u>: Of Pericles' three

speeches in Thucydides the first (I. 140-4), in the winter before the war began, justified Athens' resistance to Sparta's demands and Thucydides' view of the causes of the war; the second, the funeral speech after the first year's fighting (II. 35 - 46), set out an Athenian ideal; this last speech, delivered when the war and the plague have begun to weaken the Athenians' resolve, reasserts the priority of the community over its individual members, and justifies most forcibly the endurance of suffering in the short term in order to preserve Athens' empire. As always, we cannot be sure how closely it corresponds to what was actually said: it is not the humble appeal for mercy which Dionysius of Halicarnassus thought Pericles should have made (923-7). *Thuc.* 44-7), but it is the kind of speech which might have been made to achieve the result which is known to have followed, a revival of the Athenians' determination to persevere in the war.

65. 2. <u>instead of continuing their approaches to Sparta</u>: See 59. 2 n.

<u>The common people . . . The rich</u>: Contrast the allegation of [Xen.] *Ath. Pol.* 2. 14 that "the farmers and the rich in Athens tend rather to yield before the enemy, but the people, knowing well that nothing of theirs will be burned or cut down, live fearlessly and do not yield." It is true that those who had no property, or none except inside the city's fortified area, did not stand to lose directly from the invasions, but even they stood to lose indirectly, and many of "the people" did have some property, however little, outside the fortifications (cf. 14 - 16). Both Thucydides and Aristophanes represent the men of Acharnae, whose land was ravaged in 431, as particularly eager to fight (cf. 20. 4 n.).

<u>handsome possessions</u>: Cf. 38. 1 n.

65. 3. <u>he had been sentenced to a fine</u>: Probably he was deposed from office, either by a special decree of the assembly or through the opportunity provided in each prytany for depositions (*Ath. Pol.* 43. 4, 61. 2), and then was prosecuted, perhaps on a charge of deceiving the people. This episode is mentioned by Diod. Sic. XII. 45. 4, Plut. *Per.* 35. 4-5: deposition occurs in both; a fine of 80 talents in Diodorus, of 15 or 50 in Plutarch (if the fine was paid, 15 is the most credible figure); three different prosecutors (one of them Cleon), from three different sources, are named by Plutarch. Thucydides says nothing of deposition: it may but need not be implied by the statement of 59. 3 that at the time of his last speech "he was still in office".

This episode often is, but ought not to be, confused with

the trial for embezzlement mentioned by Plut. *Per*. 32. 3-4, which presumably resulted in acquittal, and which (although Plutarch links it with the outbreak of the war) is to be dated *c*. 437 (F. J. Frost, *JHS* 84 (1964), 69 - 72).
65. 4. as the masses are apt to do: I.e. to change their mind without any justifying change in circumstances.
elected . . . entrusted: The elections were conducted "by the first prytany after the sixth in whose term of office there are good omens", i.e. in the spring (*Ath. Pol*. 44. 4), and took effect in the new year, *c*. July: many have thought that Thucydides implies a shorter period out of office for Pericles, ended by a special reappointment, but we cannot be certain. There is no need to infer from Thucydides' language that when Pericles was restored to office he was given more power than was normally given to a member of the board of generals (cf. 13. 1 n.).
65. 5. presided over the city in peace: He had been active in politics since the late 460s; Plut. *Per*. 16. 3 artificially divides his career into a period when he was one politician among many, and a period, after the ostracism of Thucydides son of Melesias in or about 443, when he was unrivalled. His leadership was not in fact unchallenged even after Thucydides' ostracism: cf. e.g. the second paragraph of the n. on 65. 3.
its greatest height: In the funeral speech Pericles attributes this collectively to his own genration (36. 3 with n. on 36. 2).
65. 6. He lived on for two years and six months: Apparently, from the outbreak of the war, i.e. to *c*. September 429 (cf. Diod. Sic. XII. 46. 1): Thucydides does not mention his death in its chronological place. According to Plut. *Per*. 38. 1-2 he caught the plague, and was weakened though not immediately killed by it.
65. 7. the Athenians would prevail if: Cf. 13. 2 nn. and, on the significance of the naval expeditions of 431 and 430, 25. 1 n. "Keeping quiet" (*hesychazein*) here is not the same as "avoiding trouble" (*apragmosyne*, e.g. 63), though the verb is used in that sense by Alcibiades in VI. 18. 2 and *hesychia* refers to neutrality in II. 72. 1, but must be equivalent to "avoiding a hoplite battle with the enemy": Gomme's insertion of "with their hoplites" may be correct.
they did the opposite of all these things: They risked, and were defeated in, major hoplite battles at Delium in 424/3 and at Mantinea in 418; they did not fail to look after their fleet; they tried to add to their empire in Sicily in 427 - 424 and 415 - 413 (III. 86. 4, IV. 65. 3; VI. 6. 1, etc.); they put

the city at risk, particularly by committing large forces to Sicily in 415 - 413, and by provoking the hostility of Persia through their support of the rebel Amorges about the same time (VIII. 5. 4-5, cf. 19. 2, 28. 2-4). Thucydides returns to the great Sicilian expedition in §11.

and did still other things which appeared irrelevant: It is not obvious which actions Thucydides would condemn under this head. To redress the balance, it should be stated that things were done after Pericles' death which he seems not to have contemplated and which were or could have been beneficial. The occupation of Pylos in 425 and Cythera in 424 were beneficial, but there was no attempt to hold fortresses in Spartan territory in 431 - 430 (see especially 56. 6 n.); Athens with her allies of 431 could not hope to match a full army of Sparta and her allies, but attempts on Boeotia on its own in 426 and 424/3 might with better planning have succeeded, and the alliance in 420 with Argos and other Peloponnesian states might not have led to defeat in 418.

private individuals: *Idiotai* are normally private citizens, in contrast to men in an official or semi-official position, and the appearance of the word here impressed a scholiast and worried Gomme (who proposed "themselves individually"). I do not think the manuscripts' text impossible.

65. 8. strong in . . . intellect and . . . incorruptible: Cf. the beginning of the last speech, where Pericles makes these claims for himself (60. 5 n.).

speak against them and provoke their anger: Some editors take the meaning to be, "speak up against their anger".

65. 9. in theory democracy but in fact rule by the first man: It is hard for us to get behind Thucydides' admiration for Pericles and make a dispassionate assessment. Constitutionally, Pericles was never more than one of a board of ten generals: he had to stand for re-election every year (if we may believe Plut. *Per*. 16. 3, he was elected for each of the last fifteen years of his life) and to present his accounts every year, and in 430 he was deposed and fined. The membership of the council of five hundred, the body which prepared business for the assembly (a body with which the generals seem to have had a privileged relationship during the Peloponnesian War: see 22. 1 n.), changed every year; the assembly which took all major and many minor decisions was open to all adult male citizens, and individuals would range over the spectrum from regular attenders to regular non-attenders. Even when a strong man had a consistent policy which he wished to pursue, he could not guarantee that the council and assembly would consistently decide in

accordance with that policy, and Connor, *Thucydides*, 60 n. 26, stresses that this comment is made at the point when Pericles has been deposed from office.

Allusions to Pericles' aloofness (cf. 44. 1 n.) are at any rate compatible with Thucydides' picture of a Pericles who did not try to curry favour with the people. Plutarch's claim may be true, that he did not incessantly make speeches, and propose decrees in his own name, but reserved himself for major occasions and otherwise had supporters who would speak and propose as he wanted (*Per.* 7. 7-8, *Praec. Ger. Reip.* 811 C - 813 A). It is not true, even of the later part of Pericles' career, that he was *de facto* the unopposed ruler of Athens (cf. §5 n.), and, for instance, in the two days of debate on Corcyra and Corinth in 433 it is likely (though Thucydides gives us no help: cf. Introduction, p. 11) that he did not change his mind but the opinion of the majority was at first against him but finally with him (I. 44. 1). However, although we cannot be sure that each particular thing which the Athenians did was what Pericles wanted done, we may assume that the general line of policy pursued by Athens from the 450s until his death was his policy.

65. 10. <u>The leaders who followed Pericles</u>: It was to be a commonplace in the fourth century that Athenian politics and politicians had changed for the worse in the late fifth: Pericles is sometimes regarded as the last of the old politicians, sometimes as the first of the new. There has been argument among scholars as to who, if any one, is to be regarded as his direct successor. In the schematic list of democratic and aristocratic leaders in *Ath. Pol.* 28 Pericles is followed by Cleon on the democratic side and Thucydides son of Melesias by Nicias on the other; A. B. West argued that it is Nicias who was Pericles' successor, while Cleon was leader of a "breakaway radical wing" (*CP* 19 (1924), 124-46, 201-28); Gomme emphasised the similarities between Cleon and Pericles and considered Nicias one of the *apragmones* whom Pericles condemned (*JHS* 71 (1951), 74 - 80 = *More Essays*, 101-11). It is better not to award the prize to either. Both accepted the democracy and the empire; both were second-generation rich men and first-generation politicians; Nicias made himself acceptable to those who liked the aristocratic style of leadership, while Cleon was ostentatiously populist; in their attitude to the war Nicias seems to have been more afraid of failure than eager for success, while Cleon favoured a more adventurous strategy than Pericles.

65. 11. <u>That involved</u>: The Sicilian expedition was certainly the greatest departure from Periclean strategy (§7 n.). The reader of books VI - VII is likely to conclude that there was a

fundamental "error of judgment" (Athens could have succeeded in the short term but could not have retained possessions in Sicily for long against opposition: notice the remarks in speeches in VI. 11. 1, 86. 3), and that the possibility of short-term success was lost through errors made on the spot by Nicias, whereas there was no failure in subsequent decisions at home unless the recall of Alcibiades to stand trial on religious charges, and the refusal to recall Nicias when he was ill and asked to be recalled, are regarded in that light. This is the most serious inconsistency in Thucydides' history. It shows that, at an absolute minimum, even if the whole work as we have it was written up after the end of the war, the whole work is not the result of a single spell of thinking; and it gives strong support to those who believe that the whole work is not the result of a single spell of writing. The earlier part of ch. 65, or something approximating to it, may have been written shortly after Pericles' death, but this later part must have been written after the end of the war; VI - VII, with their different view of what went wrong with the Sicilian expedition, were probably written not long after 413, when Thucydides realised that the expedition could be treated in detail as a distinct and significant episode. Cf. Introduction, pp. 14 - 16.

the accusations made against individuals: On charges of sacrilege: many were put to death or went into exile, and had their property confiscated (cf. VI. 27-9, 53 - 61). The scandals broke out in 415, shortly before the expedition was due to sail. Whoever were the perpetrators and whatever were the purposes of the sacrilegious acts, the acts were used as an opportunity to attack Alcibiades and others. Alcibiades, the most enthusiastic advocate of the expedition and one of the generals appointed to command it, was allowed to sail but was recalled later in the summer to stand trial; he fled to Sparta; in 412/1 he fell out with the Spartans and made his way back to the Athenian side; and his career continued in chequered fashion (cf. last n. on §12).

65. 12. falling into a state of dissension in the city: In 411 the democracy was replaced by what turned out to be an extreme oligarchy; later in the same year that gave way to an intermediate régime; in 410 the full democracy was restored. Distrust persisted between democrats and different kinds of oligarchs, and Athens was to undergo another bout of oligarchy in 404 - 403, after the end of the war.

eight years: The manuscripts' "three" cannot be right unless it is referred to the period 411/0 (constitutional upheavals) - 408/7 (before the arrival of Cyrus), which is not the most

natural interpretation: the revolt of the allies, mentioned before Cyrus, began in 412. A period of time is appropriate here, and probably Thucydides thought that the Athenians held out for the eight years 412/1 - 405/4, and succumbed in the ninth, 404/3 (reckoning according to Thucydidean years).
those from Sicily who joined them: Not many (cf. 7. 2 n.).
their allies, who revolted against them: Cf. above. On the whole, Athens recovered control of the Aegean islands and the cities from the Bosporus to the Hellespont, but was less successful on the mainland coast of Asia Minor.
Cyrus: Sent in 407 to support the Peloponnesians and exercise supreme command in western Asia Minor. The war against Athens was waged most effectively when he was supporting Lysander of Sparta; but the Persian satraps Tissaphernes and Pharnabazus had been supporting Sparta, if not always whole-heartedly, since 412 (cf. 65. 7 n., on Athens' support for Amorges).
stumbled over themselves: In 405 the last fleet which Athens could afford to send out was defeated in the Hellespont, at Aegospotami; during the winter Athens was blockaded by Sparta, and Cleophon, who wanted to continue fighting, was condemned to death; in 404 Athens sued for peace: her defeat can be sufficiently explained in those terms. Thucydides, however, as above on the Sicilian expedition, blames disunity within Athens: he is perhaps thinking particularly of the Athenians' failure to be reconciled again with Alcibiades immediately before Aegospotami (his information on and evaluation of Alcibiades suggest that he derived some of his material from Alcibiades himself or from some one close to him).
65. 13. would very easily prevail . . . on their own: I.e. without having to face in addition their own allies, the Sicilian Greeks and the Persians. On Pericles' strategy cf. 13. 2 nn., 25. 1 n., 65. 7 nn.: if that had been strictly followed the Athenians would have avoided defeat, but they would not have won a decisive victory, and the problem of Athens' power and Sparta's fear of it would not have been solved.

With this premature obituary notice Pericles disappears from Thucydides' history, apart from one cross-reference in VI. 31. 2; and in the remainder of book II Thucydides reports Athenian decisions baldly, without focusing on individual political leaders.

66 - 69. The Summer's Campaigns (ii)

66. 1. a hundred ships: The largest Peloponnesian naval force

attested in the Archidamian War (cf. 7. 2 n.).

Zacynthus: As with Cephallenia, to the north, Thucydides indicates the island's location (cf. 30. 2 n.). According to Paus. VIII. 24. 3 the *oikistes* (the man presiding over the foundation) of the settlement was an Arcadian; he says nothing about Achaean involvement. Zacynthus is listed among Athens' allies in 9. 4.

66. 2. Cnemus: Still in office in summer 429 (80-2, 84 - 94), but not otherwise attested. Sparta had a single navarch in command of the fleet, who once he had retired from the office could not be reappointed to it (Xen. *Hell.* II. 1. 7). The view that it was an annual office beginning in the autumn, accepted by Gomme, does not work for the whole of the late fifth and early fourth centuries: possibly it began in the autumn until 409, in the spring from 407 (J.-F. Bommelaer, *Lysandre de Sparte*, 66 - 79; see also R. Sealey, *Klio* 58 (1976), 335-58, in German).

67. 1. Aristeus: The Corinthian most active in support of Potidaea in 432 (I. 60-5). His father Adimantus commanded the Corinthian contingent in the Greek fleet fighting against the Persians in 480 (Hdt. VIII. 5, 59 - 64, 94).

Aneristus, Nicolaus and Pratodamus: Hdt. VII. (133 -) 137 tells this story in connection with Aneristus son of Sperthias and Nicolaus son of Bulis (and also mentions the Corinthian, whom he calls Aristeas), because Sperthias and Bulis offered themselves to the Persians for execution in atonement for Persian heralds put to death in Sparta, but they were spared whereas on this occasion their sons' lives were taken. Nothing is known of Pratodamus.

Timagoras . . . Pollis: Nothing is known of either. Pollis, presumably a member of a pro-Spartan faction in Argos, goes as a private individual because his city is technically neutral and traditionally unfriendly to Sparta (cf. 9. 2 n.).

Sitalces: Cf. 29.

Potidaea: Last mentioned in 58; its capitulation will be recorded in 70.

Pharnaces son of Pharnabazus: Satrap of north-western Asia Minor, with his capital at Dascylium, near the Propontis. The family seems to have had a hereditary interest in this appointment (cf. I. 129. 1, VIII. 6. 1).

67. 2. Learchus . . . Aminiades: Nothing is known of either.

Sadocus: Cf. 29. 5 n. Herodotus does not mention him, but attributes the betrayal to Sitalces and his brother-in-law Nymphodorus.

67. 3. while they were travelling through Thrace: According to Herodotus this happened at Bisanthe, on the Propontis (but he says Hellespont).

67. 4. without holding a trial: Only Athenian citizens, and metics present in Athens or citizens of states with which Athens had made a judicial agreement, were in law entitled to a trial in Athens. Heralds, sent not to negotiate but to make a solemn proclamation, were normally considered inviolate (cf. 1 n.: this is why Sparta felt guilt over the killing of the Persian heralds), but envoys were not similarly protected, and these men had no legal grounds for complaint.

68. 1. the Ambraciots: As before, Thucydides does not seem to think geographical notes necessary for the mainland of northwest Greece (cf. 30. 1 n.). The places mentioned in this chapter lie around the large Gulf of Ambracia: Ambracia itself, a colony of Corinth (9. 2 n.), to the north; Argos, whose legendary origin is given in this chapter, to the east, Amphilochia being the whole region to the east of the Gulf; Acarnania, Greek, and in alliance with Athens (9. 4 n.), the whole region to the south of the Gulf (its legendary origin will be given in 102). Argos was probably on the right bank of the H. Ioannes branch of the River Betoko (N. G. L. Hammond, *BSA* xxxvii 1936/7, 128 with 129 fig. 1 = *Studies*, 471 with 473 fig. 21); but Gomme placed it at the south-east corner of the Gulf, where Hammond locates Limnaea (80. 8 n.).

68. 3. Amphilochus: As usual, Thucydides accepts the outline of the legendary account: cf. 15. 1 n. and other passages cited there. Amphilochus was a brother of Alcmeon (cf. 102. 5 n.).

68. 5. learned to speak Greek . . . barbarians: Thucydides does not offer an explanation of the fact that the people of a region "founded" by a Greek were barbarian, i.e. not Greek-speaking. The natural conclusion for us is that Argos and the rest of Amphilochia were indeed barbarian, and were attached to the story of Amphilochus because of a similarity of name. As often, N. G. L. Hammond is more credulous than most scholars: he accepts the foundation legend (*Epirus*, 391) and believes that the Argives later changed from "a provincial dialect" of Greek to Doric (419). It is likely enough that Argos was hellenised under the influence of Ambracia.

68. 6. In time: Presumably, a few years before the outbreak of the Peloponnesian War; but Hammond, *Epirus*, 496-7, argues that it was before Pericles' campaign of the 450s (evidence 102. 2 n.), possibly in 456/5. It is particularly frustrating that, although he gives us so much background, Thucydided does not

say when this episode took place: on his omissions cf. Introduction, p. 11. The episode resulted in close ties between the
Acarnanians and Phormio (cf. below).

In 433 Athens supported Corcyra against Corinth and sent
ships to Sybota, north of the Gulf of Ambracia; and on their
return journey the Corinthians got possession of Anactorium, in
Acarnanian territory on the south side of the Gulf (I. 24 - 55,
cf. II. 9. 2 n.).

68. 7. Phormio: Cf. 29. 6 n. For the remainder of his career,
in which he commanded a squadron of ships based on Naupactus
and again supported Acarnania, see 69. 1, 80 - 92, 102-3 and
103. 1 n.

68. 9. the Chaonians: Living on the west side of Mount Pindus,
north of the Gulf.

they returned home: Strictly this episode, as a local war in
north-western Greece with no involvement of the other Greeks,
does not form a part of the Peloponnesian War, but it is mentioned because the participants in the Peloponnesian War are to
be involved in subsequent episodes in the region. For the next
stage see 80-2.

69 - 70. Second Winter (430/29)

69. 1. Naupactus: Cf. 9. 4 n. It is surprising that this measure was not taken earlier (cf. 25. 1 n.).

the Gulf of Crisa: The Gulf of Corinth, east of the strait between Rhium and Antirrhium (86. 2-3 n.).

Caria and Lycia: Caria is at the south-western corner of Asia
Minor, and Lycia is the region on the south coast immediately
to the east of Caria; both contained cities which were included
in the Delian League (cf. 9. 4 n.).

to raise money there: The same language is used in III. 19 and
IV. 50. 1, where it probably refers to special imposts rather
than the collection of the regular tribute. In this remote corner of the League many states seem not to have paid tribute except when special pressure was put on them, and it is probably
pressure of that kind that is referred to here.

merchant shipping: Athenian imports of dates and wheat-flour
from Phoenicia are taken for granted by the comedian Hermippus,
fr. 63. 22 (ed. Kock or Edmonds).

69. 2. Melesandrus . . . was killed: Nothing else is known of
him, but Pausanias saw his memorial in the Ceramicus (I. 29. 7:
not necessarily an exception to the rule of ch. 34), and the
name Melesandrus appears on a stele from Xanthus, *TAM* i 44, *a*

45 (but W. E. Thompson, *Hesp*. 36 (1967), 105-6, thinks this was another Melesandrus, active there in 414/3).

70. 1. Potidaea: Continued from 58, cf. 67. 1.
Xenophon . . . Hestiodorus . . . Phanomachus: Xenophon had been hipparch in the 440s (*IG* i^2 400 = i^3 511) and general in 441/0 (Androt. *FGrH* 324 F 38); nothing else is known about the other two. For the death of Xenophon, and very probably the others, see 79.
70. 2. two thousand talents: Expenditure on Potidaea is mentioned, but not quantified, in 13. 3. Diod. Sic. XII. 46. 4 gives the cost of the siege as more than one thousand talents.
70. 3. one outer garment . . . a fixed sum of money: The rest of their possessions were to be left behind as booty for the Athenians.
70. 4. found fault: But, apparently, did not go to the extent of recalling, deposing and punishing them (cf. 79. 1 n.).
on whatever terms they liked: I.e. the city was so desperate that they could have insisted on its unconditional surrender.
some of their own people: Diod. Sic. XII. 46. 7 says a thousand. The Chalcidians based on Olynthus remained hostile to Athens: for the next campaign in this region see 79.

71 - 92. Third Summer (429)

71 - 78. *The Siege of Plataea*

71. 1. did not invade Attica . . . Plataea: Thucydides does not say why. Two likely reasons are that they were afraid of catching the plague, and that they were under pressure from Boeotia to take action against Plataea (against which no move had been made since the Theban attack of spring 431: 2 - 6). On Thucydides' detailed treatment of Plataea see 6. 4 n.; a further reason for the amount of detail given here may be that by the standards of the time this was a technologically advanced siege, with great ingenuity shown on both sides (76. 4, 77. 1 nn.), and that Thucydides had access to eye-witnesses who escaped before the fall of the city (III. 20-4), and as with the plague (47 - 54) welcomed the opportunity to set out a detailed account. Cf. G. B. Grundy, *JHS* 18 (1898), 218-31, esp. 223-8, who notes that Thucydides has tried to create an impression of scale where the facts do not justify it. Resemblance to tragedy can be seen in the exchange of speeches and the seeming inevitability of the fall of Plataea.

We learn from 79. 1 that the Peloponnesians went to Plataea "when the corn was growing ripe", in May (cf. 78. 2 n.). In the short account of this episode in [Dem.] LIX. *Against Neaera*, 101-2, the attacking army is said to comprise a two-thirds levy from the Peloponnese and a full levy of the Boeotians and their allies in central Greece; nothing is said of the attempt to take the city by force after the failure of the diplomatic approach and before the setting-up of the blockade.
They were commanded: Archidamus is given the same formal introduction as at the beginning of the previous years' campaigns (10. 3, 19. 1; 47. 2).
the . . . battle fought in our territory: The battle of Plataea, in 479.
he made sacrifice: In addition to what is stated here, we learn from III. 58. 4 that the Plataeans agreed to look after the graves of the Greeks who fell in the battle. Diod. Sic. XI. 29. 1 mentions before the battle, and Plut. *Arist*. 21. 1-2 mentions after it, an undertaking to hold an annual festival and quadrennial games at Plataea, in celebration of the freedom of the Greeks, and to continue the war against Persia; but the continuation of the war arose rather from the naval campaign of 479, and the celebrations have been projected back to the fifth century from the Hellenistic period (see Rhodes, *The Athenian Empire*, 9 - 10).
71. 3. courage and spirit: The same qualities are attributed to the Plataeans in Hdt. VIII. 1. 1.
the opposite: Cf. 65. 7, where Thucydides complains that the Athenians pursued the opposite to Pericles' policies after his death.

72. 1. who on that occasion . . . and who are now: Not many of the member states of the Delian League had fought on the Greek side in 479, but they included Aegina (Hdt. IX. 28. 6), dispossessed by Athens in 431 (27).
to liberate them: Cf. 8. 4 n.
we have already called on you: Not mentioned previously by Thucydides.
72. 2. their children and women were there: Cf. 6. 4; also 78. 3.

73. 3. since we became allies: Cf. 2. 1 n.
will help you with all their might: It was in fact incompatible with Pericles' strategy for Athens' land forces (13. 2 n.) that they should do so, and apart from the small garrison sent in 431 (6. 4 n.) no Athenian help was sent. It seems clear to the modern reader that it would have been advantageous to Plataea

251

to accept Archidamus' offer, and that a Plataea under siege was of no strategic advantage to Athens and was bound to be starved into surrender unless the war quickly came to an end.

74. 2. the local gods and heroes: There is a list in Plut. *Arist.* 11. 3. In 424 the Spartan Brasidas in the Thraceward region tries to win over the members of the Delian League and then calls on the local gods and heroes to witness that he has made a fair offer before taking hostile action (IV. 87. 2).

75. 1. come out to attack them: Gomme prefers "escape", but there can have been little likelihood of that while the enemy were present in force.
a mound: In fact a ramp, to enable men and battering-rams (76. 4) to reach the top of the city wall. It was presumably on the south, uphill, side of the city.
75. 3. †seventy† days: Although the Peloponnesians may have spent four months altogether at Plataea (78. 2 n.), this is far too long a period; but it is impossible to recover the correct figure.
75. 6. fell against it: While the mound was being built, it would slope downwards to the wall from its highest point: cf. 77. 3. It was therefore feasible for the Plataeans to open a hole in the bottom of their own wall to reach this part of the mound.

76. 2. For a long time . . . failed to detect: We are not told what action they took when they did detect it, but they were eventually able to take a battering-ram up the ramp: cf. §4.
76. 4. machines: Battering-rams, called "rams" (κριοί) by Xenophon (*Cyr.* VII. 4. 1) and subsequently. This was the most advanced kind of siege machinery known in the fifth century, and was perhaps a novelty in the siege of Plataea: the major technological advances were to be made in the fourth. See especially Marsden, *Greek and Roman Artillery*, [i.] *Historical Development*.

77. 1. circumvallation: Blockading by means of a circumvallation is what is normally denoted by "besiege" (πολιορκεῖν) in the fifth century and earlier. Until more effective siege machinery had been developed it was rare for a walled city to be taken by force, though Cleon was to succeed against Torone in 422 (V. 2 - 3); but if a city could be cut off from all contact with the outside world it could in time be starved into surrender. It was to guard against this that Athens and other cities a short distance inland had built long walls linking themselves to their harbour towns (for Athens cf. 13. 2, 7 nn.).

77. 3. against the rest of the city: I.e. against the city wall, on each side of the mound.

77. 4. the largest . . . that any one had ever seen: On superlatives in Thucydides see Introduction, pp. 3 - 4.

77. 6. it is said: Cf. 18. 5 n.: Thucydides will not vouch for the truth of this lucky chance, and H. D. Westlake, *Mnem.*⁴ 30 (1977), 345-62, at 354, suggests that he is uneasy about something which might be taken as a sign of divine intervention.

78. 1. by cities: By city contingents within the attacking army.

78. 2. complete: A detailed account of the wall is given, in connection with the escape of some of the Plataeans, in III. 21.

the rising of Arcturus: Its heliacal rising, i.e. the time when the star can first be seen rising before the sun, after the period of forty days in which it rises invisibly, after sunrise: *c.* 20 September. On Thucydides' use of common-sense and of astronomically precise terms as indications of date see 1 n., 2. 1 n. If the Peloponnesians had set out in May (cf. 79. 1 with 19. 1 n.), they will have spent about four months at Plataea.

78. 3. women to act as bakers: Possibly slaves.

78. 4. That was the total number: Cf. I. 65. 1, where in 432 Aristeus advises leaving five hundred men to defend Potidaea against Athens.

79. *An Athenian Campaign in the North-East*

79. 1. the Thraceward Chalcidians and the Bottiaeans: Potidaea had surrendered to Athens in winter 430/29 (70), but the Chalcidians based on Olynthus remained hostile and undefeated. On the Bottiaeans see 99. 3, 100. 4 nn.

Xenophon . . . and two others: Probably Hestiodorus and Phanomachus, as in 70. 1: this campaign, in May (78. 2 n.), will fall within the same Athenian year, 430/29. The Athenians "found fault" with these generals after they had accepted the surrender of Plataea (70. 4), but evidently did not depose and punish them.

79. 2. Spartolus: To the north-west of Potidaea, and apparently inland. See B. D. Meritt, *AJA*² 27 (1923), 334-9; Meritt *et al.*, *The Athenian Tribute Lists*, i. 550.

79. 5. the Athenians withdrew: If the manuscripts' text is correct, there is a very awkward change of subject, so possibly we should read with Gomme " . . . a fresh attack on the Athenians, who were exhausted by the battle and were withdrawing . . . ".

<u>79. 7. they had lost . . . all their generals</u>: This battle foreshadows the fourth century in the successful use of light-armed infantry and cavalry on the level ground where hoplites were normally considered the most effective kind of soldier. For a further campaign in this region, in which the Athenians fail to take part, see 95 - 101.

Thucydides seems to use each of the campaigns of this year to make a particular point. The Athenians' hoplite army is so weak that at Spartolus it is defeated by cavalry and light infantry; at Stratus the Peloponnesian hoplites are let down by the indiscipline of their barbarian allies (80-2); but at sea the battles in the Gulf of Corinth demonstrate the overwhelming superiority of Athens (83 - 92). In the following winter the audacious Brasidas prompts the Peloponnesians to attempt a raid on the Piraeus, but their nerve fails them (93-4); the huge Thracian army of Sitalces overruns Macedon but achieves nothing (95 - 101).

80 - 82. *A Spartan Campaign in the North-West*

<u>80. 1. the Ambraciots and Chaonians . . . persuaded the Spartans</u>: Continued from 68. Here we have an adventurous Spartan decision which is not attributed to Brasidas (though he will appear before long: 85. 1).

<u>80. 2. Cnemus</u>: See 66. 2 n.

<u>80. 3. the state from which Ambracia had been settled</u>: See 9. 2 n.

<u>80. 4. Phormio . . . at Naupactus</u>: See 69. 1.

<u>80. 5. Thesprotians</u>: Living in the coastal region north of the Gulf of Ambracia and opposite Corcyra (cf. I. 30. 3). Although Thucydides calls them barbarian, they were in fact Greek-speaking. See Hammond, *Epirus*, 423, 525-31; and, on all the tribes which joined Sparta, 500-2.

<u>80. 6. Molossians</u>: Living in the Pindus range, north-east of the Thesprotians; they too were Greek-speaking. Although they were on the Spartan side on this occasion, Tharyps was educated at Athens, was made an Athenian citizen, and civilised his people as Archelaus (100. 2) civilised the Macedonians (Tod 173, Plut. *Pyrrh*. 1. 4-5, Just. *Epit*. XVII. 3. 9-13).

<u>Atintanians . . . Paravaeans . . . Orestians</u>: Other tribes

of the Pindus region. For the Orestians cf. 99. 3 n.

<u>80. 7. Perdiccas</u>: Last mentioned in 431, when he changed to the Athenian side (29): presumably at this point he was still nominally an ally of Athens. R. L. Beaumont, *JHS* 72 (1952), 64, suggested that his purpose here was to show the Peloponnesians that they could reach the north-east without travelling through pro-Athenian Thessaly.

<u>80. 8. Limnaea</u>: Located by Hammond at the south-easternmost point of the Gulf of Ambracia, south of Argos. He believes that Cnemus will have assembled his army near the coast of the Gulf, north-west of Argos, and have marched southwards from there. See *BSA* 37 (1936/7), 132 with 129 fig. 1 = *Studies*, 476 with 473 fig. 21; *Epirus*, 246 with 675 map 16.

<u>Stratus</u>: On the right bank of the Achelous, about half-way between the Gulf of Ambracia and the Gulf of Corinth: Hornblower, *Thucydides*, 201, describes it as "the key to Akarnania". Cf. 102. 2.

<u>81. 1. did not rally to support Stratus</u>: Although Cnemus had not waited for the arrival of the fleet which was to engage the attention of the coastal Acarnanians and prevent them from supporting Stratus. The casual remark of Diod. Sic. XII. 47. 5 that the Acarnanians did unite is probably a careless error.

<u>Phormio</u>: Cf. 69. 1.

<u>81. 3. the men with them</u>: It is not clear who these were: Gomme suggests Acarnanians hostile to Athens.

<u>82. to the River Anapus</u>: Not identified, but apparently south of Stratus.

<u>Oeniadae</u>: At the mouth of the Achelous: cf. 102. 2. From Oeniadae he went to Leucas: 84. 5.

    80 - 82 is one of the passages used by Hornblower, *Thucydides*, 194 - 204, in his concluding chapter, "Thucydides' Virtues Illustrated": he presents it as a passage in which Thucydides' emotions are not intensely engaged, and as one carefully organised to provide a descent from the very general to the very particular.

83 - 92. *Naval Battles in the Gulf of Corinth*

<u>83. 2. in an open space</u>: Cf. Phormio's speech, 89. 8. The gap between Rhium and Antirrhium (86. 2-3) is at the western end of a long narrow stretch, in the western half of which Naupactus is situated, so Phormio would wait to catch the Peloponnesians in the wide Gulf of Patras to the west of that gap.

These battles are discussed by Morrison & Coates, *The Athenian Trireme*, 68 - 76 (that book and Morrison & Williams, *Greek Oared Ships, 900 - 322 B.C.*, will be cited by authors' names). Chs. 83 - 92 are studied also by Hunter, *Thucydides, the Artful Reporter*, 43 - 60: as in chs. 10 - 22 (cf. p. 190, above), she argues that Thucydides has inferred intentions from results, and, in particular, that he "makes Phormion predict the unpredictable" (p. 54).

83. 3. more as transports: The ships would be more heavily laden, and so slower and less manoeuvrable, than when used for fighting.

from Patrae: A short distance south-west of Rhium. They would have to make the crossing from the Peloponnesian to the northern coast of the Gulf there if they did not want to cross a very wide expanse of open water.

Chalcis and the River Evenus: North-west of Patrae.

83. 4. the Corinthian generals: Nothing else is known about them.

83. 5. in as large a circle as they could: To prevent the Athenians from using the tactic known as *diekplous*, sailing through their line and turning on it (cf. 89. 8, and see Morrison & Williams, 136-9, 313-6, Morrison & Coates, 42-3). The same defensive tactic was used by the less skilled Greeks, and met with the same response from the more skilled Persians, at Artemisium in 480: Hdt. VIII. 10. 1, 11. 1, 16. 1.

and also their five best-sailing ships: These will in fact have been wasted, imprisoned inside a contracting circle.

84. 2. would not stay in formation: Being less confident and less skilled than the Athenians, they would be forced by Phormio's encircling movement to contract their own formation and fall foul of one another.

84. 3. their poles: A trireme would carry two or three poles: Morrison & Williams, 293.

their officers: A *keleustes*, as his title implies, is an officer who shouts commands to the oarsmen: Morrison & Williams, 196, 200-1, 266-7, Morrison & Coates, 111-2, 130.

the helmsmen: Morrison & Williams, 195, 200-1, 266-7, Morrison & Coates, 111-2, 130-2, 174-6.

holed: The verb καταδύειν is normally translated "sink", but the triremes of which it is used, though too waterlogged to be of further use, did not sink to the sea bed (Morrison & Coates, 128-9).

Dyme: The westernmost city in Achaea, before the mouth of the Gulf of Patrae is reached.

84. 4. **Molycrium ... Rhium**: Molycrium was at or near (Antir)rhium, the northern headland at the channel's narrowest point.
dedicated a ship: One of the ships they had captured: cf. 94. 5; and Hdt. VIII. 121. 1, after the battle of Salamis in 480.
85. 1. **sent Timocrates, Brasidas and Lycophron ... as advisers**: On Brasidas see 25. 2 n.; Timocrates was to commit suicide after the Peloponnesian defeat (92. 3), but nothing else is known about him or Lycophron. The Spartans were particularly given to appointing advisers for commanders — even kings — who had not come up to scratch: cf. III. 69. 1 (Brasidas again), V. 63. 4, VIII. 39. 2. In general the commander seems to have retained the final authority (III. 79. 3), but in 86. 6 below Thucydides names Brasidas with "Cnemus ... and the other Peloponnesian commanders".
85. 2. **greatly surprised**: On *paralogos* as a theme running through Thucydides' history see J. H. Finley, *HSCP* Supp. 1 (1940), 273-81 = *Three Essays on Thucydides*, 140-9: until they overreached themselves in the Sicilian expedition of 415 - 413 the Athenians surprised conventional judges by the strength which they displayed.
the first time: The first during the war, but there is no need to suppose that Thucydides must have spelled that out and that a phrase has been lost. The last naval battle against Athens in which we know the Peloponnesians had been involved was the battle of Cecryphalea, *c*. 459, another Peloponnesian defeat (I. 105. 1).
long experience ... short period of training: In I. 121. 4 the Corinthians claimed that with practice the Peloponnesians would soon reach the level of the Athenians; in I. 142. 6-9 Pericles denied that.
85. 5. **added to the commander's instructions**: It is surprising, but must be accepted despite W. R. Connor's emendation of the text to obtain a reference to the well-known Athenian Nicias, that the commander is not named.
Crete: Occasionally, but only occasionally, drawn into the main stream of Greek history in the classical period. Gortyn was an inland state in the centre of the island, Cydonia on the north coast at the west end of the island (colonised by Athens' enemy Aegina: Hdt. III. 59), and Polichna inland from Cydonia. Thucydides' account is frustratingly brief: we want to know why the Athenians chose to involve themselves in Crete while fighting the Peloponnesian War; and why, having so chosen, they decided to use the ships urgently needed by Phormio rather than to send

a separate force. Thucydides mentions no other Athenian ships in use this year, though presumably some travelled between Athens and Potidaea (cf. 70, 79), and large forces should have been in preparation, but were not in fact sent, for a winter campaign in the north-east (95. 3, 101. 1); it is not until the following year that he refers to the Athenians' being in financial difficulties (III. 19). The ships' arrival at Naupactus will be mentioned at 92. 7.

Thucydides does not overtly criticise this Athenian decision, but his narrative makes it appear grossly irresponsible. Peloponnesian forces will take part in a war in north Africa on their way to Sicily in 413, but they go there because they are driven off course by the wind (VII. 50. 1-2).
proxenos: Cf. 29. 1 n.

86. 1. Panormus: East of Rhium, but not as far into the narrow channel on the south side as Naupactus on the north.
86. 2. Molycrian Rhium . . . the other Rhium: The first was on the north coast (cf. 84. 4 n.), the second was on the Peloponnesian coast. The actual distance between them (which is not likely to have changed significantly since the time of Thucydides) is about $11\frac{1}{3}$ stades (for the stade cf. 5. 2 n.), but no one in antiquity will have made an accurate measurement of this distance across water.
86. 5. open water . . . a confined space: Phormio had placed himself between the enemy and the open Gulf of Patras.
86. 6. Cnemus, Brasidas and the other Peloponnesian commanders: See 85. 1 n. Probably Brasidas is mentioned because Thucydides knew or thought that the plan for attacking the Athenians was his.
spoke as follows: On Thucydides' speeches in general see Introduction, pp. 8 - 9. The antithetic rhetoric of the Peloponnesian speech is not what we should think either appropriate to the occasion or characteristic of Sparta; and, although it was appropriate for Phormio to stress the skill of the Athenians before he led them into battle against a fleet four times the size of his, the Athenians ought not to have needed the lesson in tactics which he gives in 89. 8. Speeches before a battle are not the kind of speech of which any one is likely to remember more than the general thrust and the occasional vivid phrase: these speeches will have been composed by Thucydides, without much concern for "what was actually said", to highlight this remarkable contest between numbers and skill.

87. 2. fight a battle . . . make a journey: Cf. 83. 3 n.
we had considerable bad luck: Cf. Pericles in 61. 2-3 on fac-

tors which cannot be foreseen. Thucydides uses *tyche* sometimes of fortune in that sense, sometimes in the sense of all that happens to a person or state: cf. Introduction, p. 12. The claim made here may be rhetorically appropriate in the circumstances, but nothing in Thucydides' account of the first battle does in fact suggest that they had bad luck: they would be more justified in complaining of their luck when the Athenians turned defeat into victory in the second batle (though there too Thucydides represents them as incompetent: 91. 4).

87. 3. our spirit was not forcibly defeated: Cf. V. 75. 3 (the Spartans' victory at Mantinea in 418 showed that their previous setbacks had been due to chance, not to lack of spirit); also VI. 11. 6, 72. 3.

87. 4. superiority in boldness . . . the enemy's skill: Contrast Pericles' claim, in 40. 3, 62. 4 and elsewhere, that the Athenians have a more secure boldness because it is grounded in understanding of what they are doing. Phormio will say in 88. 3 that Athenians and Peloponnesians are each bolder in the element where they are more experienced.

87. 6. in front of friendly territory with hoplites present: For the importance of this factor cf. VII. 36. 5, 53. 1, 62. 4. Achaea must have joined the Peloponnesian side since the beginning of the war: cf. 9. 2 n.

88. 2. there was no force of ships so large: For twenty ships (83. 1) to risk a battle with seventy-seven (86. 4) was indeed daring, and it was not absolutely necessary for Phormio to take this risk: the Peloponnesian fleet was no longer aiming to support an army in Acarnania, and it would have been sufficient for him to defend Naupactus. Cf. the remark attributed to him in 89. 5.

spoke as follows: For the degree of authenticity in this speech see on 86. 6.

89. 4. they would not otherwise have attempted another battle: This is hardly cogent: they might very well have thought that with better preparations and nearly four times as many ships as the Athenians had they could hardly fail.

89. 8. a confined space will not be to our advantage: Because of the Athenians' skill rather than because of their small numbers: ability to manoeuvre is wasted without space in which to manoeuvre.

to ram: To attack the enemy's side or quarter with the bronze *embolon* or set of *embola* at the prow of the ship: Morrison & Williams, 280, Morrison & Coates, 35-6, 168-9.

sail through the line and turn on the enemy: Cf. 83. 5 n. *Ana-*

strophe is the sequel to *diekplous*.
<u>an infantry battle</u>: One in which the fighting was done by armed men on the decks of the ships, the older style which had preceded the development of skilled manoeuvres (cf. I. 49. 2). In 413 the Corinthians (VII. 34. 5) and the Syracusans (VII. 36. 2-5) successfully use the older style against the Athenians, strengthening their ships for ramming rather than manoeuvre and forcing the Athenians to fight "an infantry battle from their ships" (VII. 62. 2, 4). Cf. Kitto, *Poiesis*, 305-6.

89. 9. <u>by your ships</u>: Not on board, in position with their oars and tiring themselves unnecessarily, but ready to embark and sail as soon as the order is given.

<u>discipline</u>: More commonly thought of as a Spartan virtue (cf. 11. 9 n.); but the Athenians' naval skill depended on discipline, and in this battle it will be the Peloponnesians whose discipline fails when they think the victory has been won (91. 2-4).

89. 10. <u>either you will extinguish . . . or you will bring closer</u>: If the Peloponnesians cannot win this battle, they cannot hope to win any naval battle; but, if they do win this battle, they may go on to win battles in which the odds are not so heavily in their favour.

90. 1. <u>deployed their ships in four columns</u>: The Peloponnesian ships had been anchored in line, four deep; they turned right to sail in column, four abreast, north-eastwards towards the interior of the Gulf.

90. 2. <u>The twenty best-sailing ships</u>: These now headed the columns. Phormio's ships were against the north coast, but their starting position was further west than the Peloponnesians', and they could not move until they saw what the Peloponnesians were doing, so it was reasonable to hope that they would not be able to reach Naupactus before the Peloponnesians attacked.

90. 3. <u>reluctant as he was</u>: Reluctant to be drawn into the narrow channel to the east of his starting position.

<u>the Messenians' infantry</u>: A detachment of soldiers from the Messenians living in Naupactus (9. 4 n.), who must have marched out to support his fleet as the Peloponnesians had sent an army to support theirs (86. 1, 4).

90. 4. <u>in line</u>: They turned left, but probably not through as much as ninety degrees, and sailed across the channel against the Athenian column.

<u>as quickly as each of them could</u>: Gomme estimates that it will have taken them at most half an hour to cross the channel and attack the Athenians.

90. 5. the open sea: Not the open water to the west of the gap between Rhium and Antirrhium, the sense in which Thucydides has used such expressions above, but the relatively open water in the middle of the channel as opposed to the water close to the shore.

91. 3. the Athenian ship: Probably Phormio will have been sailing on the leading ship, so this ship will not have been his: we are not told who was responsible for the order which turned defeat into victory.

91. 4. this unexpected and amazing occurrence: Cf. 85. 2 n. This snatching of victory out of defeat exemplifies the Athenian characteristics alluded to by the Corinthians in I. 70. 2-5.
they had fallen into disorder: Cf. 89. 9 n.

92. 2. recovering those of their own: Possibly the ships towing Athenian ships were the slowest and most easily caught; more probably they abandoned the Athenian ships in order to get away.

92. 3. The Spartan Timocrates: One of the three Spartan advisers (85. 1).

92. 5. The Peloponnesians also set up a trophy: Although the episode had ended in a humiliating defeat, they had a success to celebrate, and the Athenians were not likely to sail across to the Peloponnesian shore to interfere with their setting up a trophy.

Later the Peloponnesians were to gain in skill and confidence. In 413 at Naupactus the Athenians consider eighteen of their own ships too few to fight against twenty-five Corinthian, and when the Athenians' numbers are increased to thirty-three there is an evenly balanced battle (VII. 31. 4-5, 34).

92. 7. The Athenians from Crete: Cf. 85. 5-6. The effect of this brief note, placed after the account of the battle, is to remind us how badly Phormio needed these ships: cf. Kitto, *Poiesis*, 203-6.

So the summer ended: The story of the Peloponnesian fleet is continued in 93-4, that of Phormio and the Athenians in 102-3.

93 - 103. Third Winter (429/8)

93 - 94. *The Peloponnesian Fleet*

93. 1. Athens' harbour: Thucydides is not writing for Athenian readers only: cf. Introduction, p. 10.
guarded or closed: To prevent an enemy fleet from sailing in.

Mytilene in 428 built moles to narrow its harbour entrance (III. 2. 2); one of the things Athens was to do in 378 on adopting an anti-Spartan policy again was "build gates for the Piraeus" (Xen. *Hell*. V. 4. 34).

93. 2. <u>his oar, cushion and strap</u>: This is one of the texts which proves that a trireme had as many oars as oarsmen; the strap was a leather loop to hold the oar to the tholepin on the hull of the ship. See Morrison & Williams, 268-9, Morrison & Coates, 111, 136.

<u>Nisaea</u>: Presumably there were no triremes currently available at Cenchreae, Corinth's harbour on the Saronic Gulf.

93. 3. <u>There were no ships on guard there</u>: Thucydides returns to the point made at the end of §1 (where this material would more appropriately have been placed). There should have been many ships in the harbour, including if it is to be accepted as authentic the special detachment of a hundred ships kept in reserve for such an emergency as this (24. 2 n.), but evidently there were none manned and ready for immediate use. After Phormio's victories during the summer it must have seemed even less likely than before that the Peloponnesians would dare to attack the Piraeus by sea. We learn from §4 that there were some soldiers and three ships at Cape Budorum, on Salamis; but their purpose was to blockade Megara, not to defend the Piraeus.

<u>did not expect them to risk it even openly</u>: A sudden, unpremeditated attack, though more likely to catch its victims unprepared and so perhaps more likely to succeed, is regarded as an act of greater daring, less likely to be undertaken by the Peloponnesians.

93. 4. <u>it is alleged</u>: Thucydides contemptuously rejects this excuse: cf. 94. 1, and H. D. Westlake, *Mnem.*⁴ 30 (1977), 345-62, at 352.

<u>the headland of Salamis facing Megara</u>: Named as Budorum in 94. 3; probably the more northerly of the two prongs embracing the long promontory south-east of Megara.

94. 1. <u>torch-signals</u>: There was probably a rudimentary code: accroding to a scholiast torches held still indicated the approach of friends, torches shaken indicated the approach of enemies.

<u>as great as any in the war</u>: On Thucydides' fondness for this kind of superlative cf. Introduction, pp. 3 - 4. This was probably written with reference to the Archidamian War only: for later panic in Athens see VI. 28-9, VIII. 1. 2, and (fear for the Piraeus again) VIII. 92. 3 with 94, 96; in 413 at Syracuse

after the Athenian defeat in the great harbour "the immediate result was a panic as great as at any time" (VII. 71. 7).
that could easily have happened: There is no discussion of what the attackers had thought of doing, or of how much they could have done, before large numbers of Athenians assembled to resist them: an obvious thing to do would have been to set about damaging or destroying Athenian ships and equipment.
and no wind would have stopped them: Thucydides rejects the excuse mentioned in 93. 4.
94. 3. were not water-tight: Ancient ships needed frequently to be hauled ashore, dried out and recoated with pitch: Morrison & Williams, 135, 279-80, Morrison & Coates, 231. The point is relevant here because waterlogged ships will have been slower and more likely to be caught if pursued.
94. 4. taking other precautions: Diod. Sic. XII. 49. 5, possibly from guesswork or possibly on the basis of genuine information, mentions a better garrison on Salamis.

95 - 101. A campaign by Sitalces the Odrysian

95. 1. Sitalces: Cf. 29, 67.
Perdiccas: Cf. 29, 80. 7.
the Thraceward Chalcidians: Cf. 79.
95. 2. Perdiccas . . . had made a promise: We are never told what promise Perdiccas had made to Sitalces and had failed to keep.
restore his brother Philip: Athens had supported Philip and a cousin called Derdas against Perdiccas *c*. 433/2 (I. 57. 2-3): Derdas was king of Elimea (on which see 99. 2 n.; the Derdas of Xen. *Hell*. V. 2. 38 will be his grandson), and it appears from the places mentioned in 100. 3 that Philip had controlled the Axius valley.
making him king: Either restoring him to the kingdom he had ruled previously or backing him in a direct challenge to Perdiccas. The second is envisaged below for Amyntas.
had undertaken to the Athenians: Cf. 29. 5.
95. 3. Philip's son Amyntas: Presumably Philip had recently died.
Hagnon as commander: Cf. 58. 1 n. This ought to mean that Hagnon was general in 429/8: it is so interpreted by Davies, *Athenian Propertied Families*, 228, but not by those who have compiled lists of Athenian generals, e.g. Beloch, *Die attische Politik*, 290, Fornara, *Hist*. Einzelschrift 16 (1971), 55.

96. 1. between Mount Haemus and Rhodope: An approximately rhomboid area bounded by Mount Haemus (running from west to east: Stara Planina), the Black Sea coast from Mesambria (Nesebür) to the Bosporus, the Propontis and the Aegean coasts from the Bosporus to Abdera, and Mount Rhodope (running from south-east to north-west: Rodopi Planina).
the Scythians: North of the Danube.
96. 3. Paeonian tribes: To the north of Macedon and Chalcidice.
River Strymon: The Struma, entering the Aegean at Eïon. (The ancient name is now used for this and the other rivers where they flow through Greek territory.)
Mount Scombrus: Rila Planina, in the area where Haemus and Rhodope meet. All the tribes mentioned in §§3-4 lived in this region.
96. 4. River Oscius: The Iskŭr, rising south-east of the Strymon but flowing north into the Danube.
Nestus: The Mesta, rising near the Oscius and flowing south to enter the Aegean opposite Thasos.
Hebrus: The Maritsa, rising near the Oscius and flowing first east and then south to enter the Aegean at Aenus.

97. 1. from the city of Abdera: Abdera, and other Greek cities on the Thracian coast, were tribute-paying members of the Delian league. Apart from the marriage-link mentioned in 29 we do not know in what relationship they stood to the Odrysian kingdom, but in the fourth century some cities were simultaneously members of the (much weaker) Second Athenian League and tributary to the Thracians (*IG* ii^2 126 = Tod 151: improved text Meritt *et al.*, *The Athenian Tribute Lists*, ii. 104, T 78d). In §3 Seuthes is credited with ruling Greek cities, if the emendation adopted is correct.
the shortest time . . . is four days and four nights: Herodotus gives similar accounts of the Black Sea and its exit (IV. 86) and of Scythia (IV. 101). Gomme estimates that at Herodotus' rate of 700 stades (of 176 metres or 193 yards: cf. 5. 2 n.) in a day and 600 in a night (IV. 86. 1) this time should have been about right, if the journey were not lengthened by the current in the Hellespont.
eleven days: At Herodotus' rate of 200 stades a day (IV. 101. 1) this is an underestimate: the actual distance is about 420 km., 260 miles, or 2370 stades. For the route see Isaac, *The Greek Settlements in Thrace*, 74.
97. 2. to the Laeaeans and the Strymon: I.e. to the source of the Strymon. At Herodotus' rate this is about right.
97. 3. and the Greek cities which they ruled: See §1 n.

Seuthes: Nephew of Sitalces (101. 5). He, rather than Sitalces' pro-Athenian son Sadocus, succeeded late in 424 (IV. 101. 5).
four hundred talents of silver: Comparable with the prewar tribute of the Delian League (13. 3 n.). Diod. Sic. XII. 50. 2 gives his total annual revenue as more than a thousand talents.
princes: Rulers of the separate tribes within the Odrysian kingdom.

97. 4. **the opposite custom to that of the Persian empire**: The Persian kings collected far more in revenue than they needed to spend, and were accustomed to reward their favourites with lavish gifts (e.g. Xen. *Cyr.* VIII. 2. 7-10).

97. 5. **the Ionic Gulf**: Nothing to do with Ionia, but named after the legendary wanderings of Io: the Adriatic Sea, and especially the southern part of it.

97. 6. **if one single people is to be compared with another**: The Persian empire as a whole may be stronger, but none of the individual nations within it is. Hdt. V. 3. 1 had said that the Thracians were the largest nation after the Indians, and would be the strongest if they were united.

98. 1. **Mount Cercina**: Ograzden Planina, well inland. For Sitalces' route from there see Hammond [& Griffith], *A History of Macedonia*, ii. 127-9 with 128 map 4 (that volume will be cited by authors' names).

98. 3-4. **a hundred and fifty thousand . . . a third were cavalry**: Diod. Sic. XII. 50. 3 has 120,000 infantry and 50,000 cavalry. Cf. his minor variation on the numbers of Athenian hoplites at the beginning of the war (13. 6 n.).

98. 4. **The most warlike infantry**: de Romilly is probably right to delete "armed with daggers" as a gloss repeated from 96. 2.

99. 1. **Lower Macedonia**: The low country around the Thermaic Gulf: "coastal Macedonia" in §3.

99. 2. **Lyncestians, Elimiotians**: In the hill country to the west of Lower Macedonia: Hammond [& Griffith], 66 map 2.

99. 3. **Perdiccas' father Alexander and his forebears**: The legendary account is given by Hdt. VIII. 137-9. The royal house of Macedon, the Argead dynasty, claimed at least from the beginning of the fifth century to belong to the Temenid (Argive) branch of the descendants of Heracles (Hdt. V. 22, Thuc. V. 80. 2): this connection with the Temenids is accepted by Hammond [& Griffith], 3 - 4, but many scholars are less willing to believe that the evidence which convinced fifth-century Greeks would have convinced us. According to some ancient texts the Argeads derived their name from the Argos in Orestis (cf. 80. 6), on

the upper Haliacmon (App. *Syr.* 333), and Argos and Orestis were so named because they were visited by Orestes in his wanderings after the killing of Clytemnestra (Strab. 326. VII. 7. 7): what Appian (or his interpolator) says may be correct. Alexander I was king in the early fifth century, and in 480 - 479 submitted to Persia but remained friendly to Athens and was used as a go-between.

expelling the Pierians from Pieria: The region on the west side of the Thermaic Gulf, east and south of the lower reaches of the Haliacmon. Whether or not the Argeads came from Argos in Orestis, they probably arrived from Orestis. It was first suggested by Hammond, *A History of Macedonia,* i. 156-8 with 124 map 12 (that volume will be cited by Hammond's name alone), that Aegeae, the original capital of Macedon, was at Palatitsa (Vergina), in Pieria near the Haliacmon, and this has been confirmed by the excavations of M. Andronikos (e.g. *AAA* 10 (1977), 1 - 72). On the expansion of Macedon see Hammond, 430-41.

still called the Pierian Gulf: "Now" would be more appropriate (contrast §5 n.).

the Bottiaeans: In the region around Pella (100. 4 n.), between the Haliacmon and the Axius (Vardar).

who are now neighbours of the Chalcidians: Living to the north of the three prongs of Chalcidice (cf. Hdt. VII. 127. 1).

99. 4. a narrow stretch of Paeonia: The lower part of the Axius valley.

Mygdonia: North of the Bottiaeans' new home, on a line from the Axius mouth to the Strymon mouth. Most of the Edonians moved to the north of Mount Pangaeum (cf. Hdt. IX. 75), but a few settled in Athos (Thuc. IV. 109. 4).

99. 5. the Eordians: Having described coastal Macedonia from west to east, Thucydides goes back to deal with regions further inland (Hammond, 436-7).

is now called Eordia: "Still" would be more appropriate (contrast §3 n.).

Physca: In Mygdonia.

the Almopians: North-west of Pella.

99. 6. Anthemus: The valley containing the river of that name, flowing into the Thermaic Gulf from the east.

Grestonia: Elsewhere called Crestonia; east of the Axius (cf. Hdt. VII. 124, 127. 2).

Bisaltia: East of Grestonia (cf. Hdt. VII. 115. 1). Some Grestonians and Bisaltians migrated to Athos (Thuc. IV. 109. 4).

and much of Macedonia also: Upper Macedonia, the upland region to the west of Pieria and Bottia, containing the tribes mentioned in 2. As Hammond points out (437), Thucydides' order in

98-9 is (a) Sitalces, (b) Perdiccas, (c) Upper Macedonia, (d) Lower Macedonia; (d) Lower Macedonia, (c) Upper Macedonia, (b) Perdiccas, (a) Sitalces.

100. 1. These Macedonians: Presumably, all those subject either directly or indirectly to Perdiccas.
100. 2. Archelaus: An illegitimate son who murdered the legitimate sons (Pl. *Grg.* 471 A-D) to succeed Perdiccas and reign from 413 to 399: he was consistently pro-Athenian, and attracted a circle of writers and artists which included Euripides.
stronger cavalry, infantry and other forces: The main strength of the Macedonian army was in the cavalry (cf. §5), and it was not until the reign of Philip II (360/59 - 336) that Macedon built up an effective infantry force.
the eight kings who had reigned before him: Listed in Hdt. VIII. 139. Nothing reliable is known about the kings earlier than Alexander I (on whom see 99. 3 n.).
100. 3. on leaving Doberus: Cf. 98. 2.
Philip's kingdom: Cf. 95. 2 n.
100. 4. Pella: On what subsequently became a lake but was originally a north-western recess of the Thermaic Gulf (Hammond, 152-3 with 141 map 14): it was made the capital of Macedon in place of Aegeae by Archelaus (cf. Xen. *Hell.* V. 2. 13).
Cyrrhus: North-west of Pella (Hammond, 159-60 with 141 map 14).
They did not continue . . . to Bottia and Pieria: So "left" above is from the viewpoint of an invader proceeding southwards down the Axius (but see 101. 1 n.). We should expect the old home of the Bottiaeans to be given the same name in 99. 3 and 100. 4: in 101. 5 their current home is called *Bottike*.
100. 5. did not even think of resisting with infantry: Cf. §1 n.
their allies in the interior: This perhaps includes both the tribes of Upper Macedonia, which are "allies and subjects" in 99. 2, and Paeonian tribes to the north.

101. 1. since the Athenians had not arrived: The sequence of thought which leads Thucydides to use "since" is not clear: perhaps he is explaining why, when Sitalces moved on to act against the Chalcidians, he did so on his own.
Since the Athenians' current interest was in the Chalcidians (95. 2), and the last mentioned position of Sitalces was to the north of Chalcidice, we should assume that the Athenians had been intended to sail to Potidaea; but Hammond [& Griffith], 124-9, dates to this winter the first Athenian decree for Methone, on the west coast of the Thermaic Gulf (M&L 65 = IG i^3 61, 3-32, more commonly dated 430), takes Sitalces west

when he first reaches the mouth of the Axius (contrast 100. 4 n.), and supposes that the Athenians were intended to operate from Methone. Sitalces had made his alliance with Athens in 431, and there is no record of his doing anything since then to support the Athenians beyond allowing them to capture Peloponnesian envoys on his territory (67), but it should have been easy enough for the Athenians to learn about the movements of his great army now.

101. 3. Panaeans . . . Dersaeans: Inland tribes between the Strymon and the Nestus.

101. 4. the Greeks who were opposed to Athens: Athens' enemies in the Peloponnesian War. Later we find Athens using Thracian mercenaries in Chalcidice (IV. 129. 2); Cleon at Eïon tried to obtain Thracian mercenaries, and the Spartan Brasidas at Amphipolis succeeded in obtaining some (V. 6); and in 413 Thracian mercenaries reached Athens too late to be sent to Sicily (VII. 27 - 30). Athens' Thracian alliance did not bring her significant help in the Peloponnesian War.

101. 6. returned home quickly . . . stayed thirty days in all: The great invasion achieved nothing worthwhile (possibly more would have been achieved if the Athenians had gone to Potidaea). It is only marginally relevant to the history of the Peloponnesian War; but it provided Thucydides with the opportunity to copy Herodotus by giving an account of places and peoples remote from the experience of most Greeks, and the region was one with which he had personal connections (cf. Introduction, p. 1). In IV. 101. 5 there will be a bald note of the death in battle of Sitalces and the succession of Seuthes.

102 - 103. Phormio in Acarnania

102. 1. Astacus: The tyrant Evarchus was expelled by Athens in summer 431 (30. 1) and restored by Corinth in winter 431/0 (33. 1-2). He must have been ousted again since then, as Astacus was clearly not hostile to Athens now.

Athenian hoplites from the crews of their ships: The regular *epibatai*, of whom there were ten on each ship (cf. 23. 2 n.): Thucydides has not allowed for the losses in the second battle in the Gulf of Corinth (90. 5-6).

Stratus: Cf. 80. 8 n. and 81.

Coronta: The city, Cynes and Theolytus are unknown.

102. 2. had always been hostile to them: In the 450s Pericles attacked Oeniadae and failed to take it (I. 111. 3), but according to Diod. Sic. XI. 85. 2 (with Dindorf's emendation) he

did win over all Acarnania except Oeniadae. Phormio's son Asopius was to make an unsuccessful attack on Oeniadae in summer 428 (III. 7), and it was finally forced into the Athenian alliance by Demosthenes in 424 (IV. 77. 2).
<u>Dolopians, Agraeans</u>: In the mountainous country between the Gulf of Ambracia and Thessaly.
102. 3. <u>this will happen to all of them</u>: It has not yet done so. The phenomenon which Thucydides describes will have been unfamiliar to many readers, since alluvial land at the mouth of a large river is not a common feature of Greece.
102. 5. <u>Alcmeon son of Amphiaraus</u>: Amphiaraus was one of the Seven against Thebes, attacking Oedipus' son Eteocles on behalf of Oedipus' son Polynices: knowing that he was doomed to die, he ordered his children to avenge his death on his wife Eriphyle, who had compelled him to take part in the campaign. Thucydides has given part of the story of Alcmeon's brother Amphilochus in 68. 3.

103. 1. <u>At the beginning of spring</u>: Normally the beginning of spring is the beginning of Thucydides' summer (cf. 2. 1 n.), but he is less rigid than some scholars would make him: the episode mentioned here belongs to this year of the war although chronologically it runs into the next, so Thucydides bends his framework to accommodate it at the end of the winter.
<u>they sailed back to Athens</u>: After the overwhelming defeat of the Peloponnesian fleet, it presumably seemed safe to leave Naupactus without a naval guard.

Phormio plays no further part in Thucydides' narrative, and in summer 428 his son Asopius is sent to Naupactus "because the Acarnanians urged that a son or kinsman should be sent to them as commander" (III. 7. 1). According to Androt. *FGrH* 324 F 8 (cf. Paus. I. 23. 10) Phormio was once sentenced in his *euthynai*, the examination of his conduct after a year in office, to a fine which he could not pay, and so he withdrew from public life; when the Acarnanians demanded him as general he said that he could not serve; so the Athenians found a way of paying his fine for him. It could be inferred from Diod. Sic. XII. 48. 3 that although the final result was victory Phormio was criticised for risking the second battle in the Gulf of Corinth. Androtion's story shares with Thuc. III. 7. 1 a demand by the Acarnanians, but the point of it is that Phormio was enabled to serve after all: unless it is badly garbled, we must assume that it refers to some earlier occasion and that by the summer of 428 he was ill or dead (since he had a son old enough to serve as general, probably aged thirty or more, he will not have been a young man). It is, alas, all too typical of Thucydides that he alludes to Phormio's disappearance from the scene in this frustrating way: possibly when he wrote III. 7 he thought that he had said here what became of Phormio, and failed to check (cf. Introduction, pp. 11, 15).

103. 2. That was the end of the winter: The ending of one of the eight books here is due not to Thucydides himself but to a later editor (cf. Introduction, p. 17), but for books II, III and IV the editor has based himself on Thucydides' years (cf. 1, 2. 1 nn.), assigning three years to each of these books.

APPENDIX

Athenian Population Figures

It cannot be demonstrated with certainty which is the most appropriate demographic model to use, but the different models which have been used recently do not yield markedly different results. In the table on page 272 I give

(a) figures calculated for me by Dr. J. P. Coleman from the U.N. *Age and Sex Patterns of Mortality*, pp. 18 - 19, table 7, model 35 (males, expectation of life at birth 24.68), alluded to by Patterson, *Pericles' Citizenship Law of 451-50 B.C.*, 40 - 81;

(b) figures from Coale & Demeny, *Regional Model Life Tables*, p. 824: model South, males, mortality level 1 (expectation of life 19.917), female gross reproduction rate (mean age 29) 4.000 = growth rate 7.04 per 1,000, cited as one extreme possibility by R. P. Duncan-Jones, *Chiron* 10 (1980), 101-9;

(c) figures from Coale & Demeny, p. 842: model South, males, mortality level 10 (expectation of life 40.626), gross reproduction rate 2.250 = growth rate 11.47, cited as the opposite extreme possibility by Duncan-Jones;

(d) figures from Coale & Demeny, p. 128: model West, males, mortality level 4 (expectation of life 25.260), growth rate 5.00 = gross reproduction rate 2.808, cited by Hansen, *Demography and Democracy*, 11 - 12;

(e) convenient approximations which I have extrapolated.

It is certain that the total liability for military service in Athens was ages 18 - 59, and that the "youngest" class was 18 - 19 (*Ath. Pol.* 42. 1 with 53. 4). It is usually believed that the "oldest" class was 50 - 59 (e.g. Gomme, *Population of Athens*, 5, cf. *Commentary*, ii. 34; Duncan-Jones; Hansen, 17, 40), but A. H. M. Jones believed it was 40 - 59 (*Athenian Democracy*, 163-5).

If we assume that the 1,000 cavalry (Ar. *Eq.* 225: with 200 mounted archers they make up the 1,200 of 13. 8) were men of hoplite census and of an age to serve in the field army, they should be added to the 13,000 hoplites of 13. 6 to yield a total field army of 14,000. So, if the field army was ages 20 -

	a	b	c	d	e
0 - 17	40.86	45.31	39.81	42.54	42
18 - 19	3.80	3.76 (3.96)	3.58 (3.74)	3.85	3¾
20 - 39	32.16	29.73	29.68	31.44	30¾
40 - 49	10.94	9.80	10.76	10.33	10½
50 - 54	4.02	3.74	4.41	3.85	4
55 - 59	3.09	2.97	3.74	3.00	3¼
60 +	5.13	4.70	8.01	5.00	5¾
	100.00	100.01	99.99	100.01	100
20 - 39	32.16	29.73	29.68	31.44	30¾
18 - 19 + 40 - 59	21.85	20.27	22.49	21.03	21½
20 - 49	43.10	39.53	40.44	41.77	41¼
18 - 19 + 50 - 59	10.91	10.47	11.73	10.70	11
30	1.61	1.48	1.48	1.57	1½
59	0.53	0.51	0.68	0.52 (0.51)	0.6

All age classes are inclusive: e.g. 18 - 19 denotes those who have reached their 18th birthday but have not yet reached their 20th birthday. Figures represent males in the stated age class as a percentage of all males. Duncan-Jones and Hansen do not state, but it can be discovered, how they arrive at figures for such classes as 18 - 19:

Duncan-Jones takes 18 - 19 to be 40% of the 15 - 19 class; Hansen takes 18 - 19 to be 20% of the 15 - 24 class, 30 to be 10% of 25 - 34 and 59 to be 10% of 55 - 64. I prefer Hansen's method: in columns b and c I use figures obtained by that method, but for the 18 - 19 class I give Duncan-Jones's figures in parentheses below my own; for the last entry in column d I give Hansen's figure in parentheses below my own.

49, the youngest and oldest numbered about 4,000, and the 16,000 reserves of 13. 6 included about 12,000 metics; if the field army was ages 20 - 39, the youngest and oldest numbered about 9,800, and the reserves included over 6,000 metics (Jones by more rudimentary means reached approximately the same conclusion for a field army of ages 20 - 39). 3,000 metic hoplites served in the invasion of the Megarid in autumn 431 (31. 2), but this figure can be used only as a minimum, since that number may have been mobilised to compensate for the 3,000 citizen hoplites at Potidaea, and in any case we might expect a mobilisation of metics to be less efficient than a mobilisation of citizens.

To most scholars who have considered the population of Athens, 12,000 metic hoplites (even if they came from the whole age range 18 - 59) would be a startlingly large number: Gomme suggested that the reserves included unfit citizens of age for the field army and that the number of metic hoplites was 5,500 or 6,500 (*Population*, 5; *Commentary*, ii. 36). Duncan-Jones, however, is prepared to accept that there were over 12,000 metic hoplites, and adds that metics are likely to have formed a higher proportion of the non-hoplite than of the hoplite population, so that altogether there could have been as many metics as citizens. Hansen in his book is concerned primarily with fourth-century figures: on pp. 29 - 33 he notes that 10,000 metics were registered in Demetrius' census according to Stesiclides, *FGrH* 245 F 1 *ap*. Ath. VI. 272 C, but comments that we cannot tell whether this is a population figure or an army figure. In *SO* 56 (1981), 19 - 32, he pressed the grammar of 13. 7 to argue that the 16,000 reserve troops were drawn from a larger total number in the categories there mentioned, and that the "oldest and youngest" citizens from whom reserve troops were drawn included thetes, so that it is impossible to calculate the number of metic hoplites from the 16,000. I do not think this is right, but even if it is right it will not invalidate the calculations which follow, which are all based on a field army of 13,000 hoplites + 1,000 cavalry.

The standard objection to Jones's assumption that the field army consisted of ages 20 - 39 is that the army which fought at Delium in 424/3 included Socrates (e.g. Pl. *Ap.* 28 E), aged about 45 (cf. Diog. Laert. II. 44). On that occasion a full levy of citizen hoplites numbered 7,000 (IV. 90. 1 with 94. 1). Gomme, believing in a field army of ages 20 - 49, thought this figure surprisingly small, and to explain it suggested that we should allow not only for some hoplites serving elsewhere but also for an exceptionally large number of unfit after the plague (*Population*, 6). Jones, to include Socrates, thought that by 424 the upper age limit must have been raised from 39 to Socrates' age or above, and suggested that because of the secrecy of the operation not all the men liable for service received their summons in time (p. 178). Duncan-Jones, however, argues that a field army of 7,000 in 424/3 is plausible only if the upper age limit was the same then as in 431.

It seems that we must either accept a field army of ages 20 - 49, with the very large metic population inferred by Duncan-Jones, or explain the presence of Socrates at Delium. I wonder if we should do the second rather than the first. In the major wars of this century, many men who were eager to serve in the British forces but were not of an age to do so falsified their ages so that they could serve. It would not surprise me if for the Delium campaign some men above the upper age limit, and Socrates among them, joined the army although they were not legally liable. In what follows I shall keep open the possibility both of a field army of ages 20 - 39, implying about 24,000 hoplites of ages 18 - 59 (including the 1,000 cavalry), and of a field army of ages 20 - 49, implying about 17,750 hoplites of ages 18 - 59.

I assume that the 13,000 and 16,000 of 13. 6 are paper strengths, from which if the full army were mobilised we should have to deduct the temporarily unfit and the holders of major offices; but to obtain the total number of adult male citizens we have to add the permanently unfit (I imagine), the men of 60+ and the thetes. Hansen suggests that it is probably too optimistic to assume that no more than 20% of the citizens were (permanently or temporarily) unfit (pp. 18 - 21), so I suggest that to allow for the permanently unfit it would be reasonable to add 10% to the paper strength of the army. An estimate of the proportion aged 60+ can be obtained from my table. Thus the total number of adult males of hoplite census in 431 should be about 29,000 if the field army was aged 20 - 39, or about 21,650 if the field army was aged 20 - 49.

Estimating the number of thetes is very much harder. A full discussion is beyond the scope of this Appendix, and here I give simply a brief review of the principal items of evidence, which are often cited but which do not enable us to reach a firm conclusion. (*a*) Herodotus had a conventional figure of 30,000 for the Athenian citizen body (V. 97. 2, VIII. 65. 1), and believed that in 479 there were 8,000 Athenian hoplites at Plataea (IX. 28. 6) while at the same time Athens was contributing an unknown number of ships to the Greek fleet of 110 ships (VIII. 131. 1). We do not know how accurate his figures are, nor what proportion of the body of hoplites aged 18 – 59 was sent to Plataea. (*b*) According to a fragment of Philochorus, when the Athenians received a gift of corn from Psammetichus of Egypt in 445/4, 4,760 false claimants to citizenship were exposed and 14,240 men were given corn (*FGrH* 328 F 119, cf. Plut. *Per*. 37. 4); but we do not know what proportion of the citizens were intended to receive or did receive corn, and even in this poorly documented period it is hard to believe that if nearly five thousand men were deleted from the registers we should have so little trace of it. (*c*) Since we do not know what proportion of the oarsmen in Athens' navy at any time were Athenian citizens, we cannot even calculate a minimum from the largest number of ships known to have been in use simultaneously (over 218, requiring over 40,000 men, in 413, after the citizen body had been reduced by war casualties and the plague: 24. 2 n.). (*d*) In 403, after the end of the war and the troubles which followed, there were about 5,000 citizens who owned no land (Dion. Hal. 526. *Lys*. 32); but presumably some thetes did own a little land. (*e*) In 321 9,000 citizens satisfied a property qualification of 2,000 drachmae, while either 12,000 or 22,000 failed to meet that requirement and were disqualified (Plut. *Phoc*. 28. 7, Diod. Sic. XVIII. 18. 5). Both figures for the number disqualified have had their champions (I have supported the higher in *ZPE* 38 (1980), 191 – 201), and we cannot be sure how closely the 2,000-drachmae line approximated to the line between hoplites and thetes.

Athens was certainly more populous and more prosperous in 431 than in 479 or in 321, but we cannot be sure by how much. If we guess — and I stress that this is only a guess — that in 431 there will have been at least as many thetes as hoplites, and that there will not have been more than twice as many adult male citizens as in 479 or in 321, we shall look for a total number of adult male citizens in the range 45,000 to 60,000. I do not think we should rule out a field army aged 20 – 39, which would imply a total citizen body at the upper end

275

of that range.

Acharnae is said by Thucydides to be the largest Athenian deme (19. 2), and is known from inscriptions to have had the largest number of representatives in the council of five hundred (twenty-two in the fourth century). According to the manuscripts of 20. 4, Acharnae contained 3,000 hoplites. Commentators have been right to reject that as virtually impossible (W. E. Thompson, *Hist.* 13 (1964), 400-13, has argued that it is not beyond the bounds of possibility, but he fails to establish that it is likely). If Acharnae was correctly represented with twenty-two councillors, it should have had 572 men in a field army of 14,000, a total of 1,047 active hoplites aged 18 - 59 if the field army was aged 20 - 39 or 780 if the field army was aged 20 - 49, and a grand total of 1,278 or 953 adult males of hoplite census (and perhaps about the same number of adult males below hoplite census). Acharnae may have been underrepresented in the council, or represented by a different number in the fifth century, and it is possible that representation was based on total citizen population and that Acharnae had an unusually high proportion of hoplites among its citizens, but it is still inconceivable that there should have been as many as 3,000 hoplites in this one deme. That "hoplites" in 20. 4 is a corruption of "citizens" (ὁπλῖται for πολῖται), suggested by F. Polle, *NJhB* 135 (1887), 109-11, would on the figures presented here and the assumption of a field army aged 20 - 39 be possible but not very likely; that 3,000 is a corruption of 1,200 (XXX for XHH), considered by Gomme, *Commentary*, ii. 74 and accepted by Whitehead, *The Demes of Attica*, 397-9, would on the figures presented here and the assumption of a field army aged 20 - 39 be possible but cannot be considered certain.

Postscript

On previous occasions when I have written about population figures I have extrapolated from suitable tables in Mitchell, *European Historical Statistics, 1750 - 1970*, in order to argue on the same terms as E. Ruschenbusch. In *ZPE* 38 (1980), 191 - 201, I accepted the estimates of Ruschenbusch, *ZPE* 35 (1979), 173-80, that males aged 18 would be 3% of all males aged over 18, males aged 30 would be 2.3% and males aged 59 would be 0.6 - 0.9%, and I further calculated that males aged over 60 would be 11% of males over 18 and that males aged 30 would be 3% of males aged 18 - 59. The corresponding figures from the table on

p. 272, above, are:

% of 18 +	a	b	c	d	e
18 (½ of 18 – 19)	3.21	3.44	2.97	3.35	3¼
30	2.72	2.71	2.46	2.73	2.6
59	0.90	0.93	1.13	0.90	1
60 +	8.67	8.59	13.31	8.70	10
% of 18 – 59					
30	2.98	2.96	2.84	2.99	2.9

In an article on Sparta in *Hist.* 30 (1981), 498 – 502, I estimated that males aged 30 were within the range 2.8 – 4.0%, and probably 3.2 – 3.5%, of males aged 20 – 54. The corresponding figures from the table on p. 272, above, are:

3.42	3.42	3.33	3.44	3.4

Strong objections have been expressed (e.g. by Hansen, 9 – 11) to the use of statistics such as those collected by Mitchell rather than computerised models. In fact the extrapolations which Ruschenbusch and I have made yield results very close to those obtained from the models selected by Patterson, Duncan-Jones and Hansen (and the arguments which I have based on those extrapolations, in the articles cited above, can stand).

INDEX

This Index is not exhaustive: in particular, it omits men named only as the fathers of men involved in the narrative, and some places, peoples and rulers, especially in north-west Greece and Thrace, which receive only a single mention. References are to pages, mostly in the Introduction and translation; a reference to the Commentary is sometimes added to guide readers to the principal discussion of a subject which occurs at several points.

Abdera   73, 167
Acarnan   177
Acarnania   11, 25, 30, 47, 49, 75, 77, 125, 141-7, 175-7
Achaea   49, 145-61
Acharnae   11, 65-7
Achelous, R.   175-7
Aegaleos, Mt.   65
Aegina   15, 23, 71-3, 75
Aenesias (of Sparta)   39
Agatharchidas (of Corinth)   147
Alcmeon   177
Alexander (of Macedon)   171
Alope   71
Ambracia   3, 25, 49, 123-5, 141-5
Aminiades (of Athens)   121-3
Amphiaraus   123, 177
Amphilochia   123-5
   See also Argos
Amphilochus   123
Amyntas (of Macedon)   165, 173
Anactorium   49, 141-5
Anapus, R.   145
Aneristus (of Sparta)   121-3
Anthemus   171, 173
Antirrhium   149, 151
Archelaus (of Macedon)   15, 171
Archers   57, 69
Archidamus (of Sparta)   3, 9, 24, 51-5, 63-5, 93-5, 127-33

Argos (Amphilochian)   25, 123-5, 143
Argos (in Peloponnese)   14, 28, 39, 49, 73, 121, 123, 171
Aristeus (of Corinth)   121-3
Aristonous (of Larisa)   69
Asopus, R.   43
Astacus   75, 77, 175
Atalante   77
Athens *passim*; in particular:
   Acropolis   7, 55-61
   Archers   57, 69
   Archons   39
   Cavalry   57, 63, 67, 75, 105, 139
   Empire   9-11, 13-15, 21-5, 49, 51, 55, 81, 111-9, 129
   Enneakrounos   59-61
   Finance   24, 55-7, 69, 123, 193-6
   Funerals   10, 29, 77-93, 101
   Generals, appointment and powers of   10, 11, 55, 67, 105, 107, 117, 192, 206-7
   Kallirhoe   59-61
   Light-armed infantry   75, 139
   Metics   57, 75

Navy 20-1, 24-5, 29, 49, 57, 63, 69-71, 75, 105, 107, 125, 145-61, 163-5, 173, 175-7
Pelargikon 61
Population 57, 65, 75, 271-7
Sea-power 24, 83, 87, 111-3, 141, 149-57, 163-5
Synoikia 59
Temples 7, 55-7, 59, 61, 101
Walls 15, 24, 57, 61-3
Attica, invasions of 11, 24, 29, 49-55, 63-9, 93-5, 105-7, 125, 127
Axius, R. 171

Black Sea 165-9
Boeotia 26, 49, 53-5, 63, 137
  See also Plataea; Thebes
Bottiaeans 139-41, 171-5
Brasidas (of Sparta) 26, 71, 149-51, 163
Brilessus, Mt. 69
Budorum 163-5
Byzantium 7, 21, 167

Carcinus (of Athens) 69
Caria 6-7, 49, 125
Cavalry 49, 57, 63, 67, 75, 105, 139, 169, 173
Cephallenia 47, 75, 77, 141
Chalcidice, Chalcidians 75, 107, 127, 139-41, 165, 171, 173-5
  See also Potidaea
Chalcis (in Aeolis) 147
Chaonians 125, 141-5
Chios 2, 49, 105
Chronology 14-15, 39, 63, 73, 75, 77, 93, 107, 125, 127, 137, 139, 161, 163, 177, 179-81

Chrysis (of Argos) 39
Cithaeron, Mt. 133
Cleopompus (of Athens) 71, 107
Cnemus (of Sparta) 121, 141-5, 149, 151, 163
Corcyra 11, 13, 23, 25, 47, 49, 69
Corinth 11, 23, 25, 29, 49, 121, 141-3, 145-61, 163-5
Coronta 175
Cranae 75, 77
Crete 11, 149-51, 161
Crisa, Gulf of (Corinth, Gulf of) 11, 25, 125, 145-63
Cropia 65
Cydonia 149-51
Cyllene 149-51
Cynes (of Coronta) 175
Cyrus (of Persia) 15, 121

Danube, R. 167
Daulis 7, 73
Delos 21, 47-9
Democracy 1-2, 13, 81-3
Diemporus (of Thebes) 39
Diodorus Siculus 19-20
Doberus 169, 171
Dorians 49, 103, cf. 47
Dyme 149

Earthquakes 3, 13, 47-9
Echinades, Is. 175-7
Eclipses 3, 13, 73
Eleusis 59, 63-5
Elis 49, 71, 121, 149
Ephorus 18-19
Epidaurus 105
Euboea 57-9, 71, 77, 105
Eumachus (of Corinth) 77
Euphamidas (of Corinth) 77
Eurymachus (of Plataea) 39, 45
Evarchus (of Astacus) 75, 77
Evenus, R. 147

Fire 155-7

Getae 165-7, 169
Gortyn 149-51
Graea 69
Grestonia 171, 173

Haemus, Mt. 165
Halieis 105
Hellanicus 2-3, 19
Hellespont 49, 121-3, 165
Heralds 39, 41, 45, 53
Hermione 105
Herodotus 2-3, 5, 8, 12
Hestiodorus (of Athens) 127, cf, 139-41
Homer *See* Poets

Ionia, Ionians 21, 49, 59
Ionic Gulf 169
Isocrates (of Corinth) 147

Javelin-throwers 139

Laconia 73
    See also Methone; Prasiae; Thyrea
Laeaeans 167
Laurium 10, 105
Learchus (of Athens) 121-3
Legends 2, 6, 59, 73, 123, 177
Lemnos 95
Lesbos 49, 105
Leucas 49, 141-3, 149, 159-61
Light-armed infantry 75, 139
    See also Archers; Javelin-throwers; Peltasts; Slingers
Limnaea 143
Locris (Opuntian) 49, 71, 77
Lycia 125
Lycophron (of Sparta) 149

Macedon 15, 25, 73-5, 143, 165-75

Machaon (of Corinth) 147
Megara 23, 49, 75, 163-5
Melesandrus (of Athens) 125
Melesippus (of Sparta) 53
Melos 9-10, 16, 49
Meno (of Pharsalus) 67-9
Mercenaries 77, 167
Messenia *See* Methone
Messenians in Naupactus 49, 71, 159
Methone 69-71
Molycrium 149, cf. 151
Mygdonia 171, 173

Natural phenomena 3, 7, 12-13, 43, 47-9, 73, 95-105, 137, 147, 155-7, 163, 175-7
Nauclides (of Plataea) 39
Naupactus 11, 49, 125, 141, 143, 145-61, 175, 177
Navies 20-1, 24-5, 29, 30, 49, 57, 63, 69-71, 75, 105, 107, 121, 125, 141-3, 145-61, 163-5, 173, 175-7
Nicias (of Gortyn) 149-51
Nisaea 75, 163-5
Nymphodorus (of Abdera) 73-5

Oaths 45, 127-31
Odrysians *See* Thrace
Oeniadae 145, 175-7
Oenoe (in Attica) 63
Olynthus 139
    See also Chalcidians
Opus 77
Oracles 12-13, 47, 61, 67, 103
Oropus 15, 63

Paeonians 167, 169, 171
Palaerus 75
Pangaeum, Mt. 171
Panormus 151, 161
Parnes, Mt. 69

Patrae 147-9
Pausanias (of Sparta) 6-7, 16, 21, 65, 127-9
Pella 171, 173
Pellene 49
Peltasts 75, 139
Pentelicon, Mt. See Brilessus
Perdiccas (of Macedon) 25, 73-5, 143, 165-75
Pericles (of Athens) 1-3, 8-9, 11, 13-15, 24, 27, 29, 53, 55-7, 75, 77-93, 105, 107-21
Persian Empire 6-7, 15, 22, 26-8, 47, 95, 111, 121, 169
Persian Wars 2, 6, 21-2, 57, 61, 67, 127, 129, 131
Phanodemus (of Athens) 127, cf. 139-41
Pharnaces (of Persia) 121
Phaselis 125
Pheia 71
Philip (of Macedon) 165, 171-3
Phocis 49, 73
Phormio (of Athens) 11, 15, 30, 107, 125, 141-3, 175-7, 269-70
Phrygii 67
Pierians 171, 173
Pindus, Mt. 175
Piraeus 15, 24, 57, 63, 95, 163-5
Plague 3, 5, 10, 12-13, 27-9, 75, 95-105, 107, 111, 115
Plataea 13, 16, 26, 29, 39-47, 49, 63, 127-39
Plistoanax (of Sparta) 65, cf. 22-3
Poets 2, 6-8, 12, 87
Polichna 151
Pollis (of Argos) 121-3
Polybius 19-20
Polymedes (of Larisa) 69
Potidaea 23, 25, 39, 55, 75, 107, 121-3, 125-7, 139

Prasiaea 105
Pratodamus (of Sparta) 121
Proteas (of Athens) 69
Proxenoi 73, 149-51
Pythangelus (of Thebes) 39
Pythodorus (of Athens) 39

Rain 13, 43, 137
Reasoning 6-7, 85, 109, 113
Religion 12-13, 83, 95, 101-3, 115, 129, 131
See also Oaths; Oracles; Temples
Rhium (in Achaea) 151, 161
Rhium (in Ozolian Locris) See Antirrhium
Rhodope, Mt. 165-7, 169

Sadocus (of Thrace) 73-5, 121-3
Salamis 3, 163-5
Scombrus, Mt. 167
Scythians 3, 167, 169
Seuthes (of Thrace) 175
Sicily 3, 8, 10, 15-16, 26, 28, 47, 119-21
Sicyon 49, 141
Sieges 26, 107, 133-9
Sitalces (of Thrace) 25-6, 30, 73-5, 121, 165-75
Slingers 145
Socrates (of Athens) 69
Sollium 75
Sparta *passim*; in particular:
  Ephors 9, 39
  Kings as commanders 9, 22, 24, 51-5, 63-5, 93-5, 127-33
  Navarchs 121, 141
  Xenagoi 133
Spartolus 139-41
Speeches 4, 8-9, 14, 16-17, 51-3, 79-93, 107-17, 127-33, 151-3, 155-7, 217, 227-8, 258, cf. 55-7
Stratus 143-5, 175

Timagoras (of Tegea) 121–3
Timocrates (of Sparta) 149, 161
Timoxenus (of Corinth) 77
Troezen 105
Trophies 67, 141, 145, 149, 161
Treaties and truces 23–8, 39, 45, 47, 67, 131, 139, 145

Unexpected, the 12, 53, 111, 115, 149, 155–7, 163

Wind 137, 147, 163
Women 41, 43, 47, 71, 77, 93, 129, 137

Xenophon (of Athens) 127, 139–41
Xenophon (historian) 14, 18

Zacynthus 25, 47, 49, 121, 141

Strymon, R. 167, 171, 173

Tegea 121
Teres (of Thrace) 7, 73, cf. 121, 165
Tereus 7, 73
Thebes 26, 29, 39–47, 129
    See also Boeotia
Theopompus 18–19
Thera 49
Therme 75
Thermopylae 173
Theseus 59
Thessaly 67–9, 173
Thrace (Odrysian kingdom) 3, 7, 25–6, 27, 30, 73–5, 121–3, 165–75
Thraceward region 1, 25, 49, 107, 123, 139–41, 165, cf. 23, 55, 127, 173
Thriasian Plain *See* Eleusis
Thronium 71
Thyrea 15, 73

Other Greek texts in this series include:

Aeschylus	*Eumenides* ed. A.J. Podlecki [1988]
Aristophanes	*Acharnians* ed. Sommerstein
	Birds
	Clouds
	Knights
	Peace
	Wasps
Euripides	*Alcestis* ed D. Conacher [1988]
	Electra ed. M.J. Cropp [1988]
	Orestes ed. M.L. West
	Phoenician Women ed. Elizabeth Craik
	Trojan Women ed. Shirley Barlow
Hellenica Oxyrhynchia ed. P.R. McKechnie & S.J. Kern [1988]	
Menander	*Samia* ed. D.M. Bain
Plato	*Meno* ed. R.W. Sharples
	Phaedrus ed. C.J. Rowe
	Republic 10 ed. S. Halliwell [1988]
Sophocles	*Antigone* ed. A.L. Brown
Thucydides	*Pylos 425 B.C.* ed. J. Wilson